STRANGERS & CITIZENS

A Positive Approach to Migrants and Refugees

Edited by
Sarah Spencer

IPPR/Rivers Oram Press

First published in 1994 by
Rivers Oram Press
144 Hemingford Road, London N1 1DE

Published in the USA by
Paul and Company
Post Office Box 442, Concord, MA 01742

Set in 10/12 Sabon by EXCEPT*detail*, Southport
and printed in Great Britain
by T.J. Press (Padstow) Ltd, Padstow, Cornwall

Designed by Lesley Stewart

British Library Cataloguing in Publication Data
A catalogue record for this book is available from the British Library

ISBN 1-85489-050-6
ISBN 1-85489-051-4 pbk

CONTENTS

Contents

TABLES AND FIGURES

Tables

Figures

ACKNOWLEDGEMENTS

IPPR would like to thank the Joseph Rowntree Charitable Trust for its generous support for this project, without which it would not have been possible. Our thanks also to the Friedrich Ebert Foundation and the Anglo-German Foundation for their support for a seminar on the social and economic impact of migration, in March 1993, and to the participants at that seminar which made a significant contribution to our thinking.

Many individuals and organisations have assisted with ideas and information, some by attending the seminars at which the papers prepared for the project were presented. In particular we would like to thank Kathryn Cronyn, Alf Dubs, Don Flynn, Werner Menski, Shamit Saggar, John Seymour, John Solomos and Ranjit Sondhi for papers which they contributed; Professor Kevin Boyle for organising a joint seminar with IPPR at the Human Rights Centre, University of Essex, at which many of the papers in this volume were discussed; the officials in the Home Office Immigration and Nationality Department and in the Foreign and Commonwealth Office who were most helpful when they met with us to discuss the issues; and Ken Mayhew, Nuala Mole, Ceri Peach, Philip Rudge, John Salt, David Smith, Philip Trott and staff of the British Council for their valuable advice and comments.

Most of all we thank the contributors to this volume who have given generously of their time, meeting frequently to discuss and revise their papers and, for some, updating them to take account of developments in Europe and the recent UK Asylum and Immigration and Appeals Act. While there was much agreement among the contributors on the conclusions to be drawn and recommendations made, there were also differences of opinion. The conclusions and recommendations in the final chapter are therefore my own, with all of which each of the contributors may not necessarily concur.

Sarah Spencer, *October 1993*

NOTES ON CONTRIBUTORS

Ann Dummett is Consultant on European Affairs at the Commission for Racial Equality and author of a number of books on immigration issues including *Subjects, Citizens, Aliens and Others* with Andrew Nicol (Weidenfeld, 1990).

Dr Allan Findlay is a senior lecturer and Director of the Applied Population Research Unit, Department of Geography, University of Glasgow. He previously carried out research for the ILO in Geneva and has written reports on migration issues for OECD and UNECWA. His current ESRC funded research project is concerned with emigration from Hong Kong.

Dr Reuben Ford is a researcher at the Policy Studies Institute, London. His doctoral thesis was on aspects of skilled international migration. He co-authored the UK chapter of the *Handbook of International Migration* (W.J. Serow et al., eds, Greenwood, New York) and aided the UK correspondent in the compilation of the 1988 and 1989 OECD *Continuous Reporting System on Migration (SOPEMI)* reports.

Laurie Fransman is a barrister specialising in immigration and nationality cases. He is a consultant at Tower Hamlets Law Centre and an Associate of the New York firm of immigration attorneys, Allen E. Kay. His publications include *Fransman's British Nationality Law* (1989). He was the first Chair of the Immigration Law Practitioners Association and is currently a member of the Ad Hoc Council of Europe Committee of Experts on nationality (advising Hungary).

Geoff Gilbert is a Senior Lecturer in Law at the Human Rights Centre, University of Essex. His interests are refugees, minority rights and international criminal law.

Elspeth Guild is a solicitor with Baileys, Shaw and Gillett and Secretary of the Immigration Law Practitioners Association. She is a member of the Council of Justice.

Anne Owers is Director of Justice and a former General Secretary of the Joint Council for the Welfare of Immigrants. She has been a member of the Board of the Centre for Research into Ethnic Relations and of The Church of England Board of Social Responsibility, Race and Community Relations Committee.

Bhikhu Parekh is Professor of Political Theory at the University of Hull. He is a former Deputy Chair of the Commission for Racial Equality (1985–90) and Vice-Chancellor of the University of Baroda, India (1981–84). He is author of several books including *Marx's Theory of Ideology, Contemporary Political Thinkers, and Gandhi's Political Philosophy*. He has frequently broadcast on race-relations in Britain and has written extensively on the subject.

Chris Randall is a partner with Winstanley Burgess, a firm of solicitors which specialises in immigration and refugee law. He is an Executive Committee member of the Immigration Law Practitioners Association and one of the two UK representatives for the European Legal Network on asylum.

Sarah Spencer is a Research Fellow at the Institute for Public Policy Research and a former General Secretary of the National Council for Civil Liberties. She has published on a wide range of human rights and constitutional issues, most recently co-editing (with Robert Reiner) *Accountable Policing: Effectiveness, Empowerment and Equity* (IPPR, 1993).

Dr Hugo Storey is a lecturer and deputy Director of the Centre for the Study of Law in Europe, Department of Law, University of Leeds. His publications include studies of the interconnections between immigration controls and the welfare state and immigration law and human rights.

GLOSSARY OF ABBREVIATIONS

ASIL	American Society of International Law
BDTC	British Dependent Territories Citizen
BNA	British Nationality Act
BN(O)	British National (Overseas)
BOC	British Overseas Citizen
BPP	British Protected Person
CA	Court of Appeal
CMLR	Common Market Law Reports
CRE	Commission for Racial Equality
CSCE	Conference on Security and Co-operation in Europe
CUKC	Citizen of the UK and Colonies
ECHR	European Convention on Human Rights
EHRR	European Human Rights Report
ELR	Exceptional Leave to Remain
EOC	Equal Opportunities Commission
ETS	European Treaty Series
Excom	Executive Committee of the UNHCR Programme
F.2d.	Federal Reporter, Second Series
FCO	Foreign and Commonwealth Office
HRC	Human Rights Commission
HRLJ	Human Rights Law Journal
ICCPR	1966 International Covenant on Civil and Political Rights
ICJ	International Court of Justice
ICLQ	International and Comparative Law Quarterly
IDSS	Institute of Defence and Strategic Studies
IGO	Inter-governmental organisation
ILO	International Labour Office
ILPA	Immigration Law Practitioners Association
INS	Immigration and Naturalisation Service, USA
INT.LEG.MAT.	International Legal Materials

IOM	International Organisation for Migration
IRR	Institute for Race Relations
JCWI	Joint Council for the Welfare of Immigrants
NLJ	New Law Journal
NOP	National Opinion Polls
NYIL	Netherlands Yearbook of International Law
OAS	Organization of American States
OAU	Organization of African Unity
ODIHR	Office of Democratic Institutions and Human Rights
OECD	Office for Economic Co-operation and Development
OJ	Official Journal of the European Community
ORCI	Office of Research and Collection of Information
SEA	Single European Act
SEC	Secretariat of the European Community
UNGA	United Nations General Assembly
UNGAOR	United Nations General Assembly Official Report
UNHCR	United Nations High Commissioner for Refugees
UNTS	United Nations Treaty Series
YEL	Year Book on European Law

INTRODUCTION

Sarah Spencer

Of the 46 million passengers who arrived at the borders of the United Kingdom in 1991, 267,000 intended to stay for a year or more and were therefore classed as 'immigrants'. The vast majority, however, (43.8%) were British citizens while a further 11.6% were nationals of other European Community countries, exercising their right to freedom of movement within the Community. The remainder were nationals of Commonwealth and foreign countries outside the EC and thus subject to immigration control. In the same year, 239,000 people emigrated from the United Kingdom, leaving a net immigration of 28,000.

For non-EC nationals there are four principal means of immigration to the UK:

☐ *to work*, with a work permit, or to accompany a worker as a dependent.
   52,000 work permit holders and their dependents were admitted in 1992.

☐ as a *family member*, for marriage or family re-union.
   18,500 spouses and 3,000 children were admitted in 1992 and 2,600 fiancé(e)s.

☐ as a *student* or to accompany a student as a dependent.
   202,000 students from outside the EC entered in 1991. There were 84,600 students studying in public sector institutions in 1992 and an estimated 490,000 in the private sector.

☐ as an *asylum seeker*.
   There were 24,600 applications for asylum in 1992 (including applications from individuals already in the country), a fall from 45,000 in 1991.

Just over 3,000 people were removed as illegal entrants or overstayers in 1992 and nearly 2,500 people were deported (for breaching conditions attached to their leave in the UK, because they had committed a criminal offence or their presence was 'not conducive to the public good').

Largely from among existing residents, 52,600 people were accepted for settlement in 1992, that is, they had the conditions attached to their stay removed. In 1991, 58,000 people were granted British citizenship.[1]

For each category of people seeking entry to the UK, different 'push and pull' factors predominate in the decision to migrate and each requires a different policy response. In relation to most migrants, the government is free to determine who should be allowed to enter according to its perception of the country's interests, although it may choose to be generous on humanitarian grounds. Only in certain cases, (e.g., of dependent young children seeking to be reunited with their parents), will its obligations under international law effectively require that entry is permitted.

This situation is reversed, however, in the case of asylum seekers. Under the UN Convention on Refugees (1951, and 1967 Protocol) the Government must grant asylum to individuals who have a well-founded fear of persecution on the grounds of their race, religion, nationality, membership of a particular social group or political opinion. This definition of refugee is, of course, far narrower than that in common usage, but government is free to choose how to respond to applications from asylum seekers who fall outside the UN definition, for instance because they are fleeing not from personal persecution but from civil war. (In this chapter and in the Conclusion I shall use the term 'refugee' in its broad common usage, except when clearly referring to the narrower category who qualify for UN refugee status).

The UK Government's policy on immigration and nationality is set out in the briefest of statements in the Report of its Immigration and Nationality Department, part of the Home Office. It is to:

- allow genuine visitors and students to enter the United Kingdom;
- give effect to the 'free movement' provisions of European Community law;
- continue to admit the spouses and dependent children of those already settled in the United Kingdom;
- subject to the above, to restrict severely the numbers coming to live permanently or to work in the United Kingdom;

- maintain an effective and efficient system for dealing with applicants for citizenship.

The Government seek to pursue this policy firmly and fairly while making efficient use of resources and providing a courteous, helpful service.[2]

There is no similar statement of asylum policy but, in summary, it is:

to meet the UK's obligations towards refugees under the UN Convention while reducing the scope for misusing asylum procedures. Where an individual does not qualify for refugee status, their individual circumstances will be taken into account and leave to remain granted in exceptional cases.[3]

These policies have developed as ad hoc responses to the perceived crises caused, first, by successive influxes of migrants from the New Commonwealth and latterly of asylum seekers. Government itself acknowledges the piecemeal way in which immigration policy has developed:

Immigration law in this country has developed mainly as a series of responses to, and attempts to regulate, particular pressures rather than as a positive means of achieving preconceived social or economic aims.[4]

Government policy on asylum seekers is similarly reactive. Moreover, the UK has no coherent refugee policy; that is, no coordinated policy which addresses the causes of refugee flows as well as the symptomatic arrival of asylum seekers at our borders.

There is much scope for questioning, first, whether current procedures do fulfil the stated objectives. Do current rules actually ensure that genuine visitors and students can enter the UK? Can the policy be said to be implemented 'fairly' when, in Bangladesh, spouses seeking entry to the UK may wait up to 6 months for their first interview while those in other countries wait only one day? Is it legitimate to claim that the UK is giving effect to the free movement provisions of EC law while border controls are retained?

In the IPPR study which led to this report we have, however, done more than ask whether the UK is meeting its existing policy objectives. We have considered whether its policies are appropriate for the situation the UK will face in the next decade. Is it adequate to have a reactive system which responds to those seeking entry rather than a pro-active approach with clear social and economic policy objectives? Is it sufficient to maintain an 'effective and efficient' system for dealing with applicants for citizenship in the absence of any sense of what a citizenship policy should be trying to achieve? Most fundamentally, will such a reactive approach equip the UK to deal with the complex and potentially overwhelming migration pressures to which it will increasingly be subject in the years ahead?

Global migration pressures

The global, long-term context in which Britain's immigration and refugee policy must now be situated is very different from the post-war, post-colonial era in which its current policies were formulated.

Until the 1970s, Europe was a net exporter of people and Africa, for instance, a net importer. European countries were encouraging or tolerating labour migration to compensate for domestic labour shortages, until the rise of anti-immigrant feeling and the economic downturn in that decade led many countries to tighten controls. Nevertheless, the movement of people was still considered manageable and containable. Twenty years later that is no longer the case. With the exception of asylum seekers the UK has, until now, largely avoided the principal immigration pressures confronting many European States. However, it is questionable whether the UK can remain immune from the migration pressures which are certain to increase in the years ahead.[5]

The world's current population of 5.5 billion will increase by 10% by the year 2000. Twenty-five years later, when today's primary school children reach middle age, it will be around 8.5 billion. Ninety-five per cent of that growth will be in developing countries where available resources already cannot sustain existing populations. The labour force of the less developed countries will increase by 730 million in the next 20 years, compared to a total labour force in today's industrialised world of 586 million. Thus, to maintain present levels of (under)employment in the South an additional number of jobs greater than the total now available in the developed world would have to be created.[6] The question is whether the people can achieve satisfactory living conditions within their own countries or whether they will choose to emigrate.

Political instability, war and now 'ethnic cleansing' in former Yugoslavia have fuelled the most dramatic increase in human movement in recent years, that of asylum seekers. While the vast majority are supported within the poor, developing countries, the number who reached Western Europe in 1992 was three times the organised intake of foreign workers. Mass communications and the relative ease of international travel are two further push factors which have led to South-North and, to a lesser extent, East-West migration.

The acceleration in migration to developed countries had become quite marked by the mid-1980s and was stronger and gaining ground by 1990 and 1991.[7] Despite the economic downturn in Europe and the restructuring of the European economies which has substantially reduced the demand for unskilled labour, the emigration push factors in the South and East look likely to over-ride the absence of the strong pull factors which once existed.

International migration experts argue that, if appropriate action is not taken, emigration for many in developing countries will be seen not as a question of choice but as one of survival. 'Explosive potential' and 'out of control' are the terms used by the civil servants running two of the proliferating international bodies attempting to come to terms with this 'uncontrolled, large scale international migration (which) is threatening social cohesion, international solidarity and peace'.[8]

In the first half of 1993, 80–90 inter-governmental meetings on migration issues were held in Europe, involving up to 40 States, compared with half as many two years previously.[9] This flurry of activity reflects the level of governmental concern in Europe but it has not yet led either to coordinated action nor to the systematic development of policies designed to tackle the root causes of migration and asylum flows. Experts criticise the 'scattered and unco-ordinated machinery' and lack of systematic thinking taking place at the international level which recognises the linkages between population growth, migration, inequality and security, on the one hand and policies on defence, human rights, development aid, trade, debt and the environment on the other. European immigration policies developed in the aftermath of the Second World War and little developed since, need, they argue, to be re-thought to reflect the entirely new global migration patterns in which Europe now finds itself embroiled.[10]

IPPR study

A sense that UK immigration policy has not adjusted to the new and potential migration pressures was one of the reasons IPPR decided to initiate a study of UK policy. A second motivation was an awareness of the contrast between the UK's reactive approach and that of so called countries of immigration which adopt a pro-active immigration policy in line with wider social and economic policy objectives. We felt some concern that the UK should so often be at odds with its European partners on these issues of mutual concern, and at its failure to press for policy solutions at the European level which reflect the international human rights standards to which the UK Government is committed. Finally, we felt it essential to find a means of alleviating the distress caused to UK residents by some of the current immigration controls, while recognising that purely humanitarian considerations cannot alone form the basis of a sound immigration policy.

IPPR's concern to consider the economic, social and political implications of immigration as well as the international legal framework led us to bring together experts knowledgeable about very different aspects of these issues: geographers studying migration patterns, economists considering their economic impact, voluntary organisations and lawyers working with immigrants and refugees, political philosophers, experts on European policy and others studying refugee law, policy and practice. The papers they prepared were discussed at seminars to which many others were invited; many of them are published here. The concluding chapter draws together their principal conclusions and advocates a new approach to immigration and refugee policy which IPPR believes the British Government should adopt.

In order to emphasise that government must not focus solely on immigrants and asylum seekers, the result of migration pressures, but adopt a holistic approach, we look first at the causes of refugee flows in Geoff Gilbert's chapter, 'Tackling the Root Causes of Refugee Flows'. Gilbert examines the reasons why there are 20 million refugees in the world and a further 25 million displaced persons, 90% of whom, it must be remembered, stay in developing countries. Armed conflict is the largest single cause but is not directly covered by the international definition of refugees. Gross human rights violations may amount to 'persecution' but those fleeing systematic and widespread violation have to show that they had a personal, well-founded fear. Natural disasters, famine, flooding and pollution, are clearly outside the definition of refugee as currently interpreted, although Gilbert argues that persecution ought to be read more widely. States have chosen a narrow interpretation in order to restrict the number of those eligible to claim asylum.

Gilbert argues that refugee flows are the responsibility of the country of origin not only of the receiving state and the international community. He is critical of States and international bodies which, with a few exceptions, have made little attempt to develop the comprehensive approach to refugee policy which is clearly needed; an approach which recognises the connections between policies on defence, human rights, aid, trade and environmental issues. The UK lamentably fails to make these connections. Within the Foreign Office there is no unit responsible for coordinating action on refugees. It was put to us by a Foreign Office official (in 1992) that a committee to coordinate policy with the Overseas Development Agency, Department of Trade (sale of arms) and Home Office would be giving the issue 'more priority than it deserved'.

Gilbert sets out the measures which exist to remove the causes of refugee flows or ameliorate their worst effects, in particular the human rights protection mechanisms in international law. He considers why these have largely failed and why the international standards and enforcement mechanisms to protect minority rights are particularly ineffective, as the situation in former Yugoslavia demonstrates. His recommendations, equally valid at a national and international level, range through means of enhancing international human rights protection, arms control, early warning mechanisms, debt forgiveness, means of avoiding natural disasters and institutional changes to enable an integrated policy approach to be implemented.

In 'Current and Future Migration Flows', Reuben Ford looks at the outcome of migration pressures as they affect the United Kingdom, describing the major change which has taken place in each of its principal migration streams: migration for settlement, temporary labour and asylum. Dismissing the popular misconception that immigrants to the UK are primarily job seekers and family members from the New Commonwealth, Ford explains the shift in emphasis towards professional and managerial employees; the fact that UK citizens remain the largest group of immigrants and that, throughout the years after 1960 when immigration was of heightened political concern, the UK was a net exporter of people. Almost two-thirds of employed immigrants are highly skilled and only 12% of immigrants are over 45 years old. While asylum seekers are the most rapidly expanding source of potential settlement migration in Europe, the numbers entering the UK are relatively small compared to those received by some of our European neighbours.

Highly critical of the absence of data on immigrants, Ford

nevertheless attempts to look ahead, providing a series of forecasts until the end of the century. Acknowledging the major assumptions on which they are necessarily based, he concludes that the most likely scenario is that the number of asylum seekers will continue to increase, but that no accurate estimate could possibly be made; that there will be a continuing increase in inward migration of the highly skilled, with some increase of both skilled and unskilled EC nationals; and some limited increase in the number of non EC nationals entering for marriage and family re-union (a number which would be greater were entry controls relaxed). He argues that the emphasis by certain other countries on selecting 'quality' migrants may mean that the UK's labour migrants will be drawn from a pool of migrants of diminishing skill levels; the UK, having shown no interest in competing for these workers in the past, could now find it difficult to do so successfully. In its haste to discourage immigrants with few skills it may find that it has lost out on attracting those with higher skills as well, an issue explored more fully by Allan Findlay in his chapter on the economic implications of immigration. Critical of successive governments' reactive approach, Ford argues for a new policy designed to achieve positive objectives. Whether the aim is to defend the existing policy, however, or to monitor the success of a new approach, a more reliable system of data collection on stocks and flows is urgently required.

The number and kinds of immigrants reflect not only migration pressures but the State's policy on entry and settlement. The immigration policy which is adopted reflects the State's perception of itself and, in particular, the extent to which it accepts or rejects a multicultural identity. Before examining current British policy and its impact, it is therefore worth stepping back to consider the perception of the UK on which that policy is based and whether that perception itself ought to be revised. This task is undertaken by Bhikhu Parekh in 'Three Theories of Immigration' in which he argues that modern States' conceptions of themselves fall into one of three categories— *liberal*, *communitarian* and *ethnic*—leading to different types of immigration policy, albeit that they overlap in practice.

Parekh argues that all three conceptions have been part of Western self-understanding, capture some aspects of historical reality and are plausible in different degrees, but that all are unsatisfactory. His analysis of the communitarian view is perhaps most pertinent to a consideration of future immigration policy. Communitarians believe that a state is united by the shared understandings, history, values and loyalties of its members; it is a distinct ethical and cultural unit. To preserve this identity, it must be selective about whom it allows to become members. Outsiders can only be admitted on the basis of their capacity and willingness to acquire these common characteristics. Parekh argues, however, that communitarians greatly exaggerate the extent to which such a common identity exists. They fail to recognise the diversity across class and gender and in different parts of the country. He agrees that there is a need for a level of agreement about how to live together and resolve our differences; a level of consensus on political values and institutions. But this consensus does not need to extend into the whole of social and private life. He concludes that Western societies can tolerate diverse ways of life and benefit from that diversity.

Immigration policy is interlocked with and shapes the way in which *former* immigrants are treated. If the policy excludes or discriminates against a particular group, it implies that they are undesirable, encouraging the majority to believe that they are not acting wrongly if they treat them badly. It follows that, where a government wants to end discrimination, its immigration policy must assist rather than hinder that objective, an argument I take further in my chapter on the implications of immigration policy for race relations.

The State must recognise that it is not the individual but the family which is the principal unit of migration and not force families apart or interfere in an individual's choice of marriage partner. The ways in which current UK immigration policy can infringe these principles is explained in Hugo Storey's 'International Law and Human Rights Principles'. Storey sets out the principal international rules affecting immigration and their various means of monitoring, supervision and enforcement. The fact that they set only minimum standards is, he argues, both their weakness and their strength. While, on the one hand, the rules fail systematically to safeguard the full range of human rights, on the other hand most States have found that they can live with these rules which have prevented greater deterioration in the treatment of immigrants and asylum seekers.

The UK, however, lives uneasily with these standards, in many cases failing to ratify a treaty, derogating from parts of it, failing to comply with the standards it sets or responding negatively to adverse findings by the supervising bodies. In this context the UK government's enthusiasm for inter-governmental (as opposed to EC) cooperation in this area of policy comes as no surprise. International law advances should, Storey argues, be the cornerstone on which reform of our immigration and asylum law is based and he sets out a programme of reform on that basis.

Frustration with the UK's preference for inter-governmental agreements runs through Ann Dummett's chapter 'Objectives for Future European Community Policy'. In it she demonstrates the Government's confused and contradictory attitude to EC policy making: on the one hand signing the Single European Act giving the EC policy making powers in this area and allowing free movement of EC nationals across our borders; on the other, resisting what it perceives as infringements on British sovereignty and refusing to remove border controls. It is not clear to what extent the Government fails to understand the commitments it has made and to what extent it wants to resist its legal obligations. The UK's negotiators, she argues, seek ad hoc decisions pursuing the Government's short-term aims and interests rather than engaging in long-term policymaking for twelve countries. There is no concept of basic principles or international law to be respected nor of burden sharing among partners.

Dummett explains the nature of the UK's existing commitments within the EC and inter-governmental machinery and the likely developments post-Maastricht. She sets out the changes needed in British immigration and nationality policy to provide British residents with the same rights as their European counterparts; and the developments in EC policy on migration and asylum for which the British Government should be pressing.

One of the significant respects in which the UK's approach differs from many other European countries is its unwillingness to recognise that immigration, in part, reflects labour market needs and that immigration policy should, therefore, be part of forward economic planning. This argument is taken up by Allan Findlay in his 'Economic Audit of Contemporary Immigration' in which he examines the economic impact of contemporary immigration and evaluates the economic basis for current immigration policy. He considers the consequences of persisting with the government's current—limited—policy tools and the economic case for policy reform.

An assessment of the economic impact of immigration is severely hampered by the paucity of data on current flows and recent arrivals. In stark contrast to the quality of data in countries which do monitor the relationship between immigration and the economy, Britain collects little data on immigrants; data on ethnic minorities—often second or third generation immigrants—is often substituted in the debate. Given 'the fundamental switch which has occurred in the way in which the international migration system is organised', and the impact of discrimination (reducing the contribution which members of ethnic minorities can make to the economy), using such data seriously distorts the picture.

Findlay demonstrates that countries which share many common economic characteristics with the UK have had a starkly different view on the economic desirability of immigrants: while Western Europe has been attempting to close its doors, North America opened its doors a little wider. This is not because of different economic conditions but because its self-image and its ideology are different. Immigration is seen as contributing to the vitality of a multi-cultural nation while in Europe resistance to multi-culturalism remains strong. The social context is critical to whether immigration is perceived to be of economic benefit.

Findlay examines the relationship between immigration and economic growth, finding that economic growth no longer guarantees an expanding labour market (and hence scope for immigration). Nor, however, does labour market stagnation preclude immigration, as the policy in North America shows. Significantly, of course, North America has not opened its doors to all-comers but selectively to those in managerial and professional grades. Why, when the UK has looked so often to America for inspiration on other economic policies, did it not follow America's lead on immigration?

While British politicians still associate immigration with unskilled flows from former colonies, the growth in skilled, transient, migration to the UK is now a significant and expanding form of migration affecting Britain. While substantial numbers of migrants are unlikely to be needed to fill labour shortages, there is clear evidence that demand exists for these skilled workers. However, existing controls give priority to protecting the indigenous work force rather than to the possible long-term economic benefits of allowing these workers to come and to remain. Is this the right policy for the long term?

Findlay addresses the primary economic concerns about immigration: that it will increase unemployment, the burden on social services and on the social security system. Limited existing research suggests that unskilled immigrants do not in general displace existing workers but take the jobs which they will not do. The Government, he argues, should have the data to support or refute this and, for instance, to assess the impact of any increase in unskilled immigration. Without such research, it cannot simply assume a negative impact.

Is it in fact the case that our ageing working population may need to be supplemented by immigration in the decades ahead? Findlay largely rejects this view but notes that the trend towards a greater proportion of skilled professional and managerial jobs within the labour market means that job vacancies cannot immediately be filled by higher participation rates: training takes time and planning and in the meantime immigration may be a necessary source of labour.

Findlay concludes that government policy does not maximise the economic benefits which could be achieved and sets out the changes which he believes are needed in the Government's approach, data collection and research, in order to adapt the system and bring it within mainstream economic planning. He is clear, however, that economic goals should not be the sole objective of immigration policy nor economic criteria the sole basis for entry clearance. Moreover, the government should not assume that individuals who are allowed to enter on humanitarian grounds cannot also make a positive contribution to the economy. He noted how refugees, for instance, could be helped to become economically productive more quickly. This is not, however, the approach currently adopted.

In his chapter 'An Asylum Policy for the UK', Chris Randall demonstrates that the ideology of the recent Asylum and Immigration Appeals Act was highly restrictive. The emphasis, at a time when the number of asylum seekers has increased dramatically, is on how to reduce the number who gain access rather than to ensure that genuine refugees are protected.

Randall considers the obligations which the UK has towards asylum seekers, and its policy and procedures, in the context of recent European developments and the 'characteristically undemocratic' way in which policy in Europe is being harmonised. The problem, he argues, is that the UN Convention and related documents are virtually silent on determination and appeal procedures. The willingness of the UN High Commissioner for Refugees (UNHCR) to compromise on procedures because of its own political difficulties in a hostile world has been unhelpful for those pressing for higher standards.

Whatever policy is adopted, some will be excluded. We must, however, recognise that those who fall outside the narrow UN definition of refugee, like those fleeing civil war, are not 'bogus' refugees. The number who are nevertheless given Exceptional Leave to Remain (ELR) in the UK demonstrate that there are many non-UN refugees who are nevertheless in need of sanctuary. In the present climate however, it would not be helpful to seek an amendment of the UN definition.

Randall considers the major issues of access to British territory: the imposition of visas and carrier sanctions. Both of these measures keep out genuine asylum seekers, yet to remove visa requirements for asylum seekers would encourage migrants to claim asylum in order to enter the country. It is only the current political climate, he notes, which makes indiscriminate exclusions from the country so much more acceptable than indiscriminate access. He explores the alternatives to both policies and suggests some limited reform.

In a detailed, tabular analysis, Randall compares current British determination procedures with those recommended by UNHCR, Amnesty International and the European Consultation on Refugees and Exiles. This makes the inadequacy of the new Act clear and emphasises the steps needed to make procedures fair and efficient for both the applicant and the State.

Asylum seekers were not the only group adversely affected by the recent Act. Elspeth Guild's chapter 'Future Immigration Policy' picks out three aspects of policy—family life, students and visitors, and appeals—to suggest the principles on which such policy should be based and the reforms which she believes are necessary.

Guild notes that the importance of the family as the fundamental unit of society is recognised by the UK's political parties and is protected by international law. But it is in conflict with the desire to keep to a minimum the numbers allowed to enter for settlement. Her chapter sets out to balance these objectives.

The family is an elastic concept and immigration policy must find the right balance between a policy which is firm while respecting the emotional and economic ties between family members. EC law provides a more generous definition of family than UK law, discriminating against EC and UK nationals who have not exercised their right to live and work in another EC country and thus cannot benefit from EC provisions. A policy which excludes a disproportionate number of family members from ethnic minority communities similarly discriminates in an unacceptable way; moreover they cannot settle successfully unless they have security of residence and rights of family reunion. The State has the right to adopt measures to prevent abuse of that right, but these must be proportional to the mischief they are seeking to prevent. Current intrusions into privacy, not least officials reading the love letters of marriage partners, fail that test.

Guild suggests a more satisfactory test of a genuine marriage; argues against using DNA tests unless there is strong evidence of abuse and makes the case against expulsion of spouses after marital breakdown.

Guild's argument in relation to students and visitors takes us back to those in Findlay's chapter: the government is failing to recognise the economic benefits which these temporary migrants bring and is 'cutting the country short' by making it difficult for them to enter. The commercial benefits which visitors bring as tourists, as well as socially and culturally, are hard to measure and the sums lost through the deterrence of visa costs or refusal of entry have not been calculated.

In relation to overseas students, Guild argues that the Home Office and Department of Employment regulations deter students from coming and make it more difficult for UK institutions to compete with others in the lucrative overseas student market. Even leaving aside humanitarian considerations, the case for reform is strong and Guild sets out the changes which are needed.

On appeals, current policy is measured against the standards set in the official report of 1967 which argued that it was inconsistent with the rule of law that the power to take decisions affecting an individual's whole future should be vested in officials against whose finding there is no appeal. Guild shows how UK policy falls far short of this standard. She explains the vital role which appeal rights play in regulating the consistency of decision making by public officials and the implications for a family, and for the sense of insecurity in a community, if an individual is expelled without a fair appeal on his or her case. Yet she fears that the recent reduction in appeal rights in the Asylum and Immigration Appeals Act is only a first step towards future, piecemeal, dismantling of the appeal system.

Anne Owers considers a further aspect of UK policy on immigrants in 'The Age of Internal Controls?' in which she questions the growing assumption that a relaxation of border controls would necessitate greater internal checks for illegal immigrants, including identity cards. As third-country nationals living in other EC States do not have the right to live and work here, and external border controls in those States may not be very effective, the potential for significant numbers of unauthorised people to enter or over-stay in the UK is undoubtedly there. But Owers questions, first, whether it is feasible to prevent this and, secondly, whether the moral panic over their presence is necessary.

Given the 'growing, possibly irresistible pressure for a system of internal checks', Owers examines how such a system might operate in practice, what problems it might be expected to solve and the effects it could have. She explains, first, the existing means of personal identification used, for instance by benefit agencies and hospitals; a system which is not comprehensive nor subject to central direction. It focuses on black alleged illegal immigrants and largely ignores, for instance white Americans and Australians.

Extending sanctions on employers who exploit illegal workers is dismissed as impractical in a country where many foreigners need no permit to work and misguided given that European countries which have such sanctions have more illegal workers. ID cards are a more real possibility but as a means of immigration control, they would not be feasible because of the need to carry out a census of the immigration status of every individual in the country, recording frequent changes. Were this done, it could only prove a gateway to further checks as immigration status is a moving target; it would thus provide no protection for those vulnerable to discriminatory police attention and intrusive questioning. Non residents would have no ID card, including the thousands of temporary visitors each year, the group from which most 'overstayers' come. She concludes that ID cards would be of no value in controlling those people over whom there is most concern.

Is it sensible to set up a hugely expensive and intrusive system which is both disproportionate to the problem and may anyway miss its target? Moreover, should men and women, invariably working for very low wages, be considered a sufficient threat to justify even the police raids which currently take place. As Ann Dummett says in her chapter 'illegal immigrants are not a separate, sinister type of human being and should not be classed with criminals'. Both agree that there should be a reasonable policy of checks which neither infringe human rights in general nor impinge disproportionately on particular communities. Owers sets out some principles to which such a system should adhere.

The impact on existing minority communities in the UK should also be a principal concern in devising citizenship policy. In fact, many of the concerns in the other chapters reappear in Laurie Fransman's chapter 'Future Citizenship Policy': the need to recognise that we are no longer devising policy for the post-colonial era but for a State subject to accelerating global migration patterns; the importance of looking ahead to harmonisation of policy throughout Europe; the value of seeing the inter-connections between different aspects of government policy, for instance the implications of citizenship policy for a healthy, participatory democracy; and the harm caused by officials' wide discretion and the absence of appeal rights.

Fransman summarises the history of British nationality law and the key provisions of the current 1981 Act, explaining the generosity (by today's standards) with which Commonwealth citizens were able to acquire British nationality only to have their rights curtailed by successive legislation culminating in the 1981 Act; the way in which the component parts of nationality such as right of abode have been separated and moved around like the inter-connecting units of a child's toy; and the weakening over time of the concept of allegiance (e.g. with the relaxation of objections to dual nationality).

Crucially he draws a distinction between the legal status of nationality and the more fluid concept of citizenship rights (civil, political and social) which can be possessed to varying degrees by non-nationals. Political rights, he notes, are normally restricted to those with the legal status of nationality although in the UK they are also enjoyed by citizens of Commonwealth countries and Ireland.

Fransman sets out a list of 13 principles which he argues should form the basis of UK nationality policy and policy on nationality related citizenship issues. Looking to the security of minority communities and to the health of our democracy, he insists it is right that citizenship rights, including the right to vote should be enjoyed by a wider group than UK nationals and Commonwealth citizens. He questions whether right of abode should, once more, be separated from nationality status so that those who do not become British nationals can nevertheless obtain security of residence and, most important, have access to European citizenship. Granting nationality status should be seen not as a privilege but a right for those who have established a sufficiently close connection with the State. It is in our interests for long-term residents to become citizens and government policy, and the procedure, should not deter them.

That immigration policy cannot be devised in isolation from the pursuit of economic and social objectives must now be clear. The final chapter considers the implications of UK immigration policy for one particular area of social policy, race relations, refuting the assertion of successive governments that the current system of immigration control is good for race relations and proposing an alternative approach.

Governments argue that 'strict immigration control' is necessary to avoid fuelling anti-immigrant feelings. The primary objective of immigration policy since the early 1960s has indeed been to reassure the electorate (although some research suggests that the emphasis on controls helped to create the anxieties it was intended to calm). More immigrants would, government argues, lead to pressures on employment, housing and welfare resources, and thus increase resentment; but it has not carried out the research necessary to enable it to establish whether, and to what extent, some immigrants have a negative impact on these resources and to what extent they are of positive benefit.

In 'The Implications of Immigration Policy for Race Relations' I argue that, far from placating the electorate, the form which immigration control has taken and the presentation of policy have served to reinforce prejudice rather than to enhance race relations. By accepting in political statements that grievances, not against all immigrants, but against black and Asian immigrants, are justified, and imposing controls disproportionately against these immigrants, government policy has given legitimacy to the view that black and Asian people are undesirable and should be excluded wherever possible.

If the damage which immigration policy causes to race relations is to be removed, a series of changes are proposed to the content, presentation, and extent of public debate on immigration and asylum policy.

The need to investigate the socio-economic impact of migrants on British society, to understand any genuine conflicts which may exist between the interests of existing residents and those who want to come, and to develop new policies based on that understanding, are themes which recur throughout this volume. In it we have not attempted to study every aspect of these complex issues. The primary (though not sole) focus is on migrants and asylum seekers from outside of the EC (so that little is said, for instance, on Irish immigrants). Due to lack of available empirical research, we have not explored the potentially important questions around housing, for instance, nor in detail the use by migrants of social welfare and health services. Our aim has not been to propose comprehensive alternative immigration and refugee policies but to suggest the *approach* which should be adopted in developing such policies; an approach which, as the final chapter proposes, should be based on the kind of data and research evidence which was not available to us in our enquiry.

1 TACKLING THE CAUSES OF REFUGEE FLOWS

Geoff Gilbert

There has been an unprecedented rate of increase in the number of people seeking asylum in Western Europe and North America during the past five or so years. Some change to the procedures for dealing with asylum applicants is therefore essential if the system is not to collapse under the sheer weight of numbers. The focus of this paper, however, is not with the applicant for asylum but rather with the initial causes of refugee flows and their prevention or amelioration. The events in Yugoslavia and the former Soviet Union reveal that these issues, while predominantly related to Africa, South-East Asia and Central America, have a European perspective as well.[1]

There is no doubt that a new policy is needed to cope with the growth in applications being experienced in Europe and the rest of the industrialised world. Nevertheless, if that were to be the sole or primary response to the worldwide refugee crisis, it would be equivalent to a doctor prescribing pain-killers to a patient with a broken limb without trying to set the bone so that the fracture might heal. Concentrating on the asylum-applicant in Europe is to become preoccupied with the 'symptoms' of 20 million refugees worldwide (and that figure ignores a further 25 million people displaced within the borders of a state of which they are a national[2]) instead of trying to deal with the causes of refugee flows. A reduction in the number of people having to leave their own state, the source state, would necessarily cut down on the numbers seeking asylum in Europe[3] and, more importantly, it would focus attention on the 90% of refugees in the Third World rather than the relatively small number in Europe. This approach shifts the focus from immigration policies to international relations, aid and development:

> The Executive Committee [of the UNHCR]...[welcomed]...
> the strengthening of joint international efforts to deal with
> causes of flows of asylum-seekers and refugees in order to avert
> new flows.[4]

The Swedish Ministry of Labour's Summary of its Bill on Active Refugee and Immigration Policy[5] makes the point that refugee movements cannot be 'successfully handled' without measures aimed at eradicating the causes of refugee flows. The Bill calls for the integration of refugee and immigration policy with foreign trade and development assistance so that there is less cause to move to escape famine or poverty. It also proposes a wider and stronger role for the United Nations High Commissioner for Refugees, involving co-ordination of relief work by Inter-Governmental Organisations (IGOs) and Non-Governmental Organisations (NGOs). The Swedish Government has thus taken a holistic view of the refugee crisis and has attempted to create a framework that will deal with causes and symptoms.

It is the aim of this paper to examine the fundamental causes of refugee flows, to propose appropriate steps to prevent flows and to recommend measures for when they arise. It takes the view that refugee flows are an international issue and the concern of all states, not just those which might experience future asylum applications. As such, there is a need to co-ordinate foreign policy, aid and trade policy, human rights and humanitarian affairs in a way that does not currently fully exist in the United Kingdom. A coherent and co-ordinated refugee policy obviates the need to treat each case on a crisis by crisis basis.

The causes of refugee flows

Before one can try to prevent flows, one has to be aware of their causes. If regard is had to the 1951 Convention Relating to the Status of Refugees,[6] the only recognised cause of refugee flows in international law is persecution of the individual:

> [The] term 'refugee' shall apply to any person who...owing to a well-founded fear of being persecuted for reasons of race, religion, nationality, membership of a particular social group or political opinion, is outside the country of his nationality and is unable or, owing to such fear, unwilling to avail himself of the protection of that country.[7]

The definition is not at first glance appropriate to meet the situation of mass trans-border influxes and there are those who believe that a new definition will have to be created to deal with the changed position since 1951. However, while that may well be a useful long-term goal, in the immediate future *de iure* refugees will be those who can be classified as suffering persecution.

Traditionally, states in Europe have defined persecution narrowly in order to restrict the number of successful applications for asylum, but it could be interpreted more widely:

> The essence of the Convention/Protocol is not just the notion of well-founded fear of persecution; not just race, religion, nationality, membership of a particular social group; not just *non-refoulement*; not just danger to life or freedom. It relates to the broad field of individual and community rights which require protection, not excluding the right of communities, bound by ethnicity, culture or language to decide for themselves, the economic, social, cultural and political framework most conducive to maintaining their identity.[8]

Persecution is undefined in the 1951 Convention and 1967 Protocol, allowing it to be interpreted in a flexible manner suitable to the needs of any given situation. Nevertheless, it is based on the idea of the state of origin having breached fundamental rights, as set out in international instruments[9]. At that point, it is legitimate for an individual to seek protection from another state. Article 14(1) of the Universal Declaration of Human Rights expresses the proposition in the following terms, 'Everyone has the right to seek and to enjoy in other countries asylum from persecution'. However, in order to protect as many people fleeing involuntarily as possible, it may be necessary to broaden the grounds for persecution[10] to include violations of economic, social and cultural rights as well as civil and political rights. The reason for their absence from the original list is that the Soviet bloc did not participate in the drafting of the 1951 Convention,[11] leaving the West free to define human rights but that definition should now be reconsidered. If it is accepted that persecution connotes violation of fundamental rights, then the corollary is that, where the state cannot provide those minimum guarantees to its citizens, whether in terms of civil and political or economic, social and cultural rights, and as a result an individual leaves the country, s/he should be treated as a refugee.[12]

There are in fact cases under the Convention as it is now applied where the 'social group' category has been held to permit the granting of refugee status to those fleeing economic disadvantage.[13] In the

Réfugie sur Place case,[14] the Supreme Court of the Federal Republic of Germany held, *obiter*, that capitalists and traders constituted a social group for the purposes of the 1951 Convention.[15] The US Court of Appeals in *Dunat* v. *Hurney*[16] was prepared to accept that preventing someone earning a living might amount to persecution:

> There is no basis for thinking that physical persecution requires or connotes the use of intense physical force applied to the body with all the dramatics of the rack and wheel. The denial of an opportunity to earn a livelihood...is the equivalent of a sentence to death by means of slow starvation and none the less final because it is gradual.[17]

In *Kovac* v. *INS*,[18] the 'deliberate imposition of substantial economic disadvantage' was held to qualify an applicant for refugee status. Thus, those denied a basic minimum standard of living due to the social structure of their society can qualify as refugees where it impinges on their fundamental human rights. Persecution within the 1951 Convention and 1967 Protocol might be interpreted, therefore, in a manner wide enough to embrace all objective causes of refugee flows, but this is unlikely in Europe.

However, when we are not considering refugee status but the protection of all those fleeing involuntarily and the elimination of those factors causing them to flee, a wider interpretation is justified: future references to refugees must thus be read to refer to all *de facto* refugees. It is necessary to examine those causes in order to decide how to prevent mass trans-border influxes. The usual causes of flows can be summarised as gross human rights violations,[19] war and 'natural' disaster:

> The root causes of the phenomenon of refugee migration are, of course, the grand evils of the world: civil and international war, communal violence, famine and drought, the repression of military and other dictatorial governments, natural disasters and the frightening gap between the richer and the poorer world.[20]

Human rights violations have, to a certain extent, been covered, but it is necessary to make a few, brief further points. Although state practice is still developing in this field, it ought not to matter whence the persecution emanates, whether it be from the state or some third party. Discrimination, the underlying rationale behind the grounds for persecution in Article 1 of the 1951 Convention, is often perpetrated by persons other than the state authorities, either at the latter's behest or because those authorities are incapable of exercising proper control. Second, some rights are non-derogable, such as torture, but others, including powers of detention, can be derogated from in an emergency. Breach of a non-derogable right should be equated with persecution automatically, but other rights will also count if there is no sufficient emergency, if no derogation has been entered by the state or if, despite the derogation, the act in question is not justified by the state of emergency.[21]

Armed conflict

Armed conflicts are probably the largest single cause of refugee flows. The 1989 Swiss inter-ministerial strategy group on refugee and asylum policy noted that many of the developing countries were subject to internal conflicts:[22]

> [Thanks] to foreign support, repressive regimes often succeed in remaining in power for years, if not decades, and in annihilating the opposition in their countries, unless they succeed in forcing part of their population to emigrate. Tens of millions of people have already lost their countries of origin as a result of armed conflict and civil war. The war in Vietnam, the conflicts in the Horn of Africa, in Latin America, Eastern Africa and in the Persian Gulf are some examples of the refugee misery caused during recent years by national and internationalised conflicts.

Despite the obvious need to protect such a large group of persons fleeing across international boundaries, the 1951 Convention is deemed not to cover those escaping from armed conflicts per se.[23] The *UNHCR Handbook*[24] is particularly stringent in this regard:

> Persons compelled to leave their country of origin as a result of international or national armed conflicts are not normally considered refugees.

Nevertheless, if the invading or occupying force carry out persecution of the applicants' group, then there is no reason why they should not qualify as traditional 1951 Convention refugees. However, if the object of the exercise is not to assess individual cases but rather to design systems and procedures to prevent refugee flows, whether or not those fleeing would count as traditional *de iure* refugees, then a wide interpretation must be put on persecution, as argued above, such that armed conflicts are acknowledged to be a major contributor to the 20 million persons involuntarily outside their borders. Added to the list of tasks alongside ending human rights violations, therefore, is ceasing all armed conflicts—would that Hercules had had it so easy.

Natural disasters

Finally in this list of causes, regard must be had to 'natural' disasters. While earthquakes and volcanoes cannot be predicted with any degree of certainty, other 'natural' disasters such as famine, flooding and large scale pollution can, in part, be attributed to the activities of man. Over-intensive cash-crop farming creates dust-bowls unable to grow subsistence-crops for the local population. Flooding and mud-slides in delta regions are often the result of intensive, hardcurrency producing logging operations in the highlands. Contaminated land and water supplies ensue from lack of proper safety standards in factories or from the dumping of hazardous waste by first world states.[25] Some of these disasters are exacerbated by an unprecedented growth in populations, especially in the developing world, and movements from rural areas to large cities. Another source of deprivation is over-consumption by the first world.[26]

Natural, economic and ecological factors thus add to the numbers of persons outside their country of origin. They cannot claim to be victims of persecution, but a comprehensive refugee policy designed to reduce mass trans-border influxes must create procedures to cope with movements resulting from these causes.

Tackling the root causes

It would be unbelievably optimistic to suggest that all refugee flows would be prevented if the following proposals were to be adopted. The object behind putting forward these ideas is to create conditions where flows are less likely to occur, to reduce the size of flows when they do arise and to ameliorate the conditions for those fleeing. Having established the principal causes, the most appropriate responses can properly be drawn up taking into account all pertinent areas of law and policy.

Gross human rights violations

In the years since the Second World War, human rights have been given a prominence in international law that would not have seemed possible during the earlier part of this century. There have been worldwide and regional human rights conventions of both a general and specific nature. Yet abuses continue undiminished. Some benefit must attach to encouraging more states to accede to these agreements, but further steps might increase their effectiveness in practice. The pervading influence of the concept of the sovereign equality of states in international relations, however, prevents total guarantees under international instruments ever being granted to individuals, inhibiting intervention even where the violations are gross. Furthermore, apart from the agreements themselves, there is a need for greater support for international human rights organisations in countries with a poor human rights record.[27]

Human rights agreements are only as good as their enforcement mechanisms and procedures. Without the means to force the state to abide by its obligations, promises to uphold human rights are readily forgotten.[28] Weight is sometimes given to the view that states are strongly influenced by their standing in international public opinion, but given the British Government's dealings with the People's Republic of China after 'Tiananmen Square', human rights cannot rely solely on such ephemeral mechanisms. Political pressure to comply with human rights obligations is used to some effect but is inadequate on its own. States can also use threats to restrict aid,[29] but direct action under the relevant convention with its attendant publicity is more useful in the long term.

Human rights conventions tend to be administered either through judicial tribunals[30] or by means of reports to some overseeing body.[31] In both cases, the right to bring individual petitions is at the discretion of the state. Where such a right is accorded, human rights are more effectively enforced.[32] On the other hand, merely giving individuals a right to petition does not meet the issue of group discrimination against minority populations, a state practice which so often gives rise to refugee flows—for example, Croatians into Hungary as Serb forces occupied parts of Croatia. To meet this problem, the *locus standi* of the minority group itself must be acknowledged in relation to claims of discrimination or failure to protect and promote the group's culture and identity.[33] Within Europe, the Conference on Security and Co-operation (CSCE) has developed minority issues most fully in recent years.[34] The CSCE has a long history of involvement in the protection of minority rights,[35] although the principal measures have been adopted since the Vienna Meeting of 1986–89,[36] its Concluding Document stating that there is a duty to:

> create conditions for the promotion of the ethnic, cultural, linguistic and religious identity of national minorities on their territory.

The most detailed exposition of minority rights within the CSCE process came out of the Copenhagen Meeting of 1990.[37] Its principles:

> represent a significant advance over efforts to define minority rights in other international forums…. The three areas in which the Copenhagen principles contribute most significantly to minority rights are the use of minority languages, education and political participation.[38]

The Copenhagen Document affirms, for instance, the right to use one's mother-tongue in private and public,[39] and that the state should provide 'opportunities for instruction of [the] mother-tongue or in [the] mother-tongue'. Moreover, having asserted the right of persons belonging to minorities to 'effective participation in public affairs', it goes on to declare that the participating states:

> [noted] the efforts undertaken to protect and create conditions for the promotion of the ethnic, cultural, linguistic and religious identity of certain national minorities by establishing…appropriate local or autonomous administrations corresponding to the specific historical and territorial circumstances of such minorities.

The provision adopts the view that individual rights can only be properly protected where the group have political control of their own affairs.[40] Given states' reluctance to accord rights to members of minority groups, this new dimension to their promotion reveals a potentially monumental shift in thinking, even if the participating states only 'noted' it. As a long term goal, it ought to be recognised that mere legal enforceability may not be sufficient to guarantee minority rights and that political power might have to be given to the group with respect to its own affairs.[41] With regard to the German Länder of Schleswig-Holstein, for instance, there is an agreement between Germany and Denmark that the Danish minority will have seats in the assembly.[42] Domestic constitutions need to build in such protections for minority groups; regional or international arrangements are insufficient on their own.

A subsequent CSCE Meeting of Experts on National Minorities in Geneva emphasised that:[43]

> [issues] concerning national minorities, as well as compliance with international obligations and commitments concerning the rights of persons belonging to them, are matters of legitimate international concern and consequently do not constitute an internal affair of the respective state.[44]

The subsequent Helsinki Meeting[45] appointed a High Commissioner on National Minorities:[46]

> The High Commissioner will provide 'early warning' and, as appropriate, 'early action' at the earliest possible stage in regard to tensions involving national minority issues which have not yet developed beyond an early warning stage, but, in the judgement of the High Commissioner, have the potential to develop into a conflict within the CSCE area, affecting peace, stability or relations between participating states, requiring the attention of and action by the [CSCE].

If sufficient resources are provided, sufficient facilities extended, and sufficient respect paid to the High Commissioner, minority rights enforcement in Europe could receive a new and effective voice.

While legal and administrative protection and political representation might be adequate responses to the concerns of some minority groups, however, especially those termed linguistic or religious minorities, it will not satisfy the demands of those groups who see themselves as a nation or people without territorial legitimation of their identity[47]—Croats in what was Yugoslavia, for instance. In those cases, as hardline regimes crumble there will inevitably be a disintegration of previously conglomerated states. The best that can be hoped for is a peaceful establishment of new states. Towards that end, though, the current trend away from the nation-state to regional authority, as for example in the European Community, can only assist, since autonomy within the regional grouping is a less drastic step than independent nationhood for the former minority group.[48]

Inter-state cases

Another aspect of enforcement mechanisms that has a large role to play in preventing the gross violations that set off refugee flows is inter-state cases, although they must be seen as a long term remedy taken when other less confrontational measures have failed. Very few inter-state cases have been brought under the European Convention on Human Rights (ECHR) and none at all under the American Convention on Human Rights (ACHR). Nevertheless, given that the direct victims of such violations are being compelled to flee the state of which they are nationals, it falls to the international community as a whole to take measures to enforce that irreducible minimum of rights guaranteed to all citizens of all states.[49] This approach also implicitly acknowledges that refugee flows affect receiving states and gives them a direct interest in protecting human rights in a third state. Furthermore, an argument can be made that states are obliged under the ECHR[50] to bring inter-state cases to guarantee the rights of refugees who have sought asylum within their jurisdiction. Article 1 states that:

> The High Contracting Parties shall secure to everyone within their jurisdiction the rights and freedoms defined in Section I of this Convention.

According to Advocaat-Generaal Strikwerda of the Dutch Supreme Court in *Short* v. *The Netherlands*,[51] the jurisprudence of the Commission in relation to this issue is extremely broad. Quoting from a Commission decision,[52] he held that:

> It is clear from the language, in particular of the French text, and the object of this Article, and from the purpose of the Convention as a whole, that the High Contracting Parties are bound to secure the said rights and freedoms to all persons under their actual authority and responsibility, *whether that authority is exercised within their own territory or abroad.*[53]

Armed conflicts

Moving on to consider measures to reduce flows resulting from armed conflicts,[54] industrialised states ought to restrain the arms trade that fuels these conflicts.[55] Arms embargoes must be upheld, even if there is apparent injustice—the way the Security Council embargo on arms sales to Croatia was flouted called into question the authority of that organ.[56] It may be possible to make this policy more proactive and encourage a general reduction in the arms trade, if only on the cost-benefit analysis that the arms industry overall costs more than it brings in by way of export revenues.[57] At minimum, where the Foreign Office is seriously concerned about the activities of another government, whether internally or in relation to its neighbours, then it seems sensible to prohibit further arms exports via a DTI refusal of a licence—effective policing of such a ban is also a necessary improvement in the light of the Iraqi supergun fiasco.[58]

Before considering the rules of war that, if followed, might improve the lot of the noncombatant caught up in the hostilities, it has to be admitted that in the light of the means of warfare adopted in Bosnia, all the rules in the world are useless if one side decides to ignore wilfully the basic tenets of the conduct of armed conflicts. The lack of an effective sanction to deal with breaches of the laws of war as they occur, other than reprisals or some war crimes tribunal that might or might not sit in judgment in the future, means that breaches can occur with impunity, especially in internal or quasi-internal conflicts. One option increasingly available is intervention, to be considered below, but it is still in its infancy as a tool of human rights protection.

Existing international legal obligations can be effective in reducing refugee flows. By making war less inhumane and taking steps to protect civilians from the carnage, there will be less need for them to leave their homes and become refugees. The relevant materials include[59] the 1948 Genocide Convention, the four 1949 Geneva Conventions on the Laws of War and the two 1977 Protocols thereto, plus any parts thereof that constitute customary international law. Whereas the 1949 Conventions have been ratified by most states, not so many are parties to the 1977 Protocols which provide better protection to civilian populations. The UK, for instance, has ratified neither Protocol and should rectify this omission. Nevertheless, it may be possible to argue that some elements of the Protocols are customary international law.

Before looking at specific provisions relevant to refugees in times of armed conflict, one must distinguish between international and non-international armed conflicts. The former involve wars between two states and, according to Protocol I, Article 1.4, those situations where peoples are fighting for their self-determination against colonial domination, alien occupation and racist regimes. The precise scope of Article 1.4 is not clear. Non-international armed conflicts, such as civil wars, are governed by common Article 3 of the four Geneva Conventions and Protocol II. The guarantees for non-international armed conflicts are not as forthright, as detailed or as far-reaching, but it may be that some parts of the rules for international armed conflicts constitute customary international law pertinent to non-international conflicts, including those provisions relating to the protection of civilians. Furthermore, where a third state decides to intervene on the side of the rebels, the conflict automatically becomes subject to the rules of international armed conflicts: where the third state supports the incumbent government, however, such as happened when the former USSR sent troops to assist the Afghan regime, the status of the conflict is not settled.

Looking at international armed conflicts first, common Article 1 of the four 1949 Conventions and the 1977 Protocols states:

> The High Contracting Parties undertake to respect and to ensure respect for the present Convention in all circumstances.

While parties to the conflict are expected to abide by the laws of war, non-parties are empowered to take steps to enforce compliance and may be under a duty so to do. Intervention to uphold the rights of a fleeing civilian population may be required of third states. While action in the time of battle may aggravate the situation, there is scope under common Article 1 to instigate measures to prevent abuses during an occupation[60] which may give rise to refugee flows. There is also the possibility of invoking Article 90 of Protocol I and enlisting the assistance of the International Fact Finding Commission. The IFFC may also act in relation to an armed conflict between two states recognising its competence at the behest of a non-involved party.

Turning to Protocol I in detail, it contains several provisions pertinent to the protection of individuals fleeing armed conflict. While the number of states to have ratified the Protocol is not as comprehensive as it is for the 1949 Conventions,[61] nevertheless, many of the most important refugee-related measures could be customary international law applicable to all states. Article 48 requires protagonists to distinguish between civilians[62] and combatants and between civilian and military objectives. Civilian targets should be avoided at all times. On the other hand though, in the heat of battle with an army and a civilian population in full retreat, putting Article 48 into practice may prove difficult. The overriding control on all lawful attacks, however, is that they must be proportionate; this is a rule of customary international law and is an essential element of Articles 50–60.[63] Even if a moving column of refugees contained a military convoy or if a town or refugee camp was full of retreating soldiers, the attacking forces must carry out their objectives so as to avoid civilian targets.[64] Adherence to such provisions would undoubtedly protect refugees. Finally, once an area is captured and occupied by military forces, refugees who were in that area prior to the attack are to be treated as protected persons under Geneva Convention IV and Article 73 of Protocol I.

The only protection for those caught up in non-international armed conflicts comes from common Article 3 of the four 1949 Geneva Conventions, 1977 Protocol II to those conventions and from those parts of customary international law which are applicable to non-international armed conflicts. Dealing with the customary international law point first, it is unclear just how many of the measures deriving from international armed conflicts govern, legally and factually, civil or guerrilla wars. While it is probable that the use of dum-dum bullets is prohibited and can be policed, rules based on the principle of distinction may apply in law, but cannot automatically be effectively implemented because of the nature of the conflict, where combatants do not, for example, wear uniforms.

Common Article 3 provides that non-combatants be treated humanely, which includes a prohibition on violence to the person, on the taking of hostages and on outrages upon personal dignity. Protocol II[65] is slightly more detailed.[66] Unlike Protocol I, Protocol II has very little to say on the issue of the means and methods of warfare. Since the Protocol deals with non-international armed conflicts where the parties will generally be the armed forces of the state and a guerrilla group made up of nationals of the state,[67] distinguishing between combatants and civilians is much more difficult. The relevant provisions are to be found in Articles 13 to 17. Civilians are to enjoy general protection against dangers arising from military operations, so they cannot be directly attacked, and they must not be terrorised. Objectives cannot include those objects indispensable to the survival of the civilian population or those that contain dangerous forces, such as dams, dykes or nuclear generating plants. Most pertinent to the question of refugees, Article 17 states that:

> [the] displacement of the civilian population shall not be ordered
> for reasons related to the conflict unless the security of the
> civilians involved or imperative military reasons so demand.

If abided by, Article 17, in conjunction with Articles 13 to 15, would help reduce the number of persons fleeing in time of non-international armed conflict.

Ratification and accession to both Protocols has not, however, been universal. Increased recognition of the competence of the now operative International Fact Finding Commission under Article 90 of Protocol I would also be helpful. Finally, these international agreements are only effective if all persons involved in the conflict are aware of, and willing to respect, their constraints. To that end, the four Geneva Conventions and the Protocols impose a duty to disseminate their contents in peace-time and during wars to civilians and combatants alike. Encouraging compliance with the obligation to disseminate might eventually lead to conflicts being fought in such a manner that involuntary mass movements of civilians would diminish.

Beyond the laws of war, per se, several Conclusions of the UNHCR Executive Committee[68] have dealt with the issue of attacks on refugee camps.[69] The various Conclusions condemn the attacks, noting the civilian nature of the camps. They also call on all parties, including the refugees themselves, to preserve this civilian status by doing nothing that might continue the war effort from the camps; measures such as moving the camps away from the area of conflict are recommended. Third states are exhorted to provide all necessary assistance to relieve the plight of victims of attacks on camps.

Natural disasters

There are few steps that can be taken to prevent true natural disasters. However, some disasters are not wholly natural. In order to meet debt repayments, governments sometimes have to grow cash crops for export at the expense of feeding their own population with the consequence of dust-bowls and subsequent famine.[70] The extent of the debt burden for some states is highlighted by research based on UK Government statistics which reveals that £2.5 billion more flows back into Britain than goes out in all forms of aid.[71] A proper response to this finding must be, first, to co-ordinate aid and trade policy[72] so as not to promote refugee flows. Second, it is necessary to improve Britain's record in relation to overseas aid from 0.27% to 0.7% of GNP as recommended by the UN and accepted 'in principle' by the Government.[73] Finally, it has to be accepted that debt forgiveness is the only effective method of allowing proper development in third-world states; alternatives, such as the 'Toronto' terms, which restructure debts over 25 years with a fourteen-year grace period, or 50% or 66% reductions in debt do not remove the millstone, but either lighten it slightly or extend the chain around the 'neck' of the developing state.[74]

Intervention

Beyond direct responses specific to the recognised causes of refugee flows, several generalist proposals have been propounded in recent years to meet mass trans-border influxes. The first of these is intervention, which itself has several guises for various different contexts. Since 1980, following steps taken by Canada, the UNHCR and Germany,[75] there have been a series of General Assembly Resolutions and UN reports concerning 'international co-operation to avert new flows of refugees'.

UNHCR Executive Committee Conclusion No.40 on voluntary repatriation[76] stated that:

> (d) The responsibilities of states towards their nationals and the
> obligations of other states to promote voluntary repatriation
> must be upheld by the international community.

Taken together, the two processes permit intervention in the widest sense in the cause of alleviating refugee crises. Moreover, more direct powers have subsequently been adopted by the UN. In 1991, it agreed to appoint a humanitarian co-ordinator who would be able to intervene directly in a state, not necessarily with the consent of that state, in order to respond to a variety of issues,[77] including human rights abuses. In part, this decision built on the concept of safe-havens in Iraq for Kurds that developed after the Gulf Conflict.[78] Furthermore, in the CSCE process, the Moscow meeting agreed in its Final Act in October 1991 to establish an intrusive system of human rights monitoring where a state did not of its own volition seek advice in relation, inter alia, to matters affecting regional stability.[79] The Helsinki 1992 Meeting appointed the High Commissioner for National Minorities[80] and went on to appropriate to the CSCE a peacekeeping role, using the armed forces of the WEU or NATO.[81] The situation is in flux, but there is a recognition that strong measures directed at the source state will prove essential to combating refugee flows.[82] Given that either the Security Council[83] or the CSCE is supervising the intervention, then it may turn out to be an accepted form of action to be implemented against recalcitrant states, but there is a danger that certain states will appear to be international police officers' acting in their own best interests,[84] especially since the Security Council is perceived to be the tool of the five Permanent Members by some third-world countries[85]—intervention requires great care.[86]

Aid and trade

Other more general approaches are more tangential. The principal one of these is to tie aid and development assistance to the record of the receiving government: it is based on the fact that most countries that produce refugee flows are aid receivers from the industrialised states. The Swedish policy review in 1991 put it as follows:

> The Government wishes to continue attaching great importance in development co-operation to the respect shown by recipient countries for human rights. There is no excuse for regimes which kill, torture, maltreat or expel their citizens. As a basis for assessment, it is proposed that the *Riksdag* [parliament] be more systematically informed, in greater depth, of developments in the main recipient countries where respect for human rights is concerned.[87]

Democrats in the US House of Representatives have put forward a Bill to restrict aid being given by the World Bank and the IMF to countries which breach nuclear, chemical and biological weapons non-proliferation treaties.[88] The Swiss policy document, however, considers more than the human rights record in setting out those issues in the light of which the amount of aid, if any, is to be determined. It is more cautious, reflecting the competing interests at stake:[89]

> The difficulties encountered when discussing the measures to combat root causes of emigration—and notably the question of payment of the third-world debt—emphasise these conflicting interests. Even an active policy in the domain of human rights is subject to divergent interests since, while it could serve as an instrument to combat the root causes of emigration, it also tends to collide easily with other foreign policy or economic interests. No government appreciates being reminded of its duties concerning human rights.

Moreover, while tying development aid to 'good government' may seem a sensible form of indirect pressure at first glance, 'bad government' is often the result of limited development rather than its cause. Withholding aid can, therefore, continue a downward spiral. On the other hand, providing aid can prop up a corrupt and tyrannical regime.[90] Tying aid to a human rights record requires lots of detailed implementation, including the existence of truly independent NGO officers in the relevant state and advice to governments on human rights audits and the domestic enforcement of human rights guarantees. Like direct intervention, aid-targeting policies are not simple to put into practice.

The recent establishment in the British Foreign and Commonwealth Office of an independent human rights section with links to the Overseas Development Agency is to be welcomed in this regard. Nevertheless, the present loose co-ordination within the ministries is not appropriate to dealing with the growing issue of involuntary mass movements. There needs to be a co-ordinating committee bringing together the Foreign and Commonwealth Office, the ODA, the Home Office, Department of Trade and Industry and the Ministry of Defence, as appropriate. It does not need to be an overburdensome system but it needs to be put in place for long term planning and crisis management.

Measures when flows occur

Even if one were to accord unparalleled success to the proposals discussed in the previous section then, at best, the number of refugee flows would merely be diminished. Policies also need to be devised to deal with the continuing problem of mass trans-border influxes.

One of the major problems is the co-ordination of the various agencies providing assistance when there is a mass movement of peoples. The refugees will be in the territory of some other sovereign state that formally permits the work of the relief agencies.[91] However, the work will usually be performed by a host of inter- and non-governmental agencies: the principal players are the High Commissioner for Refugees, the UN Department of Humanitarian Affairs, the International Organisation for Migration, the International Committee of the Red Cross,[92] Save the Children, Oxfam, TearFund, CAFOD, the World Food Program and, to a lesser extent, the World Health Organization.[93] The UNHCR is persistently underfunded[94] constraining its efforts.[95] Nevertheless, unlike long-term aid, which may be predicated on concerns about the source state's government, when a true crisis arises funds are more readily supplied.[96]

While the emergency funding might be available, though, there is a secondary problem of channelling it to the agencies 'on the ground'.[97]

The various parties which have to be brought together include the receiving state, the UNHCR, donor states and the agencies performing the relief work. There is no established network that automatically comes into play when a mass movement occurs. There is no legal obligation on donor states to give resources to meet a crisis,[98] no agreement between the relief agencies as to which of them should carry out which types of work and in which regions of the world; and the duties of receiving countries under the 1951 Convention,[99] as has been pointed out above, are notoriously open to constraining interpretations.[100]

Improved co-ordination can be implemented through support for emergency planning through the UN Office for Disaster Relief, the UN Department for Humanitarian Affairs and the UNHCR. On the other hand, a better system would not have to rely on voluntary agencies 'on the ground' for the first news of a mass trans-border influx in order to communicate the crisis beyond its immediate locality so that donor states and receiving states can implement the respective necessary action. Masterplans that will solve unexpected crises are difficult to create. Better long term co-ordination, though, can make crisis solving more effective.

Early warning system

Too often, the relief work only begins once there are hundreds if not thousands of people already present in a neighbouring state. An effective early warning system, on the other hand, would provide time to try to tackle the causes giving rise to an imminent influx through negotiations with the potential source state, to make appropriate preparations for any refugees who do arrive and to establish those causes so that the necessary measures preparatory to repatriation at some time in the future are fully understood.[101]

The UN has gone some way along the path to creating such a system and it should be encouraged in this endeavour.[102] This intergovernmental early warning system is organised by the Department of Humanitarian Affairs and the Office of Research and Collection of Information (ORCI). Its object is to provide information to the various actors to help make the appropriate decisions in the event of a crisis. The following information would be collected:[103]

- numbers, including age, sex;[104]
- rate and direction of movement;
- character of moving population, including nature of impelling force or source of fear, e.g., violations of human rights, insurrection, war, racial strife, hunger, etc.;

- health;
- social origin, e.g., peasant, city dweller, poor, middle class, wealthy, educated, etc.;[105]
- aims of movement, including immediate shelter or protection, temporary asylum, resettlement, insurrection, etc.;

The CSCE at its 1992 Helsinki meeting also established an early warning system as part of its endeavours with respect to conflict resolution and the protection of minorities.[106] While the purpose is not identical to that of the ORCI, if the CSCE were to receive pertinent information it ought to be possible to warn the relief agencies that a flow might be expected if tensions were to continue to rise. Furthermore, the UNHCR has taken a firm position on preventive measures in recent years, providing a presence whenever there are internally displaced persons. It not only co-ordinates humanitarian relief but is also available to give technical advice on human rights and refugee law.[107]

In conclusion, if the relief effort were to be co-ordinated and had the sort of information that early warning might provide, then the practical task of meeting the needs of refugees would be rendered more effective.

State responsibility for causing refugee flows

Refugees tend to focus one's attention on the receiving state, the donor countries and the relief agencies. Little time is spent on considering the source state. This paper has gone some way to remedy this, but the nature of refugee law is to ignore the involvement of the state whence the refugee emanates. The 1951 Convention and 1967 Protocol deal with the source state only in terms of the refugee's right not to be returned there.[108] If the flow has occurred the source state is not an active participant in any solution until negotiations begin on voluntary repatriation. The reforms suggested above may change this approach. Nevertheless, given the disruption to the lives of the refugees and to the receiving state, fixing the source state with legal responsibility may help to remedy the causes of the present crisis and encourage practices less likely to give rise to future flows.[109]

States are liable for their own activities so, if the army attacks its own citizens, then the consequent refugee flow is the responsibility of the state. States are also liable if acts committed by the local populace are, 'knowingly tolerated by the authorities, or if the authorities refuse, or prove unable, to offer effective protection'.[110]

There is no difficulty in attributing responsibility where the state turns a blind eye to, or adopts the acts of, some third-party persecutors. However, there is less agreement concerning persecution by a third-party that the state is unable to prevent.[111] Given that the concept of persecution is founded in international human rights law and practice,[112] then the trend in that field would suggest that states are liable where they do not do sufficient to prevent abuses by non-state actors:

> An illegal act which violates human rights and which is initially not directly imputable to a state (for example, because it is the act of a private person or because the person responsible has not been identified) can lead to international responsibility of the state, not because of the act itself, but because of the lack of due diligence to prevent the violation or to respond to it as required by the Convention.[113]

Thus, a mass trans-border influx caused by the activities of a guerrilla group trying to overthrow the state may give rise to refugee status; if so, state responsibility may also arise if the government has not done enough to guarantee the basic rights of its citizens in part of its territory.[114] In addition, if the state's activities lead to massive pollution in an area or, exceptionally, if the state lets a private enterprise cause such widespread harm, it may be liable for any consequent flow of people across a border. It would not be appropriate to affix liability where the flow is caused by the activities of a third state during an invasion or occupation. In those circumstances it might be right, though, to treat the aggressor state as the 'source state' for the purposes of state responsibility.

The question that follows is whether a successful claim against the source state could be made by the refugees. General Assembly Resolution 194 (III) of 11 December 1948,[115] drafted by the UK Government in response to the rights of the Palestinians displaced by the emergent state of Israel and affirmed ever since,[116] is as follows:

> [The General Assembly resolves] that the refugees wishing to return to their homes and live at peace with their neighbours should be permitted to do so at the earliest practicable date, and

that compensation should be paid for the property of those choosing not to return and for loss or damage to property which, under principles of international law or in equity, should be made good by the Governments or authorities responsible.

The limitations of this resolution are that it was restricted to those deciding not to return and only for property losses. No mention is made of a general right to compensation for all those persons forced to become refugees for all the wrongs and indignities suffered by them.[117] Nevertheless, the fundamental principles upon which the refugee's right to damages for property loss are founded would readily justify compensating all other forms of loss and damage that the refugee has suffered, given, of course, that the right could be put into effect.[118]

While the right to compensation of refugees has been recognised in international law, the rights of receiving states are not as clearly defined. However, the nature of statehood is to have exclusive control over some territory. It is the duty of all other states to act in no way that would interfere with that control:

All states enjoy sovereign equality. They have equal rights and duties and are equal members of the international community.

In particular, sovereign equality includes the following elements:

(b) Each state enjoys the rights inherent in full sovereignty;

(c) Each state has the duty to respect the personality of other states;

(d) The territorial integrity...of the state [is] inviolable;

(f) Each state has the duty to comply fully and in good faith with its international obligations and to live in peace with other states.[119]

The usual rule of international law cited to prove that there is liability for causing refugee flows into a neighbouring state is the decision in the *Trail Smelter* arbitration.[120] There is an initial problem with this line of argument in that the case concerned trans-border air pollution rather than persecuted individuals but the underlying principles are deemed by most writers to hold good.[121] Both fumes and refugees are not willingly received by the injured state and both may place economic and social burdens on that state. If the disparaging analogy is disregarded, then a strong case can be put for attributing liability to the source state *vis à vis* the receiving state for activities carried out in the source state which give rise to the influx. While refugees can more easily be prevented from entering the receiving state than could fumes, it is only at the expense of the latter's humanitarian obligations. It is no defence in international law to argue that the plaintiff state could have avoided loss by breaching its own obligations:

> [The] wilful flooding of other states with refugees constitutes not merely an inequitable act, but an actual illegality, and *a fortiori* where the refugees are compelled to enter the country of refuge in a destitute condition.[122]

Other grounds for upholding liability include the fact that the source state has denied its citizens their nationality contrary to international law and that the social burden placed on the receiving state gives quasi-contractual rights.

Assuming that state responsibility to other states as well as to the refugees exists, how might it be effected? If the International Law Commission's Draft on state Responsibility is ever adopted, then it is likely that behaviour that causes flows would be characterised as an Article 19 international crime.[123] It would constitute a 'serious breach on a widespread scale of an international obligation of essential importance for safeguarding the human being'. However, Article 19 is not well-received by most states and its underlying rationale may not be best suited to dealing with a humanitarian crisis. The traditional initial response of international law would be to issue a protest to the source state[124]—Bangladesh has recently protested to Burma about the influx of 150,000 Rohingya Muslims fleeing persecution by the Burmese army[125]. The next step would ordinarily be to invoke the peaceful settlement of disputes procedure in Chapter VI of the UN Charter, including recourse to the International Court of Justice which can impose appropriate sanctions.[126]

In some circumstances and at some stages in every case, such a process may well be suitable as an immediate response to this particular influx and as a long-term deterrent. On the other hand, since it is currently the sole means of seeking a solution to the influx, it is inadequate to the task. It is an extremely confrontational approach,[127] while the object of the exercise is to encourage a negotiated agreement to achieve repatriation. To that end, new international arrangements will prove necessary which:

> mitigate the asperities and chaos of the movement by engaging state-of-origin responsibility where it is now not commonly engaged. What can be established are obligations to co-operate in

the prevention of flow, obligations to adhere to procedures for the amelioration and management of flow, and obligations to help secure voluntary repatriation. States of origin may respect procedural and substantive limitations they see as tolerable and advantageous in order to reduce the political fallout that results from outflow.

[The] institutionalisation of engagement of the state of origin must be at least as important as the development of substantive principles of responsibility...First...comes the function of early warning and monitoring. Second is the need to provide management and aid functions in relation to the state of origin. Third, the institutional apparatus must be designed to stimulate the political processes that will secure the co-operation of the state of origin, and to orchestrate any appropriate *quid pro quo* of assistance from the international community that may be needed to promote resolutions such as voluntary repatriation.[128]

The work of the Carter Foundation in the field of internal conflict resolution ought to be encouraged in this regard.

State responsibility is important in that it imposes obligations on the source state but the nature of those obligations is just as important to the desired final result. The aim must be to achieve voluntary repatriation of those fleeing in as short a time as possible—the idea that a case before the ICJ will result in such an outcome is untenable, especially given the usual background in the source state that gives rise to the flow. It is, of course, also essential to ensure that the obligations imposed on the source state do not encourage it to prevent refugees leaving the country by restricting their freedom of movement.

Conclusion

Refugee flows are here to stay and international relief will be required even where the people fleeing do not fit within the 1951 definition. Regardless of whether or not a new, broader definition of refugees is adopted, the proposals mentioned here will prove necessary to protect those who have to flee human rights abuses, armed conflicts and natural disasters. The accepted view is that voluntary repatriation is the optimum solution. That is most easily achieved if the time spent in the receiving state is as short as possible. By taking steps to prevent flows, the number thereof and their size will be greatly reduced. By implementing early warning, co-ordinated relief and state responsibility, those who flee should receive better care and should be able to go home sooner.

The United Kingdom, in particular, needs to develop a policy to deal with mass involuntary migrations and their causes, bringing together a broad grouping of ministries and departments. In the future, mass trans-border influxes will not only increase in number, but there is also a growing internationalisation of responsibility, either via the United Nations or the CSCE, which will involve the United Kingdom more directly. On a strict cost-benefit analysis in the short term, the establishment of such an inter-departmental network compared to the actual costs of dealing with the immediate crisis as it arises, might well reveal it to be inefficient, but over time a co-ordinated policy would reduce the number, size and frequency of flows and, thus, pay for itself, regardless of any humanitarian considerations.

Points for action

The following points have been made in the text of this document and are collected together here for ease of reference and as a checklist against which the success of the British Government, the EC and the UN can be assessed. Given that there is a growing commitment to a common foreign policy within the EC, recommendations for action by the British Government should, unless inapplicable, be read to include action by the EC and the other member states as well.

1. While a strict interpretation of persecution is likely to be employed when evaluating an applicant's case for asylum in the United Kingdom, where the object is to provide relief to persons displaced, whether within or without their national borders, the 1951 Convention's out-of-date definition should have no bearing. While pressing for a more applicable and more liberal definition of refugee status, the British Government should see relief work for those persons forced to leave their homes as a result of all gross human rights violations, armed conflict or 'natural' disaster as governed by factors other than strict legalism. A failure to provide relief initially to 'protectees' leads inexorably to more requests being made for asylum to those states which can provide adequate resources for their citizens.

2. To prevent flows arising, the British Government must undertake

certain steps with regard to its foreign policy:

- Encourage adherence to human rights conventions and the adoption of rights of individual petition.
- Support the work of independent human rights NGOs.
- Given that mass movements of peoples often result from mistreatment of minority groups within a state, their greater protection in international instruments, regional agreements and domestic constitutions must be promoted; such protection may be through judicial, administrative or political processes.
- With regard to displacements in the CSCE area, the work of the High Commissioner for National Minorities must be supported and receive appropriate assistance.
- Promote the use of inter-state cases as one method of enforcing compliance with human rights obligations.
- Since armed conflicts cause many of the mass movements of peoples, it would be a sensible policy to restrict the arms trade, preferably in a general manner, but at minimum to those governments about which there are serious misgivings.
- The British Government should ratify Protocols I and II to the 1949 Geneva Conventions at the earliest opportunity if for no other reason than *pour encourager les autres*.
- Third-world debt is a major factor behind many mass movements of peoples. The United Kingdom is a principal loan provider and should continue its policy of debt forgiveness— debt rescheduling merely extends the time for which the debt will be a problem.
- The United Kingdom should increase its overseas aid to the recommended level of 0.7% of GNP.
- The United Kingdom Government should play a full and constructive role in the UN and the CSCE given the greater use of direct intervention channelled through those two IGOs to prevent regional instability.
- It would be helpful to co-ordinate aid and trade policies so as to promote human rights, although the process is difficult to establish and run in practice.

3. When flows occur there is a need for proper co-ordination of those organisations involved in the relief effort. The UNHCR and the UN Department of Humanitarian Affairs are best placed to carry out this task, but to do so funding from donor governments must

be more secure; more co-ordination within the United Kingdom would also be helpful.

4. To relieve the tragic consequences of refugee flows, an early warning and action system needs to be established. The efforts of the UN's Office of Research and Collection of Information and Department of Humanitarian Affairs, the UNHCR and the CSCE to this end should be strongly supported, although those organisations need to act with more alacrity. Further, there is a need for more intrusive monitoring before the movements of persons involves the crossing of an international border so as to improve the situation in the source state before it gives rise to a trans-border influx.

5. As one more measure to try and put pressure on source states not to cause flows, actions in international law by the individual refugees and the receiving state should seriously be considered.

2 CURRENT AND FUTURE MIGRATION FLOWS

Reuben Ford[1]

Migration flows into and out of the UK must be seen as the products of three main migration regimes: settlement; temporary labour; and asylum-seeking. However, these are not always easy to distinguish since one may easily become another. Whilst settlement emigration was dominant for the UK pre-Second World War and persisted into the 1960s, bi-directional flows rose to prominence in the 1950s and 1960s. British skilled and unskilled workers were attracted to employment opportunities in growing economic regions such as the Middle East while low-skilled workers from ex-colonial New Commonwealth countries were encouraged by opportunities for work rebuilding post-war Britain. The return component of many such moves often failed to materialise, turning these flows into de facto settlement migration, and the reuniting of families in the UK together with marriage practices has engendered further settlement in its wake.

Within each regime, there has been major change over the past twenty years. Temporary labour flows have continued but with the emphasis increasingly on skilled worker flows into and out of the UK. Many of these are within the internal labour markets of multinational firms. The UK is currently a net recipient of professional and managerial workers. Manual worker flows have also seen renewed growth, the majority with other EC states. Whilst primary settlement moves are of reduced importance, asylum-seekers—always a feature of UK immigration flows—have risen to prominence. Applications for asylum have shown dramatic growth; given the curbs on other routes of entry, it is inevitable that a proportion of these applications will be from persons who would previously have entered via a different route. All these changes have occurred within a 'closing door' legislation policy, responsive rather than proactive, largely operating by political consensus.

These significant new trends and shifts in the nature of flows call for a reappraisal of policy which reviews not only the changes in the type of migration the policy is trying to control, but the purpose of the policy itself in serving the interests of the UK.

Data sources

Any analysis of stocks or flows of migrants is hampered by the absence of appropriate data sources. The principal sources listed below have been derived from surveys or registers established for other purposes:

☐ *International Passenger Survey (IPS)*
This is a continuous voluntary sample survey conducted by OPCS which covers the principal air and sea routes between the UK and overseas but excludes those between the UK and Eire. Migration flows have been monitored since 1964. Migrants are those who have been resident abroad for at least one year who on entering the UK state an intention to reside here for at least one year, or who on leaving intend to reside abroad for at least one year. The survey samples about 0.2% of inbound and outbound passengers. As only a small proportion of these are migrants, large standard errors arise when any breakdown is attempted. The 1990 estimate of 65,900 migrants entering the UK from the EC is based on only 127 interviews and is subject to a standard error of 12.2% or 8,000 migrants. Nevertheless the IPS is the only source to record emigrants.

☐ *Labour Force Survey (LFS)*
The LFS is a sample survey of all persons resident in private households. Approximately 63,000 households were sampled annually until 1992 when the sample size was substantially increased. It includes all UK and foreign citizens. Although the number of migrants picked up is larger than in the IPS, sampling error can still be high. Estimates below 10,000 are regarded as too prone to error and are not used. Migrants are defined as those living or working in the UK who were living and working outside the UK one year ago.

☐ *Home Office data on Immigration Control, Settlement and Asylum*
Home Office statistics result primarily from the process of immigration control and are not therefore strictly immigration statistics.

☐ *Department of Employment Work Permits*
The employment of people who are subject to immigration control

is regulated by the granting of work permits. Under the 1971 Immigration Act, a work permit is granted to a specific employer for a named person for a specific job. All foreign nationals who are not EC citizens, and whose primary intention is to work in the UK, must obtain a work permit. Work permit data record flows but not stocks of foreign workers.

☐ *Department of Social Security (DSS)*
DSS statistics are based on a 100% extraction of data on non-UK nationals arriving from abroad who register or re-register for NI (National Insurance) purposes during each year. The data pick up many not included in other surveys but they have never been properly verified.

☐ *OPCS Census*
The decadal 100% survey of the UK population provides information on place of birth and (from 1991) ethnic group. The most recently published results (at the time of writing) are those of the 1981 Census and these are too dated to be used here. The Census does not record information on nationality.

With each source, the different sample bases used reflect the purposes for which data are collected and comparison is difficult. Home Office data apply to acceptances for settlement and grants of asylum and citizenship over a different timescale to the point sampling of the two surveys. Estimates cannot easily be matched.[2] Since work permit and DSS data apply solely to incoming foreign workers, a comparison is only possible by reference to their estimates of foreign worker flows into the UK. Varying estimates of these flows are shown in Figure 2.1, and for non-EC foreign workers (those requiring work permits) in Figure 2.2. The discrepancy between DSS and other estimates may be accounted for by the need to register for NI no matter how short the period of employment and because a number of non-work-permit-holders who enter the country legally for other purposes later take up work and pay NI as do a number of illegal immigrants. The LFS consistently estimates about half the number of non-EC foreign workers suggested by the IPS (which excludes the Irish) and this may be due to the IPS recording incoming 'migrants' who fail to find employment or to complete their first year of stay, and the LFS until 1992 excluding persons not resident in households.

Thus, although the sources chosen are the 'best available' at the present time, less than full confidence can be expressed in their ability

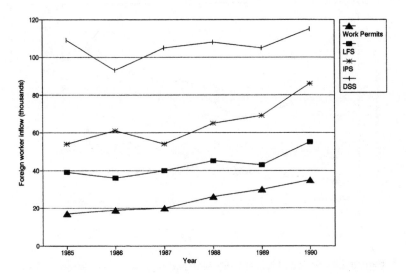

Figure 2.1   Flows of Foreign National Workers: Different Data Sources
(1985–90)

Sources: International Passenger Survey (IPS) data from OPCS 'Overseas travel and tourism', *Business Statistics Office Business Monitor MA6*, 1981–92 annual, HMSO; Labour Force Survey (LFS), Department of Social Security (DSS) and Work Permit data derived from J. Salt, International Migration and the United Kingdom', unpublished report of the United Kingdom SOPEMI correspondent to the OECD, 1991.

to construct an accurate and comprehensive representation of migration stocks and flows in the UK today.

UK migration system in context

Flows into and out of the UK cannot be seen in isolation. Sets of options for potential immigrants and emigrants are influenced by the policies of other potential destination countries. Each of the three components of the migration system affecting the UK is influenced by the UK's membership of the EC and the provisions of the Treaty of Rome and the Single European Act (SEA) with respect to freedom of movement. EC citizens (and from December 1993, citizens of the European Economic Area) are free to enter, settle and work in other member states and thus little control can be exerted over one major component of migration flows into the country. At the same time, other EC countries will represent attractive destinations for UK

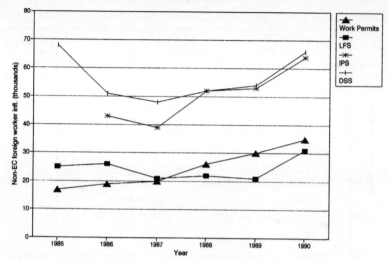

Figure 2.2 Flows of Non-EC Foreign National Workers: Different Data Sources (1985–90)

Sources: International Passenger Survey (IPS) data from OPCS 'Overseas travel and tourism', *Business Statistics Office Business Monitor MA6*, 1981–92 annual, HMSO; Labour Force Survey (LFS), Department of Social Security (DSS) and Work Permit data derived from J. Salt, 'International Migration and the United Kingdom', unpublished report of the United Kingdom SOPEMI correspondent to the OECD, 1991.

emigrants. Pressures for international migration at a global level impinge upon the UK, though to varying degrees. These pressures include the demographic, economic, political and environmental forces now increasing the emigration potential from Eastern Europe and the South. Countries in these regions account for between 42% (LFS) and 50% (IPS) of the UK's foreign citizen immigrants and it is these pressures which drive immigration policy at the European level. As a member of the EC, the UK is inevitably drawn into the debate on the harmonisation of entry control and integration. Beyond Europe, it is by no means clear what will be the effect on the UK and other European countries of the increasing emphasis on migrant quality being placed by Australia, Canada and the USA.

The European perspective

The Treaty of Rome (Article 52, effective from 1968) guarantees EC nationals the freedom to move to any other member country to seek

Table 2.1 Composition of Resident Population in EC States by Broad Nationality Breakdown (1990) (per cent)

Country of Residence	Non-EC Foreigners	EC Foreigners	Nationals
Belgium	3.5	5.5	90.9
Denmark	2.6	0.5	96.9
Germany	4.8	1.8	93.4
Greece	1.7	0.5	97.7
France	4.1	2.3	93.6
Italy	1.1	0.3	98.6
Ireland	0.5	1.2	98.3
Luxembourg	2.0	25.7	72.3
Netherlands	3.5	1.1	95.4
Portugal	0.8	0.3	99.0
Spain	0.5	0.7	98.8
United Kingdom	1.9	1.4	96.7
Total	2.7	1.4	95.9

Source: Eurostat Demographic Statistics, 1992; Labour Force Survey, 1993.

and take up work and residence. The SEA provides the basis for policies to remove remaining barriers to the freedom of movement of capital, goods, services and labour between EC members. One outcome, although not yet fully supported by all member states, would be for a 'ringfence' to be created within which intra-EC moves will remain unchecked. The principal 'internal' migrants have been the highly-skilled, the young and those undertaking retirement moves. There is little evidence to show that freedom of movement has led to substantial increases in these flows. Immigration from elsewhere— Turkey, Yugoslavia and North Africa—has grown in the 1980s through networks based on proximity, old colonial ties and policy differentials. Non-EC foreigners in EC countries accounted for 2.7% of the EC's population in 1990 (Table 2.1).

The uneven distribution of asylum applications across EC countries has already been highlighted. Inherent in this asymmetry are disparities in regions of origin (Figure 2.3). Applications to European countries increased fivefold between 1983 and 1991. Concurrently, there has been a decline in the proportion granted full refugee status. With the SEA in mind, some initiatives in harmonising asylum policy, such as the Dublin Convention agreement, have been achieved. Centralisation and computerisation of information concerning asylum

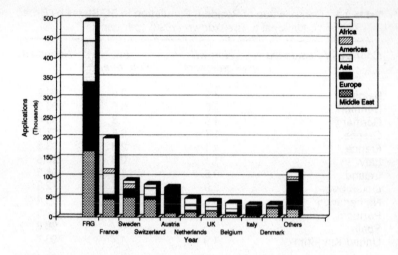

Figure 2.3 Asylum Applications by Region of Origin: Destinations in Europe (1983-9)

Source: Derived from B. Hovy *Asylum Migration in Europe: Patterns, Determinants and the Role of East-West Movements*, paper presented to conference on Mass Migration in Europe, Implications for East and West, Vienna, 5–7 March 1992.

applications should reduce the number of multiple asylum applications.

The complex nature of the EC's internal and external migration flows precludes simple harmonisation of other policies towards immigration. Political unrest and tension could follow any moves which disadvantage minority immigrant groups. Agreement has yet to be made upon the movement within the EC of third-country nationals. Many broader policy concerns exist such as over the role of aid budgets in stemming migration pressure and how this burden should be apportioned between member states.[3] Along with indecision over voting rights for intra-EC and other immigrants, many issues remain to be resolved before full freedom of movement within the 'ringfence' will be possible.

Migration stocks and flows

The United Kingdom has throughout its history experienced gains and losses through migration. For example, Jews and Moors arrived from Spain in the fifteenth and sixteenth centuries and Huguenots from France in 1685. Imperial Britain lost population as administrators, dissenters, convicts, economic migrants and the military departed for the colonies. Towards the end of the eighteenth century, around 10,000 British citizens were emigrating to North America every year. In the middle of the nineteenth century, Britain was a country of net emigration but by the late nineteenth century the position was reversed.

Effective UK legislation concerning immigration is largely a twentieth century phenomenon. It has been a country of emigration for much of its history, actively encouraging it in the nineteenth and twentieth centuries for both internal and external political reasons— reducing the numbers of rural poor and increasing the UK's dominance of the Empire and later Commonwealth.[4] Large-scale immigration began only after the Second World War, from Eire and the New Commonwealth. Irish citizens have never been subject to immigration control (except during wartime) and estimating their flows is difficult but it is safe to say that net immigration has been positive and high throughout the post-war period, peaking in 1966 when the Irish born comprised 2% of the population of England and Wales. Irish immigration, predominantly labour migration, has been permitted to continue despite the introduction of legislative controls on immigration from all other former colonies.

Thus, current migrations affecting the UK cannot be seen in isolation. They will stem in part from the past patterns of settlement of UK, Commonwealth and foreign citizens. Similarly, the factors generating current flows should not be dissociated from the factors acting to mobilise populations in the recent past or even long ago.

Total flows

Observed migration flows consist of variable components defined by citizenship, country of origin and occupational status. Thus, after an initial overview, an attempt will be made as far as the reliability of sources permits, to break down flows to show trends in each of these components. According to the LFS, 127,000 foreign nationals who were living in the UK in 1990 had been living abroad a year earlier. The broadly equivalent figure from the IPS, that for entry in 1989, was 145,300 (excluding Irish citizens). Both sources have their faults, and so it is because the IPS figures record both inflows and outflows that these are used in the following section (except where otherwise indicated).

Flows and citizenship

Figure 2.4 illustrates how net migration levels have fluctuated over recent years. Figures 2.5 and 2.6 show how these balances are the result of very different trends in the migration of British and non-British citizens. The large net outflows of British citizens in the 1960s have declined due to a decline in emigration and increase in immigration among British citizens. The first recorded year in which inflows came close to matching outflows was 1985. Flows of non-British citizens have remained remarkably consistent over the period, suggesting that fluctuations in net migration are due more to the patterns of migration of British citizens, than the decisions and actions of foreigners. Britons still form the largest single group of immigrants and the majority of emigrants (Figures 2.7 and 2.8). Although rates of non-British emigration have been rising since 1984, increases in inflows have more than compensated, leading to increases in net immigration of foreigners in the latter half of the 1980s.

The combined effect of British and non-British citizen flows is a complex picture. Britain was a country of net emigration from the inception of the IPS in 1964 up to 1978, and again in 1980–2 and 1987–8. For seven of the past eight years, however, it has been a country of net immigration.

High standard errors prevent all but a cursory examination of general trends in flow composition. Although non-British immigration and emigration have been increasing throughout the 1980s, there has been considerable variation in the flows of other nationals (Figures 2.9 to 2.12). Substantial increases in EC (excluding Irish) citizen entry and exit have occurred (Figure 2.9), partly in response to freedom of movement within the Community, though it is doubtful that migration will be increased further by the SEA. Nearly two-thirds of non-Irish EC immigrants are workers (many young) and it can be assumed that return migration following completion of temporary work commitments in the UK accounts for some of the lag seen between increases in immigration and emigration. The immigration of Old Commonwealth citizens has tripled over the decade, overtaking the relatively stable emigration rate of this group (Figure

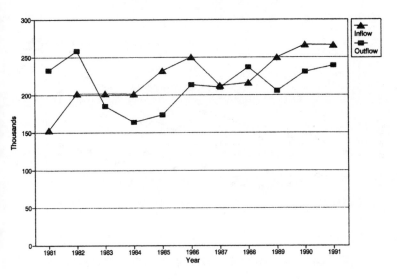

Figure 2.4 International Migration (1981–91): All Citizenships

Source: OPCS 'Overseas travel and tourism', *Business Statistics Office Business Monitor MA6*, 1981–92 annual, HMSO.

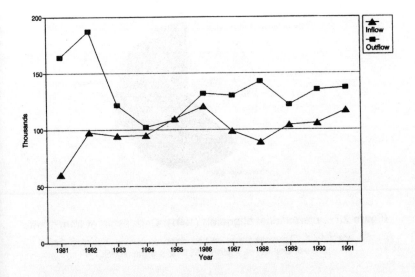

Figure 2.5 International Migration (1981–91): British Citizens

Source: OPCS 'Overseas travel and tourism', *Business Statistics Office Business Monitor MA6*, 1981–92 annual, HMSO.

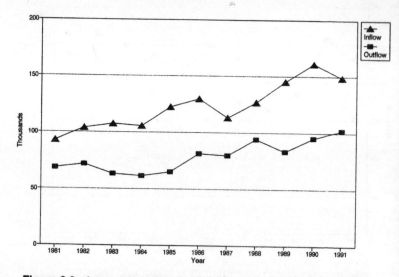

Figure 2.6 International Migration (1981–91): Non-British Citizens

Source: OPCS 'Overseas travel and tourism', *Business Statistics Office Business Monitor MA6*, 1981–92 annual, HMSO.

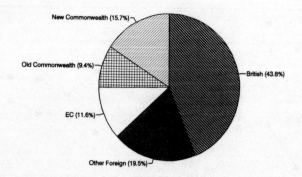

Figure 2.7 International Migration (1991): Citizenship of Immigrants

Source: OPCS 'Overseas travel and tourism', *Business Statistics Office Business Monitor MA6*, 1981–92 annual, HMSO.

2.10). Over 80% of Old Commonwealth immigrants are workers and thus labour migration would account for much of these flows. Others are working holiday makers. Flows of New Commonwealth citizens

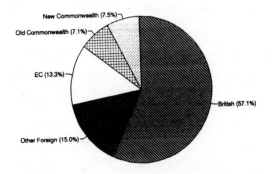

Figure 2.8   International Migration (1991): Citizenship of Emigrants

Source: OPCS 'Overseas travel and tourism', *Business Statistics Office Business Monitor MA6*, 1981–92 annual, HMSO.

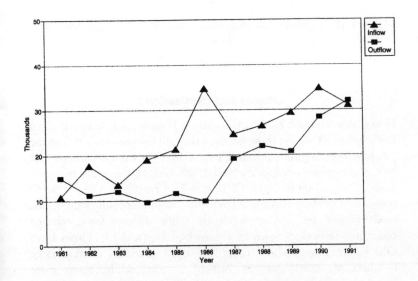

Figure 2.9   International Migration (1981–91): EC Citizens

Source: OPCS 'Overseas travel and tourism', *Business Statistics Office Business Monitor MA6*, 1981–92 annual, HMSO.

were relatively stable throughout the 1980s (Figure 2.11). Net immigration has been high as outflows remain at around half the level of inflows.

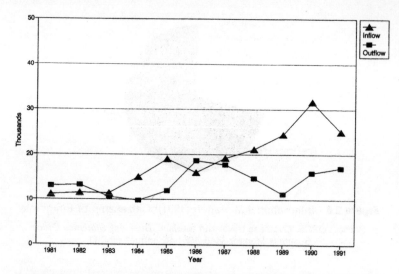

Figure 2.10 International Migration (1981–91): Old Commonwealth Citizens

Source: OPCS 'Overseas travel and tourism', *Business Statistics Office Business Monitor MA6*, 1981–92 annual, HMSO.

Origins and destinations

Flows between the UK and EC countries (Figure 2.13) have remained fairly balanced, whilst those between the Old Commonwealth and the UK have been anything but so (Figure 2.14). The exodus from the UK to this region subsided in the mid-1980s only to rise again in recent years. Comparison of Figures 2.10 and 2.14 reveals that only a small proportion of these flows comprise Old Commonwealth citizens; this tendency can be seen more clearly when inflows from selected countries are broken down by citizenship (Figure 2.15). Flows from Old Commonwealth and other developed countries contain large numbers of 'other' (mainly British) citizens, whilst flows from Bangladesh, India and Sri Lanka are composed almost entirely of citizens of those countries. Flows to and from the New Commonwealth and other countries are shown in Figures 2.16 and 2.17.

Age and sex

Sample size prevents good demographic data on migrants being collated. From the IPS, however, it can be seen that immigrants and

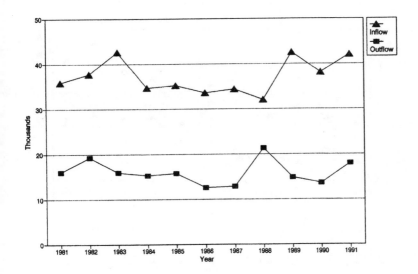

Figure 2.11 International Migration 1981–91: New Commonwealth Citizens

Source: OPCS 'Overseas travel and tourism', *Business Statistics Office Business Monitor MA6*, 1981–92 annual, HMSO.

emigrants have similar age structures (Figures 2.18 and 2.19). It does seem that flows in both directions are dominated by the young. Less than 12% of both inflow and outflow were aged over 45, compared to a third of the population as a whole. In the absence of substantial temporary labour migration, gender differences in flows are small (Figures 2.20 and 2.21).

Thus the UK can be seen to be involved in a perpetual and increasing exchange of population with its European neighbours and other economic partners. It currently experiences net gains of population from New Commonwealth countries and net losses to the Old Commonwealth. It is, however, a net recipient of citizens belonging to both the former and the latter. To assess the implications of these trends, it is necessary to examine in more detail the different migration systems to which such flows belong.

Labour migration

It has already been shown that estimates of the size of labour inflows depend upon the source used (Figures 2.1 and 2.2). Yet only by using

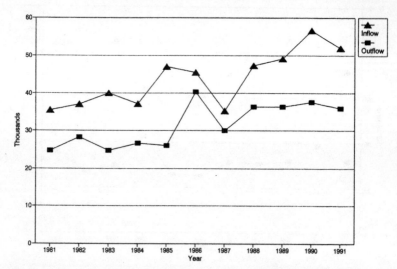

Figure 2.12 International Migration (1981–91): Other Foreign Citizens

Source: OPCS 'Overseas travel and tourism', *Business Statistics Office Business Monitor MA6*, 1981–92 annual, HMSO.

different sources can an adequate impression of the composition of flows be achieved.

An age and regional breakdown of newly entering foreign workers is possible using DSS data (Tables 2.2 and 2.3). The flow is young, predominantly centred on the South East, with 40–50% of workers coming from the EC. The composition of non-EC flows can be examined in more detail by reference to work permit data. In 1990, 34,627 work permits were issued, the holders being accompanied by 13,400 dependents. At the same time, according to the IPS, 126,400 non-EC foreign nationals entered the UK. As 60,800 of the latter group are accounted for by housewives, students and children, we can estimate that a minimum of some 30,000 adults entered the country from non-EC countries with no specified job to go to.[5] In addition, over half of work permits issued were for short-term work or training and will not have been granted to those defined as migrants by the IPS but to entertainers and sports people (accounting for four-fifths of short-term issues) and to business travellers or short-term secondees staying in the UK for less than one year.

According to the IPS, almost two-thirds of gainfully employed immigrants are accounted for by the highly skilled (Figure 2.22).

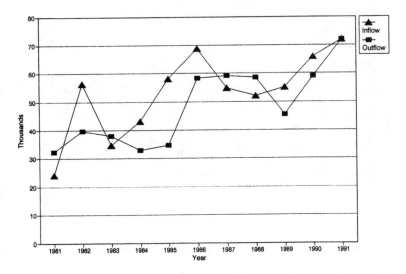

Figure 2.13 International Migration (1981–91): To and From EC Countries

Source: OPCS 'Overseas travel and tourism', *Business Statistics Office Business Monitor MA6*, 1981–92 annual, HMSO.

Whilst this inflow of professional and managerial workers has doubled over the decade, the number of such emigrants has shown no overall trend (Figure 2.23), fluctuating at around 70,000 for much of the decade. Evidence for an extensive 'brain drain' is thus weak. Nevertheless, fears are expressed over the loss of very high level manpower which cannot be picked up by a survey such as the IPS.[6] The UK has, however, been a net recipient of many categories of migrant who are not economically active as conventionally defined: students, children, housewives and other adults.

Work permit flows indicate a highly specialised type of labour migration. Seven countries account for over a third of long-term work permit issues (USA, Japan, Australia, Hong Kong, India, Malaysia and China). At the same time, over 80% of long term work permit issues—those of most importance in labour migration—are for professional or managerial work. Since 1985 (when data became available) there has been consecutive increase—in 1990 of 6%—in permits issued to workers transferring internationally from one work position to another whilst remaining with the same employer. About four in ten permits are issued to people moving within the internal

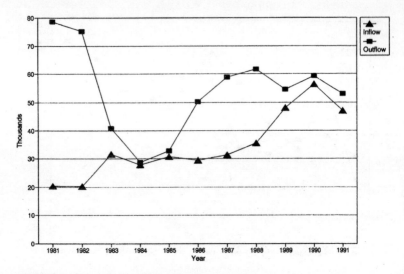

Figure 2.14 International Migration (1981–91): To and From Old Commonwealth Countries

Source: OPCS 'Overseas travel and tourism', *Business Statistics Office Business Monitor MA6*, 1981–92 annual, HMSO.

labour markets of firms in this way, down from 60% a few years ago, although this may be an artificial' fall for technical reasons. The system has also recently been streamlined to simplify entry for this group.[7] During the 1970s and 1980s, numbers of work permits granted have been inversely correlated with levels of unemployment, although this apparent 'sensitivity' of work permit policy to labour market conditions[8] has not held for more recent years.

The UK has thus acted to ensure that labour migrants from beyond the EC are highly-skilled. Whilst it is evident that labour migration from EC and other countries does bring a substantial number of low-skilled workers into the country, it is impossible to assess from current data sources the likely impact of such flows on the UK labour market.

Family reunion and marriage

The door for new low-skilled labour migration from Commonwealth countries was effectively closed by the 1962 and 1971 Immigration Acts, but continuing provision for family reunion (dependents and spouses of primary labour migrants) and patrials has ensured a

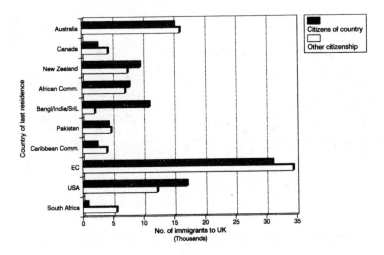

Figure 2.15 Citizenship of Immigrants from Selected Countries of Last Residence (1990)

Source: OPCS (1991) Birth Statistics 1989, series FMI No.18, HMSO.

continuing net immigration flow of citizens from these countries. The need for fiancé(e)s and spouses among the UK immigrant population, with its youthful age-structure, is likely to generate many more such immigrants under existing marriage practices. In total, spouses account for 27,240 (over half) of all acceptances for settlement from all regions. Children account for a further 8,250 acceptances (16% of the total).

Asylum seekers

Britain is one of over 100 states acceding to the 1951 Convention Relating to the Status of Refugees adopted by the United Nations in 1951. Originally it applied only to those acquiring refugee status prior to 1951. Together with the 1967 Protocol which lifted this time restriction, the Convention forms the principal legal instrument to benefit refugees. The major impact upon the UK of observance of the terms of the Convention and Protocol, aside from accommodating the population displacements of the immediate post-war period, has been as a result of the complex refugee problems arising in the developing world since the 1970s. The 1970s saw small numbers of applications

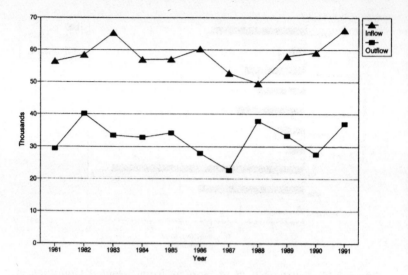

Figure 2.16 International Migration (1981–91): To and From New Commonwealth Countries

Source: OPCS 'Overseas travel and tourism', *Business Statistics Office Business Monitor MA6*, 1981–92 annual, HMSO.

and refugees entering the country, other than the 23,000 Ugandan Asian refugees given leave to enter the UK in 1973. In 1979 there were only 1,563 applications to the UK from all sources.

Applications have increased substantially in recent years (Figure 2.24) but are relatively small compared to applications made to other European countries: West Germany had 256,000 applications in 1991. Whilst many applications are linked to specific regional pressures—in Iran, Sri Lanka or Turkey—many are not, either coming from countries where problems are chronic rather than acute (India, Pakistan, Ghana) or where acute problems have since subsided. Only 45 applications were made from Angola in 1988 during the civil war, while there were 3,300 applications in 1991 (12.9% of the UK total).[9] The increase in applications from many countries where no concomitant increase in threat can be perceived has prompted many, inside and outside government, to see a large proportion of recent applications as unfounded, or from 'economic refugees'.

It is difficult to relate applications and decisions since grants do not automatically relate to the year of application due to a lag in dealing with claims. Those that are accepted are granted asylum or, increas-

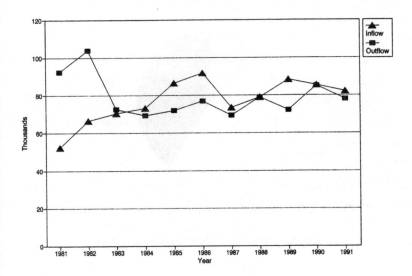

Figure 2.17 International Migration (1981–91): To and From Other Foreign Countries

Source: OPCS 'Overseas travel and tourism', *Business Statistics Office Business Monitor MA6*, 1981–92 annual, HMSO.

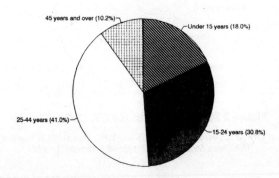

Figure 2.18 Migration to the UK (1991): Age Group

Source: OPCS 'Overseas travel and tourism', *Business Statistics Office Business Monitor MA6*, 1981–92 annual, HMSO.

ingly, exceptional leave to remain while applications are dealt with. The latter status can be applied where it is unreasonable or impracti-

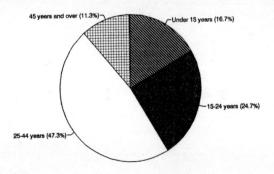

Figure 2.19 Migration from the UK (1991): Age Group

Source: OPCS 'Overseas travel and tourism', *Business Statistics Office Business Monitor MA6*, 1981–92 annual, HMSO.

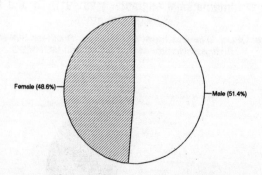

Figure 2.20 Migration to the UK (1991): Gender

Source: OPCS 'Overseas travel and tourism', *Business Statistics Office Business Monitor MA6*, 1981–92 annual, HMSO.

cable to enforce the applicant's return. Those granted refugee status can remain for four years and have the right to family reunion during this time. After four years they may apply for indefinite leave to remain, or settlement. Those granted exceptional leave to remain may apply for family reunion after four years and indefinite leave to remain (on a discretionary basis) after seven years. Some 1,100 applicants were granted asylum in 1992 whilst 15,300 were granted exceptional leave to remain. The principal nationalities to receive

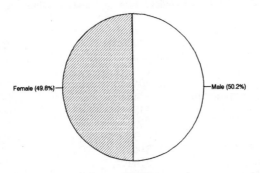

Figure 2.21 Migration from the UK (1991): Gender

Source: OPCS 'Overseas travel and tourism', *Business Statistics Office Business Monitor MA6*, 1981–92 annual, HMSO.

Table 2.2 Age Distribution of Newly Registering Foreign Workers 1990–91

Age	Number	Per cent
Under 18	1286	1.2
18–24	55541	48.5
25–34	41561	36.3
35–44	10073	8.8
45–54	3925	3.4
55–59	1135	1.0
60–64	706	0.6
65+	294	0.2
TOTAL	114521	100.0

Source: J. Salt, 'International Migration and the United Kingdom', unpublished report of the United Kingdom SOPEMI correspondent to the OECD, 1991.

grants were Sri Lankans, Ugandans, Lebanese and Indians.

As a member of the EC, the UK has accepted the Dublin Convention on dealing with asylum claims. At present, though, collective agreement over its EC-wide implementation and further harmonisation of asylum policy seems remote. The war in Yugoslavia has shown the policy vacuum that now exists in Europe. It may be argued that the EC system for dealing with refugees has become arthritic as a result of recent mass applications. Even such a major

Table 2.3 Regional Distribution of Newly Registering Foreign Workers

	1989/90 Numbers	%	1990/91 Numbers	%
Northern	1049	1.0	1130	1.0
Yorks and Humberside	1745	1.7	2094	1.8
E. Midlands	1451	1.4	1608	1.4
E. Anglia	2000	1.9	2189	1.9
South East	54753	2951.9	55126	48.2
South West	3148	3.0	3612	3.2
W. Midlands	2189	2.1	2710	2.4
North West	2925	2.8	3351	2.9
Scotland	1861	1.8	2538	2.2
Wales	1050	1.0	1401	1.2
Northern Ireland	346	0.3	472	0.4
Not known	32949	31.2	38290	33.4
TOTAL	105466	100.0	114521	100.0

Source: J. Salt, 'International Migration and the United Kingdom', unpublished report of the United Kingdom SOPEMI correspondent to the OECD, 1991.

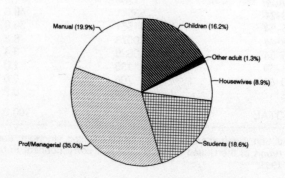

Figure 2.22 Migration to the UK (1991): Occupation

Source: OPCS 'Overseas travel and tourism', *Business Statistics Office Business Monitor MA6*, 1981–92 annual, HMSO.

crisis on the EC's doorstep is unable to elicit a co-ordinated response.

Asylum seekers represent the most rapidly expanding source of potential settlement migration in Europe. Increases in applications can be attributed both to changes in immigration policy over recent

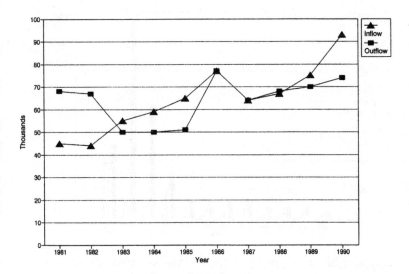

Figure 2.23 International Migration (1981–90): Professional/
Managerial Workers

Source: OPCS 'Overseas travel and tourism', *Business Statistics Office Business Monitor MA6*, 1981–92 annual, HMSO.

years and to a rising need to migrate among the persecuted. In either
case, refugees who arrive and settle have implications for systems of
future settlement migration and this must be embraced in the
establishment of any new asylum policy.

Present migration stocks

The stock of foreign nationals living in the UK in 1991, according to
the LFS, was 1,750,000, 3.1% of the total. There were 740,000 EC
nationals, 42.3% of all foreigners. The Irish continue to be the biggest
foreign contingent, their 469,000 being 26.8% of all foreign nationals
and 63.3% of those from the EC. The adoption of alternative
methods of recording Irish nationality in the 1991 LFS, particularly in
Northern Ireland, reduced the proportion of Irish nationals recorded
substantially from 638,999 in 1990. Nonetheless, the Irish have long
been the UK's unsung gastarbeiter, a fact that has attracted surprisingly little attention. Indians (136,000) and Americans (87,000—
excluding armed forces) were the two other major national groups.

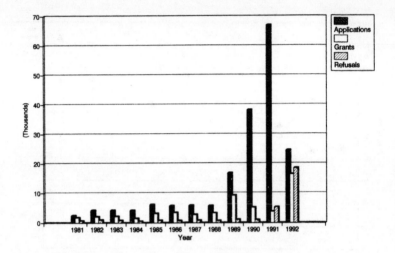

Figure 2.24 Applications to UK for Asylum (1981–92): Grants and Refusals

Source: Home Office, Asylum Statistics: United Kingdom 1992, Statistical Bulletin 19/93, HMSO.

All columns to 1991 include dependants. For 1991, these are Home Office estimates. Data are not available on applications for dependants in 1992.

Amongst those EC nationals not from Eire, the Italians (86,000) were the most numerous.

In the late 1980s the LFS recorded a rise in the number of foreign nationals at work in the UK from 744,000 in 1984 to 914,000 in 1989—more recent data show a drop to 828,000 in 1991, 3.2% of all those working. About half are EC nationals (398,000, of whom 242,000 are Irish). Based on three-year averages, the stock of foreign workers between 1986–8 and 1989–91 rose less fast than that of UK nationals (4.9% versus 6.4%). EC national stocks rose 1.3%. Foreign workers in 1990 were more likely to be in professional and managerial occupations than the UK population as a whole (24.7% compared with 21.6%). It can be seen from Table 2.4 that foreign labour is a major element in professional and managerial stocks but that substantial numbers of foreign nationals perform manual work.

Ethnic origins

Data on the ethnic minority population of the UK are available from the LFS. Some 1.6 million people (4.7% of the population) are

Table 2.4 Socio-economic Groups 1990 (thousands)

a) Numbers	Professionals, employers, managers	Other non-manual	Manual	Other	TOTAL
Total					
All nationalities	5792	8840	11833	193	26658
UK	5526	8507	11326	182	25541
Foreign nationals	230	268	426	10	933
EC (exc. Eire)	36	43	72	4	150
Eire	64	96	158	4	322
Rest of the world	130	129	195	6	420
Men					
All nationalities	4258	2760	7923	140	15090
UK	4076	2650	7609	131	14466
Foreign nationals	165	87	262	7	520
EC (exc. Eire)	26	12	41	1	79
Eire	43	27	107	3	181
Rest of the world	96	48	114	1	259
Women					
All nationalities	1524	6080	3910	54	11568
UK	1450	5858	3717	50	11075
Foreign nationals	64	182	164	3	413
EC (exc. Eire)	11	31	31	0	73
Eire	20	69	52	0	142
Rest of the world	33	82	81	0	199
b) Percentages					
Total					
All nationalities	21.7	33.2	44.4	0.7	100.0
UK	21.6	33.3	44.3	0.7	100.0
Foreign nationals	24.7	28.7	45.7	0.9	100.0
EC (exc. Eire)	23.8	28.5	47.7	0.0	100.0
Eire	19.9	29.8	49.1	0.2	100.0
Rest of the world	28.3	28.0	42.4	1.3	100.0
Men					
All nationalities	28.3	18.3	52.5	0.9	100.0
UK	28.2	18.3	52.6	0.9	100.0
Foreign nationals	31.7	16.7	50.4	1.2	100.0
EC (exc. Eire)	32.9	15.2	51.9	0.0	100.0
Eire	23.8	14.9	59.1	2.2	100.0
Rest of the world	37.1	18.5	44.0	0.4	100.0

Table 2.4 *continued*

	Professionals, employers, managers	Other non-manual	Manual	Other	TOTAL
Women					
All nationalities	13.2	52.6	33.8	0.4	100.0
UK	13.1	52.9	33.6	0.4	100.0
Foreign nationals	15.5	44.1	39.7	0.7	100.0
EC (exc. Eire)	15.1	42.5	42.5	0.0	100.0
Eire	14.1	48.6	36.6	0.7	100.0
Rest of the world	16.7	41.4	40.9	1.0	100.0

Source: J. Salt, 'International Migration and the United Kingdom', unpublished report of the United Kingdom SOPEMI correspondent to the OECD, 1991.

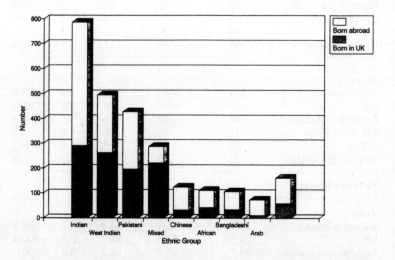

Figure 2.25 Ethnic Minority Population of Britain by Place of Birth

Source: J. Haskey (1990) 'The ethnic minority populations of Great Britain: estimates by ethnic group and country of birth', *Population Trends*, 60, pp. 35–38.

defined as belonging to an ethnic minority. Whilst the majority of this population was born abroad (Figure 2.25), 45% were born here. The high total period fertility rates (TPFRs) of overseas-born mothers are likely to lead to an increase in the UK-born proportion. TPFRs for most groups have come down during the 1980s, however (Table 2.5).

Table 2.5 Live Births and TPFRs by Country of Birth of Mother

Country of birth of mother	All live births						
	Thousands				TPFR (not 1979)		
	1979	1984	1988	1989	1984	1988	1989
UK	554.2	556.5	612.5	607.2	1.7	1.8	1.8
Outside UK	83.3	80.2	81.0	80.4	2.5	2.4	2.3
TOTAL	628.0	636.8	693.6	687.7	1.75	1.82	1.80

Source: OPCS *Birth Statistics*, 1991, series FMI, No. 18, HMSO.

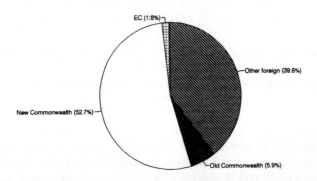

Figure 2.26 Acceptances for Settlement in the UK by Nationality (1992): Total = 52,570

Source: Home Office (1993) *Control of Immigration Statistics: Third and Fourth Quarters and Year 1992*, Statistical Bulletin 14/93, HMSO.

Settlement and naturalisation

The trend in settlement is now fairly stable at around 50,000 a year. Small increases between 1987 and 1991 reflect technical and administrative changes in entry criteria and procedures. About half originate from New Commonwealth countries (Figure 2.26). Acceptances on arrival have been declining, particularly in the case of those from the New Commonwealth.

Naturalisation and citizenship are of growing policy concern in Europe in the light of millions of disenfranchised but legally resident foreign nationals. The UK has traditionally had a more relaxed

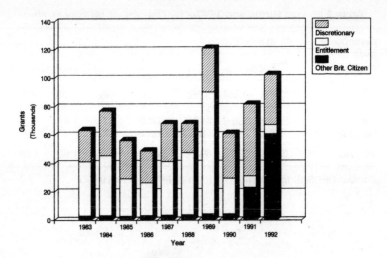

Figure 2.27 Grants of British Citizenship: Acceptance Category (1983–92)

Source: Home Office (1993) *Persons Granted British Citizenship: United Kingdom, 1992*, Statistical Bulletin 16/93, HMSO.

attitude towards naturalisation than many of its neighbours. This is mainly due to past colonial influences. Grants issued in the UK averaged around 60,000 per year for much of the 1980s and in 1992 dropped to 42,000 (Figures 2.27 and 2.28). An exceptional year was 1989 which saw a 'beat the deadline' rush (by Irish and New Commonwealth citizens in particular) before the transitional entitlements in the 1981 Nationality Act expired. In 1991 and 1992 there were large increases in grant issue in Hong Kong following the Tiananmen Square incident and enactment of the British Nationality (Hong Kong) Act 1990. This has swollen the number of 'other issues' in Figure 2.27 above the number of grants in the UK for the first time in many years. Residence is the most frequent basis for acquiring British citizenship in the UK, accounting for 18,200 grants (45%). Marriage to a British citizen accounted for 13,900 (35%) of grants.

In 1992, 6,100 people were removed from the UK under the enforcement powers of the 1971 Immigration Act, up from 4,280 in 1990. The number detected as illegal entrants increased to 5,600 in 1992; 3,600 people were removed in this category. Overstaying is likely to be more prevalent than illegal entry, but there is little information as to its extent.

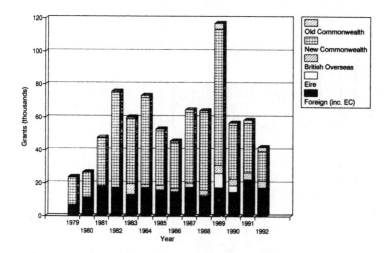

Figure 2.28 Grants of Citizenship in the UK by Previous Citizenship (1979-92)

Source: Home Office (1993) *Persons Granted British Citizenship: United Kingdom, 1992,* Statistical Bulletin 16/93, HMSO.

Demographic trends and immigration

Many, contemplating the demographic and economic consequences of an ageing population in Western Europe over the coming decades, have called for a compensatory increase in immigration. Calls stem from the dual concerns of the implications for pensions, the dependency ratio and other welfare costs of a growing elderly population and the anticipated shortfall in the number of school-leavers and subsequent entrants into the labour force.

In the UK for the short and medium term, however, the number of pensioners is determined more by fluctuations in the age structure than long-term ageing. Because of birth rate fluctuations, the next fifteen years will remain unexpectedly favourable in terms of age structure (Figure 2.29). No immediate crisis is in evidence but the cost of pensions will be of much greater concern in 20-30 years time.

Similarly, the size of the work-force is expected to remain constant, at around 27 million, for the rest of the century. The current demographic sensation is the trough of small cohorts born since the early 1970s which create a novel shortage of young workers. Such a sharp fall in potential teenage recruits is without precedent and is a near universal prospect for developed nations. It was the subject of an

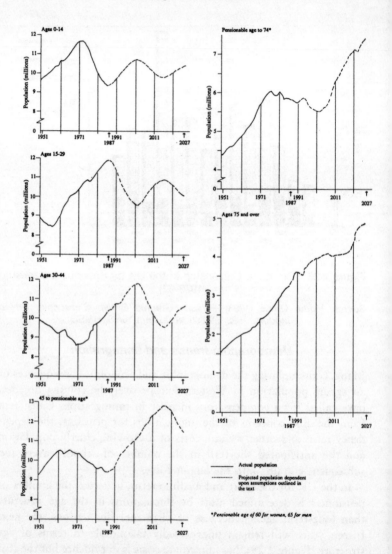

Figure 2.29 Actual and Projected Home Population by Age Group (in millions) England and Wales (1951–2027)

Source: OPCS Monitor, 14 February 1989.

OECD conference which also addressed the role to be played by migration in maintaining levels of labour force participation. The conference conclusions are worth quoting in detail:

One of the main conclusions...is that the seemingly simple proposition of increasing the intake of young migrants to compensate for the slowdown of population growth and for ageing would in practice encounter a number of formidable difficulties....This is not to say that it would be impossible in principle to overcome these difficulties. But the political will to succeed would need to be so strong and the policy change so difficult that the chances of finding acceptable solutions would seem to be small in pluralistic societies. A review of current country positions and their migration assumptions in population projections reveals that such a political will does not exist at present.[10]

In addition to these reservations in destination regions, such a policy would be likely to engender technical and political problems for sending countries. It is unlikely to be favoured where alternatives exist:

Nonetheless, migration would not be the only option for improving labour supply trends. This...raises the question about the role of migration policy relative to a whole range of other supply-enhancing policy options (higher female labour-force participation, deferred retirement, upskilling, etc.).[11]

It has been argued elsewhere that migration would not be justified in labour market terms if more attention were paid to levels of unemployment, retraining programmes for those with redundant skills and the increasing of labour force participation rates.[12] Given freedom of movement, these are issues which must be addressed at a European level.

Within the EC as a whole in 1990 there were 12 million unemployed, 4 million of whom were under 25. The comparable figures for the UK in the first quarter of 1992 were 2.7 million and 790,000. In addition, there is a 'hidden' labour force of people of working age who do not participate in the labour market. Many of these people might enter the labour market if participation rates were raised. This group, mainly married women, has been estimated to total 33 million in the EC, equivalent to 15% of its working age population.[13] Comparison of the participation rates for married women aged 25–39 in the UK (64.5%) and Denmark (90%) indicates the extent of the increase that is possible, and the considerable effect this would have if repeated across Europe (Table 2.6).

Whilst there is some scope for an increase in EC productivity rates

Table 2.6 Activity Rates for Women by Marital Status and Age: EC 1988

Country	Age group				
	14–24	*25–34*	*35–44*	*45–54*	*55–64*
a) *Unmarried women*					
Belgium	25.9	84.3	79.0	63.5	22.1
Denmark	67.7	84.3	89.1	81.2	48.7
West Germany	53.9	84.7	89.9	87.0	43.4
Greece	30.4	83.1	72.3	49.1	29.5
Spain	40.1	84.4	78.9	67.3	51.6
France	35.4	87.8	86.8	82.0	45.3
Eire	42.0	87.6	77.1	65.9	40.2
Italy	40.5	78.2	76.9	63.9	22.7
Luxembourg	45.6	87.9	84.6	75.3	49.9
Netherlands	46.8	79.9	78.8	62.6	44.8
Portugal	52.3	88.6	85.4	76.4	34.8
UK	59.8	83.2	80.3	76.3	34.8
EC TOTAL	45.5	84.1	82.9	74.0	37.9
b) *Married women*					
Belgium	72.3	71.9	57.9	33.3	9.6
Denmark	76.4	90.1	90.7	82.0	43.3
West Germany	59.7	68.5	57.5	51.5	23.2
Greece	36.1	50.0	49.3	40.6	29.1
Spain	45.0	45.0	33.6	25.9	16.2
France	67.1	68.5	69.1	58.8	25.6
Eire	51.4	45.5	29.7	25.6	13.5
Italy	45.6	54.5	49.4	34.8	14.8
Luxembourg	58.9	48.5	39.0	25.1	8.9
Netherlands	66.3	72.0	66.2	49.9	30.9
Portugal	56.9	50.5	52.4	41.4	14.3
UK	62.6	64.5	74.5	69.9	36.8
EC TOTAL	58.2	59.1	58.5	48.1	23.1

Source: Eurostat Demographic Statistics 1991, Luxembourg, EC.

compared with those of Japan, investment in retraining is likely to gain greater public acceptance than a similar expenditure to integrate an expanded immigrant labour force. New technology dictates that any changes in labour market needs will be towards skills selectivity rather than mass demand. It is thus evident that immigration cannot be seen to offer a 'quick fix' for demographic shortfalls.

One important lesson to have emerged from the present work is the difficulty of sustaining a positive impact of migration on the age structure over the longer term. The most appropriate option would be a steady intake of a regular size relative to the total population. This would contribute to overall population growth and possibly slow down (even if only temporarily) the ageing process. It would essentially be a delaying tactic and the short-term adjustment problems arising from a constant intake should not be underestimated. There is a clear message from migration history: migration is a process which develops its own inherent dynamics. It cannot be administered in a stop-go fashion.[14]

Future trends

It is necessary to be cautious in interpreting future trends. Past trends are a product of the interaction of many different migration systems. Flows occur in response to economic, political, religious and social pressures, as part of the working of the international labour market, and due to family reunion and retirement. Extrapolation assumes that the perceived opportunities for individuals and the structural con-straints upon them that acted in the past, will act upon them in a way that produces a similar outcome in the future. The role of legislation then becomes ambiguous. Whilst the periodic imposition of increas-ingly restrictive legislation will have influenced past trends in flows, will extrapolating from those flows imply maintenance of a policy status quo, or of a continuing imposition of periodic restrictions? Unforeseen legislative changes elsewhere may affect rates of emig-ration from Britain and also of immigration to Britain, while movements of asylum-seekers will be influenced by the frequency, severity and location of unknown future political upheavals in the developing world and elsewhere.

There are many different ways of analysing and forecasting time series data such as migration flows. All have inherent methodological and theoretical problems. Given the scope of the present work, only two methods can be considered here. The first is fairly simple and crude yet can prove robust. This is the extrapolation of trend curves based on past experience, either flows or applications, as preferred by the Home Affairs Committee.[15] Fitting of curves is often advocated where it is unlikely to be worthwhile fitting a complicated model to past data as the model may change in the future.[16] The second is a subjective forecasting based on intuition and established knowledge.

Under the latter approach likely migration patterns can be hypothesised based on a series of possible scenarios.

Trend curves

At least seven to ten years' historical data are required for the extrapolation of trend curves and Harrison and Pearce[17] suggest that 'one should not make forecasts for a longer period ahead than about half the number of past years for which data are available'. Thus, with 20 years' data available since the Immigration Act of 1971 sought finally to curb Commonwealth immigration, a forecast up to the year 2000 is theoretically possible. If it is assumed that net migration levels are the combined result of several different migration streams affecting the UK which act independently of one another, then the fitting of several curves is necessary for forecasts of future trends to be applicable at both the level of individual streams and on the UK's migration status overall. However, even if one considers only the most fundamental (and least erratic) components of flows: British and Foreign citizens in and out of the country, immediate problems are faced in choosing the appropriate trend curves to apply. No logical basis for choosing among the curves exists except for criteria of goodness-of-fit. Unfortunately, several curves can be found which fit the data equally well.

Figures 2.30 to 2.34 illustrate this problem. IPS estimates of flows each calendar year are shown with forecasts based on past trends. The outflow of British citizens has shown a general downward trend throughout the past decade, but several departure 'peaks' are evident. One could hypothesise that a cyclical pattern should also be taken into account—especially since peaks seem to coincide with times of relatively high unemployment in the UK. Recent data do not support this hypothesis however. As the data do not indicate a trend which is obviously multiplicative[18] or additive,[19] Forecast 1 in each case is based on an eight year cyclical trend which is multiplicative, whilst Forecast 2 is based on an eight year cyclical trend which is additive. Forecast 3, crude exponential smoothing, ignores any cyclical effect and is based solely upon the most recent observations.[20] The effect is taken to be multiplicative and hence the curve tends to follow the mean trajectory of recent observations whilst tending towards stationarity in the absence of reinforcement by observations. In all forecasts, the hypothesised gradient is applied to the previous year's observation (or forecast). A four year cycle has been used to produce inflow

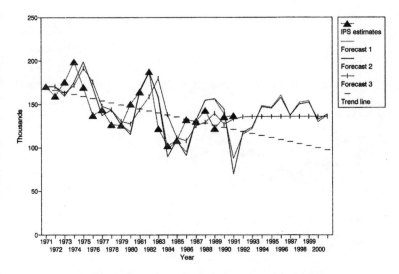

Figure 2.30   British Outflow: Various Forecasts

Source: Derived from OPCS 'Overseas travel and tourism', *Business Statistics Office Business Monitor MA6*, 1981–92 annual, HMSO.

Forecasts 1 and 2. A least-squares regression line is also fitted to indicate linear trend.

If a cyclical pattern is hypothesised to continue in the emigration of British citizens, this will have a dramatic impact upon forecast migration balances over the next ten years. Similarly, a relatively stable trend-line applied to inflow betrays the substantial but gradual decline in migration of Britons to the UK in the 1970s and the doubling of inflow between 1981 and 1986 (Figure 2.31). It should be noted that OPCS population and Department of Employment labour force projections into the twenty-first century assume nil net migration.

Trend curves can be fitted to Non-British immigration and emigration which indicate either that steady growth in flows in both directions over the past two decades will continue (regression line), or that the growth rate in immigration itself is beginning to increase (Forecast 1). Net immigration scenarios thus reflect these diverse estimates (Figure 2.34). The variation in observed and hypothesised trends implies an increased need for flexibility in policy approach.

These models based on past flows require broad generalisations as to the trends and cyclical patterns observed. A better model of past

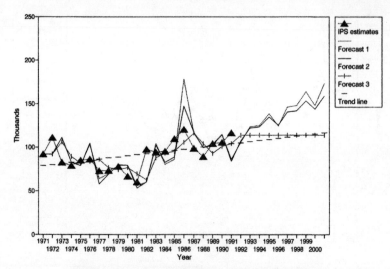

Figure 2.31   British Inflow: Various Forecasts

Source: Derived from OPCS 'Overseas travel and tourism', *Business Statistics Office Business Monitor MA6*, 1981–92 annual, HMSO.

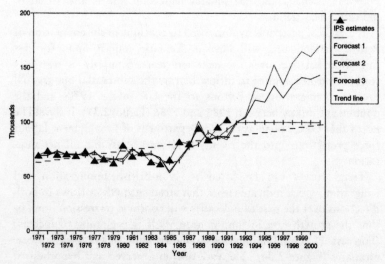

Figure 2.32   Non-British Outflow: Various Forecasts

Source: Derived from OPCS 'Overseas travel and tourism', *Business Statistics Office Business Monitor MA6*, 1981–92 annual, HMSO.

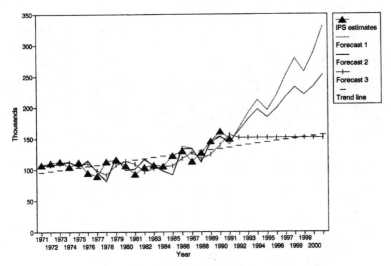

Figure 2.33   Non-British Inflow: Various Forecasts

Source: Derived from OPCS 'Overseas travel and tourism', *Business Statistics Office Business Monitor MA6*, 1981–92 annual, HMSO.

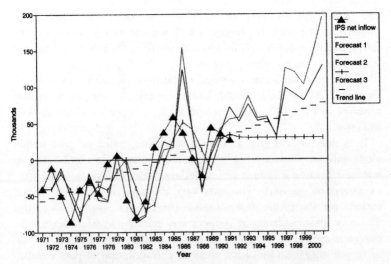

Figure 2.34   Net Immigration: Various Forecasts

Source: Derived from OPCS 'Overseas travel and tourism', *Business Statistics Office Business Monitor MA6*, 1981–92 annual, HMSO.

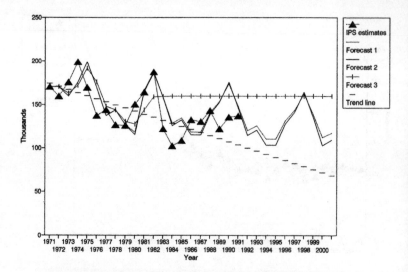

Figure 2.35 British Outflow: Various Forecasts from 1981

Source: Derived from OPCS 'Overseas travel and tourism', *Business Statistics Office Business Monitor MA6*, 1981–92 annual, HMSO.

trends may be possible by embracing a broad range of potential 'pull' and 'push' factors but, as many of the latter are 'chance' or unpredictable events, any forecasts will be subject to substantial error. Extrapolating models as forecasts can multiply the effect of inappropriate assumptions about previous trends. Figures 2.35 to 2.39 illustrate how the models applied to produce plausible outcomes in Figures 2.30 to 2.33 would have forecast the migration trends observed in the 1980s. Few forecasts accurately predicted any growth in flows.

It is thus evident that statistical modelling based on past trends alone will not produce reliable forecasts of future inflow and outflow, not least because it cannot accommodate future changes in legislation or migration pressure. Forecasts vary dramatically in their implications for the future depending on the criteria assumed to apply. There is little evidence to support any purely statistical approach. Forecasts are thus better based on intuition and established knowledge of future migration pressures, than on extrapolation of past trends.

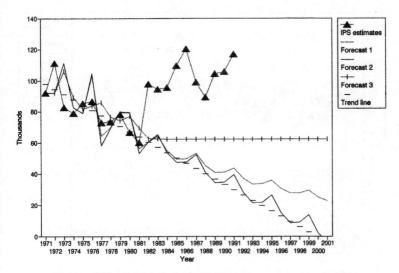

Figure 2.36 British Inflow: Various Forecasts from 1981

Source: Derived from OPCS 'Overseas travel and tourism', *Business Statistics Office Business Monitor MA6*, 1981–92 annual, HMSO.

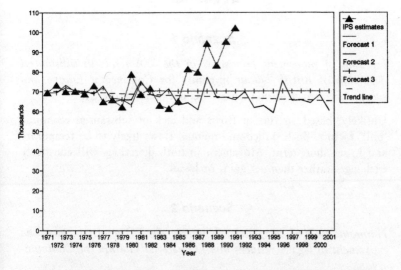

Figure 2.37 Non-British Outflow: Various Forecasts from 1981

Source: Derived from OPCS 'Overseas travel and tourism', *Business Statistics Office Business Monitor MA6*, 1981–92 annual, HMSO.

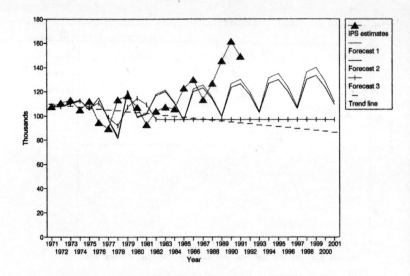

Figure 2.38 Non-British Inflow: Various Forecasts from 1981

Source: Derived from OPCS 'Overseas travel and tourism', *Business Statistics Office Business Monitor MA6*, 1981–92 annual, HMSO.

Scenarios

Scenario 1

Freedom of movement provisions in the SEA result in substantial departure of British labour migrants for Continental Europe and substantial arrival of non-British EC nationals in the UK.

Unlikely, based on current flows and lack of substantial economic 'pull' factors. Both skilled and manual flows likely to be temporary and losses short-term. Movement in both directions will constitute exchanges rather than net gains or losses.

Scenario 2

Harmonisation of entry controls within the EC results in increased movement of legally resident non-EC nationals within the Community.

Such movement is highly likely between existing immigrant communities in the EC, with movement based on proximity, existing

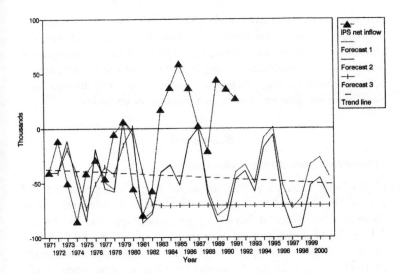

Figure 2.39 Net Immigration (1971–2001): Various Forecasts from 1981

Source: Derived from OPCS 'Overseas travel and tourism', *Business Statistics Office Business Monitor MA6*, 1981–92 annual, HMSO.

national groups and perceived opportunities. Given the distinctive origins of the UK's settlement migrants compared to those elsewhere in the EC—from distant ex-colonies rather than the more proximate regions of Turkey, Eastern Europe and the Maghreb—the attraction of such settlers to the UK seems unlikely.

Scenario 3

Harmonisation of entry controls results in increased movement of non-legally resident persons within the Community.

Large numbers of non-EC nationals from non-European bordering countries have been able to enter the EC and find work within the informal economies of countries such as Italy, Spain and Greece. An estimated one million such foreigners illegally inhabit these countries.[21] The porous nature of some of the EC's external borders, combined with the opening up of its internal borders would enable significant numbers of illegal immigrants, once in, to migrate to work anywhere in the EC region. The extent of such flows would depend on the demand for such 'informal' workers and the extent to which external border controls could be enforced. The maintenance of immigration control on intra-EC movement to curb such flows is strongly favoured by the present government. Without immigration control, a UK government wishing to exclude 'informal' workers may be encouraged to seek alternatives such as the introduction of a population registration system, or sanctions on employers.

Scenario 4

Applications from asylum-seekers increase.

Highly likely based on recent rates of increase. The problem is posed not only by the number of refugees who need to be admitted, but in the escalating financial burden of processing applications. Figures 2.40 and 2.41 show the trend in applications to the UK and Europe in recent years. However, applications to the UK dropped substantially in 1992. To obtain even a reasonable forecast of numbers would require a detailed study of the political events which give rise to claims. In addition, it is only by addressing such causes that any permanent solution will be found. Serious debate about the impact of asylum seeking is deterred by the lack of data, especially on the number of such applications which are not duplicated elsewhere, and the characteristics of applicants.

Scenario 5

Eastern European labour migrants seek work in Western Europe, perhaps as a result of joining EC.

Over 1 million Eastern Europeans have moved West since 1989 but the UK has largely avoided the impact of these migrations. This is partly because immigration control applies to Eastern Europeans and partly because the country lacks the traditional links to the East of countries like Austria and Germany. Applications for asylum from Eastern European countries have declined and substantial immigration is not foreseen.

Scenario 6

Substantial proportions of Britain's ethnic minority population continue to seek family reunion, fiancé(e)s and marital partners abroad.

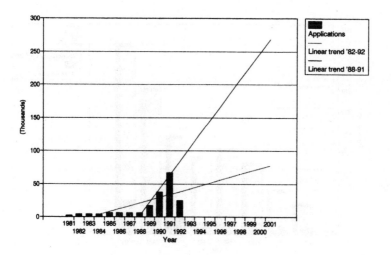

Figure 2.40 Applications to UK for Asylum (1981–2001): Various Forecasts

Source: Derived from Home Office (1993), *Asylum Statistics: United Kingdom 1992*, Statistical Bulletin 1993, HMSO.

All columns to 1991 include dependants. For 1991, these are Home Office estimates. Data are not available on applications for dependants in 1992.

The size of these flows will be a product of demographic and social trends among Britain's ethnic minority population. The demand for family reunion is closely linked to the sex ratio of primary settlers and how recently the group has arrived. Britain's most recent arrivals from Bangladesh have an age structure and fertility rate such that 51% of the population is aged under 16 years.[22] Among earlier post-war arrivals, however, such as those of West Indian origin, marital family size is decreasing. Asian fertility is also declining. Some evidence exists that immigration of fiancés and brides is of diminishing importance. A combination of legislative change and altering marriage preferences has meant that the recent increase in size of the young UK-born Asian population has not produced a corresponding increase in migration for purposes of marriage.[23]

Scenario 7

The international migration of the highly skilled continues to increase.

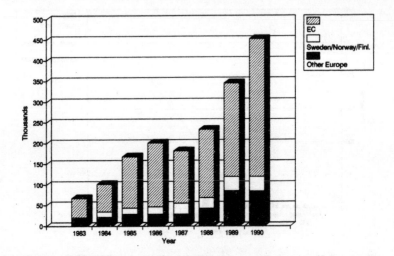

Figure 2.41 Applications for Asylum (1983-90) to European Countries

Source: Derived from B. Hovy, *Asylum Migration in Europe: Patterns, Determinants and the Role of East-West Movements*, paper presented to conference on Mass Migration in Europe, Implications for East and West, Vienna, 5–7 March 1992.

Movement is largely temporary and within the internal labour market of firms. It can be seen as the outcome of the redistribution of manpower within such companies as much as international migration per se. Moves are usually highly visible and thus easy to control. Britain is currently a net recipient of professional and managerial workers whose contribution to the economy is generally perceived as positive.

Scenario 8

Mass flight from Hong Kong in 1997 or white exodus from South Africa.

Some 50,000 Hong Kong residents had the right of abode in the UK in 1992. Whether this is taken up will depend in part upon how the actions of the Chinese Government are perceived and anticipated over the next four years. It is unlikely to be in the interests of the Chinese Government to create a situation whereby these individuals feel pressured to leave the colony. In 1993 800,000 British patrials in South Africa had right of abode in the UK.

Scenario 9

Immigration policies centred on the 'quality' of migrants in Australia, Canada and the USA result in increasing pressure on European states to accept remaining migrants, with fewer qualifications or larger numbers of dependents.

Quality has become an issue in countries of continuing settlement migration. A fear expressed in Europe is of its labour migrants being drawn from a pool of potential migrants of diminishing skill levels. This theme of an immigration market in which developed nations compete for migrants has been pursued by Borjas.[24] If such a market exists however, it is one in which the UK may have difficulty competing. Current indications are that it has no intention of trying to do so. With such a policy, it may find that in its haste to discourage the immigration of those with few skills, it has lost out on attracting those with higher skills as well.

Likely combination: 4 (asylum seekers), 7 (highly skilled), and 1 (EC nationals), 2 (non EC nationals) and 6 (family reunion), to some extent. The UK Government has adopted what it terms a 'firm but fair' approach to immigration policy. This has assumed a finite capacity of the UK to absorb further immigration. In the face of increasing immigration pressure, the approach has been typified by frequent tightening of regulations and increasingly sophisticated requirements for asylum seekers which aim to reduce the number of applications lodged. It is in this context that these likely future sources of immigration are advanced. Were controls to be dropped, Scenario 6 would rise in prominence, with likely increased flows of low skilled labour into the UK.

Conclusion

Due to existing high levels of immigration control, the UK is unlikely to see any substantial increases in net settlement or labour immigration over the next ten years. Whilst labour exchanges with Europe can be anticipated to increase and bridal exchanges with New Commonwealth countries can be forecast to continue for many years, the days of the UK as a country of low-skilled labour and settlement immigration have largely drawn to a close. The exception to this trend is the growth in refugee applications in recent years. Little evidence exists to suggest the numbers of persons displaced by war, famine or political pressure will decline. One view was that refugee numbers were kept up by proxy wars fought by the superpowers. A present view is that 'as empires fall, people flee' and that as new nationalisms expand so do the numbers of asylum seekers. Similarly, with the income gap between the developed and developing showing no signs of closing, the number of applications is unlikely to fall. Most of these application-generating situations are those which migration does little to solve other than temporarily. Whilst the need for other solutions is pressing, for the UK to be seen to continue to play an active role in accepting a share of the displaced and dispossessed (borne in large part by neighbouring countries) an effective policy stance is required.

Migration regimes affecting the UK are in a state of flux where it is impossible to predict future trends. Up until the time of writing, the UK Government's response has been reactive and based on perceptions of domestic unease over further immigration. It attributes to its own emphasis on immigration control the relative absence of immigration issues from the domestic political agenda and the weak standing of British anti-immigration political parties[25] compared to those in France and Germany. There is a danger in such arguments of immigration policy being used to diffuse domestic racist or xenophobic prejudice by accommodating it rather than tackling it. If future policy is to seek to achieve positive objectives, a more proactive stance is required. Either way, to defend existing policy or to monitor the success of any new approach, a much more reliable system of data collection on stocks and flows than exists at present is required.

3 THREE THEORIES OF IMMIGRATION

Bhikhu Parekh

Every modern state claims to enjoy the right to control immigration and emigration. Many writers question this claim on the ground that the earth and its resources belong to humankind, and that the morally arbitrary modern states are not justified in parcelling out the earth among themselves and interfering with an individual's natural right to move freely across the globe.

Even if this argument were valid, it would be too abstract and ahistorical to be politically significant. For over three hundred years states have claimed and exercised the right to control immigration and emigration, regarding it as an integral part of their sovereignty and a vital precondition of their survival as cohesive communities. There is no realistic hope of their giving it up. It would therefore be best to begin by accepting the right as an inescapable fact of contemporary life.

Although all states claim the right to regulate immigration and emigration, their exercise of it has varied enormously. Until the early years of the twentieth century, most Western states restricted both. Liberal democracies restrict immigration but not emigration. While insisting on their sovereign right to restrict emigration, they argue that it should only be exercised in rare circumstances and that the citizens should generally be left free to emigrate at will. Although there is no contemporary example of it, many earlier polities restricted emigration but not immigration. They defined their identity in ethnic rather than territorial terms. They did not mind outsiders settling in their areas, but discouraged and in some cases disallowed their own members from leaving.

Different countries follow different immigration policies. They do so because they entertain different ideas about their identity, and different concomitant notions of who should and should not be their members. In this paper I am concerned to do three things. First, I shall argue that modern states' conceptions of themselves fall into three

91

categories, and that these entail three different types of immigration policy. Second, I shall critically examine these conceptions and conclude that none is wholly satisfactory. Third, I shall tease out several general principles that in my view should guide the immigration policy of the modern state.[1]

In its widest sense immigration refers to an act by which outsiders seek the permission of the state to enter its territory. They may wish to pass through it, come as tourists, visit their friends and relatives, study in its educational institutions, come and settle in it, or to become its citizens. Most states have no objection to all but the last two categories of people. They do not mind short- or long-term visitors and even encourage them, but feel strongly about those seeking to come in for long term residence (what is sometimes called settlement) or to become its citizens. Although in its broadest sense every outsider entering the jurisdiction of the state is an immigrant, in its narrow sense the term is reserved for prospective settlers and citizens. In this paper I shall use the term in its narrow sense. States vary greatly in their attitudes to long term residents who do not become its citizens. Some encourage them to become citizens, some discourage them, yet others are indifferent. Some confer full rights of citizenship on them, others confer fewer rights. In either case they are rightful residents of the state in which they are settled. In this context I use the term 'state' to mean a group of people occupying a territorial unit and united in terms of their common acceptance of a public authority. I shall use the term 'members of the state' to refer to both its full citizens and to its non-citizen residents.

An immigration policy refers to the state's official attitude on who should be allowed to become its members, under what conditions, and of what kind. A state's conception of who should be its members depends on its conception of itself, of the kind of polity it thinks it is and how it believes itself to be constituted and held together. Its immigration policy is therefore an expression of, and ultimately grounded in and legitimised in terms of, its definition of its identity. Broadly speaking, modern states conceptualise their identity in one of three ways which for convenience I shall call *liberal, communitarian* and *ethnic*. Each entails a distinct view of who can and cannot become its member. Since the advocates of the three views of the identity of the state have not always spelt out what kinds of immigration policy logically follow from their views, I shall do it for them.

The liberal view

According to the liberal view, the state exists to create conditions in which its autonomous and self-determining citizens can freely pursue their self-chosen activities. It is not their guardian telling them how to run their lives, nor some kind of supra-personal entity pursuing its own distinct purposes and values to which their goals are to be subordinated. The state is basically a civil association, voluntary in its nature and almost like a club, held together by a general agreement on how its collective affairs are to be conducted and the decisions taken which are binding on all its members.[2] To be its member is to acknowledge the established structure of authority, to obey the laws, and to participate in the conduct of its collective affairs in the spirit of 'civility' or 'liberal conversation'.[3] Nothing more can be required of its members, both because this is enough to secure the basic conditions of civil life, and because anything more inevitably compromises their moral autonomy.

The liberal view of the state implies that any outsider satisfying the minimum requirements of its membership is qualified to be its member. No other criteria, such as her religion, race, ethnicity, political beliefs or even acceptability to the rest of the citizens should enter into the consideration. This does not mean that every eligible applicant must necessarily be admitted. If a state is passing through bad times, has large-scale unemployment, or can be shown to be overcrowded, it might not admit outsiders. But if it does need outside labour, professional skills, or talents, it must admit them solely on the basis of whether or not they meet the economic requirement and satisfy the minimum membership qualifications.

Some liberals see no need to restrict immigration. The classical economists of the eighteenth and nineteenth centuries championed free trade, including an unrestricted movement of labour, goods and capital. They thought that people would only go to a country if there were jobs, and that they would leave it if or when there were none. In their view, as reported by Henry Sidgwick, the sole duty of the government is 'to maintain order over [a] particular territory, but not in any way to determine who is to inhabit this territory, or to restrict the enjoyment of its natural advantages to any particular portion of the human race'.[4] Some contemporary liberals and neo-liberals share this view, and point to the success of the European Community and the recent launching of the free trade area between Canada and Mexico.

The liberal view of the minimum qualifications required for the membership of the state has been interpreted differently over the years. Until recently most liberals have taken it to exclude only convicted criminals and politically subversive activists on the grounds that the former have proved their inability, and the latter have declared their unwillingness, to respect the laws of the land. In recent years many liberals have taken a more restrictive view. In the aftermath of the rise of Muslim 'fundamentalism' and the Rushdie affair, some of them have argued that those unwilling to subscribe to liberal values could legitimately be denied admission by a liberal state. Many British liberals including Roy Jenkins, Fay Weldon and Anthony Burgess took this view, but this was largely an angry reaction to the threat on Rushdie's life and has not resulted in a political campaign. The American liberal theorist, Bruce Ackerman, who pleads for unrestricted immigration on liberal grounds, has argued that the *only* reason for restricting immigration is to protect 'the ongoing process of liberal conversation itself'.[5] It is not entirely clear what he means by liberal conversation, and whether it excludes groups who do not share secular rationalist values but are otherwise law-abiding. Although he vacillates, he too does not wish to exclude such people so long as they refrain from an open advocacy of violence.

The communitarian view

The communitarian view of the nature of the state has a different thrust. Although formulated differently by different writers, it basically insists that the state is not just a collection of men and women united by a body of rules and subscription to a common authority, but a group of people united by shared understandings, meanings, interests, values, sentiments, loyalties, affections and collective pride. It is distinguished by a common ethical life, a body of ideals and moral self-understanding, in terms of which its members define their collective and even individual identity and by which they seek to regulate their lives. They perceive themselves as bound to each other by ties of unarticulated but deeply felt sympathies and affections. As Walzer puts it, they have 'some special commitment to one another and some special sense of their common life'.[6] They have a common history, a shared understanding of their past, common collective memories, shared ceremonies and rituals in which these memories are preserved and renewed, common traits of temperament and character, and so on. They constitute, and know that they constitute, a single community, a distinct ethical and cultural unit with a clear shape and character, marked off from other communities in ways which they instinctively recognise but may not always be able to state clearly and explicitly. They have a strong sense of collective 'we', such that 'we' is not a plural of 'I' but rather that 'I' is a singular of 'we'. The state is an integral part, and a custodian of, their shared way of life. It is a political expression and articulation of the collective identity of the community and neither is, nor ever can be, like a club or a voluntary association.

The communitarian view obviously entails a distinct conception of who can be the member of a state, but that conception has not so far been clearly stated by its advocates. Being a distinct ethico-cultural unit, every state wishes and is entitled to preserve, its identity. 'Admission and exclusion are at the core of communal independence', argues Walzer.[7] It cannot, therefore, admit outsiders indiscriminately, thus raising the vital question as to whom to admit and reject. By definition, outsiders do not share the unspoken sympathies, under-standings and sentiments that characterise the state, and which can only be acquired after a long residence in it. They can only be admitted on the basis of their capacity and willingness to acquire these. But how does one determine this? Neither Walzer nor any other communitarian has a clear and coherent answer. By and large they seem to point to such criteria as whether the members of a state are able to identify with the potential immigrants, recognise their ways of life as similar to their own, have historical ties with them, and regard them as their national 'relatives' or 'kith and kin'.[8] All this is extremely vague and cannot form the basis of a coherent immigration policy. Walzer and others give preference to the relatives of those already settled. But since they do not want the state to become self-reproducing, it is not clear how they propose to choose among the rest.

The ethnic or nationalist view

Although the ethnic or what might also be called the nationalist view of the state overlaps with and is sometimes indistinguishable from the communitarian view, it is basically quite distinct. In Britain it is advocated by the New Right, but has a much wider appeal.[9] It conceptualises the state as a 'hereditary' group of men and women who, through centuries of living together and intermarriages, have come to be related to one another by 'ties of blood'. They have common 'ancestors' or 'forefathers' to whom they are bound by sentiments of 'filial piety', as well as common 'descendants', 'posterity' or 'grandchildren' to whom they have special parental obligations. The unity of the state is based on the 'unity of stock', a sense of 'kinship', 'shared collective instincts', on loyalty to people of a 'common kind'. As John Casey puts it, 'There is no way of understanding English patriotism that averts its eyes from the fact that it has at its centre a feeling for persons of one's kind.' In the ethnic view, the state is a family, a kinship group, not just a community let alone a club. Although the ethnic view resembles the crude racist view of Gobineau, Chamberlain and others and even occasionally uses the language of race, it is quite different. The racist view divides mankind into distinct races, considers them natural and unalterable, and disallows close biological contacts between them. The ethnic view rejects all three. It sees ethnic groups as products of history and born out of close social contacts and shared experiences. It regards almost every long-established and cohesive state as a distinct ethnic group, and generally stays clear of the ideas of biological purity and pollution. While the racist views the state as the expression and historical creation of a distinct race defined naturalistically and independently of the state, the advocate of the ethnic view reverses their relationship.

In the ethnic view of the state, its membership is necessarily restricted to those connected to it by ties of kinship. This means two things. First, no one lacking such ties may be admitted. And if they are admitted, because of the shortage of labour or professional skills or international pressure, they cannot be its full members. At worst they remain guest workers. At best they become full members of the *state* and enjoy all the rights of citizenship, but they remain marginal to the *nation* and its collective life. They are ethical and cultural outsiders whose values, sensibilities and deepest emotions find no expression in the ethical life of the country. This is why the New Right in Britain opposes black and brown immigration and insists that, if those already settled cannot be 'repatriated', they should be turned into 'guest workers' by retroactive laws or 'thoroughly assimilated' into the British 'national life'.[10] The advocates of these policies acknowledge that these are not 'civilised', but insist that they are required by the 'survival of the British race' and represent a 'necessity of the state'.

Second, in the ethnic view all outsiders who happen to be related to the state by ties of kinship belong to it in principle, and have an inextinguishable claim to its membership. The boundaries of a state do not, and need not, coincide with those of the relevant ethnic group. Not all Germans live in Germany. The fact that some do not cannot deprive them of their claim to the unrestricted hospitality of their 'ethnic' or 'national' home. It is on the basis of the ethnic view of the British state that Margaret Thatcher and the New Right justified the war with Argentina. The Falklanders were 'British by every conceivable test, by language, custom and race', and had a moral claim on British support. Indeed, thanks to their 'strong feeling of kinship', the British people 'spontaneously' felt a passionate concern for their aggrieved 'kith and kin' and rushed to their defence.

Conceptions of the state and immigration policy

I have briefly and hurriedly sketched three influential ways of understanding the nature of the state and explored their criteria of admission to its membership. All three views have been a part of Western self-understanding for a least two centuries, capture some aspects of historical reality, and are plausible in different degrees. It is therefore hardly surprising that many writers including the most talented sympathise with all three and promiscuously draw upon them to support their political preferences. Michael Walzer is a good example.

Basically, Walzer is a communitarian. He explains the nature and unity of the state in terms of shared understandings, sentiments, and so forth, rather than in the ethnic and purely procedural terms characteristic of the other two views. Yet the influence of the latter two is pervasive and unmistakable. He defends the citizen's right to emigrate on the liberal ground that the state is like a club whose members cannot be prevented from leaving it. He does not appreciate that if the state is a long-established and cohesive community bound by the deepest ties, its citizens may not leave it as easily as they leave a club. They have obligations and loyalties to their fellow-citizens which they may not disregard and off-load on others without powerful reasons and without incurring at least some public disapproval. Brain drain, leaving the state or transferring one's capital or savings abroad when it is passing through bad times and selling one's scarce skills abroad for better remuneration are surely acts of communal disloyalty and must be disapproved of by a communitarian. Walzer talks like a communitarian when immigration is involved, but like a liberal when emigration is concerned. To explain this away by invoking the alleged asymmetry of immigration and emigration is unconvincing, for the asymmetry must be established not just assumed and its implications must be spelt out.

Walzer also talks like a liberal when he argues that, since Australia has vast empty spaces, the starving people of the densely populated lands of South-East Asia would be justified in fighting their way into it. 'I doubt that we would want to charge the invaders with aggression'.[11] This is strange. From the communitarian point of view Australia is a community based, like Walzer's America, on shared understandings, sympathies, and so forth, and entitled to preserve its 'character'. The fact that it has large unoccupied areas is of no consequence. Walzer's liberal concern for the poor South-East Asians undercuts his argument about the rights to communal self-maintenance and rich social citizenship grounded in his communitarian view of the state. I wonder if Walzer would allow the poor Latin Americans to occupy the vast and empty American spaces.

The communitarian view easily slips into the ethnic view, and again this is evident in Walzer. As we saw, the latter implies both that those without biological ties to the state may not be admitted to it, and that those with such ties may and indeed must be. Walzer rightly rejects the first but not the second. He observes:[12]

> In time of trouble, the state is a refuge for members of the nation, whether or not they are residents and citizens. Perhaps the border of the political community was drawn years ago so as to leave their villages and towns on the wrong side; perhaps they are the children or grandchildren of emigrants. They have no legal membership rights, but if they are persecuted in the land where they live, they look to their homeland not only with hope but also with expectation. I am inclined to say that such expectations are legitimate. Greeks driven from Turkey, Turks from Greece, after the wars and revolutions of the early twentieth century, had to be taken in by the states that bore their collective names. What else are such states for? They don't only preside over a piece of territory and a random collection of inhabitants; they are also the political expression of a common life and (most often) of a national 'family' that is never entirely enclosed within their legal boundaries.

The ease with which Walzer slips into the ethnic vocabulary and turns the state into an ethnic homeland, the 'political expression' of a 'national' family is disturbing. He does not see that if the state is viewed in this way, he cannot consistently complain against non-ethnic citizens being reduced to a second class status and denied an equal right to participate in and reshape the ethical life of the community.

Critique of the ethnic view

Of the three views of the nature of the state, the ethnic view is the least satisfactory. To start with, it does not make sense in relation to any Western state, all of which are products of considerable ethnic intermingling and cannot pretend to belong to a single ethnic stock. This is obviously the case with such countries as the USA, Canada and Australia which are made up of immigrants drawn from different parts of the world. It is not true either of such allegedly homogeneous states as Great Britain and France. Britain consists of at least three major ethnic groups and there is no ethnic group called the British. Each of these three in turn is a product of much ethnic mixture. For those interested in this kind of thing, a distinguished genetic anthropologist, using blood grouping and other variable protein markers, has recently traced and charted the heterogenous and highly mixed origins of the British population.[13] The process of evolution of the British stock did not end with the creation of Great Britain. It went on to absorb such other ethnic groups as the Huguenots, the Irish, the Jews and even the eighteenth century black slaves and produced a most varied stock without damaging the unity of the British state. There is no reason why the process should not continue in the future.

A state might and generally does include one or more dominant ethnic groups. But *qua* ethnic groups they are politically irrelevant and the state cannot take political cognizance of them. It must transcend ethnic identities and treat its members in a uniform manner. If a state identified itself with and saw itself as a 'political expression' of a specific ethnic group, then it would necessarily discriminate against those not belonging to that group and end up violating the principle of equal citizenship that lies at its basis. If Germany were a state of the ethnic Germans, then its ethnically non-German citizens would be cultural and ethical outsiders. Their moral relation to the state would remain unequal and they cannot be bearers of equal rights and subjected to equal obligations.

The state cannot *both* identify itself with an ethnic group and ensure equal citizenship. This is why the concept of an ethnic or a nation state contains a contradiction. The state stands for openness and equality, the nation signifies closure and exclusivity. The two are uncomfortable bed-fellows and their tensions have been a source of much intolerance and violence during the past three centuries of European history. Thanks to the influence of the ethnic view of the state in Germany, non-ethnic Germans are virtually excluded from citizenship and in Belgium non-ethnic Belgians cannot join the armed forces and occupy certain offices of the state even after becoming its naturalised citizens. A state might begin as a nation as several of them have done, but it must and in many cases does succeed in liberating itself from its national origins and basing itself on its own independent foundation. Unless it does so, it cannot ensure equal citizenship to all its citizens, with all the problems that entails.

Contrary to what the New Right asserts, and to which Walzer seems to lend his support, the state has no 'relatives' and is not a 'national family'. It is not based on ties of blood or ethnicity and is not a quasi-biological entity. Its members might and do have relatives outside its boundaries, but only in their private capacity. *Qua* citizens they are public persons enjoying a state-derived identity and can, by definition, have no kinship ties either with one another or with outsiders. They may and do feel interested in those they consider to be their fellow-ethnics living abroad. But the feeling is often exaggerated for dubious political purposes.

For years the Indians in India took little interest in the Indian diaspora settled in over twenty countries abroad, and the attempts to arouse their interest met with little success. The reverse was and is just as true. Overseas Indians who have lived abroad for generations have evolved autonomous life-styles and self-definitions; many of their values, practices, social institutions, habits, and traits of temperament and character are often quite different; some of them have married locally; they often do not speak any of the Indian languages, and have little more than a vague emotional attachment to their ancestral place of origin. Since they and India have developed in different directions, their undoubted similarities often conceal their deeper differences and create the dangerous illusion of belonging to a shared community. As many an overseas Indian has painfully realised, they are likely to be misfits and miserable in India, in much the same way that the British settled abroad for decades often find Britain a strange and bewildering place. With such profound differences it does not make much sense to say that the overseas and indigenous Indians belong to the *same* ethnic group. And even if it did make some sense, their cultural and other differences often outweigh such similarities as are derived from their shared ethnicity.

The fact that one's great great grandfather was born in a particular country is not enough to generate even emotional ties, let alone moral. If the overseas Indians were to be expelled from their respective countries, it is wrong of them and of world opinion to think that India is their ethnic home and owes them hospitality as a matter of ethnic or racial obligation. It might, and perhaps will, welcome them, but if it did not, it would not stand convicted of ethnic disloyalty or impiety. That we do tend to think in these terms only shows the continuing influence of the untenable ethnic view of the state. What is true of India and the overseas Indians is also true in different degrees of other countries and their diaspora and there is no moral basis for giving the latter a preferential treatment for immigration purposes. If the ties between the two have remained deep, and if the diasporic community has continued to contribute to the development of the country concerned and thereby behaved as its virtual citizens, there is *some* moral basis for their claim but even then the claim is weak and can be overridden by other considerations. The state is the home of those who live and are allowed to come to live in it. It cannot be an 'ethnic home' for the outsiders whose ancestors might once have lived in it.

Critique of the communitarian view

Unlike the wholly untenable ethnic view of the state, its communitarian cousin contains many valuable insights. Every long-established community has a distinct way of life and a recognisable character. Its members define themselves and relate to each other in specific ways, share in common a body of practices and goals, traits of temperament and character, ways of conducting their affairs, interests, institutions, and so on, and have some sense of their collective identity. To spend a day in New York is a very different kind of experience from spending a day in Bombay or London, and to teach in an American university is quite different from teaching in a French or a German university. While all this is true and well-said, the communitarian view exaggerates its depth and importance, and is open to a number of objections. I shall only discuss those relevant to immigration.

First, although members of a polity share a sense of collective identity, and define themselves as British, Americans, Indians and so on, there is generally far less agreement on what the collective identity means and involves than is suggested by the communitarians. Take British identity. Its content has changed considerably over the centuries and it is not defined today in the same way as it was before the Second World War. The Scots define it quite differently from the way the English and the Welsh do. Moreover, within each group, the definition tends to vary with class and gender. This is inescapable, for any attempt to abridge a highly complex and rich way of life is necessarily selective and involves a good deal of myth-making. What is selected depends on who is selecting, in what context, for whom and for what purpose; and all such constructions are contested and deconstructed by those who feel marginalised by them, or whose life-experiences are inadequately articulated by them. Indeed, at any given point in time, the identity of a community is defined in several different ways, each capturing some aspect of it but ignoring the others and its public life is marked by an endless debate between them.

One might go further and wonder if the concept of national identity is not a source of unnecessary confusion. A society's way of life generally does have a recognisable character or *individuality*. But to talk of its *identity* is to introduce a risky and misleading concept. The concept reifies and homogenises what is distinctive to a society and suppresses diversity and fluidity. It also arrests history and implies that a society's character has persisted more or less unchanged over time. It implies a notion of the 'other' against whom the identity is to be protected and that, for a society to deviate from what is taken to be its identity, is to be untrue to oneself and to lack integrity. Even the concept of personal identity is problematic and ignores the vital fact that an individual is a bearer of multiple, evolving and dialectically related identities. To attribute identity to a community of millions spread over vast expanses of space and time makes even less sense.

Second, the communitarian emphasis on shared understandings, values, interests, attachments, affections and loyalties implies too homogeneous and unrealistic a view of the community. Common understanding does not necessarily imply common values. Members of a society may share a common system of meanings and know how to behave in specific situations and to interpret each other's conduct, but disagree about values. Caste-Hindus and the untouchables, or slave-owners and the slaves, do understand each other and know what is expected of them, but the latter group in each case does not share the values of the former. Similarly, members of a society may share common values, yet their interests may be fundamentally opposed as in a deeply divided society. The fact that they agree on what is good and desirable does not mean that they are willing to share it. The British people share common values, but there was little moral outrage, let alone a concerted action, when the number of the unemployed reached an all time high, when their welfare benefits were drastically reduced, or now when the homeless sleep in card-board boxes in bitter cold. Again, shared values and interests do not necessarily imply shared sentiments, attachments and affections. Members of a society may share a set of moral values and interests and act in accordance with them, without developing emotional bonds either towards one another or towards their shared institutions. In short, the communitarian view lumps related but basically quite different things together and naively imagines that all imply each other.

Furthermore, the references to shared understanding, values, and so forth find only a limited support in reality. In spite of centuries of living together, women in every society have complained that they sometimes have a great difficulty making sense of the motives and behaviour of men. Freud reflected the views of many men when he complained that, even after years of study, he remained ignorant of 'what women really wanted and felt'. Similar gaps in mutual understanding obtain between classes, generations, religions and races. Indeed, each individual is a world unto him or her self and carries areas of darkness which remain opaque not only to others but sometimes even to him or her self. Members of even the most integrated and self-conscious society are never fully transparent to one another. They *do* understand each other well enough to live together, but the understanding is necessarily limited in range and depth and is never wholly free of large areas of incomprehension and misunderstanding.

The same is the case with values. Every modern society is characterised by moral pluralism and diversity, and its members entertain different beliefs both about how they should live as individuals and how their society should be organised. Yet they have to live together and need to agree on the best way to debate and resolve their differences and on the principles that should guide the laws and policies of their polity. This calls for a broad consensus on a family of political values and more generally on their conception of a good polity. In all western and some non-western societies, these values include such things as equality before the law, the rule of law, equal citizenship, certain basic rights, respect for privacy, popular accountability of the government, free press and the right of dissent. The consensus is embodied in their legal and political institutions and gives the polity a distinct character. Although it is relatively stable, the consensus is open to debate and change. It is broadly accepted by most but not by all, for there are always people who think that it either goes too far or not far enough, and advocate either hierarchical and fascist or fully participatory systems of values and institutions. The general support that the consensus does enjoy is the product of an interplay between such different factors as genuine consent, social pressure, ideological conditioning, inertia and coercion.

The bulk of the values common to the society as a whole are thus politico-legal in nature. They pertain to the state, that is, to a specific aspect and not to the totality of social life. As the history of most countries shows, it is the state that self-consciously sets about uniting its otherwise diverse members by educational, industrial, cultural, symbolic and other means. Far from the state being the expression of a pre-existing community as the communitarian view maintains, there is in most societies very little cohesive community prior to or outside of the state. Most nation-states are really state-nations, nations created by states in the dubious pursuit of cultural and moral homogeneity. This partly explains why every modern communitarian is a nationalist and assigns to the state a dubious community-maintaining role.

Like common values, the common attachments and affections also cover a wide spectrum. Different members of society are attached in different degrees to different aspects of it. It is rare for all of them to be attached to all aspects of it in equal degrees. Their attachment, loyalty to and affection for their society, in a word their patriotism, is therefore not homogeneous and uniform, but differently derived and constituted, has a different texture, and covers a wide spectrum ranging from 'watery' fidelity to a fiercely blind commitment. Many public rituals and ceremonies that deeply move some sections of society evoke only indifference, contempt or bitter historical memories among others. Attitudes to the past also vary widely. Some Britons view their imperial history with intense pride sometimes bordering on racist narcissism; others with a mixture of pride and shame; yet others feel nothing but embarrassment and guilt. Again, some Britons are deeply attached to their way of life, whereas others find it parochial, smug, even oppressive. Members of a society form a series of concentric circles or layers, relating to their way of life in different ways, sharing it in different degrees, and viewing it with different degrees of enthusiasm and commitment.

The communitarian, then, is right to maintain that the state implies a body of shared values, some conception of common interests and 'identity', some measure of shared understanding, and some degree of attachment and loyalty. However it grossly exaggerates their degree, importance and interconnections. The shared understanding is limited; the shared values are minimal and largely politico-legal in content; the evocative power of the cultural pool of images and myths is limited in its range and depth; the prevailing way of life is really a federation of diverse ways of life; and it evokes different degrees and forms of attachment and loyalty such that some members of a society are little different from the outsiders.

Since this is the case in all Western societies, the communitarian criteria for membership of the state need radical revision. Western society contains and can tolerate diverse ways of life and hence it is not necessary that the immigrant's way of life should be similar to that of the host society. The members of a society are attached and feel loyal to each other and to their way of life in different degrees, and hence it is also not legitimate to require that they should all be able to identify with the potential immigrants and recognise them as part of a common national or cultural family. What is more, the host society is not a homogeneous 'we' but made up of several 'we-s', and its different sections identify with different groups of immigrants. Many religious Britons feel that they have more in common with the devout, pious and family-centred Muslims and Hindus than with many of their aggressively secular, complacent, or effortlessly superior upper-class countrymen. For basically the same reasons, it is equally illegitimate to demand that the immigrants should have long historical ties with the host society. All that can be legitimately required of the new-comers is that they should satisfy the minimum conditions of the membership of the polity and these consist of adhering to its common politico-legal values. This does not necessarily mean accepting or believing in them as a matter of intellectual conviction, but rather that one should be willing and able to conform to them in practice. Muslim immigrants to Britain may not believe in universal franchise, but so long as they conform to it in practice and do not stop women from voting, they fully qualify for its membership.

One can go further and argue that the communitarian view fails to appreciate the vital significance of cultural differences in the life of a society. They widen the range of life-styles open to all its citizens, enabling them to borrow from others whatever attracts them and to enrich their way of life. They also bring different traditions into a mutually beneficial dialogue and stimulate new ideas and experiments. A creative interplay between the ethnic minority musical, literary, culinary and artistic traditions on the one hand, and those of the British society on the other, has led to many exciting developments and enriched both. New ways of life also bring with them new talents, skills, sensitivities and ways of looking at things, different kinds of imagination, new psychological and moral resources, new sources of spiritual energy, and give the receiving society a cultural breadth and depth. The way in which successive waves of immigrants have vitalised and built up such societies as the USA, Canada and Australia and even such long-established societies as Britain and France testifies to this. Far from being a handicap, the fact that an immigrant's way of life is different is often a factor in her favour. It is true that she may be illiterate in the cultural grammar and idioms of the host society and that may provoke some initial resentment. The answer to that lies, not in obturating the door to difference, but in explaining its importance, devising programmes of better mutual understanding, minimising the likely causes of tension, and giving those involved the time and the encouragement to negotiate their relationships.

Critique of the liberal view

As for the liberal view of the state, it need not detain us long, for many of its strengths and limitations are the obverse of those of its communitarian rival. It fails to appreciate fully the cultural and historical basis of the state. Every state represents a distinct way of life with its own common politico-legal values, political vocabulary, manner of debating and conducting its collective affairs, traditions, and so forth. It involves shared historical experiences and memories, some sense of community, shared myths and common understandings. Unlike clubs and other voluntary associations, it aims to endure in time and its members perceive it as a more or less permanent feature of their collective life. As such they see it as their homeland, their political home on earth, and feel possessive about it. Contrary to what the liberal often tends to assert, individuals are not abstract atoms endowed by nature with certain basic desires and the powers of reason and will, but cultural beings structured and shaped by their society in a particular manner. Furthermore, they are integral parts of, and can only flourish and fashion their identities within, the framework of emotionally secure and happily unself-conscious quasi-voluntary communities based on familial, kinship, neighbourhood, ethnic, religious and other ties. The liberal stresses voluntary associations at the expense of these communities and ignores the latter's significance.

While the liberal can be faulted on these and other grounds, he has grasped several crucial features of the modern state that are ignored or inadequately appreciated by the other two views of the state. He is acutely aware of the fact that moral, ethnic, religious and other forms of diversity are the necessary consequences of the modern conception of the self and a permanent feature of modern life. As such, any conception of society that ignores this fact in pursuit of a morally and culturally homogeneous community is unrealistic and fraught with problems. The liberal is also aware of the historical specificity and the unique character of the modern state. Unlike the Greek, the Roman and the medieval polities based respectively on the unity of the *ethnos,* the *cultus* and faith, the modern state's source of unity lies within itself. It grew out of bitter religious, ethnic, moral, linguistic and other conflicts, and represents a distinct and historically unparalleled mode of creating unity out of plurality. It requires only limited unity, that is, unity in the politico-legal area of social life and leaves the other areas to the free play of plurality. The distinction between state and society lies at the basis of the modern state. Society is not a mere background to the state or a raw material to be shaped in its image. And nor is the state merely an extension of society. Since the two are separate, the modern state is not only able to tolerate plurality in a way that the earlier polities could not, but also derives strength and energy from it.

Furthermore, the modern state relies on its own resources to create such unity as it needs. It sets its own criteria of membership, has its own autonomous source of authority, and has its own distinct goals and objectives. Unlike its predecessors, the modern state therefore does not require unity of race, ethnicity, religious, moral doctrines or even language to maintain itself in existence. So long as its members subscribe to its authority, obey its laws, conform to the basic values inherent in its structure and debate their differences in a civil manner, its unity is assured. It does, of course, help if they agree on common purposes and share a common culture, and every state develops both these. However, they are subject to constant debate and negotiation between its different sections. In a world as fluid and porous to external influences as ours, neither the common purposes nor the common culture can be treated as the political *a priori* of the modern state. The common purposes are constantly questioned and periodically reformulated and the internally differentiated common culture is forever undergoing subtle and deep changes. Every modern state lives with diversity and leaves its members free to develop their own different forms of communal life. As the liberal maintains, the modern state can in principle accommodate *any* outsider, leaving the individual free to find his or her own niche in its capacious and diversified structure.

The liberal rightly argues that all forms of life are human creations, that they necessarily share several crucial features in common, that all human beings have the capacity to create and to appreciate each other's cultures, and that there is none to which they cannot adjust, however different it might be from their own. Once admitted, no outsider for long remains an outsider. Given time and encouragement, the individual learns how to find his or her way around in the life of the host society and to acquire at least moderate competence in its conceptual grammar and vocabulary. This does not mean that the society concerned may not limit the number of outsiders, ask them to make a genuine effort to learn its language, customs, history, and so on, and expect them to be sensitive to the fears and genuine anxieties of the indigenous people. But this relates to what the state does to them once they have become its members and here many liberals have shown an unjustified preference for a policy of assimilationist cultural engineering.[14] It does not, however, damage the basic liberal thesis that in principle the membership of the state should be open to all who satisfy the minimum conditions of civility.

Conclusion

In the previous sections I briefly commented on three currently dominant views of the state and their theories of immigration.[15] If my criticisms, and the implied view of the modern state, are correct, they entail several general principles.

First, the state is not a family, the national home of a specific ethnic group, or based on the unity of race. No state should therefore admit, reject or prefer immigrants on ethnic or racial grounds.

Second, the state is not based on the substantive unity of moral, political, religious and other kinds of beliefs. It should not therefore admit, reject or prefer candidates for its membership on the grounds of their religious, political or moral beliefs or sexual orientation.

Third, although a state represents a distinct way of life, it is an open and formal association capable of accommodating diverse ways of life. Furthermore, every sane human being is capable of adjusting to and participating in its way of life. No outsider may therefore be denied admission on the ground that her way of life is different from or renders her incapable of sharing that of the host society.

Fourth, the immigration policy of a state must be acceptable to all its citizens and not reflect the biases and preferences of a dominant group. They all have to live with the new members (or without those who are excluded), and must have an equal say in shaping the rules of admission.

Fifth, the immigration policy must be seen not in narrowly economic terms but also as a means of enriching the cultural diversity of the country. Immigration brings in not only new skills, not only new people, but also new cultures which broaden and deepen the prevailing way of life. As such it has a vital cultural dimension that deserves to be taken into account in deciding whom to admit and even encourage or invite. The humanitarian admission of refugees and asylum seekers is best defended as an integral part of the moral culture of the receiving country. It not only helps the needy but also tests, reinforces and deepens the spirit of humanity and universality of the host society.

Sixth, the immigration policy of a country is interlocked with and shapes the way its citizens treat the immigrants already settled among them. If the policy discriminates against, or places disproportionately stringent restrictions on, specific ethnic, cultural or religious groups, it implies that the latter are undesirable, unwanted, and to be admitted only when there is no other alternative. This casts them in a negative light and encourages the majority to believe that it would not be acting wrongly if it ill-treated or discriminated against them even after they become their fellow citizens.

Finally, the right to marry and to have children is universally recognised as a basic human right. Hence to admit individuals is also to undertake to admit their spouses and children. Not the individual but the family is the unit of immigration. This means that no state may deny the immigrant admitted to its membership the right to marry wherever s/he pleases and to bring in her or his spouse. If the state doubts the genuineness of the marriage, the onus of proof should be placed on it, not on the immigrant, as required by the normal principles of justice. In admitting an immigrant, the state incurs an obligation to facilitate the entry of his or her spouse and children. If their entry were to be delayed beyond a reasonable period of time or subjected to humiliating inquiries, the state would be guilty of deliberate obstruction and even perhaps of the perversion of the course of justice, and owes the immigrant an explanation and even perhaps compensation. The now notorious British practice of making black and Asian immigrants wait for years before uniting them with their spouses and families, and making them cross all manner of perverse bureaucratic hurdles, is valid neither in law nor morality.[16]

4 INTERNATIONAL LAW AND HUMAN RIGHTS OBLIGATIONS

Hugo Storey

To create a just immigration policy able to meet the challenges of the 1990s and beyond will require major overhaul. Far more is involved than improving human rights guarantees. But a cornerstone of any real reform must be that our laws and policies on entry, stay and expulsion adequately reflect contemporary international law and human rights standards.

In 1984 the European Commission of Human Rights stated in relation to UK Immigration rules on marriage that:

> It has not been shown that the measures in question enhance good race relations, for, although they may respond to the fears of a certain section of the population, they may create resentment in that part of the immigrant population which views the policy as unfair.[1]

In these few lines a supranational human rights body rejected the contention of the UK Government that sex-discriminatory measures taken against the foreign husbands of wives settled in the UK served to protect the rights of others. In repudiating an ideology central to post-1962 British immigration policy, the European Convention on Human Rights (ECHR) machinery at Strasbourg showed the very valuable role that international human rights law can play in helping gain a clearer perspective in an area of policy so often bedeviled by emotive argument. This historic case—which was followed by an adverse European Court of Human Rights judgment against the UK in 1985[2]—has been one of many developments pointing towards the need for a more systematic reform of UK immigration policy founded on international human rights standards.

In this paper I examine why and how this could be done given the present state of development of international human rights law relating to immigration control. Throughout this paper, the term 'immigration' is used broadly to cover issues of emigration, immigration and asylum; although it leaves many matters of nationality and asylum (and the European Community) to be dealt with in greater depth in other papers.

Cornerstone of reform

Having been hammered out by policymakers and legal experts from many different states, the international rules on immigration are based on rational and objective criteria, particularly in the way they have been interpreted and applied by various international judicial bodies.

The second reason why international human rights standards should be built into UK immigration policy is that this is a policy area where there are inadequate checks and balances to ensure that basic human rights are not abused. There are no powerful unions or interest groups. There is no adequate media scrutiny; rather a persisting degree of media hostility. Fears about foreigners can easily be stirred up by populist politicians or others for base ends. Virtually all empirical studies identify 'foreigners', 'aliens', 'migrant workers' and 'refugees' as particularly vulnerable groupings.[3]

Immigration has long been and continues to be an emotive area of policy. It is accordingly vital that any reform should include human rights protection tied to international supervisory machineries. We know enough from the two World Wars, from the tragic events in former Yugoslavia as well as from the disturbing signs of resurgent racist and xenophobic tendencies in several other states in Europe,[4] to see the wisdom of requiring our own reforms to conform to minimum international standards.

Third, great strides have been taken post-war in the development of international instruments that directly or indirectly protect individuals who are the subject of adverse immigration measures. Yet international rules relevant to immigration still amount to little more than a set of minimum standards.[5] Even so, when applied to the UK in the last three decades they have revealed many shortcomings. During this period relevant Strasbourg case law under the ECHR[6] has censured UK immigration law for *inter alia* (the names of leading cases are given in brackets):

- racial discrimination (*East African Asians Cases*);
- sex discrimination (*Abdulaziz; Min*);

- failure to respect the rights to family life (*Uppal, Fadele, Yousef, Lamguindaz*);
- lack of effective appeal remedies (*Abdulaziz*);
- lack of enforceable rights (*Alam; Amekrane*);
- overdependence on executive discretion (*Abdulaziz*);
- inadequate economic and social justification behind rules governing key categories of entrants (*Abdulaziz*);
- inadequate safeguards that ensure procedurally fair expulsion policy (*Caprino, Zamir*).

Those hurt by immigration decisions are not only the immigrants themselves. A wife, husband, parent, adult son or adult daughter, sometimes themselves British citizens, can suffer greatly from the exclusion or expulsion of a spouse, child or elderly parent. Under our immigration law such 'indirect victims' often lack adequate legal remedies.[7]

The UK's gradual integration into a framework of European law has served to magnify our shortcomings, since the latter is built on a firmer conceptual footing which establishes enforceable rights and effective remedies.[8] There is a danger of exaggerating the UK's poor performance in comparison with some other developed democracies;[9] but that is scarce justification for it.

By reforming our own laws in line with international standards we also improve the chances of any new 'Greater Europe'[10] achieving viable pluralist democracies based on the rule of law and respect for human rights. With or without the Maastricht Treaty, our immigration laws are likely to be brought into greater harmony with those of other EC states in a common European code on immigration rules. This trend may result in greater immigration justice, particularly if this development takes place primarily within the normal EC law-making process. If however this harmonisation process is pursued through intergovernmental 'paracommunitarian'[11] channels, such as the Schengen Convention, then the result may be less immigration justice. Whereas the former process has broadly respected human rights guarantees in the sphere of immigration, the latter has not.[12] The chances of harmonisation reflecting proper standards will also be far greater if our own national law is based on these standards. With some EC member states feeling mounting pressures externally from refugees and internally from resurgent neo-nazi forces, it is a crucial time to reassert UK respect for fundamental human rights values.

Ensuring that our reforms include international safeguards will also inspire confidence amongst our own ethnic minorities. For them, such safeguards will offer a shield (e.g., against arbitrary expulsions) and sometimes a sword (e.g., to secure just policies on family reunification). They will offer a way of linking concern to preserve their own cultural identity with increased civic pride and sense of *British* identity. If our reforms can ensure easier access to British citizenship for permanent residents,[13] and thus access to European citizenship, then that will invest them with a more secure sense of *European* identity.[14]

Finally, making international human rights obligations central to UK immigration reform will enhance the ability of the UK to promote human rights abroad without double standards or hypocrisy. Events in former Yugoslavia serve as a dire reminder that human rights guarantees are no shield against bullets and mortars, even when the eyes of the world look on. But there is considerable evidence that international legal obligations can reduce the incidence of gross human rights violations. As Geoff Gilbert argues in his chapter, they can assist by creating fair and understandable systems for regulating transnational movements of people. They may help allay or reduce refugee flows at source and to reduce tensions in fledgling democracies by affording resident national minorities firm guarantees about rights to family reunification. This key role of human rights is becoming more accepted as an integral part of UK[15] (and EC)[16] foreign policy. For the UK to put its own house in order would lend the UK greater stature in the world and in the eyes of developing countries in particular.

The current state of international rules on immigration

It remains an axiom of international law that states have a right to control the entry, residence and expulsion of aliens. This is fully recognised by human rights courts, including the European Court of Human Rights in Strasbourg. But so is the precept that this right is subject to their treaty obligations.[17] Largely by and through treaties,[18] nation states now accept more international limits on their immigrations policies than ever before. We live in a part of the globe where the level of mutual acceptance by democracies of such limits is higher than anywhere else.

It surprises most people to learn that there are currently over 70 international instruments relevant to this area of policy. Most have come into being during the post-war period. An increasing number have become the subject of ratification by virtue of which states bind themselves legally to protect human rights. A significant and growing number now include mechanisms of supervision, monitoring and enforcement. Old models of international law saw states, and not individuals, as true legal actors. That has changed. In particular, the right of individuals to complain about breaches of international rules has come to be seen as an essential propeller for any system claiming to secure practical and effective enjoyment of fundamental human rights.[19] The right of individual complaint as well as distinct supervisory mechanisms has had many effects. A key one is that there now exists a great deal of established case law.[20] The textual rules have thus been fleshed out quite significantly.

The number of rules made within the framework of the Council of Europe is itself quite remarkable.[21] These international rules as given concrete shape and form by case law have done much to keep up standards. Of the utmost importance is the fact that, contracting states to treaties, despite accepting international limits on their powers and increasingly giving practical effect to these rules, have found that they can work and live with them. The requirement that they adopt policies based on objective and rational criteria of justice in the form of definite and identifiable rules, has proved compatible with restrictive and stringent immigration controls as well as with a more liberal and flexible approach. The rules have not prevented shifts from one approach to another. States have not experienced them as imposing too tight a legal 'corset' upon them. No studies of those Council of Europe states which have incorporated the ECHR disclose evidence of any serious difficulty caused by the Convention or Strasbourg case law to their policies on immigration nor to the authorities which operate their immigration controls.[22]

For those who wish to promote greater protection for the human rights of foreigners this is seen as a weakness of the case law, reflecting patchy and incomplete safeguards and undue tolerance of double standards on the part of states.[23] Others see such case law as a spur to myriad reforms not only in countries that incorporate the ECHR[24] but also in countries like the UK where the influence of ECHR case law traces back as far as the *Alam* v. *UK* case in which the UK formally committed itself to the introduction of an independent appeals machinery (brought into force in a 1969 Statute).[25]

Whether or not criticism is valid, the fact that states have found the international rules manageable is highly significant. It demonstrates a preparedness to live by, as well as swear by, such rules and the standards they enshrine.

UK failure to comply with international human rights standards

In general, the UK has a good record of compliance with international human rights standards.[26] In the sphere of immigration policy, however, this has not been so. Evidence to this effect is threefold:

- The UK continues to avoid taking on immigration-related obligations imposed by some of the key universal and regional international instruments.
- The UK appears particularly reluctant to give full legal effect to those obligations which it has undertaken in this sphere.
- In relation to immigration the UK has singularly failed to remedy effectively a number of breaches of its international obligations identified by international bodies whose jurisdiction it has accepted.

The appendix to this chapter lists the principal international instruments relevant to UK immigration policy and, for the first time anywhere in print, brings together details on the UK's position in respect of non-ratification, reservations and interpretative declarations.

A state seeking to avoid or minimise treaty obligations can make use of a number of methods. It can sign but not ratify a treaty; or ratify only bits of it; or enter reservations; or make interpretative declarations; or derogate from one or more provisions. In extreme instances it can denounce a treaty.

The UK has achieved international notoriety for its continuance under the 1966 International Covenant on Civil and Political Rights (ICCPR) of a blanket reservation covering immigration and nationality.[27] Coupled with its non-ratification of the Optional Protocol to this Covenant[28] (which grants an individual right of complaint), this has prevented any judicial testing of its immigration policy by the UN Human Rights Committee. This flaw appears more serious when one examines the three Human Rights Committee 'state report' scrutinies conducted so far under Article 40 of this Covenant.

Thereunder the UK's record in the sphere of immigration has been the object of pointed criticism.[29] Collaterally, the UK has shown little enthusiasm for UN attempts to remedy some of the deficiencies in international standards by the creation of new Conventions (e.g., the 1990 Convention on the Protection of the Rights of All Migrants).[30]

Similarly, the UK has avoided making commitments concerned with migrant workers under various instruments which other developed democracies have had no qualms about embracing. In justification, the UK Government has often claimed that its own observance of international standards in this field was ensured by its commitments within the European framework.[31]

If one examines the position the UK has taken up in respect of the major European human rights system, the ECHR and its Protocols, however, there has been a singular concern to avoid the few obligations that do expressly safeguard immigration rights. It has no intention of ratifying the ECHR's Fourth Protocol,[32] something not even another island state—Eire (also part of our 'Common Travel Area')—has found problems with.[33] It may be argued that UK worries over Hong Kong might necessitate making a reservation in relation to the provision concerning the admission of a state's own nationals; but that is no argument against ratification. Provisions of the Fourth Protocol also include a right often seen as one of the most fundamental of all rights: the right to leave any country, including one's own. This has long seemed a strange omission to the former Soviet and Eastern bloc states whose denial of exit rights to their own citizens the UK had so regularly and properly denounced. The Fourth Protocol also prohibits collective expulsion of aliens. Recently the UK has declared its intention of ratifying the ECHR's Seventh Protocol,[34] which, *inter alia*, adds a number of minimal procedural safeguards to do with expulsion of aliens. This was designed to ensure greater correspondence between the range of ICCPR and ECHR protections.[35] But this still remains a promise only. Until we ratify it and do something about the Fourth Protocol any argument that our European obligations render superfluous our failings in respect of the ICCPR sounds weak.

Additionally, the UK has failed to make a declaration under Article 63 of the Convention extending its jurisdiction to cover all of the territories for whose international relations it is responsible, in particular Hong Kong. As a result, controversial measures undertaken by authorities there, e.g., expulsions back to China of persons active in the 1989 Tiananmen Square protests, cannot be contested by them at Strasbourg, despite the issues touching on fundamental human rights—the right to life and the absolute prohibition on torture or inhuman and degrading treatment.[36]

Things stand no better under another major European human rights instrument: the 1961 European Social Charter. During the course of parliamentary proceedings on the Asylum Bill 1991, the Government announced its intentions of derogating from key parts of the Charter that impinge on migrant workers and their families.[37] There is also no sign of any UK intention to ratify the 1977 European Convention on the Legal Status of Migrant Workers.[38]

Such negative aspects to the UK's human rights record in the immigration sphere must be read in conjunction with its current enthusiasm for the 'paracommunitarian' (inter-governmental) machineries developed amongst leading members of the EC.[39] A prime feature of the paracommunitarian instruments to date is their silence on any international obligations except the 1951 Convention on Refugees and its 1967 Protocol.[40]

Lack of incorporation into UK law

The problems of the UK in securing human rights in the immigration sphere are compounded by the approach it has adopted towards achieving internal legal effect for such obligations which it has been prepared to undertake. The Government has incorporated into domestic law the four Geneva Conventions concerned with the context of war which include provisions affording protection against expulsion.[41] Certain other statutory provisions ensure full legal effect is given to international rules affecting the immigration position of special categories, such as diplomats, visiting forces and certain categories of persons involved in shipping, aviation etc.[42] Otherwise the only statutory provisions currently made relate to clauses requiring no action contrary to UK obligations under the 1951 Refugee Convention. The first of these arose in an isolated context which concerned exemption from a limited right of appeal imposed on overstayers[43] and the provision involved appears to have been inserted only as a result of a formal commitment given before the European Commission of Human Rights in the course of the *Kandiah* case, the so-called 'Kandiah concession'.[44]

UK Immigration Rules have from inception incorporated the 1951 Convention on refugees.[45] But the legal status of these Rules is an anomaly and they do not confer fully enforceable legal rights.[46] From this angle the fact that some asylum law has now been put onto a statutory footing is a positive step; but the Asylum and Immigration Appeals Act 1993 is widely criticised for its failure to conform to UNHCR and human rights standards.[47]

The UK Government continues to resist giving our courts any legal powers to ensure the internal legal effect of human rights safeguards in this sphere. The courts for their part adhere to the doctrine of transformation, under which, for a treaty to be accorded internal legal effect, Parliament must enact legislation to this end. Normally therefore, UK treaty obligations do not create enforceable legal rights for individuals who claim the UK has violated international law in their case. Certainly, judgments on immigration cases are amongst those in which espousal of this doctrine tends to be given its most robust expression.[48]

This problem is compounded by the absence of any fundamental constitutional law (apart from Community law) by reference to which English courts can invalidate or disapply domestic immigration law thought to contravene human rights treaty obligations.

Although rules of construction adopted by our courts permit limited recourse to international treaty texts where there exists ambiguity in the law,[49] in the field of immigration and asylum law such recourse has rarely been made. There are limited signs that some judges now view it as part of their function to examine international law standards. The lobby in favour of incorporation of the ECHR into English law now includes the Master of the Rolls (Lord Justice Bingham).[50] In the absence of any Parliamentary initiative, however, there can be no substantial change of approach by English judges.

UK response to adverse findings

Although the UK generally enjoys a good reputation as a state that complies with findings against it made by international organs of adjudication established by treaty, its record in the immigration field has been dismal. The following examples are in point.

Despite Human Rights Committee (HRC) report queries (noted earlier) our immigration laws, rules and policies continue to preserve rules that discriminate on the basis of sex, e.g., there is no provision for husbands to accompany female students during their period of study. There is some provision for settlement by unmarried daughters aged 18–21 but none for comparable sons. Some female British Overseas Citizens who have no other nationality are still denied a non sex-discriminatory statutory scheme governing their admission to the UK.[51]

Despite the findings of UK non-compliance with the 1961 European Social Charter made by its competent supervisory organ, the Committee of Independent Experts, the UK has still failed to put right matters raised over more than one cycle of previous reports. Some improvements have occurred but in the latest report available (1988–9), this Committee concluded that the UK was not fully complying with Article 19 paragraph 8, specifically in respect of its much-publicised 'Three Advisers' procedures. The Committee:

> has found the United Kingdom in violation of this provision as there is no right of appeal to a court or to any other independent body against a deportation order made by the Secretary of State on political or national security grounds (see *inter alia* Conclusions V, p.139 and Conclusions XI-1, p.167).
>
> The United Kingdom report contains no new information on this issue. The Committee reiterated its negative conclusion because the panel of three advisers, even assuming that it is an independent body, has only the competence to make non-binding recommendations to the Secretary of State.[52]

It also noted that it was unable to say whether the UK was or was not complying with Article 18 (on liberalised regulations for those wishing to engage in gainful occupation) or Article 19(6) (on family reunion). Under scrutiny in the former instance were undue restrictions on the self-employed and of persons admitted to the UK on the basis of short-term work permits. Under Article 19(6) the cause of concern was the continuing failure of the UK to afford to dependent children between 18–21 the right to enter the UK for the purpose of family settlement.[53]

With regard to the ECHR, the UK's commitment during the course of Strasbourg proceedings to eliminate discrimination from immigration legislation has still not been completed over seven years after an adverse judgment by the Court (in 1985)—in the *Abdulaziz* case.[54] Nor must the manner of the UK's compliance with the *Abdulaziz* judgment be forgotten. For husbands and fiancés wanting to be joined by foreign wives or fiancées it amounted in all but one aspect to a levelling-down of their position to that of women. It also resulted in the repeal in 1988 of s.1(5) of the 1971 Immigration Act (which had conferred privileges on Commonwealth wives and children). That response met the letter of Convention law. But its spirit, which requires non-restriction, maintenance and further realisation of rights, was flouted.

International standards as sources for reforming measures

We know that it is possible for a democratic country to make conformity to international obligations one of its stated aims in the immigration sphere: e.g., The Canadian Immigration Act 1978 opens with fulfilment of international obligations as one of its listed objectives. But how could or should this be done in the UK and European context?

Because of the considerable body of international case law that now exists, there is significant scope for drawing on international materials to cure deficiencies in our present immigration and asylum law and practice.

First, priority might be given to altering our law in those aspects which have been the subject of condemnation by established international machineries whose supervisory jurisdiction we have accepted. Those pinpointed by the Human Rights Committee of the ICCPR and the Committee of Independent Experts of the 1961 European Social Charter should be first on this part of the agenda. From established ECHR case law on complaints lodged against the UK in Strasbourg, it is further possible to identify a number of specific problems with existing law and policy.

The great value of the accumulated case law is that it has established *distinct methods* for testing national immigration law and practice to see if any Convention violations are involved. In terms of the substantive rights guaranteed, it is established under Articles 2 and 3 that in relation to expulsion, for example, a state has to show that it has ensured that any person subject to extradition or deportation measures will not, if returned, face a real risk of harm to his or her life or be subject to inhuman or degrading treatment.[55]

In relation to Articles 8, 12 and Protocol No. 1 Article 2 which deals with rights to respect for family life, private life and to education, immigration measures may give rise to a breach either by failing to respect the right, or by unjustified interference with it.

Unjustified interference is examined by reference to various factors including:

  (i) the strength of a person's connections [with the UK], particularly as established by residence, broader family ties, citizenship, service, etc.;

 (ii) the extent of his or her connections elsewhere (usually in the country of origin);

(iii) the extent to which the person concerned knew that immigration difficulties lay in store for him or her, before exercising the right guaranteed;

(iv) the extent to which the person is responsible for the adverse measure taken against him or her;

 (v) the extent to which there exist serious and practical obstacles to his or her being able to enjoy the rights elsewhere.[56]

In seeking to justify any immigration decision being challenged, the UK must show that the action pursues one of the legitimate aims specified in the restriction clauses (if any) attached to the right guaranteed; and that one of these aims *is* a valid reason behind the immigration measure in any particular case. It must also demonstrate that pursuit of this aim is proportionate and meets a 'pressing social need'. There is the further possibility of breaching the rights by way of discriminatory restrictions, under Article 14.[57] Thus, for example, the Commission has noted that in family settlement cases financial restrictions that discriminated against poorer applicants could give rise to a violation under Article 8/14.[58]

On the procedural side, case-law has been robust in requiring a state to show that it possesses an effective multi-level system of remedies. It is true that the recent Court judgment in the *Vilvirajah* case concerning Tamil asylum seekers from Sri Lanka narrowly ruled that UK judicial review did comply with Article 13 (on effective remedies). This judgment, however, does not destroy this approach, since it did not detract from Commission identification of flaws in other levels of UK immigration legal remedies, especially as regards UK over-reliance on executive discretion.[59]

Another key feature of this case-law is that it requires that decision-making is made subject to procedural safeguards.[60] Equally important to those Strasbourg cases involving the UK, is the ECHR case law formulated in cases taken against other states. A prime example is the Court's judgment in the *Berrehab* case against the Netherlands. Under the ECHR system of 'collective enforcement' each state is required to take account of every Court ruling even when it arises in a case against another state. Thus the *Berrehab* ruling highlighted the need to fill a gap in existing UK immigration rules which presently do not cater for a foreign parent who may have strong family reasons for needing to settle in the UK to be with his or her children. That gap remains unfilled.[61]

By examining UK shortcomings highlighted by immigration cases taken to Strasbourg, and scrutiny of our law and practice in accordance with Strasbourg's method of approach as revealed by its case law, much improvement could be made, even without reference to other international law materials.

Implications for immigration decision-makers

More concrete measures should be taken to ensure that all involved in the administration of our immigration controls as well as in immigration appeals and in judicial review make full use of established international materials in the course of their decision-making. Under our present system governing asylum cases for example, judges do not always accept that they must apply provisions of the *UNHCR Handbook* or the Conclusions of its Executive Committee; at best these are seen to supply 'helpful guidance'.[62] Given the UK's obligation, long-written into our immigration rules, not to act contrary to our obligations under the 1951 Refugee Convention, this simply will not do.

We must expect to meet some resistance to the new approach championed here. There will be those who will say that international rules are somehow beyond the ken of our immigration officials. The judicial stamp of approval for this attitude was given some years ago by Lord Denning:

> I desire, however, to amend one of the statements I made in the Bhajan Singh case. I said then that the immigration officer ought to bear in mind the principles stated in the [ECHR]. I think that would be asking too much of the immigration officers. They cannot be expected to know or apply the Convention. They must go simply by the Immigration Rules laid down by the Secretary of State and not by the Convention.[63]

This attitude can no longer be sustained. Whilst it is true that some

ECHR provisions are opaque, the case law has done much to elaborate specific transparent rules.[64] In any event it is scarcely beyond the wit of those who draft our rules to adapt these particular provisions. If PACE (Police and Criminal Evidence Act 1984) codes and social security rules can be transformed into relatively clear rules for officials and public alike (at least in their public leaflet form), so can international rules on immigration distilled from treaties and case law.

Giving international standards greater effect within domestic law

Drawing to a greater extent on international materials to rewrite our own rules will not in itself guarantee better levels of protection. First, this is because immigration is an area of administration where there is often a need for careful weighing of individual circumstances. Even if the exercise of discretion is made subject to human rights criteria it will simply not be possible to prescribe for all 'fact situations'.

Second, even if Lord Denning was wrong to label the ECHR as too woolly, it is correct to note that its text contains rules expressed in broad and universal language. That is part of its character as a human rights code. International instruments establish general principles which are to govern the criteria elaborated in more particularised ground-level rules. As such they act as beacons that light up the path for changes in those rules which must necessarily be made and remade to meet new situations, and to prevent backsliding (a crucial aspect in Europe with the dangers posed by those seeking authoritarian solutions to migration and asylum issues). In this regard, special mention should be made of Article 17 of the ECHR which provides that:

> Nothing in this Convention may be interpreted as implying for any state, group or person any right to engage *in any activity or perform any act aimed at the destruction of any of the rights and freedoms set forth herein or at their limitation to a greater extent than is provided for in the Convention.* [emphasis added]

For this reason, use of provisions in major human rights treaties for the purpose of filling gaps in our existing immigration rules can never render redundant their role in furnishing objectives and general principles.

Third, the supervisory bodies established under some of the major international human rights instruments, the European Court of Human Rights in particular, have adopted a 'dynamic' approach to interpretation of the Convention rights. This approach has ensured that, whilst the rights guaranteed are expressed as inalienable and fundamental, their content has been able to change over time in response to scientific and other changes. There is no reason to think that Strasbourg's future case law on immigration issues will cease to try and maintain and further standards both in the UK and in other contracting states, even if practitioners experience disappointment in some important cases. It is crucial therefore to ensure that our rules and practice can respond immediately to developing case law from Strasbourg.

Incorporation of the ECHR

Much of my argument so far would seem to lead directly on to a conclusion that the UK should incorporate the ECHR into domestic law either in lieu of, or in addition to, adopting a distinct British Bill of Rights or various Acts of Parliament which cover the same ground.[65] I confine comment on this much-debated[66] area here to four major points:

First, any variant of incorporation of the ECHR (and indeed other key human rights instruments that touch on immigration) will improve our overall standards of immigration justice.

Second, it would be unwise to urge any selective identification of particular ECHR rights as substitute for incorporation of the ECHR. In the absence of incorporation of a full set of human rights guarantees, it is difficult to see how the disadvantaged situation of foreigners and settled residents can ever be comprehensively tackled. It is striking, when one looks at those who have taken applications to Strasbourg over the past three decades, how many are foreign nationals or persons of foreign origin. Most are raising complaints quite unrelated to immigration.[67] This well illustrates that it is a fallacy to imagine that one can solve 'immigration' problems without bringing into play the broader principles of equal treatment and justice enshrined in the international instruments.

Third, without across-the-board incorporation, access to justice for the ordinary individual will not be available from the courts and tribunals of our land. In order to get it, s/he will continue to have to tread 'the long road to Strasbourg', where an outcome can sometimes take years.[68]

Fourth, whilst the UK record of compliance with judgments on non-immigration cases by the European Court of Human Rights has generally been good, it must be doubted in the light of its response to the *Abdulaziz* judgment, that its compliance with any future judgments in the immigration field[69] might not be similarly narrow and slow.

To rely entirely on ECHR incorporation or a Bill of Rights would not be prudent. One sure lesson of the past is that 'immigrants' are often the first casualties of failure to implement justice and human rights reforms. Thus it is imperative that immigration reform proposals should not be made contingent upon more generalised measures of reform. It is necessary to pursue specific immigration measures independently of any broader package. In any event the ECHR and the other major human rights treaties do not and were not designed to cover directly most immigration issues.[70] There remains a need for implementation of international rules into *specific* immigration and asylum laws and policies. Nothing less can create the climate of long-term security and stability so necessary to promote a more positive role in British society for our ethnic minorities, as well as to provide a rational basis for broad consensus in the population at large.

It is also increasingly vital that any such immigration reforms be closely linked to the existing and projected EC system and with our own ideas for the greater realisation of immigration justice within that system.

An agenda for reform

The first task should thus be a reappraisal of the basis for the UK's existing record of nonratifications, reservations and derogations, with particular regard to its blanket reservation to the ICCPR.[71]

Particular issues may still require special measures e.g. if exclusion orders under Prevention of Terrorism legislation are to be preserved, or further provisions made dealing with the future of Hong Kong residents. But they will require specific justifications, based on carefully analysed data and by reference to reasoned criteria. The burden of proving their ongoing necessity must be imposed squarely upon the UK.

Will such an approach impose undue constraints on the UK Government? Here it is important to recall my earlier point about the manageability of existing international obligations. Being drawn up and freely entered into by governments themselves, it is not surprising that most of the main international instruments recognise the need for a balancing of individual rights and the interests of the state. The 1977 European Convention on the Legal Status of Migrant Workers, for example, contains a clause allowing for temporary derogation in certain situations where a contracting state may face problems in complying with Article 12 dealing with family reunion.[72]

Article 15 of the ECHR, similarly, includes a set of established rules designed to prevent unnecessary or arbitrary derogations. These rules have proved manageable standards for democratic states. Some would argue that they are too manageable and that international standards need raising.

Save in relation to nonderogable and absolute human rights such as the prohibition on torture most of the rights protected under instruments relevant to us allow for permissible restrictions, albeit in prescribed form. The main discipline imposed by human rights law on states is thus, in essence, a holding fast to the fundamental thesis of human rights law in respect of limitations on rights. The latter are always to be restrictively interpreted; otherwise they erode the very nature of these rights as rights.[73]

Viewed in this light, much of the discipline imposed by human rights law is better seen as prudent and positive guidance on how to ensure a fairer and more just immigration policy. Thus, when it comes to the task of reconciling human rights guarantees with more planning of immigration policies as argued elsewhere in this volume it is necessary to ensure that any resultant framework of law *avoids applying a quota system to 'humanitarian' categories* such as displaced persons and refugees. Any such step could create undue obstacles to meeting human rights obligations.[74]

Thus, if certain rules or policies are made to limit numbers in a particular immigration category, e.g., those coming for marriage or family settlement, it will be important to ensure that the aim behind such measures is legitimate (e.g., because it genuinely does preserve 'economic well-being') and also that they are proportionate to the aim (e.g., because they truly do serve a 'pressing social need'). That will and should require sound empirical data in justification.[75] This approach has proved workable in other countries.[76]

The second task will be the need to formulate clear criteria for selection of the international rules to be incorporated into UK law. If the present basis of the UK Government's ratification of treaty provisions relating to immigration seems *ad hoc*,[77] can a programme of incorporation be essayed on a better footing?

In an ideal world a developed democracy might simply treat all international human rights rules as automatic parts of domestic law. But even systems that subscribe to this approach find its practical realisation a hard objective. UK policy makers must be able to consider the practical implications of various international instruments. They must act in the national interest, as perceived at any given time. Whilst it may be true that almost all, if not all, of the human rights provisions relating to immigration could be 'implemented' within UK law without necessarily entailing a rise in overall numbers accepted for immigration, they would certainly entail adjusting categories. Some selection among international instruments would thus seem almost unavoidable. If our reform avoids too many international commitments, however, and is simply confined to economic, social, housing and environmental planning conceived of in purely utilitarian terms, there would be no guarantee that the outcome would uphold justice, the rule of law or other basic democratic values.[78]

For this purpose we first of all need a full *inventory* of existing and international law and human rights treaties and other international and European instruments relevant to immigration which must be kept up to date. It should also be published and disseminated to all interested parties. Only then will there exist any proper framework within which to make a selection.

Selection of relevant international rules

Selection criteria must not be too rigid. They should allow for prompt response to new developments where conditions are favourable, on the basis that every provision brought in is a gain. Thus, for example, it might currently be thought wise to encode in our law the UN Convention on the Rights of the Child (which the UK has just ratified with a reservation concerning immigration) on the basis that this could remedy present immigration rules which contain no provision for bringing a child to the UK for the purposes of adoption. Arguably, a small number of children might thereby be spared distress. The current immigration rules dealing with adoption are increasingly out-of-step with recent legislation on children which gives first consideration to the welfare of the child.[79]

The following criteria for selecting international rules to incorporate particularly suggest themselves:

Fundamental character

Chief amongst existing global instruments should be the ICCPR along with its Protocol granting individual right of complaint. So long as our European equivalent—the ECHR—fails to match all its guarantees (e.g., concerning discrimination; right to a passport (the latter through HRC case law)[80] it should be a priority to give this Covenant more direct effect.

Chief among European instruments should be the ECHR, including the Fourth Protocol and Protocol No.7, the two Protocols which deal expressly with immigration subject matter.

Supervisory character

It is essential to accord full weight to treaties having implementation machineries which have supervisory powers whose legal effects the UK Government recognises. This criterion would also cover the ICCPR, whose Article 40 report machinery has periodically identified actual or possible UK breaches of the Covenant in respect of immigration matters. In the regional sphere it would also cover Articles 18 and 19 of the 1961 European Social Charter, two articles under which (as already noted) our immigration law has regularly been found to lack compliance.

Long-standing usage

This type of criterion was doubtless one of the factors behind the decision to incorporate the 1951 Refugee Convention into our earliest set of immigration rules.[81] It argues strongly for more attention to ILO instruments affording basic protections to migrants and other special categories of transnational workers.[82] On the regional plane it would also pick out such vintage instruments as the European Convention on Establishment.[83]

EC nexus

More controversial but cogent nevertheless would be a criterion aimed at ensuring that our national reforms were in harmony with Community law. Arguably, the existing Community legal regime places a duty of convergence upon us already. The recent judgment of the European Court of Justice in the *Surinder Singh* case[84] has confirmed a trend towards harmonisation of this kind. Without firmer efforts to marry Community and UK norms, we shall continue to see the development of Community law create only a deeper divide between the (privileged) Community citizen and the permanent resident, and to tolerate anomalies which allow for example, a Greek woman but not a British citizen woman to live here with a 'third-country' husband without facing the 'hoop' of our 'primary purpose' or self-sufficiency rules. Even if any full UK Government's response to *Surinder Singh* were to end this anomaly, many others are likely to continue, even when they are seen to lack real justification. The extension of free movement of workers and/or other rights to EFTA states[85] and in new association and co-operation agreements[86] can only deepen this anomaly.

It must not be forgotten that international obligations unlikely to be selected may still have a useful role to play. The mother of all post-war human rights treaties—the 1948 *Universal Declaration of Human Rights*—continues world-wide to inspire and guide nations. It covers some immigration subject-matter.[87] Currently the human rights dimension of the *CSCE process* is emerging as a major part of the new arrangements for democratisation of the old and new states of Central and Eastern Europe. Significantly, the major agreements reached within this process include a diverse range of guarantees relevant to immigration.[88] As one of over 50 participating states the UK has committed itself *inter alia* to provisions dealing with: freedom of movement,[89] family reunification and family visits,[90] refugees and displaced persons[91] and nationality rights.[92]

Even if international standards relating to immigration form no part of our law, they should be treated as valuable reference points, by officials, appeals authorities and judges. They should be kept in view when discretion is exercised or where extra-statutory rules are at issue. It would seem perverse for a Home Office official not to review refusal to extend leave to remain on grounds of a technicality (e.g., a young student from an Eastern European country) when the UK Government has promised under CSCE provisions to facilitate greater 'human contacts' by way of cultural and educational exchanges.

The precise mechanics for ensuring selection of the international rules to be given direct force in our law is largely a matter for the drafters. But they in turn must be given more concrete guidelines for instance on the extent to which greater codification of immigration rights should be in statute, in delegated legislation or in rules and policy; and the extent to which exercise of discretion, including that of a Minister, should be made subject to limits imposed by human rights criteria.[93]

A programmatic approach

There is no reason why a human rights broom cannot work swiftly to rid our immigration law of cobwebs. But some issues are inherently complex and technical and any coherent linking of international standards with other parts of our reform programme will take time (e.g., better planning of economic and social impact on the UK). Certain things could be done immediately, such as providing internal effect within immigration law for the ECHR. Others will require medium and longer-term consideration.

Internal monitoring

The process of reform will require reorganisation of the various government departments. Such reorganisation must entail far greater co-operation between the Home Office and the Foreign and Commonwealth Office which despite overlapping responsibilities[94] regularly speak in different tongues.[95] Any new governmental arrangements might do well to consider adopting the model of an advisory 'Bureau of Immigration Research' along the lines of the Australian body of that name set up in May 1989.[96]

Reforms in this sphere could be stillborn unless there were, placed over the administration, an independent monitoring body charged with the task of ongoing review. This is not to belittle the valuable service performed over the years by some of the parliamentary committees. The defunct Standing Committee on Race Relations and Immigration and the present Home Affairs Select Committee have done much to improve scrutiny.[97] Only meagre awareness of these international standards was shown by the Home Affairs Committee, however, in its recent examination of the issue of Migration Control at External Borders of the European Community.

An immigration watchdog

A new immigration watchdog body should be established, perhaps modelled on US and Australian monitoring bodies. Recent immigration legislative reforms in these countries have created statutory bodies with responsibility for ongoing monitoring (a nine person Immigration Committee under the US Immigration Act 1990,[98] the Australian Joint Select Committee on Migration Regulations respectively).[99] There are also analogues within our existing law, e.g., the Social Security Advisory Committee[100] that might offer some lessons on choice of an appropriate structure.

In terms of resources, this proposal is unlikely in functional terms to add significantly to overall costing of our national immigration system since such a Committee will perform various tasks which would otherwise fall to civil servants—except that in this model, the machinery ensures a measure of independent review.

If international standards are to be a cornerstone of reform it is imperative that any such body be placed under a duty to ensure full effect is given to international rules chosen according to our earlier proposals. That would end the sorry phenomenon of Parliamentary Committees paying little attention to UK responsibilities in this respect. The international dimension would reinforce the need for such machinery to possess full independence from executive interference or pressures, otherwise such machinery could itself fall foul of international standards of fairness. This watchdog would best ensure proper scrutiny in the light of such standards by including among its members one of more independent experts in the field of international law and human rights.

Human Rights Commission

Proposals for immigration reform cannot be sensibly considered in isolation from reform of our legal system, in particular the growing pressures for the establishment of a national Human Rights Commission.

The existence of a separate international law and human rights watchdog body would do much to enhance the carrying through of effective reforms in the immigration sphere. Leading studies of UK immigration law bear strong witness to the need for such a complementary system, identifying a great proneness within the UK at administrative, appellate and judicial levels for both judicial review and human rights principles to be applied less robustly in the field of immigration than they are in other areas of administration and social policy.[101] The broader perspective which would be brought by this type of watchdog could help end such disparities. It could be argued that the role just outlined could best be made part of existing or revamped 'equal treatment' bodies (CRE, EOC). That would carry the advantage of avoiding unreal divorce of immigration and equal treatment subject-matters. But past experience suggests that such bodies find it difficult to focus sufficiently on the complexities of a subject-matter not predominantly confined to domestic issues of discrimination.

Public participation

With regard to the immigration watchdog, there seems one very important lesson to be drawn from Canadian and Australian experiences. In Australia, the bodies set up to investigate and monitor reform of immigration policies have sought with some success to ensure a significant level of public consultation, from interested persons and organisations across the political spectrum.[102]

The scope for ensuring not only public participation in, but membership places for various bodies representing interested groups should be considered. That depends on the importance that is attached to linkage of immigration reform with a plan to make our ethnic minorities fuller actors in our democratic destiny. Public participation exercises should extend to cover the views not only of the ethnic minorities but also the voice of people who view foreigners and ethnic minorities in negative terms.

Conclusions and recommendations

Prime focus in this chapter has been upon the rationale for making international law obligations a cornerstone of immigration reform. The crux of this idea is that UK immigration controls would thereby secure for the first time at least a minimum floor of basic rights and thus put an end to decades of policies marred by fitful failures to secure fundamental protections for those who are affected by such controls.

To anchor this idea, it will be necessary to enact new legislation that sets out in statutory form observance of international law safeguards as a primary objective. For such an objective to be given concrete shape it is essential to gain a clearer understanding of the current state of international rules on immigration and how it is both desirable and feasible to expect a country like the UK to take on international obligations that do place certain limits on its freedom of action to impose whatever type of controls suit the political order of the day.

Similarly, it is crucial to review the UK's record of performance in relation to international rules on immigration, both as regards obligations that have been taken on and those that have been avoided. UK immigration policy has conspicuously failed to measure up to international law and human rights standards.

The second part of the chapter suggests how UK law and policy could be brought up to standard, bearing in mind that *Realpolitik* might push governments of the day in different directions at different times. It is recommended that priority be given to remedying the shortcomings already identified by international bodies whose legal jurisdiction we have accepted, in particular the Human Rights Committee (established as part of the ICCPR machinery); the Committee of Independent Experts (established under the 1961 European Social Charter) and the supervisory organs forming the Strasbourg machinery (established under the ECHR), the European Commission of Human Rights and the European Court of Human Rights.

It is further recommended that all levels of authority involved in the administration of our immigration controls should make fuller use of all relevant international legal materials in the course of their decision-making. They must strive to see in such materials not so much obstacles to be surmounted as valuable yardsticks that help ensure proper standards.

Nevertheless, this chapter warns heavily against imagining that any full remedying of UK human rights shortcomings can be achieved simply by complying with international rulings made against the UK and making more regular recourse in decision-making to relevant international standards and case law. Further action is needed to give greater internal legal effect to such international rules.

One of the central recommendations flowing from this analysis is incorporation into our law of the major European treaty supervising human rights performances of the UK and other member states of the Council of Europe: the ECHR (and its protocols in full). Bearing in mind the broad spectrum of debate on this topic, this chapter confines itself to the particular advantages such a step would yield for immigration reform. At the same time, it recommends that incorporative action in relation to the ECHR (or indeed any other human rights treaty covering a very wide range of subject-matters) must be complemented by more particularised measures of immigration reform. This is seen to entail ongoing review of the UK's record of treaty ratifications and specific steps taken to exclude or reduce the level of obligations undertaken. It is recognised that the UK Government will always want to be sure that its immigration control system serves the national interest but it is proposed that any attempts by the UK to restrict relevant international obligations must be done according to the strict criteria imposed by international law as interpreted by the European Court of Human Rights in particular.

Another key recommendation centres on the concept of an inventory of relevant international law and human rights on immigration rules. To ensure systematic and inclusive awareness of applicable rules it is vital that the keeping up to date of such an inventory and the UK's position in relation to it be a clear duty, along with a duty to publish it and disseminate it to all interested bodies. An outline model for such an inventory is provided in the appendix to this chapter.

In the UK, the prevailing approach to adoption of international rules within domestic law generally appears to be cautious selection based on *ad hoc* policy considerations. Whilst it is wholly valid for a democratic state to take care that its treaty obligations serve the public and national interest, it is recommended that any selection should be carried out within a proper framework that treats human rights obligations as an aid to its own policy-making and practices. Selection should be made on the basis of clear and coherent principles. Those highlighted in this chapter seek to ensure that the UK reliably meets fundamental human rights standards that can achieve practical and effective realisation of essential protection for individuals. To emphasise the need to be aware of emerging standards, some attention is also paid to the CSCE process and its human rights mechanism.

Broad guidelines are proposed for imbuing our immigration reforms with a firm human rights underpinning. It is recommended that there be a carefully phased programme to enable 'humanitarian'[103] aspects of policy to be properly integrated into overall economic and social planning.

A brief outline is attempted of key institutional components of such a programme, starting from the premise that mechanisms for monitoring and scrutiny must be given a high premium. It is recommended that two watchdog bodies be established or that existing bodies carry out their watchdog functions including public consultation and use of human rights experts to ensure that human rights obligations are taken into full account at all stages of immigration policy and its enforcement.

5 OBJECTIVES FOR FUTURE EUROPEAN COMMUNITY POLICY

Ann Dummett

At present, each Member State of the European Community retains control over its own immigration policy towards third countries (i.e., non-EC countries) but has accepted that Community law and policy govern the movement between Member States of EC nationals.

Each state has also accepted, as an exception to its own control over third-country nationals, the provisions in EC law which give a right of entry and residence, and certain other benefits, to close relatives of EC nationals who have moved to work in EC states other than their own. Britain has abided by these rules.

EC law now provides, however, for a greater role than this in control over immigration into each Member State by third-country nationals, and at this point British Government policy appears confused and contradictory. Roughly speaking, the British line is, 'All right, we have accepted the movement of EC nationals and their families, but the Community has no business to ask more than this and we shall not accept any further encroachments on our sovereign right to control immigration.'

And yet the British Government *has* accepted further encroachment, first by signing the Single European Act[1] and getting Parliament to ratify it in 1986, and second, by ratifying the Maastricht Treaty on European Union. Journalists have reported of Mrs Thatcher's role here, as Alan Watkins put it in the *Observer* on 24 May 1992, 'she pushed the Single European Act through Parliament... but she complained afterwards that she was not told what it all meant.' Personal experience suggests that Mrs Thatcher was not alone here: many British politicians and officials seem not to understand either that Act or the Maastricht Treaty. It is not easy to say how much government statements reflect genuine lack of understanding and how much they express a Machiavellian strategy of resistance to a legal obligation, but in either case they resemble the attempts of a man who has signed a binding contract with an

137

insurance company only to object to the terms after signature.

British policy-makers appear to be pretending not only to the British public but to themselves that they can formulate immigration policy as though the 1986 and 1991 agreements had never been made. The first objective for UK policy in the EC for the future should be to study, and come to terms with, the agreements the Government has already endorsed, and think through their implications. This in turn requires developing a new style of thinking about the Community. It is not necessary to assume everything the Community thinks is good and that all independent British judgements are bad, but it *is* necessary to understand what the Community is supposed to be and to recognise that it is concerned with forward planning in the long term for twelve or more countries and not just with short-term considerations on the economic and political fronts.

The single market

In signing the Single European Act, Britain accepted that EC territory was to form an area without internal frontiers. Movement within it is to be like movement within a single state. The European Commission in 1992 reiterated in strong terms what Article 8A of the Treaty means: there are to be no controls over anyone, either an EC national or a third-country national, at internal frontiers. Controls will be maintained at external frontiers only.

This is intended to work as follows. If, for example, a plane lands at Heathrow after a nonstop flight from New York or Dacca, every passenger, whether an EC national or not, will be checked because the plane has arrived at an external frontier. If a plane arrives at Heathrow from Paris or Berlin, however, nobody, whether an EC national or not, should be checked because it has crossed an internal frontier. The assumption is that all passengers who are not EC nationals will already have arrived at some EC destination across an external frontier and will have been checked there. Within a single airport, if it deals with both domestic and international flights, there should be two channels for passengers: one for those who have come from an EC starting point and one for everyone else. The former group should walk through as easily as they would leave a train that had travelled from Birmingham to London.

Some countries are already allowing people on 'internal' journeys to pass unchecked. As Sir Edward Heath pointed out during the

Parliamentary debates on the Maastricht Bill, Britain has always had a similarly open border with one other EC country, Ireland. But Douglas Hurd has complained that other EC countries are much laxer than Britain in applying controls, and people admitted to other states will be able to enter Britain freely, even if they are terrorists, drug dealers or illegal immigrants, if our border controls are not maintained in full force. The Home Office has always been strongly opposed to any dismantling of British frontier controls for anyone.

As part of a general British strategy of blaming anything unpopular on 'Europe' wherever the opportunity arises, the Home Office has repeatedly threatened that lifting internal controls would require extra police checks in Britain on suspicious characters and, probably, the introduction of identity cards. It is vitally important that everyone should understand that these internal surveillance policies are *not* required by the EC. Internal law and order matters remain within the jurisdiction of each state. The Community requires abandonment of internal frontier controls, but has nothing to say one way or the other about how countries deal *within* their frontiers with the detection of unauthorised immigrants. The Home Office may wish for its own purposes to have greater police surveillance and/or identity cards, but there is no need for such policies to be introduced as a result of altering the frontier controls. Most Continental countries have some identity papers yet, on Mr Hurd's own admission, they have more illegal immigrants than we do; clearly, identity cards will not prevent illegal immigration. The same argument applies to police checks, which are frequent in France for example. The best answer seems to be to adopt a less hysterical attitude to illegal entry in general and to co-operate with other EC countries on a suitable policy to be applied at EC external borders.

Such a policy could be directed against terrorists and criminals on the basis of the EC's existing principles of defending public security, public health and public policy: even EC nationals can be denied the right to remain in any EC state other than their own on this basis. It is worth remembering that a country has to put up with its own terrorists and criminals and cannot send its own undesirable citizens elsewhere: there are already laws to deal with their activities within the country of citizenship, and such laws apply to non-citizens in the jurisdiction as well. If, however, it is considered a proper end for immigration policy to exclude dangerous characters who are not citizens, it should not be too difficult for countries which already operate such policies individually to agree on an EC policy here towards the outer world.

More difficult is the question of dealing with illegal immigrants moving between EC states. An illegal immigrant is a concept created by a particular country's law, and one country's desirable entrant may be another's undesirable, and vice versa. Hence a policy at the EC's external border may become the most restrictive possible, in order to meet objections from the most restrictive state on each category of person. On the other hand, some borders on the EC's outside edges are in practice more easily crossed than others—Italy's enormously long sea coast, for example—and too rigid a policy on exclusion risks actually creating more illegal immigrants because people prevented from entering legally will, under pressure, do so illegally. This argues not so much for fiercer restrictions as for aid to sending countries and tough action against employers who exploit illegal residents. One wants to see some solution which will neither increase police powers at the expense of human rights within the EC nor attempt an unworkably harsh policy towards new entrants, and admittedly this is a very hard problem to solve.

So far as racial minorities are concerned, it should be pointed out that there are enormous advantages in lifting controls at internal frontiers. A school trip of black and white children from England to France, for instance, would no longer be haunted by worries about harassment at the point of entry into France or by immigration officers on returning to Britain. Adult tourists, of course, would get similar advantages.

The objective of UK policy here should be to accept Community policy on internal frontiers because, legally and morally, we must: we have already bound ourselves to agree to it. A corollary of this acceptance will be a reasonable policy on checks within the country, which neither infringes human rights in general nor bears unequally on racial minorities. Attitudes, as much as policies, have to change here; illegal immigrants are not a separate, sinister type of human being and should not be classed with criminals.

At the Edinburgh meeting of the European Council in December 1992, heads of government reaffirmed their commitment to the full and rapid implementation of Article 8A, but said that they had to take note of the fact that free movement could not be completely assured by 1 January 1993. Britain, Ireland and Denmark were not ready to lift their controls, and the nine other EC states (the Schengen Group) were not ready to implement their own, separate agreements on free movement, chiefly because the Schengen Information System was not yet operating. In practice, little has changed so far as internal frontiers are concerned.

Future policy on immigration from third countries

The British Government agreed at Maastricht that a common policy on immigration and asylum should be worked out between the twelve Member States by the end of 1993. Although it is unlikely that this deadline can be met, negotiations have begun. We cannot tell what is being discussed because the inter-governmental meetings involved work in secret session. However, we have some documents prepared in recent years by the Group of Co-ordinators and by the European Commission on immigration, which together with statements by spokesmen for different governments give some idea of where policy may be tending or at least what the main concerns of politicians and officials are.

The formal agreement contained in Title VI, Article K, of the Treaty on European Union provides for *co-operation* in the fields of justice and home affairs. The objectives of co-operation are set out in the Treaty, which also sets certain rules for the inter-governmental meetings. Their decisions must be unanimous.

Article K(9) provides that immigration (inter alia) may be brought within the competence of the Community institutions in future by extension of Article 100c: the decision to do this will have to be made by unanimous decision of the Council of Ministers on the initiative of either a Member State or the European Commission. This means that we are in the first of two stages. For now, a common immigration policy is being worked out by inter-governmental co-operation, outside the EC framework proper but aiming to meet goals set by the EC. Later, at some unknown date, the Community may take over the policy-making process, using the Community institutional framework instead of inter-governmental meetings. In either process, British Ministers and officials are making British policy and urging their views on Ministers and officials from other States. Leaving aside the mechanics for the moment, one must enquire what British policy is and what it ought to be.

Britain clearly wishes to maintain all its existing controls over people from non-EC countries and is likely to pursue a negative policy of resisting any attempts to change the existing British line, without having any positive, alternative policies to propose to our EC partners.

There is an important difference in approach between Britain and the other countries concerned in the way they view immigration policy. First of all, British policy-makers cannot accept the notion of policy-making for any entity except Britain itself. A Community policy is for them something which affects Britain and must be considered exclusively with British aims and interests in mind. Of course, other countries too regard their own interests first, but countries accustomed to frequent changes in land borders and to the comparative ease with which land borders can be crossed have a less entrenched and literally insular outlook than the British: they can understand that they are making a policy for a number of countries including their own. Second, Britain in the twentieth century has never formulated a clear policy on immigration as part of its forward planning. In the Home Office's own words to the Select Committee on Race Relations and Immigration in February 1971:

> Immigration law in this country has developed mainly as a series of responses to, and attempts to regulate, particular pressures rather than as a positive means of achieving preconceived social or economic aims.

In other words, when a particular group has begun to enter the UK which the Government wants to stop, it has acted to exclude that group. With minor exceptions the Government has not encouraged any form of immigration for economic reasons; indeed economic self-interest was sacrificed to racial exclusiveness in the 1960s, when despite a severe labour shortage, neither continental foreigners nor Commonwealth citizens were welcomed to fill vacancies. This attitude to immigration is quite different from the various attitudes found in other West European countries.

Germany has always regarded immigration policy as an integral part of economic policy. Her economic growth could not have been so spectacular without continual entry from outside, and there was nothing haphazard in this process: immigration for work was actively sought. Germany's difficulty has been to recognise that immigrants were not merely units on the labour market to be added or subtracted but people with families who might want to settle permanently and become part of society. France has long regarded immigration from the point of view of central planning. Immigration was encouraged in the nineteenth century to increase manpower for the armed forces. It was encouraged between the wars to meet the needs of industry, and until the late 1970s it was still regarded as essential to the economy.

Bilateral agreements were concluded with sending countries: the migration did not take the same individualistic form as migration to Britain but was part of an organised process of recruitment. Spain and Italy until very recently took a much more casual attitude to immigration, and were more concerned about emigration of their own nationals. Now, with their membership of the Schengen Group, both countries are seeking to tighten some of their controls but both have large numbers of illegal immigrants working for low pay and in bad conditions. Their situations are unplanned. If there is a common factor among many continental countries that is absent in Britain, it is that they are less paranoid than ours about entry from outside. They may have controls, they may at times impose them brutally, but they regard *some* immigration as inevitable and do not regard it as absolutely undesirable.

However, bureaucratic supervision and interference in daily life are even more pronounced in many continental countries than they are here. In Germany one must notify the police if one moves house; in Belgium the unemployed must report every day on their position. Such rules apply to whole populations, within which immigrants have to get accustomed to a degree of surveillance that many people here would find objectionable.

Unless differences like this are appreciated, negotiations on common policies will be difficult. During a general recession, Britain's restrictive attitude to all entry may be unremarkable. But Britain's lack of concern with any policy but restriction for the long-termfuture is a bad basis for negotiating with people who assume that long-term planning, taking into account likely economic and demographic changes, is essential.

The objectives set at Maastricht are of a very general kind. Member States are required to regard as matters of common interest: immigration policy, asylum policy, rules governing the crossing of Member States' external borders, conditions of entry and movement by third-country nationals, conditions of residence including family reunion and access to employment for third-country nationals, and the combatting of unauthorised immigration, residence and work by third-country nationals. A common policy is clearly intended to be not merely a matter of trade-offs between interests but a policy which takes account of the situation in all Member States and their common good. After all, it is to be a policy for a single, frontier-free area and a single market: there is a sense in which it must be considered in the same way that a national government would consider a policy suited to its varying regions. As already indicated above, the British Government starts on the wrong foot here.

Whether the common interest will be better served by liberalisation or restrictiveness the Treaty does not say: this is left to the negotiating and decision-taking machinery. However, it must be assumed that negotiators were expected to have in mind the Community's style of thinking, its acquired knowledge contained in numerous reports, its legal basis not only in the Treaty but in existing Community legislation and judgments of the European Court of Justice, and here too British Government negotiators are likely to do rather badly. Their style is not exactly *communautaire*; their knowledge is sometimes deficient and their legal habits are not geared to the legal system of the Continent: rather, they rely upon a crudely Austinian view of the sovereignty of the Westminster Parliament and a confidence in practical, ad hoc solutions for each problem as it comes up rather than a belief in basic principles and entrenched law whose precepts must be applied when new laws are made.

The other national governments have their own priorities, of course. Each is concerned with a particular group of countries of emigration, with which it has connections. Spain is unhappy about any limitations on entry from the Spanish American countries (or indeed entry by Spanish Americans from the United States); Germany's concerns arise from being in the front line for access from eastern Europe, particularly as political turmoil and economic difficulties are both impelling large numbers of people to move westwards. The western part of Germany has taken in so many people over the last three years (a million in 1990–1 alone), including ethnic Germans from East Germany and from other countries as well as foreign nationals, but still a vast number of mouths to be fed, bodies to be housed and hands to be found work, that Germany is eager for a Community policy which will work equitably around EC territory a little more than at present. Greece, on the other hand, has been pursuing a ruthless policy towards asylum-seekers, including some of Greek ethnic origin, sending them back summarily to Albania and elsewhere.

On behalf of the Community as such, the European Commission has stated a general policy of wanting future entry to be regulated but not entirely stopped, of clamping down on employers of illegally admitted workers, and of establishing an immigration observatory to study trends and anticipate likely large-scale movements into the EC. It advocates using aid and negotiation with third-country governments to persuade those governments to discourage their nationals from emigrating, and to promote social peace within the Community by rapid improvement to the rights of legally admitted third-country nationals already settled. The Commission would like to see resident third-country nationals have freedom of movement within the EC not only for visits but for work, to give them rights of family reunion and in general to bring them as closely as possible to the status of EC nationals so as to avoid a two-tier society on EC territory.[2] The Commission has moved ahead here (as it usually does) of what the EC's Council of Ministers is likely to accept. At Maastricht, the Ministers responsible for immigration in all the Member States submitted a report[3] which the Heads of Government accepted, based on work by the Ad Hoc Group on Immigration. This is the basis from which current negotiations on future policy have begun.

The Ministers' report points first to co-operation already achieved in the Dublin Convention determining the state responsible for examining requests for asylum and in the draft Convention on the crossing of External Borders. Since neither is yet in force and the latter is not yet even signed, this progress is not very striking. The Ministers next stress 'the massive increase in the number of unjustified applications for asylum' and the 'intensification of migratory pressure.' They see harmonisation of policies as a means to efficiency and speed of intervention, although they reaffirm the need to protect victims of persecution and apply the UN Convention. They intend to perform 'a sort of management and monitoring function' in implementing a harmonised programme on admissions and expulsions generally.

'It is neither judicious nor politically desirable,' say the Ministers, 'to shift migratory movements [in this case of third-country nationals] from one Member State to another; the aim is to make the problem manageable for the entire Community.' In the area of family reunion and formation, Member States' policies can and will have to be harmonised within a relatively short period and there will have to be a common approach to illegal immigration. On policy as a whole, it will be essential to define basic principles if restrictive opinions on immigration are not to dominate.

It is clearly true that a European immigration policy is of necessity restrictive, with the exception of refugee policy and family reunion and formation policies, as well as policies providing for admission on humanitarian grounds. It must however be borne in mind that the European tradition is based

on principles of social justice and respect for human rights, as
defined in the European Convention on Human Rights....For a
proper approach...it is very important to consider the various
aspects in relation to each other. Areas such as labour market
policies, human rights policies, development aid and integration
policies are all of direct importance for supporting a European
migration policy.

Since the British Home Office agreed to this report, one might
suppose it was a fair statement of British Government policy in the
EC, or at least was not directly contradictory to British policy. Given
the way British politicians and officials have behaved over earlier EC
agreements, one cannot feel at all sure of this, and indeed the style of
the report is startlingly different in places from the tone of British
immigration policy as we have known it over the last thirty years or
so.

Presumably it was as a result of British opinion, however, that the
report includes the notion that integration of immigrants already
settled can be achieved only if there is effective control over new entry.
Yet the report puts as its first point on integration policy the
importance of family reunion and formation, which is more a
Continental than a British Home Office view. It deals moreover with
rights of third-country nationals, and not just their welfare, in
discussing integration. At this point, the inter-governmental discussions and the Community's general aims are including what we in
Britain would call race relations policies under the heading of
immigration policy.

It is not surprising that they do this, for unjust discrimination
against foreigners (that is, resident migrants lacking the citizenship of
the host country), is a problem throughout the EC, and the distinction
between citizen and foreigner often has the role that the line between
black and white people has here. But it is important for us to
appreciate that the division we take for granted between immigration
and race relations is not recognised in these discussions, and that
therefore British policy on immigration in the EC will have to contain
elements of policies on equality and the protection of rights after
admission. Our own Immigration Acts are exempt from the provisions of our Race Relations Act and Equal Opportunities Act, but
this situation does not fit well into the theoretical basis of current
European discussions. There should be British legislation to correct
this blemish on our anti-discrimination law.

The problems of forecasting

The idea of an immigration observatory is an attempt to anticipate likely new sources of immigration and plan accordingly. The Ministers' report includes a section analysing the push factors in sending countries and making suggestions for tackling them: ethnic tensions abroad need tackling by political means; economic problems may be tackled by aid and co-operation programmes; sudden crises in other countries will require emergency aid; demographic explosions are harder to cope with, and so on. Overall, 'relevant human rights policies, substantial development aid, global food and environmental policies, and control of regional conflicts' are needed, but it is recognised that these measures will not affect immigration to the EC in the short term, nor deal adequately with a sudden and unforeseeable influx. An early-warning system is needed so that some measures can be taken quickly if a new, sudden influx is likely.

Considering what has happened in Europe since 1989, and looking in particular at the present situation in former Yugoslavia, these attempts to forecast immigration and plan accordingly look unrealistic. They do, however, demonstrate an approach that Britain has never tried to take in the past. It is here that the use of inter-governmental, rather than the Community machinery, is worrying, for between them the governments of the Twelve could act as a joint executive power with little responsibility to anyone, deciding on measures in any real or supposed crisis for which it would be hard to fix the responsibility, and which it would be very hard to stop. On the other hand, there is obvious merit in the principle of trying to plan for the future instead of producing a scheme which is designed either for the past or, in a hurry, to deal with a present, sudden change. This is particularly true on the (much more realistic) assumption made by Ministers jointly that *some* immigration will continue.

What should British objectives for future community policy be?

The first point is that the British Government must accept existing Community law; the second, that it must learn to develop policy as part of a common Community policy. Any other approach is unrealistic and cannot produce lasting results.

One must therefore consider two questions at the same time: what policy should Britain have for Britain and what policy should Britain have for the Community? Eventually, both policy lines will merge unless disaster overtakes the Community's progress, but for some years yet the British Government will retain responsibility for its policy towards third-country nationals from outside EC territory entering the UK. Moreover, it retains its responsibility towards the United Kingdom as a whole for the effects of its immigration policy and this needs careful consideration. There is a difference between working for the good of British society on the one hand and using national interest as an excuse for ignoring obligations in the EC on the other. The third need, therefore, is to reform British policy in a matter which simultaneously promotes British interests and the interests of those who apply for entry here. It should have an eye to convergence with other EC States' policies, recognising their justifiable demands but standing out against illiberal or unworkable ones.

In fact, British experience and style have much that is good to offer. The absence of identity cards is one example. The fact that nationals of a significant number of other countries can vote and stand for office in Britain is another. The grant of permanent residence to some immigrants after what is, in Continental terms, a comparatively short period, is now a less striking feature than it was before 1981 but is still a useful precedent. Anti-discrimination law plays some positive role, within the jurisdiction, for immigrants after admission.

The faults of British immigration law and policy are, however, much more obvious to those who work in the field. The main points to be learned from Community thinking (if not always from Community countries' practice) are respect for human rights as an element in policy and particularly respect for family reunion and formation; understanding of immigration as an element in the labour market and as a factor to be taken into account in a range of other policies, leading to forward planning and awareness of the need to co-operate with other countries.

For Britain's immigration policy, an obvious need is to reform British nationality law. This is a clear example of a measure which would simultaneously be good domestically and improve co-operation in the Community. Immigration officials on the Continent have genuine difficulty in knowing what British passports signify. Britain should establish a single form of British nationality with right of abode in the UK; its holders would then be unambiguously EC nationals and passports would be instantly comprehensible.

Such a measure would increase the numbers of people with right of free movement in the EC and the question arises whether the measure would be acceptable to our EC partners. This question has a new dimension now that the Maastricht Treaty has provided for the establishment of a citizenship of the European Union, which every person holding the nationality of a Member State will hold. Certain rights and duties will belong to European citizenship, including eventually the right to vote and stand for office in municipal and European elections (Article 8 of the revised EC Treaty). In a Declaration on Nationality of a Member State accompanying the Treaty, the Maastricht Conference declared that:

> wherever in the Treaty establishing the European Community
> reference is made to nationals of Member States, the question
> whether an individual possesses the nationality of a Member
> State shall be settled solely by reference to the national law of
> the Member State concerned.

Member States may amend their declarations saying who are their nationals, 'when necessary'. Thus, there need be no obstacle in EC law to Britain making this reform.

The second need is to reform British law on family reunion. The Joint Council for the Welfare of Immigrants and other groups have long urged that all immigrants to Britain should have the same rights to family unity as EC nationals here and this policy is now being urged by the European Commission. It would make an enormous positive difference to the British situation, and if pressed on EC partners would at the same time be in line with Community thinking and the wishes of politicians in several other Member States (notably Portugal; in Germany there would be more opposition). It is noteworthy that the immigration Ministers' report referred to above took for granted that family life enjoyed a special priority.[4] However, Community law itself, though far in advance of Britain's, does not adequately protect the rights of persons admitted as relatives of EC nationals. For example, in the event of a marital breakdown the spouse of an EC worker loses residence rights.

Third, the protection of human rights requires changes to the discretionary powers of the Home Secretary and reform of the immigration appeals system. Administrative powers could be limited by the introduction of time-limits, Community-style, on some decisions, and the immigration rules should be rewritten to provide objective criteria, rather than the subjective judgment of an immigration officer or entry clearance officer, in as many cases as possible. Powers of removal should be sharply curtailed and powers of detention without a hearing ended. Such reforms would be a basis for arguing within the EC for similar reforms elsewhere.

These three sets of changes would revolutionise British immigration law and policy, but still do not touch upon the question of immigration for work or for forward planning in general: topics which are outside the scope of this paper except in so far as Britain might be urged to adopt a more open and co-operative attitude to other EC countries on these matters.

Such a new attitude would not require the abandonment of British self-interest but a new evaluation of where that interest lies. For too long, British policy has been based on one simple, crude principle: keep outsiders (foreigners, blacks, alien subversives and poor people) out. Let some of them in only when absolutely forced to do so. Ignore the effects on the labour market of both immigration and emigration. (A new, crude principle has been added in recent years: don't attempt forward planning, which is socialistic.) Our country is not well served by this sort of policy, and could learn something from the experiences (both positive and negative) of other European countries. Now, such learning is not only desirable but imperative, because EC discussions on a common immigration policy towards the outside world need a common basis of assumptions if they are to succeed.

Asylum policy is the most urgent concern in the immigration field, and discussing it here after other immigration matters is not meant to imply otherwise. But there are good reasons for treating asylum separately. Here, the British Government is not so far out of line with the other eleven governments, who are all taking the line that many asylum-seekers are economic migrants in disguise and that entry for asylum has somehow to be limited without breaching the obligations countries have undertaken in subscribing to the UN Convention on Refugees. It is important, however, to take into account the different bases from which these countries start in formulating this view. Germany, as is well known, has had special provision in her Basic Law for refugees and admitted vastly more asylum-seekers since the Second World War than Britain. Processing of their applications takes years—sometimes ten years or more. Any call for speeding up processing looks very different, therefore, in Germany and has quite a different significance from a similar call in Britain, where asylum-seekers are often summarily turned round and quickly removed. Britain has very low figures for asylum-seekers compared with several other EC countries.

Proposals for reform of British policy are set out in detail in Chris Randall's chapter. Such reforms should then be urged on other EC States, for operation within the lines laid down in the Dublin Convention to which Britain has already agreed. That Convention determines which EC State shall be responsible for examining a request for asylum, and clearly it will be necessary to ensure that the common practices which are developed should be as decent as possible.

Looking ahead, however, it is clear that the Ministers' hopes of forecasting trends and anticipating crises face their greatest difficulty in matters of asylum. It is simply impossible to forecast with any precision where some new emergency will happen or what volume of asylum-seekers it will create. It is also obvious that the terms of the UN Convention on Refugees are inadequate to deal with all the emergencies that are already impelling mass flight. Perhaps all that Community policy can do (and so all that the British Government should be urging in current discussions) is to assume that large movements of people in desperate need of safety are going to continue for the foreseeable future from one source or another. Some of these will fit the conditions of the UN Convention while others will not but all will be deserving of some protection. Plans for immigration will thus have to allow for a permanent category of asylum-seekers whose place on the labour market and in the provision of housing and services must be taken into account.

A worrying element in the Maastricht agreement is empowerment to impose temporary visa requirements on any country from which there is a sudden influx. This is likely to harm genuine refugees. The policy ought to be to suspend visa requirements for a country where people are in serious danger and forced to flee. In practice, Britain's cynical decision to impose visa requirements on Bosnian asylum-seekers while simultaneously closing down all consular posts capable of issuing visas in Bosnia, shows how the 'common approach' on asylum threatens to develop. The terms of the UN Convention are inadequate to deal with genuine refugee crises today but governments, instead of moving forward to formulate new ways of meeting desperate needs, are pulling back.

A just asylum policy depends heavily on national policy in a much wider sense. The chance of anyone given asylum in Britain today getting permanent accommodation and a job to support life is very poor, just because the chance of the same things is poor among a large section of the indigenous population. Shortages of jobs and homes produce resentment against refugees after admission. Violence against asylum-seekers cannot wholly be explained by such resentment, but it would be foolish to ignore the part that the resentment played in causing onlookers to clap and cheer the attackers in Hoyerswerda and Rostock. The EC Ministers' report recognised that immigration policy interacted with policies for which other Departments than the immigration authorities were responsible. There is a general lesson here for the British Government which tends to conduct national policies like a competitive game between departments much of the time—for example, in the way that transport and housing policies are completely unrelated though they obviously affect each other.

British policy on migration within the EC

There is not much room for manoeuvre for the British Government now on movement within the EC because so much has already been decided at Community level by which the UK is bound. My view is that the British Government should seriously work to implement these obligations and to co-operate with Community institutions and other Member States in doing so. But new initiatives are needed on some matters.

A major British policy change ought to be to press for more competence for the Community rather than less in matters of internal migration and the rights of migrants. This would involve more decision-making by the Community institutions and less inter-governmental decisions, and hence more openness in policy-making.

This conclusion is not at first obvious: the present trend of visa policy, which is in EC competence, is restrictive and will result in greatly increased visa requirements for visitors to the UK at the wish of other countries rather than the wish of Britain. But nothing better would have emerged from inter-governmental agreement alone. For asylum-seekers, Community agreement would have been better than the inter-governmental negotiations which have produced the Schengen Treaty and the Dublin Convention: the Community as such would need to have regard to the European Convention on Human Rights and would surely, in line with the regard its legislation has generally shown for the rights of the individual, provide better safeguards.

On the rights of migrants already settled in EC territory, the European Commission has called in the strongest terms for improvement. Its aim is to assure to these third-country nationals parity or near-parity with EC nationals in access to the labour market, rights to family reunification, freedom of movement throughout the EC and, eventually, voting rights. Such proposals are most unlikely to get very far if left to national governments.

On new immigration into EC territory, it is obvious that in a single market without internal borders some single authority will need to operate quite soon: the authority of the Community institutions is the obvious repository. Attempts to harmonise national rules will prove awkward and almost certainly produce inconsistencies and anomalies. Furthermore, the various inter-governmental groups are duplicating each other's work, and it would be more efficient and less expensive, as well as better for human rights, for the Community institutions to take over.

The rights of EC nationals who migrate between states are already protected by Community law in many ways. Britain provides an additional protection under her domestic law by means of the Race Relations Act 1976. Britain should press the Community to introduce a Directive binding on all Member States outlawing unjust discrimination on grounds of race, colour, nationality (including citizenship), national or ethnic origin *and religion* (this last being omitted from our own law at present except in Northern Ireland, where the 'race' provisions of 1976 do not apply). If such a Directive were held to be impossible under the current Treaty, Britain should press for an amendment to the Treaty along the same lines. These proposed measures would be a safeguard for both EC nationals and third-country nationals in Member States. (EC nationals are already protected against discrimination on grounds of nationality in the Treaty, but not clearly or fully protected on the other grounds.)

The EC has an Association Agreement with Turkey and Co-operation Agreements with Morocco, Algeria and Tunisia under which workers who come legally to EC territory enjoy certain rights. Broadly speaking, their status falls between that of EC nationals and that of other third-country nationals. The details vary: indeed once one examines them it is evident that people resident in EC territory fall into at least seven different groups where rights are concerned: EC nationals within their own countries; EC nationals in other EC countries than their own; Turks; Algerians, Moroccans and Tunisians;

other third-country nationals with regard to Community law; other third-country nationals with varying rights under each Member State's law, and illegal immigrants. These differences have important practical applications in such matters as family reunion, access to social welfare benefits, and security of residence. From a human rights point of view, and also from a practical one, these differences should be reduced. Everyone lawfully present in EC territory should have a clear set of rights in such matters as working conditions, remuneration, family reunion, social benefits, etc.

This should, of course, mean a solid basis of rights achieved by levelling up rather than levelling down, and should not preclude new measures of liberalisation aimed at particular groups, which could be used as stepping stones towards further advances in status generally. The Lome IV Agreement, in Article 5, for example, includes a guarantee of non-discrimination for ACP nationals resident in EC territory. This may be, so far, of small practical importance, but it affirms a principle and can be used to obtain practical advances eventually towards equality for all residents.

The right to vote and stand for office is at present held in Britain by all Commonwealth and Irish citizens in local, national and European elections. But resident third-country nationals from outside the Commonwealth have no such right. EC nationals will have the right to vote in local and European elections. The implementation of these rights attached to European citizenship poses problems in several other Member States, particularly France, where the idea of any civic rights for people who are not French citizens rouses the deepest antagonism, and Germany, where a constitutional amendment would be needed. But Britain is in a strong position to point out that there is nothing to fear from granting the vote to non-citizens. The fact that ethnic minorities lacking British citizenship can vote and be elected here has been an important factor in making minority voices heard and in forcing politicians to take some notice of them.

The British Government should take action in three stages. It should accept that EC nationals can also vote and stand for office in general elections. It should extend the vote in British elections to resident third-country nationals other than Commonwealth citizens, so that people settled here from Vietnam, Poland, Colombia, the United States, etc., have civic rights. Then it would be in a strong position to urge on the Community at large a policy of granting civic rights not only to EC nationals butto settled third-country nationals too, in line with the European Commission's policy of integration.

It is for fear of strong objections from Member States rather than from principle that the Community has pressed for voting rights for EC nationals in local and European elections only, and not in national elections. There are particular difficulties in some countries, like Luxembourg, in whose case the total population is very small and the foreign residents make up 25% or more of the labour force. It can reasonably be objected that citizens' rights could be damaged in this situation. On the other hand, there is a strong argument for saying that all residents in a jurisdiction, who pay taxes and are bound by the laws of the country, should have some say in the democratic process.

Looking ahead to the single market with its frontier-free area and increased mobility for workers, it becomes even more important to ensure that people do not become disfranchised as a result of exercising their freedom of movement. Hence the Community's proposal that nationals from any EC country should be able to vote in any other.

W.R. Böhning of the International Labour Office has argued that the single market cannot work unless third-country nationals are given the same rights of movement as EC nationals within EC territory.[5] An employer with a labour force partly of EC nationals and partly of third-country nationals will not enjoy the intended benefits of the single market if mobility across frontiers is not possible for all of these employees, accompanied by right of work, residence and family unity. If this is accepted, the argument for enfranchising settled third-country nationals is strengthened too. The more that one set of rights is improved for third-country nationals, the greater becomes the impetus to bring their rights fully into line with those of EC nationals.

From the British Government's point of view, promotion of civic rights for third-country nationals would have the advantage that Commonwealth citizens' civic rights within Britain would be safeguarded for the future. At the same time, Commonwealth citizens would enjoy opportunities in other EC countries which they do not at present possess.

Concluding note: the *Acquis Communautaire*

The above recommendations urge the opposite course along every path from the one the British Government appears to be taking at present.

This is not the result of mere contrariness on my part but is an attempt to give an honest opinion on what policy ought to be. If the suggestions appear naive or unrealistic, I can only say it is actually more realistic to try to think in Community terms about British policy in the EC than to think and behave as though Britain could ignore the consequences of EC membership.

Member States are expected to observe the principles and guidelines of the *acquis communautaire*. The *acquis communautaire* goes wider than Community law, and includes non-binding rules such as Council and Commission recommendations and opinions. The Maastricht Treaty on European Union, in Title 1, Article B, says the Union shall set itself as an objective 'to maintain in full the *acquis communautaire* and build on it' with a view to revising co-operative processes (such as that dealing now with immigration policy) and 'ensuring the effectiveness of the mechanisms and the institutions of the Community'. This suggests a determination to bring immigration as soon as possible into the scope of the Community's institutions. Britain would do better to try to co-operate with this process than to resist it.

The British Government wants to widen the EC as soon as possible to include new Members, in the hope that this will slow down the growth of EC powers and of centralisation. Rapid widening will almost certainly have the opposite result, since the size of EC institutions will become unwieldy without radical redesigning. Whether enlarged or not, the Community is already steadily acquiring powers at the expense of national governments and from the most cynical point of view a national government should therefore become more closely involved in EC processes in order to press its own policies, rather than stay at arm's length.

Therefore, as a final suggestion, the British Government should study the *acquis communautaire*—and build on it.

Summary of recommendations

1. The British Government should study carefully the full range of obligations it has already agreed to be bound by in the European Community, and should co-operate with the implementation of agreements already reached.

2. The British Government should initiate changes to UK law on immigration from outside EC territory, both for the sake of

domestic policy and as a basis for urging new EC policies. These changes should include:

(a) establishment of a single British nationality with a right of abode in the UK;

(b) the same rights for non-EC migrants settled here as for EC nationals to family unity;

(c) reduction in the Home Secretary's discretionary powers and introduction of objective criteria in the immigration rules;

(d) no removal or detention without a hearing;

(e) reform of the immigration appeal system;

and for asylum seekers:

(f) repeal of the Carriers' Liability Act;

(g) improved investigation procedures and provision for a judicial decision;

(h) legal aid;

(i) waiving visa requirement in certain emergencies.

3. The British Government should *not* introduce any new police surveillance or the use of identity cards as methods of internal control over illegal immigration.

4. On new immigration into EC territory, the Government should support policies on family unity and asylum-seekers as proposed above, support admissions on humanitarian grounds that do not fit the terms of the Geneva Convention but are needed to save lives, and plan for future needs by assuming that reception arrangements will be needed for the foreseeable future for some asylum-seekers.

5. The Government should support the move to transfer the decision-making process on immigration from the inter-governmental to the Community framework.

6. In any discussions on stemming illegal immigration or taking emergency measures to deal with a sudden influx, the Government should have regard to the principles concerning human rights and social justice which are part of the *acquis communautaire*.

7. In planning for future entry into the EC, the Government should bear in mind that it is helping take decisions for the whole Community and look at labour market considerations and other factors from this point of view as well as from its own.

8. On migration within EC territory, the Government should take

steps to lift internal frontier controls, as already agreed, and should press for:

(a) an EC directive outlawing unjust discrimination on grounds of race, colour, nationality (including citizenship), national or ethnic origin, or religion so as to protect resident third-country nationals;

(b) in the future, the right to vote and stand for office at least in local and European elections, for third-country nationals as well as European citizens;

(c) an amendment to the EC Treaty outlawing unjust discrimination as under (a) above;

(d) family unity for third-country nationals on the same terms as EC nationals;

(e) free movement and the right to work for third-country nationals legally settled in any Member State.

9. The Government should introduce legislation amending the Race Relations Act and Equal Opportunities Act so that their provisions apply to British legislation generally and to acts done by or on behalf of Ministers in applying statutes and Orders in Council. There should also be British legislation to outlaw religious discrimination.

6 AN ECONOMIC AUDIT OF CONTEMPORARY IMMIGRATION

Allan Findlay

Is immigration good for the British economy in the 1990s? British immigration policy has become progressively more restrictive since the 1960s. Cultural and political considerations have been strong influences on policy formulation in this area, but the economic basis for the policy trend is less clear. The objective of this paper is to conduct an economic audit of immigration to Britain in order to re-examine the economic implications of allowing, or conversely restricting, further immigration. At a time when government has been eager to advocate policies in other areas of economic activity which favour liberalisation and international competition, it is particularly appropriate to investigate whether an economic basis exists for restricting the operation of international market forces with regard to labour supply.

This chapter commences by considering a range of issues concerned with the definition of labour immigration. It then proceeds to investigate a range of economic arguments which might be made for relaxing immigration controls. Attention then turns to evaluating the economic basis for existing immigration policy and considers the consequences for the British economy of persisting with current policy tools. The paper concludes that current British immigration policy lacks clear economic objectives and suggests that an economic argument exists for a more pro-active stance on immigration.

Numerical arguments

Confusion in economic arguments concerning immigration arises because of differences in the definitions and terms used to describe the phenomenon.

Consider for example Tables 6.1, 6.2 and 6.3 which follow three different conventions in the identification of 'immigrants'. Table 6.1

defines persons entering the UK for more than a year. Table 6.2 defines migrants relative to the concept of nationality, while Table 6.3 is concerned with one aspect of Britains's ethnic minority population, many of whom are second or third generation migrants and would not be included as a result in the statistics collated in Tables 6.1 and 6.2. Issues of statistical definition are discussed further in Appendix 6.1.

Of particular relevance to this paper is the fact that economic problems associated with immigration are nearly always presented relative to data for Britain's ethnic minorities (consider for example the tendency of the Labour Force Survey (LFS) to report annually on unemployment amongst ethnic minorities) rather than tabulations for first generation immigrants. The result has been the re-inforcement of the false image that all immigration has been similar to the economic experience of certain ethnic minorities. It can be argued that unemployment levels (Table 6.3) or wage rates for second or third-generation migrant populations are of little relevance in considering the economic implications of contemporary immigration. Instead such data should be treated as being of significance primarily in reporting the levels of social and economic discrimination which have operated over time against certain minority populations.

Historical patterns of immigration may have led to local impacts which have been to the disadvantage of the non-migrant population. Complaints about immigrant communities occupying scarce housing stock, filling jobs or depressing wages to the detriment of the so-called 'British' population are nearly always based either on experience from the early part of the twentieth century (prior to the introduction of the Aliens Act of 1919) or on circumstances surrounding second or third-generation immigrant groups. In the former case there is evidence of local competition between immigrants and non-migrants for access to limited job opportunities as reported for example in association with the 1919 dockland riots in Glasgow over the use of 'colonial labour'.[1] In the latter case, the spatial concentration of 'visible' ethnic minorities in the central areas of many English cities has undoubtedly contributed to tensions with 'white' unemployed youths who have perceived second and third-generation immigrants as one reason for their own difficulties in finding jobs. Peach[2] has examined the role of ethnicity and unemployment in accounting for the English urban riots of the early 1980s.

In practice, as Table 6.3 shows, it is the 'visible' ethnic minorities which have borne the brunt of unemployment during times of

Table 6.1 International Immigration by Citizenship, UK (1988–90) (numbers in thousands)

	British		Old Commonwealth	New Commonwealth	Foreign
	No.	(%)			
1988	89	41	21	32	74
1989	104	42	24	42	79
1990	106	40	32	38	91

Source: OPCS, International Immigration, 1992.

Table 6.2 Foreign (non-EC) Population (1989)

Country	Number	% Total Population	of which in 1989
Belgium	332,000	3.3	45% North African
Denmark	115,000	2.3	30% Yugoslavs and Turks
France	2,102,000	3.8	65% North African
Germany	3,520,000	5.7	65% Yugoslavs and Turks
Greece	123,000	1.2	
Holland	464,000	3.1	40% Turks, 30% Moroccans
Ireland	17,000	0.5	40% Americans
Italy	236,000	0.4	
Portugal	74,000	0.7	
Spain	165,000	0.4	
Britain	1,025,000	1.8	16% Indians, 13% Americans

Source: Eurostat Demographic Statistics 1992, Luxembourg, EC; Labour Force Survey, 1993.

recession. The fact that certain ethnic minorities are geographically concentrated in certain places in Britain has served to heighten the popular misconception that the descendents of former immigrant groups occupy jobs or housing stock to the disadvantage of the rest of the population. In relation to this view two points must be noted. First, it must be stressed once again that the nature of historical migration patterns associated with Britain's 'visible' ethnic minorities bears only a very limited relation to the pattern and type of immigration permitted under current British immigration policies. Second, most of the jobs occupied by the 'visible' ethnic minorities are ones which are shunned by the rest of the population. Far from there having been resentment against the recruitment of ethnic minorities to these jobs, 'staff-hungry' local authorities were often most appreciative of the services offered by these groups.[3]

A final definitional issue is the distinction between stocks and flows. Table 6.1 presented flow information about immigrant entry to the United Kingdom. It therefore reflects the outcome in migration terms of Britain's position within the contemporary international migration system. Tables 6.2 and 6.4, by contrast, refer to migration stocks. Stocks reflect the cumulative outcome of historical migration processes. It is apparent from comparison of Tables 6.1 and 6.4 that current foreign national immigration is very different from the patterns which operated in the past. Some of the differences may be due to differences in the data sources for the two tables, but there is widespread evidence that the primary reason for such differences is the fundamental switch which has occurred in the way in which the international migration system is organised. For example, immigrants from the Indian sub-continent made up 10.0% of the inflow of migrants to Britain in 1990, yet the same region accounted for 14.3% of the immigrant stock.

The implications of these contrasts for economic analysis are clear: immigration policy recommendations stemming from economic statistics relating to Britain's migration stock are of limited value since Britain's position in the world economy has fundamentally changed over the last thirty years. Economic analysis of immigration should be based on data relating to current migrants or to those who have arrived in the recent past, since it is these groups that reflect Britain's current economic position in the world and it is to groups such as these that policy should be addressed. It should be remembered that an economic analysis of this kind of data relates only to those allowed to enter the UK and not to the much larger number of people wishing to migrate to Britain.

Flow statistics and statistics relating to recent cohorts of immigrants are therefore the ones which are of greatest relevance. Immigrant flow statistics present a very different and much more favourable picture of the potential economic benefits of migration than do statistics for the least well assimilated ethnic minority populations. This point leads naturally to discussion of the nature and quality of data relating to the economic dimensions of immigration.

Economic data on immigration to Britain

Given the comments of the previous section, it can be stated that, ideally, economic data should relate to migration flow information and to the experience of cohorts of migrants arriving in immigration flows over recent years. Systematic and detailed information of this kind on the economics of immigration does not exist in Britain, nor in many other West European countries. By contrast, ample and much fuller economic data sets are collated in countries such as Australia and Canada.

The contrast is starkly evident if one compares the nature of the data sets used in two recent International Labour Office (ILO) analyses of discrimination against immigrants. The volume on Australia is replete with statistics on immigrant salaries, immigrant occupational status and employment by industrial sector, immigrant levels of educational attainment and on job training tabulated relative to place of birth and immigrant generation.[4] By contrast the volume on immigrants to Western Europe,[5] appears to rely either on piecemeal economic surveys or on data such as the Labour Force Survey's ethnically defined migrant stocks.

Since 1984 the Labour Force Survey has permitted migration to be viewed from other perspectives, but with a few notable exceptions[6] analysts have stubbornly ignored these opportunities. From 1984 the Labour Force Survey has asked about nationality and about place of residence a year earlier, and since 1985 there has been the possibility of information about migration flows. The value of the Labour Force Survey with regard to these questions is, however, limited due both to the absence of key economic variables and to the fact that the LFS is a sample survey, making it difficult to achieve statistically significant data for many immigration flows because of the smallness of the total sample size.

It should be noted that some of the specialised academic surveys which have been undertaken on the economic impact of immigration do produce interesting conclusions pertinent to this paper. For example a National Institute Survey of the 1960–66 Commonwealth influx to the UK concluded that this immigrant cohort had, on balance, helped to meet the aspirations—existing amongst policy makers and the wider public—to promote higher standards of living in Britain.[7]

Given the limited recent economic data available on immigration to Britain (at least until after the publication of the full results of the 1991 census) inferences have to be drawn about the economic implications of immigration based largely on the demographic information contained in the Labour Force and International Passenger Surveys (IPS). Useful evidence also emerges from consider-

Table 6.3 Unemployment Numbers and Rates by Ethnic Origin and Sex (Persons of working age, Great Britain 1991)

Ethnic Origin	All Persons	Men	Women
Unemployment numbers: ILO definition (men 16-65, women 16-60)– (thousands)			
All persons working age	2,263	1,417	846
Whites	2,068	1,291	777
Ethnic minority groups of which	179	115	64
West Indian/Guyanese	37	23	15
Indian	46	29	17
Pakistan/Bangladesh	47	36	11
All Others	48	28	20
Unemployment rates (% economically active persons of working age)			
All persons of working age*	8.3	9.1	7.3
Whites	8.0	9.0	7.0
Ethnic minority groups of which	15.0	16.0	14.0
West Indian/Guyanese	15.0	18.0	12.0
Indian	12.0	12.0	11.0
Pakistan/Bangladesh	25.0	25.0	24.0
All Others	14.0	14.0	14.0

* Includes those who did not state ethnic origin

Source: Labour Force Survey, 1991.

Table 6.4 All Persons working in the UK by Nationality (1988–90) (thousands)

	1988	1989	1990
All nationalities	25,540	26,417	26,658
UK nationals	24,315	25,201	25,541
Foreign nationals	871	960	933
EC countries (excl Eire)	460	497	473
Eire	307	325	323
Non EC foreign	411	463	460

Source: Labour Force Survey, 1991.

ation of the economic implications of immigration which have been charted for other developed countries where fuller economic data sets exist.

Culture versus economics in the analysis of immigration

Thus far the word 'economic' has been used extensively in this paper without the question being raised as to whether economic dimensions of migration can be studied meaningfully in isolation from other dimensions. Migrants may or may not sell their labour and they may or may not consume different goods and services in their host country. These impacts of migration have undoubted economic implications, but the cultural impact on the host society and for the migrant community is harder to assess. What weight should be placed on these cultural and social issues?

This matter is perhaps best explored by considering the contrasts which exist between different parts of the developed world with regard to the issue of immigration. Countries which share many common economic characteristics appear to hold starkly different views on the economic desirability of immigration. The history books will record how, from the mid 1970s onwards, most West European states sought vigorously to close their boundaries to many forms of labour immigration, establishing what may be described as a 'fortress mentality'.[8] The former British Prime Minister, Baroness Thatcher, declared in a television interview in the 1970s that the British fear 'being swamped by people of a different culture. [Britain] must hold out the clear prospect of an end to immigration'.[9]

John Major has vocally re-inforced these arguments in the context of the debate over the Maastricht treaty and has pointed to immigration as one of the key issues on which Britain wishes to maintain independent policies from Europe in order to 'double-bolt' the doors against immigrants. Britain therefore continues to refuse to sign the Schengen accord which would end intra-EC passport checks. Britain's suspicion of Schengen is presumably based on the unsubstantiated fear that it will lead to the inflow of large numbers of migrants who will contribute little to Britain's economic prosperity. The matter of whether certain migrant groups such as refugees could become a significant economic burden is taken up later in this paper.

While Britain has moved to make immigration more difficult, in North America, both the USA and Canada have re-defined their immigration policies to permit an increase in immigration. This has been done in such a way as to boost the immigration of highly skilled and professional staff, but certain categories of refugees have also been welcomed. This difference in strategy has been analysed by a range of academics[10] who conclude that the positive North American ideology towards immigration is fundamentally based on the belief that immigration contributes to the vitality of the nation by infusing new life blood into a multi-cultural nation, while in Western Europe resistance to multi-culturalism is strong. This has produced political tensions that have in turn generated a series of discussions about the perceived 'burden' to the welfare state associated with further immigration. Urbani and Granaglia[11] and others have shown that even within Western Europe significant differences exist in terms of the degree of openness or closure sought by both immigration and emigration policies, and the extent to which different nations have sought to restrict citizenship.

This is not the place for an extended review of European attitudes to ethnic minorities and immigration. They have only been introduced briefly to make the point that if national variations exist in terms of political responses to immigration, then it is not unreasonable to expect cultural factors to produce different interpretations of what is meant by the economic costs and benefits of migration.

To summarise the conclusions of the paper so far, differences of definition, lack of data, and contrasts in what is culturally interpreted to be the economic impact of migration, go some way to explaining why so many apparently paradoxical positions are held with regard to immigration policy.

Discussion now turns to a more detailed evaluation of trends in labour migration in relation to economic growth and to the possible labour market impacts of immigration to Britain.

West European labour migration and economic growth

It is extremely difficult to establish the nature of the relationship between labour migration and economic growth. Logic might suggest that a state will permit labour immigration to occur when economic circumstances are favourable and when labour resources within the state are scarce. The historical record shows that this is not necessarily the case. It is also difficult to establish lines of causality. For example, should one ask 'Does immigration affect rates of economic growth?' or is it more appropriate to start by asking 'Does economic growth stimulate immigration?'

The problem may be illustrated by considering patterns of economic performance in Western Europe in the 1970s. The decade began well with countries averaging between 4% and 6% growth per annum in their domestic products.[12] Böhning[13] and others have described how these rapidly expanding economies during the 1960s and early 1970s were threatened by labour shortages, resulting from the relatively low levels of labour market growth which, in turn, had been affected by the slow growth of their labour forces from natural population increase. The tight labour market situation fuelled fears of wage inflation acting as a check on economic growth. In this context labour immigration from labour surplus economies resulted. Within national labour markets upward social mobility attracted nationals away from the less desirable jobs leaving vacancies to be filled by immigrants.

The 1973 oil crisis undoubtedly brought to an end the period of continuous economic growth which most Western European countries had been enjoying, with recession affecting their economies in 1974 and 1975. However, by 1976 economic recovery was obvious, with Great Britain recording economic growth of 3.9%, and West Germany and France moving ahead even more strongly with growth rates of 5.6% and 5.2% respectively. Economic growth was sustained across most of Western Europe during the rest of the 1970s with recession not returning to most countries until 1980.

The reversal of economic fortunes in 1974/5 was associated with rising unemployment in most Western European countries, but what was significant was that these trends continued in the latter part of the decade despite the return to economic growth. Both unemployment and economic growth rates rose in the mid 1970s. Unemployment rates also soared in the late 1970s and early 1980s as the next recession made its impact. The fact that rising unemployment in 1974/5 was associated with the introduction of a range of policy measures to halt further immigration is not surprising. From 1976 onwards, renewed economic growth did not bring down unemployment and there were moves to strengthen policies on repatriation.[14]

White,[15] in a detailed analysis of immigration policies in Western Europe, notes in fact that attempts to halt labour immigration in many countries actually preceded the economic crisis. In Britain the Immigration Act was passed in 1971, while in West Germany steps were taken to stabilise immigrant stocks in the summer of 1973, before the oil crisis had occurred. Switzerland adopted a restrictive policy on immigration from 1970. Algeria banned emigration to France from September 1973 in outrage at racial attacks on Algerian migrants. Salt[16] and other academics agree that in the early 1970s restrictions on immigration were primarily initiated in response to social concerns over the size of certain immigrant communities, rather than in relation to the economic crisis. Once in place it was, however, the economic situation, and in particular the scale of domestic unemployment, which was cited as the reason for justifying the extension of restrictive immigration policies.

What conclusions can be drawn from the experience of Western Europe in the 1970s? First, it would seem that from 1974 onwards national economic growth no longer translated into labour market demand in such a way as to reduce unemployment levels and to create labour shortages of the kind which had encouraged labour immigration in the 1960s and early 1970s. Second, the introduction of restrictive immigration policies pre-dated economic decline in some countries, suggesting that social factors may be critical in initiating the political contexts in which further immigration is perceived as undesirable. Third, politicians in Western Europe cited rising unemployment as a reason for sustaining restrictive immigration controls. Rising unemployment in the 1970s and 1980s was not caused by immigration but by other internal and international forces.

Immigration and economic performance of selected non-EC states

If the European experience suggests that economic growth no longer guarantees conditions in which labour demand will grow and immigration become a desirable policy option in order to avoid wage inflation, this does not prove the inverse case: it does not prove that immigration is an undesirable labour market policy option. Indeed since it is a policy which has not been attempted since the 1960s in Britain, it becomes pertinent to ask if there is evidence from other parts of the globe that immigration can benefit advanced economies.

Table 6.5 presents a range of economic indicators and immigration flows for three non EC countries. In recent years British politicians have often looked to North America for inspiration on economic policy rather than following European models. It is therefore interesting to note from Table 6.5 that both the USA and Canada have followed much more positive strategies towards immigration. They have adopted new legislation to favour high quality immigration and have introduced policy measures which have encouraged increased levels of immigration amongst those categories of immigrant deemed to be of greatest value to their economies. The consequences of the positive ideologies on immigration held by these countries is evident in terms of the rising numbers of immigrants accepted for settlement. This is most dramatic in the Canadian case where numbers almost doubled between 1986 and 1989. Australia also supports a selective pro-immigration policy and has endorsed (1991) a new plan to expand further immigration flows.[17]

No one would suggest that the UK economy is similar in all respects to those of the three other countries listed in Table 6.5. It is however interesting to note from Table 6.5 that Britain can not excuse itself from following the immigration stance of these nations in terms of statements about Britain's weaker economic performance. OECD[18] figures show quite clearly that over the 30 year span, 1960–90, Britain experienced a very similar rate of growth in real GDP per caput as the USA and Australia, and over the last decade, 1979–90, enjoyed more rapid economic growth than any of these three states. At the same time the UK experienced lower levels of population growth and much slower rates of labour force increase than the other countries. Few would suggest that immigration to the USA, Canada and Australia has had damaging effects on these advanced economies and it is apparent from the new pro-immigration legislation of these countries that their governments certainly do not view immigration as a negative economic influence.

To summarise the debate, positive economic growth is not a sufficient condition to justify a policy favouring immigration on economic grounds. However, having examined Table 6.5 it is equally important to stress that large scale immigration should not be viewed as inconsistent with substantial economic growth in modern western societies. Even during periods of recession Canada, the USA and Australia have held to their pro-immigration stances, maintaining the view that positive selective immigration is to do with nation building and future economic well-being. Despite the introduction of highly restrictive immigration policies, British politicians continue to portray immigration as a phenomenon associated primarily with labour flows from Britain's former colonies of the kind which occurred in the first

Table 6.5 Economic Indicators and Immigration: A Comparison of UK, USA, Australia and Canada

	—Annual Growth Rate—				—InFlows of— Permanent Settlers (thousands)			
	Popu-lation Growth (%)	Labour Force Growth (%)	Real GDP p.c. Growth (%)					
	1960–90	60–90	60–90	79–90	1986	1987	1988	1989
UK	0.3	0.5	2.1	1.9	47	46	49	49
USA	1.1	1.9	2.0	1.6	602	602	643	1091
Australia	1.6	2.4	2.3	1.6	103	128	151	131
Canada	0.8	2.5	2.9	1.8	99	152	162	192

Source: OECD, 1992, *Economic Outlook 1960–90;* OECD, 1991, *SOPEMI, 1990.*

half of the twentieth century. In practice so-called 'skilled transients' have replaced 'settler migration'.[19] British politicians need to consider very carefully why their stance on immigration has not shifted in line with changes in the international migration system and why their view of immigration is so different from that of countries like Canada. A significant number of western economies with satisfactory levels of economic growth certainly view immigration as making a positive economic contribution.

British labour market trends and the implications for migration

Analysis of recent statements by the British Government on immigration issues (made in the context of the debate over granting new passports to a small number of skilled people from Hong Kong and in the wake of concern from European neighbours over the possible consequences of an influx of migrants from Eastern Europe), suggest that two economic worries are paramount; first that large scale immigration might exacerbate unemployment and second that it might place an insurmountable burden on the social services and social security systems. It is therefore pertinent to examine what trends are likely to emerge in the British labour force over the next few years, as well as extending the investigation to consider the wider economic costs of supporting a flow of immigrants.

Labour supply

Table 6.6 shows the labour force estimates used by the British Department of Employment along with labour force projections to the year 2001, based on the most recent finding of the 1991 Labour Force Survey. There has been a steady growth in the size of Britain's labour force over the last two decades from 24,895,000 in 1971 to 26,242,000 in 1981 and 28,081,000 in 1991. The 1982–91 growth which produced a net increase in the size of the labour force of 2,039,000 persons was particularly strong by European standards. Between 1985 and 1990 Britain had the third-highest average annual rate of employment growth, after Spain and Luxembourg. By contrast the Government's official labour force projections to the year 2001 show a much slower rate of growth, with nearly all the increase coming from increased female participation. Between 1992 and 2001 the male labour force is expected to grow by as little as 104,000, with net reductions in the most active male cohorts of the labour force. A reduction of 841,000 in the number of men in the labour force in the age cohort 20–34 years is anticipated by the year 2001, representing one of the most significant alterations in the supply of labour which the British labour market has experienced in recent decades.

Trends in labour force size and structure are dependent on:

- the size and structure of the total population (which in turn is determined by mortality, fertility and migration) and
- the activity and participation rates in each sex and age group.

It is useful first of all to consider the effects of demographic trends on labour supply. Table 6.7 shows the size and age distribution of the British population of working age. Population growth was the dominant force accounting for the increased supply of labour to the labour force in the 1970s and the early 1980s, but from 1983 a significant trend towards demographic decline in the number of young people entering the labour force altered this effect. By 1991 there were 769,000 fewer people in the 16–19 age cohort than in 1982. The continued effect of low birth rates will produce further reductions in the number of young people in this age cohort by the year 1994, when there will only be 2,602,000 16–19 year olds (nearly a million less than a decade earlier). It is statistics such as these which have fuelled speculation about a 'demographic time-bomb' creating fierce labour market pressures and perhaps introducing circumstances in which labour immigration might once again become an attractive policy option.

Table 6.6 Estimates and Projections of the Resident Population of Great Britain aged 16 years and over (thousands)

Age All persons	Estimates		Projections	
	1990	*1991*	*2000*	*2005*
16–19	3,109	2,943	2,829	2,844
20–24	4,419	4,364	3,368	3,430
25–34	8,571	8,717	8,144	7,890
35–44	7,699	7,718	8,443	8,589
45–54	6,335	6,441	7,519	7,538
55–59	2,867	2,852	3,152	3,279
60–64	2,828	2,809	2,793	2,769
65 and over	8,793	8,837	9,024	9,024
All ages	44,621	44,680	45,255	45,363
Working age (Men aged 16–64, women aged 16–59)	34,362	34,389	34,822	34,923

Source: OPCS.

Table 6.7 Estimates and Projections of the Civilian Labour Force in Great Britain (thousands)

Age All persons	Estimates		Projections		Change
	1990	*1991*	*2000*	*2005*	*1992–2001*
16–19	2,268	2,129	2,009	2,021	3
20–24	3,581	3,462	2,620	2,679	–698
25–34	7,049	7,142	6,914	6,722	–541
35–44	6,593	6,614	7,441	7,594	1,112
45–54	5,204	5,271	6,173	6,186	674
55–59	1,944	1,918	2,128	2,215	287
60–64	1,074	1,083	1,059	1,054	–10
65 and over	477	461	380	377	–58
All ages	28,206	28,081	28,724	28,847	768
Working age (Men aged 16–64, women aged 16–59)	27,398	27,270	27,978	28,102	802

Source: Labour Force Survey 1991 and *Employment Gazette*, April 1992.

The economic effects on the labour market of demographic change extend far beyond the crude impact on overall labour force size. Long-run financial implications of continued low birth rates and the associated ageing of the population include changes in patterns of consumption, investment and saving. Concern has arisen over how future pensions are to be financed; how career mobility is to be sustained; and how flexible employment policies are to be maintained.

It is important to note that while government population projections are based on fertility and mortality rates which are unlikely to change greatly over the short term (and where the effects take some time to impact upon the labour market), they also depend upon assumptions about international migration. For example, the British population projections prepared in 1985 assumed that Britain would continue to experience net emigration of about 17,000 persons per year, rather than having emigration and immigration held in balance. The result was the prediction of a population of working age by the year 2000 which would be 200,000 lower than without the net emigration effect.

Changes in participation rates were noted above as the second major influence affecting labour force trends. Comparison of Tables 6.6 and 6.7 indicates that demographic influences are only one dimension of labour force change. Participation rates are much more variable over time and are much harder to project with accuracy. For example, the increases which occurred in Britain's labour force in 1983–4 and 1988–9 may be explained largely by fluctuations in activity rates. In the 1980s participation rates tended to rise for women and to fall for men. It is expected that reductions in male participation rates will produce a decline of the male labour force in the years 1992–4.

Projections of participation rates of the British population are produced by the Department of Employment based on assumptions about how economic, demographic and social factors will affect activity rates. For example, an attempt is made to project the influence of changes in unemployment levels on the number of people participating in the labour force. The net effect of the Department of Employment's projections about participation rates is to produce increases in the number of women in the labour force. These increases will greatly outweigh the effect of small reductions in male participation rates. The consequence of labour force projections is first to dampen greatly the impact of demographic processes over the next decade and second to produce a further important redistributive effect on the structure of the labour force. Not only will there be fewer young people, with all the economic consequences that ensue from this, but there will also be a higher proportion of women in the labour force by the year 2001.

Comparison of current (1991) labour force projections with previous ones is particularly important for the analyst concerned with immigration issues. The 1990–1 fall in the labour force of 125,000 was double the projected figure of 67,000. This has been attributed to the fact that many fewer young people than expected entered the labour force, with a larger number staying on in full-time education. These statistics illustrate the relative uncertainty of the projection process, and indicate something of the scale of error which could arise in projections which already forecast a fairly stagnant picture in terms of labour supply.

The analysis of trends in the structure of Britain's labour force point to the 1990s as being very different from those of earlier decades. The decline in fertility levels and the subsequent reduction in the number of young people entering the labour force has been a significant influence on labour force structure. It has not, and will not of itself, create a demand for higher levels of immigration, since participation rates and the restructuring of labour demand intervene to affect labour force size and composition. Therefore, neither economic growth nor demographic shrinkage are sufficient conditions *in themselves* to *necessitate* an increase in immigration in the 1990s. Other labour supply options exist. The 1990s will however be a decade when a reduced level of new entries to the labour market from the younger cohorts of the population will oblige employers to consider all the options including immigration if they are to maintain current capital to labour ratios and to avoid wage inflation and a loss of flexible workforce practices.

Labour demand

Change in the demand for labour in Britain over the last two decades has been very great indeed. Between 1971 and 1981 employment declined by 2.5% even although positive rates of economic growth were recorded in all but three years. Reduction of demand was greatest in manufacturing (–24.3%) while service employment grew by 13.5%. The equivalent figures for 1981 to 1989 are 4.3% overall growth, but with a further 14.3% decline in manufacturing jobs and a 17.9% growth in services. The reasons for these very significant changes in employment demand have been analysed in detail by Massey[20] and more recently by Champion and Townsend[21] and Owen.[22] They include the effects of industrial restructuring in the face of increased international competition, resulting in the shedding of manufacturing jobs due to plant rationalisation, re-organisation and re-investment in more capital intensive production systems. An increase in the internationalisation of production systems has seen companies redistribute certain types of jobs across the globe to locations where wage levels were more advantageous. In particular this meant a reduction in the number of jobs in Britain in the older established labour intensive industries. While production jobs were internationalised, managerial and professional jobs remained in Britain creating Britains's contribution to what some have described as the 'new international division of labour'.[23]

The Labour Force Surveys of the 1980s show a consistent shift over the 1980s towards a lower proportion of manual and semi-skilled jobs and towards a proportional increase in professional and managerial posts. An interesting corollary to this has been the trend for job-related migration within Britain to be increasingly associated with professional and managerial staff. Owen[24] has shown that regional variations exist, but that in the case of the south of Britain job-related migrants were between 4 and 5 times more likely to be managerial or professional staff than manual workers (defined to include craft, skilled manual workers and plant and machine operators).

It seems probable that in the 1990s structural changes in the British economy will continue, although they may affect the demand for labour in a different fashion from in the past. Green[25] has suggested that employers and governments will continue to seek to raise standards of living. This will only be possible if British firms remain internationally competitive. On the one hand they must avoid undue wage inflation, and on the other hand ensure adequate investment in new technologies and in human resources. Skills appropriate to these new technologies must be acquired and an ability developed to adapt to the new patterns of work organisation which will emerge. One aspect of new work patterns will be increased job mobility, not just at a local scale, but at the international level.

The Institute of Employment Research (University of Warwick) estimate that in the UK there will be a 1.3 million (15%) increase in higher level non-manual occupations by the year 2000. By the turn of the century professional, associate professional and managerial and administrative occupations are projected to account for over one-third of all jobs (compared with under one quarter in 1971). Not only does this represent a very significant increase in specific skill and occupational categories, but the effect is increased by the spatial concentration of demand in the south of England (which incidentally also faces the tightest constraints on labour supply in terms of the supply-side processes discussed above).

The concentrated pattern of selective demand for certain types of labour leads according to Green,[26] to the key question of 'whether pressures arising from economic and geographical imbalances between prosperous centres and the rest of the community will encourage the mobility of economic activity and jobs and/or the mobility of labour.'

The reason why this international mobility arises more strongly as an option in relation to this trend than to other forces affecting the relation between labour supply and demand, is that matching labour demand for highly skilled jobs cannot be achieved in a situation of demographic decline simply by raising participation rates. Filling skilled jobs requires time for education and training potential employees. Consequently, failure to identify future needs for particular specialised and highly skilled functions well in advance may create a situation in which short- or even long-run skill shortages will arise. Such gaps can only be filled by immigration. It is in this context that the situation may well arise (and already has done) whereby a labour market experiences labour surpluses at one level (for example, of semi-skilled and certain white collar jobs) while at the same time facing severe skill shortages at other higher levels which can only be filled by some form of immigration.

This situation has been identified in a useful labour market model proposed by Lonnroth.[27] In discussing appropriate labour market policies to 'squeeze the supply and demand curves at various skill levels closer together', Lonnroth[28] advocates not only a policy of continuous upgrading of labour skills on the domestic labour market, but also international labour mobility. 'Paradoxically the gross migratory flows within free labour market areas may be too modest to meet the needs of internationalisation and labour force development. Policies should therefore promote temporary international mobility of key personnel, international trainee exchanges, education and training abroad.'[29] Before the nature of these and other possible policies can be considered in further detail, it is necessary to consider whether there is any evidence from the recent UK migration experience of need existing within the country for immigration of certain skill groups. This task is undertaken in the next section of this paper. The analysis which has been presented of Britain's labour market, has shown that demographic trends will continue to reduce the scale of new entrants to the labour market over the next decade. This effect will, however, be partly offset by rising female participation rates. Labour demand has shifted considerably over the last two decades. The restructuring of the economy which has followed is in part responsible for some of the mismatches which have occurred between patterns of labour supply and labour demand.

In the long run new skills can and should be produced as a result of adaptations to the education and training systems of the country, but in the short run and in the medium term it is possible, and indeed probable, that skill shortages may occur in certain professional and managerial positions which could be filled to the benefit of the economy by qualified immigrants. From this conclusion it follows that the issues which policy makers should address, prior to developing a migration stance, are not whether there is any domestic unemployment or whether participation rates are likely to compensate for demographic shrinkage, but whether there are selective skill shortages and how these can best be filled in the interests of economic growth and the standards of living of the resident population.

Rising demand for skilled foreign labour

The clearest empirical evidence supporting the labour demand argument for immigration can be found in trends in the number of work permits issued by the British Government to allow foreign labour to work on a short or longer term basis in the country. The work permit system is useful in demonstrating the existence of a clear economic demand for foreign labour in Britain because a work permit application should only be granted by the Department of Employment if it considers that there is no 'suitable' resident labour. The term 'suitable' is of great importance and we shall return to considering its meaning later.

Seymour[30] in a review of the UK work permit system has identified the precise objectives of the scheme. These are primarily to protect the resident labour force rather than to serve the economic interests of the economy. This prioritisation of the interests of the indigenous labour force helps to explain why so little attention is paid within the scheme to identifying the labour market needs of the economy as a whole. Although lip service is paid under the scheme to 'the interests of the

UK as a whole by assisting inward investment'[31] there is neither recognition of the possibility that the wider economy might benefit from immigration of entrepreneurs (independently from major capital transfers) nor of the economic stimulus which immigration of certain skills might produce.

The Department of Employment needs to be convinced by the employer who applies for a work permit for a foreign employee that reasonable attempts have been made to recruit a resident or EC worker (NB work permits are not needed for EC citizens) before looking elsewhere. Another significant control which seeks to ensure that foreign labour is not recruited to the detriment of resident workers is that the job must be offered at wages and under conditions which are not less favourable than those which would be granted to British staff.

Despite these many controls there has been a sustained and substantial rise in the number of both short- and long-term work permits granted over recent years (Table 6.8). The number of long-term permits granted rose by 29% in 1988 over the previous year, by 28% in 1989 and by 21% in 1990. To quote from the SOPEMI report; 'prior to 1990 the increase in permits reflected the stronger performance of the national economy. However during 1990 numbers of unemployed rose by 227,000, so the rise in work permits granted occurred despite a deterioration in labour market conditions. This suggests that either there is some fundamental mismatch between the characteristics of supply and demand, and/or that some lag effect exists between labour market conditions at home and employers' use of overseas workers'.[32]

The types of jobs for which the permits were most sought were in insurance, banking and finance, and professional services. Professional and managerial staff account for 81% of long-term work permits. Work permit data also serves to illustrate the changing nature of work organisation which has been alluded to above. This is so because it lists permits offered to persons making inter-company transfers (that is transfers within an international organisation from one location to another). Around 40% of all work permits are granted for inter-company transfers reflecting the strength of large international employers in stimulating and sustaining the system of international mobility.

Previous work by this author using the results of the International Passenger Survey[33] has researched this issue, and has shown the growing significance to Britain of skilled transient movements of staff within large companies. Japan and the USA are the two non-European countries with which Britain is most closely linked by this

Table 6.8 Work Permits Issued, UK (1987–90)

Year	Long-term permits	Short-term	Trainee	Total
1987	8063	9385	2900	20348
1988	10391	11793	3790	25974
1989	13268	12234	4228	29730
1990	16055	13760	4812	34627

Source: From J. Salt, 1992, 'International Migration and the United Kingdom' (SOPEMI) report to the OECD.

new form of international migration. Transferring staff from branch to branch in large international companies for periods of two or three years has become a major (arguably the major) element of the British migration system and one which contrasts strongly with the historical processes of settler immigration. Skilled transient movements are favoured by large companies as part of their internationalisation strategies. This not only reflects the way that strong economic forces operate within the internal labour markets of large companies to fill vacancies by internal transfers within the company (albeit by international relocation of an employee) rather than by external recruitment. It also reflects the benefits which the large company perceives to exist from promoting the circulation of human capital between different branches in order to sustain corporate identity as well as to facilitate communication between different branches of a firm. All these reasons may constitute for the firm one facet of why local labour may not be considered 'suitable' and it helps to explain why international skill mobility may seem to be highly desirable for reasons quite separate from the international matching of specific skill shortages with potential sources of qualified manpower.

There would seem to be at least two reasons why one would expect skilled transient international moves to continue to increase in the near future. First, it seems highly likely that throughout most developed and developing countries linkages between economies will grow stronger as policies favouring selective integration occurs. Nowhere is this trend more evident than in the states of Western Europe in the 1990s as they commit themselves to greater monetary and political integration. Research by Kritz and Caces[34] suggests that by the mid-1980s 4.6% of all professional and administrative workers in Belgium were foreign born, while in the UK the proportion was 6.0% and in Sweden 7.2%. An even more startling statistic is that, according to the UK 1981 census, 40% of all people defined as 'foreign born' (i.e., excluding second generation ethnic minorities) were employed in professional or administrative jobs.

The brief analysis presented here of the skilled transient immigration to Britain has shown first, that skill gaps do exist within the British economy, which employers and the Department of Employment judge to be best filled by skilled immigration. Second, analysis of work permits and complementary information from the International Passenger Survey (revealing similar trends with regard to skilled immigration to, and emigration from, EC countries) underscores the need to see immigration as fulfilling more than the simple need to match specific skill shortages. The internationalisation of both production and service activities has necessitated the increased mobility of certain types of human capital. This is so, not only because of the need of certain national labour markets to access international skill specialisms, but also to facilitate the needs of the internal labour markets of global corporations to circulate some of their highly skilled manpower between the different states in which they are operating. Third, the discussion points to the need to consider British immigration policy in the light of these new types of labour migration which differ considerably in their economic character from the settler immigration patterns of the past. In practice this switch in immigration behaviour has been recognised in part by the government in its recent review of the work permit scheme (Summer 1991).

The revised work permit scheme involves the creation of a two tier work permit system to facilitate the circulation of highly qualified staff, particularly those who are involved in corporate transfers. In the first tier, applications are dealt with fairly quickly because a simplified procedure has been introduced for dealing with those cases which are deemed clearly to merit approval by the Department of Employment. It is claimed that 75% of all applications are dealt with within eight weeks of receipt. These cases include senior transfers within Trans National Corporations (described as Inter Company Transfers), such as board level transfers, moves associated with inward investment and occupations considered to be in acute short supply. The Department of Employment does not however issue a list of short supply occupations since it is claimed that this list varies over even very short time periods. To quote Onslow-Cole[35] 'This list is amended on an almost daily basis and in view of the recession is currently very short.' All applications not falling under the first category require fuller documentation and are treated at greater length as Tier 2 applications.

In 1993 a set of parliamentary questions were posed to the Secretary of State for Employment concerning the operation of the revised work permit scheme. It emerged that no comparative statistics were available to evaluate whether the introduction of a second tier had been to the disadvantage of applicants other than those making internal company transfers. Of greater significance in response to the question 'what research and data collection is carried out by the Department (of Employment) to assess which skills are in short supply in the UK in order to guide officials who are dealing with work permit applications?' it emerged that no systematic data collection existed and that work permit requests were researched on an individual and ad hoc basis.

It should be stressed that the work permit scheme relates to temporary immigration. Although some work permit holders do apply to extend their permits or to settle more permanently, the vast majority (86%) leave before or on expiry of their work permit.[36] It is not therefore a system which in any way can be thought of as analagous to the types of skill recruitment achieved by the im-migration quotas and point system schemes operated in certain other countries, which relate to permanent settlement of skilled workers.

The significance of market demand for labour immigration

The previous section of the paper used work permit data to argue the case that there is a clear economic demand for immigrant labour in Britain. Those who contest this view will inevitably suggest that work permits account for only a small proportion of all immigration. It is important therefore to consider in more detail precisely how significant is market demand for labour immigration. This is achieved here first, by further consideration of work permit data and second, by pointing to other indicators of demand.

In 1992, the number of work permit holders and their dependants permitted to enter Britain numbered 52,000 persons. This compared with 52,600 persons accepted for permanent settlement.[37] The numbers involved are therefore highly significant. Furthermore, amongst those admitted for permanent settlement in their own right, on completion of four years residence, work permit holders were the single largest category (and almost twice the number of the next most important group—those in permit free employment). As noted earlier, work permits offer only a limited insight into the demand for immigrant skills. This is so because large flows of Irish labour as well as workers from EC countries (and from 1994 from EFTA) enter the UK without requiring work permits. It is for this reason that the analysis in this paper has frequently referred to the International Passenger Survey and the Labour Force Survey. These other sources substantiate the view that (a) skilled transient migration is now by far the dominant form of migration affecting Britain; and (b) a very significant market demand for immigrant skills exists within the British economy.

These views are supported by survey work of individual professions and skill groups. One example suffices here to make the point. Buchan, Seccombe and Bull[38] in an extensive survey of UK nurses show that the *annual* number of nurses entering the UK professional register who had previously been registered abroad was between 2,400 and 3,500 in the period 1984–91. An upward trend was identified with the importance of non-UK sources of nurses (as a proportion of all new admissions to the UK professional register) rising to one in ten in 1990/91. In nursing this strong demand for foreign nurses reflects the combination of increased demand for healthcare at a time when intake to domestic nurse training has been on the decline. Such a level of dependence on foreign nurses serves as only one example of the demand which exists in Britain for specific immigrant skills.

Other labour market dimensions of immigration

The case which has been presented in the preceding part of this paper suggests that selective labour immigration is both necessary and desirable relative to the needs of the British labour market. This has been shown to be true in terms of Britain's economic needs in relation to specific skill shortages which can best be met in the short term by temporary immigration. It is also true in relation to needs created by a switch in the organisation of the labour market which has required an increased international mobility of professional and managerial staff moving within large organisations.

Another argument, and one which is not developed in detail in this paper because it probably does not involve very large numbers of immigrants, is that immigrants create jobs rather than filling them. The USA and Canada have specialised in recruiting entrepreneurs and investors and have specifically recognised this category of migrants. Britain too has a facility within immigration regulations to allow the entry of very wealthy immigrants, but seems much less successful than its North American rivals in attracting this category of investor migrant. In Britain's case people are allowed to enter as business persons if first, they are bringing to the UK a minimum of £200,000 of their own money to be invested in a business, second they are to be occupied full-time in running the business, and third the business will provide new, full-time employment for persons already settled in Britain. Trott[39] has described the other conditions attaching to this mode of entry.

While attracting entrepreneurial immigrants is clearly desirable in economic terms, the British rules on this type of immigration have a number of problems. Trott[40] points out that it is not easy to determine what money belongs to the migrant. Does it include loans? What is the Home Office definition of a person being occupied full-time in their own business? Perhaps the greatest problem is that many businesses do not require £200,000 to be successful or may start very adequately on lower levels of capital and later expand. The government's own criteria in the 1980s and early 1990s for a British person to be seen as a successful entrepreneur, certainly did not involve a cash threshold of £200,000 for new business start-ups.

Historical evidence shows from around the globe that immigrants are often highly successful as entrepreneurs but that their success lies not in their capital stock but in their skills and motivation. For instance, one example of modern day free market success was the transfer of textile entrepreneurs from Shanghai to Hong Kong following the Communist take-over of mainland China. The entrepreneur refugees from Shanghai were deemed to have been responsible, at least in part, for the development of Hong Kong's successful textile industry in the 1950s. Many other examples could be quoted which reinforce the point that it is skills and motivation rather than capital which are the key characteristics determining the entrepreneurial success of refugee and voluntary migrant moves. The USA, in revising its current immigration policy in 1991, moved to try to increase the number of entrepreneurs coming to the US each year. In so-doing it has given more weight not only to inward investor groups, but also to those potential migrants with high inventive and creative capacities such as key scientists and leading professionals.

The difference in outlook and strategy between Britain and other countries is well illustrated by returning to the case of Hong Kong, and in contrasting the approaches taken to encourage Hong Kong skills to seek foreign passports in the run-up to 1997. In Hong Kong the number of 'immigration agencies' expanded from under ten in 1980 to over 120 by 1990. The main task of such agencies was to offer advice to the Hong Kong elite on how to gain visas and passports for immigration to other countries. The USA, Canada, Australia and New Zealand have actively developed these agencies in order to recruit potential investors and highly skilled immigrants. By contrast the UK's negative ideology on immigration and the outcry which surrounded the legislation to offer passports to a small number of highly placed Hong Kong citizens sent the inverse message to Hong Kong. While Canada emerged as the favoured destination for Hong Kong's elite, Britain found that its offer of a limited number of passports was initially not even taken up in full.

In brief, immigration can serve as a means to create jobs and investment. In Britain's case this strategy has not been pursued successfully by comparison with the results achieved in other countries.

The case for encouraging entrepreneurial migration needs to be balanced by a comment on the development implications of a 'brain drain' from less developed to more developed nations. Clearly it is unacceptable to recommend that a more developed country like Britain should seek to prosper by recruiting skills from the least developed countries of the world, where the most skilled nationals clearly have a key responsibility in helping in the development of their own country. However, where skilled persons seek entry to a country as refugees, as was the case for many East Germans fleeing to former West Germany in the 1940s and 1950s, or where migration is between countries of approximately the same level of development (as between Hong Kong and the UK—GNP *per capita* in Hong Kong and Scotland are similar) then no accusation of favouring a 'brain drain' can be sustained.

Immigration to Britain is of course permitted on non-economic grounds. No one would want to suggest that refugees should only be admitted if they have desirable skills. It is quite legitimate that migration policy should facilitate a degree of immigration associated with both the granting of asylum to a controlled in-flow of refugees and also to permit family re-unification. It is important to note that such forms of migration also have an impact on the labour market and that the nature of the impact of these forms of immigration need not be perceived as negative. This paper has argued that this form of immigration may not result in major positive economic gains, but it also does not have net negative consequences. Indeed some refugees may in fact be economically highly desirable, because of their entrepreneurial potential for the host economy. At present very little is done to foster this potential. Undoubtedly, investment in language training and similar support facilities to promote the integration of refugees would yield significant economic gains for the UK through promoting a more rapid achievement of the significant economic potential of these groups.

In the absence of detailed economic statistics by migrant cohort it is difficult to provide an overall audit of the impact on the labour market. Lack of appropriate economic data also makes it difficult to estimate with any accuracy what would be the impact of an increase in unskilled immigration. Such data is needed in order to judge whether further immigration of this kind would simply swell the ranks of the unemployed, or whether it would improve Britain's gross operating surplus (the difference between value added and wage bills). At present Britain lags way behind its competitors on this key measure of rates of return on capital (Spain 20.3%; USA 18.0%; Netherlands 17.2%; UK 10.8%). The Government should be able to assess the effect of further immigration on key economic measures such as these, and should be urged to collect adequate economic data on immigration in order to be able to make well substantiated judgements about what level and kind of immigration is appropriate to the economy. At present economic data of this kind is not available, hence precluding the possibilities of making detailed impact statements based on different immigration scenarios (of the kind produced in Canada and Australia).

Straubhaar and Zimmermann, Zimmermann and Rivera-Batiz et al.,[41] conclude that immigrants often complement native workers resulting in an increase in productivity and wages—a finding not incompatible with some of the models proposed by Borjas and Simon.[42] Straubhaar and Zimmermann's[43] work is also significant in identifying short-term adjustment costs as one of the key issues associated with immigration. They propose that the net benefits of migration can only be enjoyed if the host population is assured that adjustment costs are being fully covered. One solution is to offset short-run costs associated with immigration by imposing entrance fees and migration taxes. A substantial body of academic work exists in Germany to support the contention that net economic benefits accrue from immigration, even after short-run costs have been taken into consideration.[44]

The Labour Force Survey allows one only a few interesting comparisons between the labour characteristics of foreign nationals employed in Britain and the rest of the British work force. Table 6.9, for example, shows that foreign nationals are on average more highly skilled. The 1990 LFS suggested that 21.7% of UK nationals were in professional or managerial jobs. By contrast 23.8% of immigrants from the EC (excluding Eire) were in this socio-economic group and an impressive 28.3% of those from the 'rest of the world' were professionals or managers. The contribution to the labour force of immigration must therefore surely be interpreted as a positive one in terms of skill levels and qualifications. At the other end of the labour market, male foreign workers were less likely to be in manual jobs than UK nationals (50.4% and 52.6% respectively). It was only among female workers that foreign nationals were more likely to be involved in manual jobs. Immigrants are shown by Table 6.9 to be much less likely to fall in the 'other non-manual' category covering most white collar and semi-skilled jobs. This data suggests that for all foreign nationals, and not just those with temporary work permits, Lonnroth's pro-immigration labour market model has some validity in describing the British case.

An economic audit of immigration to West Germany has recently produced some interesting findings which bear serious consideration. A study produced by the Rheinish-Westfälische Institute (RWI) in 1991 provided a range of evidence to support the view that the immigrant community contributed substantially to the state's affluence. The 3.5 million immigrants who entered West Germany between 1988 and 1991 would not be described as skilled transients of the kind discussed earlier in this paper. Instead they were made up of refugees, economic migrants and family members seeking re-unification. Baron[45] reviewing the report notes that the new labour supply enabled German firms to extend their productive capacity and far from taking up jobs which otherwise would have been occupied by West Germans the wealth generated as a result of the immigrants created a net increase in employment (i.e., in addition creating extra jobs to match the jobs taken by the immigrants) of 20,000 jobs. The RWI also calculated an increase in economic growth of between 0.5% and 1.0% per annum which was attributed to the increase in foreign labour.

One reason that greater economic returns are not achieved as a result of immigration in countries such as Britain is the negative influence of discrimination. Racial discrimination in the labour

Table 6.9 Socio-economic Grouping of the Workforce by Nationality, UK (1990)

	Professionals Employers Managers	Other Non-manual	Manual	Other	Total
Total					
All Nationalities	21.7	33.2	44.4	0.7	100.0
UK	21.6	33.3	44.3	0.7	100.0
Foreign Nationals	24.7	28.7	45.7	0.9	100.0
EC (exc Eire)	23.8	28.5	47.7	0.0	100.0
Eire	19.9	29.8	49.1	0.2	100.0
Rest of the world	28.3	28.0	42.4	1.3	100.0
Men					
All Nationalities	28.3	18.3	52.5	0.9	100.0
UK	28.2	18.3	52.6	0.9	100.0
Foreign Nationals	31.7	16.7	50.4	1.2	100.0
EC (exc Eire)	32.9	15.2	51.9	0.0	100.0
Eire	23.8	14.9	59.1	2.2	100.0
Rest of the world	37.1	18.5	44.0	0.4	100.0
Women					
All Nationalities	13.2	52.6	33.8	0.4	100.0
UK	13.1	52.9	33.6	0.4	100.0
Foreign Nationals	15.5	44.1	39.7	0.7	100.0
EC (exc Eire)	15.1	42.5	42.5	0.0	100.0
Eire	14.1	48.6	36.6	0.7	100.0
Rest of the world	16.7	41.4	40.9	1.0	100.0

market results in 'visible' immigrant groups being unable to access the jobs for which they are trained. This results in some immigrant groups consistently occupying jobs for which they are over-qualified, and as a result reduces their productive contribution relative to what would have been achieved in the absence of racial discriminiation. Phizacklea and Miles and Miles[46] have paid particular attention to the employment conditions of immigrants at the lower end of the labour market. They have noted the concentration of immigrants in certain industries—notably vehicle production, textiles and hotels and catering. The types of jobs which they take up often share the unfortunate characteristics of unsocial hours or an unpleasant working environment. Many researchers suggest that immigrant labour in these types of jobs provide a replacement workforce for positions in socially undesirable jobs vacated by the national workforce.

There is a considerable literature on the extent to which discrimination operates against immigrants, and in particular against certain ethnic groups seeking work or promotion in the British labour force. Undoubtedly unemployment rates are higher for certain ethnic minority groups (Table 6.3), and a considerable body of research suggests that this can largely be attributed to racial discrimination.[47] Amongst the positive results of this indictment on British society are the facts that 1) immigrant young people are more likely to stay on in education than their national peer group, and 2) social pressures may be responsible for the greater entrepreneurship of immigrants. De Beijl[48] reports that no less than 16% of immigrants were self-employed compared with 12% of nationals, with entrepreneurship being particularly high among Pakistani and Indian ethnic groups. Encouraging evidence is produced by Robinson[49] from the LFS to show that amongst Pakistani, Indian, and East African Asian ethnic minorities the percentages of the population experiencing upward social mobility has exceeded that of the population of UK origin.

Finally, in relation to the labour market impact of foreign immigration it is important to discuss a 1989 survey of British employers of foreign labour.[50] The survey was concerned to establish the reasons given by British companies for using foreign labour. The survey focussed on four sectors: electronic engineering, financial services, health, and hotels and catering. Most of those included in the survey confirmed that a major reason for employing foreign staff was the existence of a local skill shortage. To quote 'either skills were not available (e.g., in software or nursing) or indigenous labour had proved reluctant to migrate'.[51]

The survey reached the very important conclusion that there was little evidence of foreign labour being introduced as a substitute for training British nationals. Employers suggested that British nationals often shunned the jobs occupied by immigrants on account of the low wage levels of these jobs or their anti-social hours. In the South East, where most of the immigrant labour was found, tight labour market circumstances during most of the 1980s ensured that other better paid work was available for local labour, while many job seekers from other parts of the UK were dissuaded from coming to the region to poorly paid jobs because of the high cost of finding accommodation. This was not true of better paid jobs.[52] Another reason given for the use of immigrant labour[53] was that some companies saw international staff transfers as part of staff training and career development, and therefore looked favourably both on temporary emigration of British staff and temporary transfer into the UK of foreign staff.

This section has shown, therefore, that there is considerable evidence that immigration has beneficial effects for the British labour market. This is not to say that all immigration which occurs should be geared to this objective, and it remains true that many second and third-generation immigrants of certain ethnic groups remain at a disadvantage within the labour market through inadequately developed language skills, lack of relevant occupational training, discriminatory recruitment policies and other factors. On average, however, the evidence suggests that immigration (and not just those on short-term work permits) has served to increase the pool of skilled labour and to relieve skill shortages in other parts of the labour market. The involvement of foreign labour has not been a substitute to training the local population nor is there any body of evidence to suggest that immigration has cost jobs for the indigenous population.

Migration and dependency burden

It has been noted earlier in this paper that one of the main reasons advanced by policy makers for minimising immigration is the dependency burden which it might impose upon the state in terms of the costs of providing services and support to the immigrant community. Increased dependency is an issue of broader concern to the British Government because of the ageing of the indigenous population and consequently the adverse shift in the ratio of active to dependent people in the population. If migration were to be shown to add to the costs of servicing and supporting the dependent population, disproportionately relative to the tax contribution made by immigrants, then this concern would have some justification.

Green[54] has compared dependency ratios across the EC for 1985 and the projected populations of the EC states in 2025. Britain stands out uniquely in this analysis as the one state which has less than 30% of its population under 15 and less than 30% over 65 (both in 1985 and 2025). By the year 2025 there will be a small increase in the population over 65 relative to the numbers of elderly in 1985 and there will also be a drop in the number of under 15s. But the key point is that, of all EC countries, Britain should have less concern than any other over the issues surrounding increased dependency because of demographic ageing.

Table 6.10   Education Expenditure by Age Group, UK (1984–5)

	Total Spending (£m)	Spending per head (£)
Schools		
3–4	500	775
5–10	4300	1090
11–15	5500	1465
16–18	900	2275
Non-Advanced Further Education		
16–24	1300	2015
Higher Education		
16–24	3500	5325

Source: Pearson, Smith and White, 'Demographic Influences on Public Spending', Fiscal Studies, 1989.

It is of course true that dependency ratios are a very crude basis for measuring the economic impact of demographic influences. It has been shown that in Britain the highest expenditure groups for local government bodies are teenagers (11–15 years) during their secondary school years and the very elderly (over 75 years), because of the high costs of health and social services support.

Pearson, Smith and White[55] have illustrated these expenditure costs in terms of their calculations of cohort specific expenditure on the education and health services (Tables 6.10 and 6.11). *Per capita* expenditure on education of those in higher education is very great, but the overall cost to the state is not so high since participation rates in higher education are only 13% for those aged 19 or 20 years, compared with 94% participation for 11–15 year olds in secondary education. These rates are calculated in terms of FTEs (full-time equivalent staff) as a percentage of persons in the relevant age cohorts. The details of pension costs in relation to demographic ageing is another important issue, but one which is not addressed in this paper.

Turning to the migrant population in particular, with reference to the service costs which have been presented, there is one important point which needs to be made from the outset. It is that emigration (of both British and non-British citizens) must to some extent offset any effect of immigration in terms of the net costs of service provision. If for the moment the differential characteristics of immigrants and emigrants are put on one side, then it becomes important to ask to what extent immigrants simply replace emigrants in terms of housing costs, education costs, health service costs etc. The

Table 6.11 Spending per Head on Health and Personal Social Services (1989–92) (£ per head: figures rounded to nearest £)

Births	1300
0–4	400
5–15	300
16–64	200
64–74	600
75+	1600

Source: Pearson, Smith and White, 'Demographic Influences on Public Spending', Fiscal Studies, 1989.

Table 6.12 Summary Age Structure of Immigrants and Emigrants, UK (1990)

Age cohort	Immigrants (thousands)	Emigrants (thousands)
Under 15	41.3	41.1
15–24	85.5	67.9
25–44	118.9	104.5
45–59/64	16.3	14.2
60/65+	4.8	3.0

Source: OPCS (1991), International Migration, 1990. For more details see Bailey.[56]

time series information made available from the International Passenger Survey shows that Britain experienced net emigration throughout the 1960s and 1970s (except 1979). Between 1980 and 1990 net emigration occurred on four occasions.

If emigrants depart having received an investment from their country of origin in the form of previous education or training, or for example medical support, and end up working elsewhere and paying taxes elsewhere, then the net benefits in terms of the economics of the welfare system will accrue to the country of destination rather than of origin. Thus it must be argued that for most of the last three decades the British economy has been a loser through the migration system, because of net emigration from Britain—the familiar spectre of the 'brain drain'. It is ironic that, now this effect has ceased, the economic arguments have been forgotten and net immigration has been portrayed as imposing a dependency burden. No substantiated evidence has ever been produced to support this view.

Given that most emigrants and immigrants are in the most active age cohorts (in 1990, 81% of emigrants from Britain were between 15 and 59–64 years of age) it can generally be accepted that a situation of net emigration (other things being equal) will mean a net loss of resources from the welfare system, while net immigration should have the inverse effect.

A more detailed examination of British emigration and immigration flows in 1990 (using IPS data published in the OPCS monitor on *International Migration*) confirms that the migration system led in that year to a net out migration of persons under 10 years of age: a small inflow of 10–14 year olds, totalling a net gain of about 3,000 (the expensive cohort for education services): a large gain of persons aged 15–34 and 40 to 44 (the most active age cohorts in labour market terms, and in terms of tax raising—including poll tax paid by the economically inactive elements of the population): a net loss of persons in the 35 to 39 cohort and an almost even balance amongst the small number of older members of the population involved in immigration.

On the basis of this data it can be concluded that in Britain migration flows yielded an increase in that section of the population due to pay more in tax than they would expect to receive in educational, health and social benefits. Thus increased tax yield more than covers the cost of the small net gain of teenagers (still assuming that immigrant and emigrant populations have the same characteristics). The same net gain to financing the welfare system appears to have occurred in the majority of years in the 1980s through net immigration. By the same logic, in the 1970s, when net emigration was taking place, the age specific character of the migration process is likely to have had a negative effect in terms of the balance of investments made in British people who became migrants.

It is now relevant to relax the assumption that immigrants and emigrants share the same characteristics. Clearly activity rates, unemployment rates, birth rates, education costs and health and welfare costs vary by ethnic group and by immigrant nationality. No recent systematic data set exists, however, to inform the researcher of the current, or recent, tax receipts versus costs of supporting immigrants and their families. In the absence of such data it is impossible to robustly argue either that immigrants impose a net dependency burden on the UK economy or that they make a net contribution to the welfare services through direct and indirect taxation and through taxation to both central and local government. As mentioned earlier in this paper, the last study of this kind known to the author was undertaken by the National Institute in relation to the 1960–6 Commonwealth influx. The conclusion was that the net impact was likely to be positive. To quote from Jones and Smith:[57]

> There is some evidence that average income per employed New Commonwealth worker is lower than the national level, but we also know that labour force participation rates are higher for the New Commonwealth than for the indigenous population, so total household income may well not deviate much from the national average....While it is not practicable to estimate the relative contributions of immigrants in the form of national insurance contributions and tax payments, it seems unlikely that, if New Commonwealth immigrants do pay less, the difference would more than outweigh their smaller share of the social services.

Since the 1960s the migration system, as has been shown, has shifted considerably towards the acceptance of a lower proportion of immigrants for settlement and an increase in the proportion of entrants on short- or long-term work permits. The implications of this must be a shift away from immigration flows with long-term cost implications as settlers age, become inactive, and look increasingly towards welfare services and retirement benefits. Current immigration involves increasing numbers of skilled transients, who contribute to the tax base of the economy during their limited stay in the UK, but make relatively little demand on the so-called 'welfare state'. In addition the suggestion made in relation to Table 6.9 on the skill levels of the immigrant stock of the UK would point to immigrants having a greater potential to pay taxes than the local population, given their higher proportional respresentation amongst professional and managerial staff.

Much more detailed information is available about the so-called 'dependency burden' and tax contributions of immigrants to Canada and Australia.[58] A study carried out by the Economic Council of Canada in relation to Canada's published Immigration plan concludes that new immigrants, through paying extra taxes, make a small net contribution towards reducing Canada's demographic dependency burden. However, the 'reduction of the tax burden for the rest of the population is quite insignificant'.[59] In other words immigration as a policy measure would not be justified solely on the basis of reducing the dependency burden on the rest of the population, but on the other hand immigrants to Canada certainly are not expected to add to that

burden. The National Population Council for Australia[60] in addressing the same issues concludes that the impact of migrants on
government revenue and expenditure is much the same as for other
Australians except for three important areas:

- Most migrants enter Australia after having completed their
  education. Thus net transfers by migrants over a lifetime are
  likely to be higher than for other Australians.
- Because the average migrant is younger than the average
  Austrialian-born person, immigration over the next forty years
  will act to bolster numbers at working age when the large baby
  boom generations are in aged dependency.
- There are significant costs to governments in providing ethno-
  specific services, such as English language training.

Similar arguments seem valid in the UK situation. In both Canada
and Australia it is also argued that the increased investment in
physical infrastructure associated with population growth by immigration favours a larger overall population size on economic efficiency
grounds. This last argument seems less appropriate in a UK context
where, first, the overall population is already much greater, second the
nature of infrastructural investment has followed a very different
economic history, and third there is a stagnant or perhaps declining
population situation.

This section of the paper has sought to present the fragmentary
evidence which exists concerning the economic dependency burden
which might be imposed by immigration. It is concluded tentatively
that migrants to the UK are likely to make a very small net
contribution to the economy in terms of the balance between the taxes
paid relative to the extra expenditure required to support them. For
most of the 1970s and part of the 1980s the main problem for the UK
welfare system relative to migration was its position relative to a
system of net emigration. The situation of net immigration which has
emerged in recent years should not be a cause for economic concern.
Net immigration, under the present conditions, is not likely to impose
any net-costs on the British economy (in terms of the taxes versus
services trade-off) and may even produce small net gains. In these
economic circumstances politicians should consider very carefully the
arguments for a more liberal immigration policy, not only of those
persons who have valuable skills to contribute to the British economy
but also of those migrants who are seeking to enter the country as
refugees and on other bases.

Policy issues

This chapter has sought to examine the economic basis for Britain's position on immigration. It has been argued from evidence relating to the work permit system that there is clear evidence that British businesses need a certain level of immigration of certain skill groups. As pointed out in an earlier section of this paper, work permits are granted for a significant number of immigrant entries to the UK each year. The full scale of labour market demand for immigration cannot, however, be judged from the number of work permits issued. First, many applications made for labour permits by employees are turned down by the government. Second, very large numbers of Europeans enter Britain to work, yet need no work permit under EC law. Hence demand is much greater than shown by work permit data. For this reason the paper referred frequently to data from the International Passenger Survey to substantiate the views that there is a broader demand from the British economy for skilled transient migration from a range of destinations. Third, independent surveys of specific occupational groups such as nurses,[61] have been referred to to illustrate the point that the British economy could benefit substantially from selective immigration of a range of skilled labour.

In addition to selective labour immigration it has been noted that entrepreneurial migration could have significant economic benefits for Britain, just as it has had for other advanced economies. It has also been argued that refugees and immigration of less skilled labour does not result in significant net costs for the economy and may in the long run result in net gains. The question which this section of the paper addresses is whether government policy on immigration maximises the economic benefits which could be achieved.

Many of the skilled transient migrants, of the kind identified earlier in this paper as being of the greatest economic benefit to the United Kingdom, enter the country under the work permit system. Up until 1991 there were long delays in dealing with applications for work permits and the revision of the work permit system has been welcomed by most members of the business community. However, it is important to ask whether the system serves the British economy as a whole or only certain privileged groups. An analysis of work permits by Salt[62] shows that by far the majority are issued to skilled workers from only two countries—Japan and the USA and that most of these permits are for people who gain employment in the South East of

England. This undoubtedly reflects the high proportion of permits which are allocated for inter-company transfers by trans-national corporations from Japan and the USA. It is only a slight exaggeration to say that the current work permit system exists primarily to serve trans-national employees wishing to enter the South East.

Why do skilled workers from other countries, and to other parts of the UK, gain so few work permits? The answer to this is complex, but includes the following elements. First, immigrants from the EC (and from EFTA countries from January 1994) are not required to have work permits. Therefore the work permit system does not fully reflect the substantial demand for foreign labour which exists in Britain, since many of the most important countries are not covered by the scheme, but International Passenger Survey and Labour Force Survey data show that substantial skill exchanges of similar types of immigrants (in professional and economic terms) take place with the EC.

Second, work permits are granted on the basis of applications by employers rather than by immigrants. Consequently, skills are more likely to be introduced from those countries with which employers have strong contacts, irrespective of whether this is the most appropriate source in terms of the benefits to the British economy. The system does not serve well those immigrants who have skills needed by the British economy, but who are not well linked to potential employers.

Third, there is no clearly established basis by which the Department of Employment determines those skills which are in acute short supply in the UK and, as noted earlier, the list of occupations appear to change very frequently and without explanation or notice. Some commentators would suggest that employers are in a better position to judge their labour requirements than the Department of Employment, and would therefore question the level of work permit refusals. The lack of transparency in the decision making process opens the system to criticism by those who fail to receive work permits.   Fourth, the scheme is not designed to assist entrepreneurial immigration of persons who may be self-employed. As noted earlier, a separate channel does exist for business immigration but this is defined on the basis of applicants proving that they have a large capital sum available for investment in job creating opportunities, rather than on evidence of entrepreneurial potential.

Fifth, one effect of the streamlining of tier one applications for work permits may simply have been to create longer delays for tier two applicants, although it is still too early to be sure about the long-term effects of the switch in the policy.

Sixth, the revised work permit scheme no longer has a section on the application form (as under the old scheme) which permits potential migrants and their employers to present economic arguments for being granted entry to the British labour market. Only the Department of Employment is effectively given the right to judge which skills are needed, with no opportunity for applicants to demonstrate their economic value.

Finally, the revised system has made it much harder for work permits to be extended than under the old scheme. Currently employers need to promote full documentation to obtain an extension to a work permit, for an employee which the Department of Employment has already judged to be of economic value in relation to the initial application. As a result the costs to a company of sustaining foreign labour has risen as a result of the revision to the work permit scheme. In summary, the work permit system used by Britain seems to serve primarily as a form of entry control, of blocking or delaying the temporary immigration of would-be migrants from outside the EC who do not have strong contacts with a large scale employer in the UK. It is not primarily a system which seeks, on a rational economic basis, to achieve labour market adjustments through immigration to meet the broader needs of the British economy.

If the needs of the economy were to be met, then a much lower priority should be assigned within the work permit scheme to protecting the resident labour force. In place of this the scheme should 'rely more on employers' judgement of their own needs',[63] implying a much lower rejection rate of work permit applications by employers. In 1991 the refusal rate for the main scheme was 19.6%; in 1990 it was 20.8%. For Commonwealth nationals, however, the refusal rate in 1991 was 35.3%, for foreign nationals only 13.5%. Initial data for 1992 suggests that the new procedures may have reduced the number of refusals.[64]

In addition greater investment would be required to research systematically the skilled needs of the British economy so that appropriate migrants could be actively encouraged to come to UK, in contrast to the current system which remains purely reactive to limited requests.

Perhaps the greatest problem for Britain is that the work permit system is concerned with temporary migrants and consequently involves work permits of limited duration. No clear migration channel exists to permit immigration of persons who are capable of making a contribution to Britain's economy on a permanent basis other than the rather exclusive business scheme for persons with £200,000 or more. Permanent settlement is assumed to relate to cases of family re-unification or persons seeking asylum in the UK. While such entrants may make a significant economic contribution, the nature of immigration legislation for these two latter categories tries to separate out 'genuine' cases from so-called 'economic' migrants, thus implying (without any evidence to support the case) that refugees and spouses are 'uneconomic' and that all other categories of permanent immigrants are to be dissuaded from entering the country, regardless of any economic contibution which they could make.

Thus, if Britain were to adopt an immigration policy which was to truly serve the needs of the economy, it would require not only an improved work permit system to cope with short-run fluctuations in demand but also a longer term strategy. Other countries operate a range of schemes selectively to recruit key workers. Most notorious are the quota systems used in North America. Poorly managed or misinformed systems run the risk of promoting permanent immigration of skills not required by the economy, but Britain's lack of any scheme for meeting the economy's long-term labour needs is equally unsatisfactory. More adequate labour market research and long-term skill needs is required, coupled to a pro-active rather than re-active system of selecting persons for permanent settlement.

If evidence from countries as disparate as Germany and Canada is to be believed, advanced economies have much to gain from permanent immigration of certain skill groups. These countries have adopted very different policies on immigration from the UK. Two aspects are highlighted here. The first is the information base on which decisions about immigration are taken. The second is the machinery used to select migrants.

The quality of cohort data for immigrant groups in Australia has already been discussed. This data has been used to good effect in advising government on alternative scenarios for future immigration, making it possible to estimate the social integration and contribution of different groups over time.[65] In Canada, cohort data is also available for immigrants by place of birth and period of immigration to Canada cross-tabulated by key variables such as language proficiency, labour force participation rates adjusted for age, unemployment levels and duration, earnings and occupational status, occupational distribution by gender, and receipt of government welfare assistance. Analysis of this detailed information makes it possible to make informed policy decisions about immigration options for Canada.[66] In Britain the Labour Force Survey gives only limited insights on some of these issues and no systematic monitoring of immigrant cohorts has been attempted in recent years to examine the overall economic impact of immigrant groups.

The second main distinction worthy of note here is that countries such as the USA and Canada select immigrants on the basis of a migration policy which decides migration quotas for each year, and selects immigrants for these quotas on the basis of a points system. Such an approach faces a range of problems, such as determining accurately in advance which skill categories should be encouraged to migrate and which should be discouraged. Another oft cited difficulty is that, while migrants may enter under one part of the quota system, (e.g. in relation to a particular skill group) it is not easy to ensure that they remain in this category after being granted entry. What is important however is that the system signals to potential immigrants the desire of the host country to mould their labour market in a positive fashion.

Britain seems to see immigration as a threat to an existing social or economic order. Immigration policy appears to be constructed largely to protect an established identity by limiting immigrant entry to privileged economic and social relations. By contrast Canadian, US and Australian immigration policy seems to view immigraton as of much greater economic benefit to the host society. Immigration is perceived as a means to build the future and immigration policy is used to select those migrants which are most likely to participate in the building of the new identities of the future.

This paper has not argued that Britain should model itself in migration terms on any other country, whether European or North American. Britain has experienced specific historical and geographical circumstances which have positioned it in a particular location in relation to the world labour market and relative to international labour migration systems. Its migration policies need to be tailored to this context. What the paper has argued, however, is that a selective immigration policy which takes greater account of the economic dimensions of international skill transfers would be rather different from the current policy. It would consider new ways to facilitate entrepreneurial immigration. It would see positive economic potential in many of the persons who apply to enter as refugees and it would switch from a philosophy of excluding potential migrants to 'protect' the status quo, to a system of positive selection of those immigrants with most to contribute to Britain.

Conclusions

This paper has tried to explore certain economic aspects of immigration. It has argued that immigration statistics should not be confused with data on certain ethnic minorities. An economic case for immigration cannot rest purely on evidence of economic growth outpacing labour force growth, nor on labour force projections which identify a reduction or stagnation in labour supply. It has been shown that these are not sufficient conditions to argue for immigration.

Three aspects of labour demand do, however, provide grounds to suggest that labour market benefits for Britain could arise from encouraging selective immigration. First, it has been argued that certain skill shortages exist within the UK economy which, in the short run at least, should continue to be overcome through immigration of persons via the British work permit scheme. Second, it has been argued that changes in the organisation of labour, in particular within large international companies, necessitate the international circulation of staff. Third, it has been mentioned briefly that there may be grounds for encouraging entrepreneurial immigration as a device which generates jobs rather than filling jobs by immigration. In the absence of robust data sets it is difficult to judge the overall economic impact of less skilled immigration to the UK. The limited survey material which is available would suggest that this type of immigration is not at the cost of the indigenous workforce, neither causing job losses nor job displacement.

Throughout this paper evidence has been produced in relation to virtually every aspect of the immigration system to show that inadequate research by government and a poor statistical base is a source of misinformation and weak policy making. Evaluation of British labour market trends led to the conclusion that policy makers need to determine urgently whether there are selective skill shortages which are damaging the UK economy and how best these can be met. In relation to the British work permit scheme it has been argued that the government has failed to invest in adequate data collection mechanisms to meet the short-run needs of the economy. In relation to the economic costs of immigration it has been shown that no comprehensive survey has been undertaken since the 1960s. In short, government immigration policy has no adequate research data base to justify its economic objections to higher levels of immigration. Nor does data exist to support the application of policy tools such as the work-permit scheme in its present form. Providing an adequate statistical base should be a pre-requisite to any further policy developments on immigration, regardless of their objectives or political orientation.

It has been argued that Britain holds a negative ideology towards immigration and may as a result gain much less in economic terms from immigration than might otherwise be achieved. It would seem that the government's current stand on immigration is not determined primarily on economic grounds. If it is to sustain its current policies, a stronger economic argument against immigration needs to be made and to be supported by economic data. In the absence of such data and in the face of the economic arguments which have been presented in favour of immigration in this paper, one is forced to conclude that current British immigration policy is governed primarily by political and cultural considerations. If Britain is to avoid the accusation of being racist in its immigration stance, then a serious economic investigation of the grounds of immigration policy seems long overdue.

7 AN ASYLUM POLICY FOR THE UK

Chris Randall

A consideration of an asylum policy for the UK raises the question of how long there will be distinctive national procedures at all, rather than a common European one. This paper proceeds on the basis that it is still important to articulate a UK policy. This is first because, in the short term at least, there will be a procedure distinctive to the UK, although European influences grow all the time on both substantive and procedural levels. Second, because whether or not the UK chooses to participate in the European developments, its policy will affect (and be affected by) the course of those developments. Third, because if the UK is to have an impact upon European policy, or even if it seeks to maintain a separate policy, it is important to be confident of our own practice.

A basic premise underlying this chapter is that to articulate an asylum policy means to accept that, for all those who would benefit from the application of the obligations and procedures proposed, there will also be those who would be excluded. It is therefore on the applicable definitions and procedures that I will concentrate. But the fact that I will do this does not mean that there should not be other aspects to the Government's policy on refugee issues, for instance preventative policies in relation to the causes of refugee flows and integrative policies for refugees who are protected here. But these issues are beyond the scope of this chapter.

I have also had to decide the extent to which any proposals should be influenced by domestic and European *Realpolitik*. I have decided to refer explicitly to these pressures throughout; trying to identify best practice but looking at the achievability of that practice given the national and European context.

I do not propose, however, to deal in detail with the European context. Some of the material is well known and the issues are being dealt with elsewhere in this volume. In addition, the European scenario is changing fast. For convenience, I shall summarise those recent European developments which must form the background of a consideration of future UK policy and illuminate the direction of developments to come.

There has been a growth of inter-governmental agreements on a variety of migration issues, many of which impinge directly or indirectly on refugees. There is Schengen, on the gradual abolition of border checks between an increasing number of mainland European countries; the Dublin Convention and draft parallel conventions, on the appropriate determining country for asylum applications; and the draft Convention on the Crossing of the External Borders. There is the pressure at community level to move to the abolition of internal border controls. There is a raft of on-going inter-governmental consultations away from public scrutiny on all these and other issues; and there is the Maastricht Treaty which continues the Europeanisation of asylum policy in a characteristically undemocratic way. Finally, there are strong European pressures towards the harmonisation of substantive asylum laws and procedures.[1]

It is important to note that these changes have not been matched by any growth in the democratic control of the developing European asylum policy, or in the establishment of fora in which differing interpretations of vital refugee concepts can be litigated. An early example of the way in which things are moving was the hawkish report in 1991 of the Ad Hoc Group on Immigration.[2] This document looks to harmonisation to achieve conformity of treatment of asylum seekers throughout Europe and specifically mentions states' concerns about the differing ease of access to de facto status (known as exceptional leave to remain in the UK). It prioritises the need for harmonisation in relation to 'manifestly unfounded (MUF) cases' and to the issues of 'first safe country' and goes into considerable detail about the definition and indicative factors of MUF applications.

The report sets out a detailed work programme of activity for European States which should be of great concern to those with the interests of refugees at heart. The work is proceeding at speed. Thus the 'Clearing House' referred to in the programme met for the first time in October 1992 and the UK presidency announced priority plans to discuss issues like MUF cases, safe countries, country of origin, harmonisation of asylum law and procedures and implementation of the Dublin Convention. These are indeed important issues and it is of course possible, if unlikely, that the discussion could lead to a liberal definition of safe countries and to rejection of the concept of MUF cases. But consider the absence from this prioritised agenda of issues such as family reunion, of strategies to oppose anti-refugee activities in countries providing protection, of the facilitation of access to protection and to the release of information which is available to governments and to advisers. It is clear that the ideology of the agenda is highly restrictive.

As we look at an asylum policy for the UK, we have to take account of how any local proposals would deal with these European developments, although we may seek to identify ways in which the UK can either hold out against or influence these trends which are generally not in the interest of the asylum seekers.

Human rights background

In addition to this political parameter, the other parameter for a UK asylum policy is the human rights framework of the 1951 UN Refugee Convention taken with other human rights standards. We must first look to the Refugee Convention itself, then to the United Nations High Commissioner for Refugees 1979 *Handbook on Procedures*, to the Conclusions of the Executive Committee of the UNHCR programme (Excom) and to the European Convention on Human Rights (ECHR).

A review of these sources finds them wanting. The Refugee Convention itself is virtually silent on determination procedures. There is relevant material in the *Handbook*,[3] but this does not go beyond 'basic requirements' and the listing of certain essential guarantees of a determination procedure (summarised below). It makes, for instance, no detailed recommendations about appeal procedures. There are specific Excom Conclusions which are relevant and to which I will allude in this chapter, although, like the *Handbook*, these are not binding on states, a point which the UK makes explicitly whenever it is faced with Conclusions which cause it difficulty. Finally, it has to be said that the ECHR has not proved to be the useful tool for migrants and particulary refugees for which many advisers had hoped (see for instance the decision in *Vilvarajah* in 1991)[4]. Mention should also be made of other instruments such as the Universal Declaration of Human Rights and the Convention Against Torture. But these instruments remain of little use for fleshing out the details of a determination procedure.

It should also be said that recently UNHCR has itself been equivocal on asylum policy issues. Some of its policy positions have been tempered by its own political difficulties in a hostile world. Certainly, its statements cannot always be relied upon as touchstones for asylum seekers. For example, in the Second Reading of the Asylum and Immigration Appeals Bill in the House of Lords, the UK Government was able to quote favourably a statement by the UNHCR Director of International Protection that 'a majority of people coming as asylum seekers into Europe are not refugees but economic migrants'.[5] There was an earlier damaging statement by the then High Commissioner Stoltenburg that less than 10% of asylum seekers arriving in Europe were fleeing persecution.[6] In one recent UNHCR document it was suggested that 50–60% of applications were manifestly unfounded.[7] This ambivalence can be seen on a more practical level in the landmark *Vilvarajah* case where the effect of the UNHCR request to European governments not to return Tamil asylum seekers to Sri Lanka was undermined by a UNHCR-sponsored voluntary repatriation programme between India and Sri Lanka for Tamils at the same time.

The increase in applications: a problem for states?

The perceived problem with which European countries and the UNHCR have been grappling can be put succinctly: the number of asylum applicants in Western Europe has risen significantly in the last five years. In the UK, the number of asylum seekers (excluding dependents) rose from around 4,000 a year during 1985–8 to 44,800 in 1991, although it fell to 24,600 in 1992 and remained at about that level in the first part of 1993. In Western Europe overall, asylum applications continued to increase in 1992, although the UK was not alone in experiencing a fall in numbers. Of the 34,900 cases decided in the UK in 1992, 3% were granted refugee status, 44% were given exceptional leave to remain and 53% were refused.[8] This increase would be of grave concern to states even if all applicants were Convention Refugees, since the increase feeds their wider concerns about migration pressures. It is however claimed by states that a large proportion of these applications are not well-founded and that slow determination procedures, a lack of expulsion powers, and the weakness of some states' wills in this respect make a speedy resolution of these applications impossible. As negative decisions are more difficult to make and harder to enforce as time goes by, asylum is seen by states as a weak link in an otherwise vigorously defended border system.

I would like to make a key distinction here which is often overlooked: that is, between fraudulent and/or abusive applications and applications which are merely not well-founded, i.e., which, on analysis, may not satisfy the narrow Refugee Convention definition. The Convention defines a refugee as someone with a well-founded fear of persecution, a definition which is far more limited than that in common parlance which includes those, for instance, who are fleeing from starvation. [9] In no sense therefore should one look at a refusal rate of Convention refugees and conclude that all those refused were in some sense bogus. Someone may have a well-founded fear of persecution but not for one of the reasons set out in the Convention. Someone may have failed the test which requires a risk of persecution to be reasonable, but only by a small margin. Equally, in the UK they may have failed to comply with a particular requirement (for instance providing fingerprints) which under the new Asylum and Immigration Appeals Act (the 'Act') can justify a refusal; or with a particular time limit. Thus an increased number of refusals is not necessarily a measure of an increase of 'bogus' applicants. However, the fact that governments have been able to claim that many applicants are not 'genuine refugees' has had a considerable impact on the debate about refugee determination procedures.

States' concern about the increase in applications ought, moreover, to be tempered by the fact that the vast majority of refugees still remain in developing countries with significantly lower standards of living than those in the West. In global terms, 'burden-sharing' has not yet even begun. The continued failure of the North to re-settle the Vietnamese refugees from Hong Kong over a period of many years is obvious evidence of this as is the failure to deal with the refugee problem from former Yugoslavia. Looked at from this perspective, 'the refugee problem' in Europe is small and Europe's reaction hysterical.

States are assisted in portraying the increase in numbers of applicants as 'abusive' by the fact that it has been mirrored by a general fall in recognition rates. A number of points need to be made about this. First, the states' inconsistent practices have a significant impact on these statistics. Substantive refugee law has not been harmonised. As a result, applications with the same factual basis, from different countries of origin may obtain different results in different countries at the same time (or even, from a cynical UK practitioner's viewpoint, in the same country at the same time).

There is no doubt, however, that recognition rates of Convention refugees are generally low (for instance Germany 20%, France 7%, Denmark 2.5%, Switzerland 2.5% and the UK 10%). But there has also until recently been a concomitant increase in the number of people denied Convention status but granted de facto status, or at least not forcibly removed from the territory. Thus as yet, the low Convention recognition rates are not matched by high expulsion rates, although there is a question as to how long it will be before the category of de facto status is also put under pressure, a process which can already be seen to be starting in the UK.[10]

We thus have a situation where it appears that a substantial proportion of applicants seeking protection in Europe under the Convention are said by states to fail to come within its terms, but where a significant number of those 'failed' applicants still obtain some sort of protection. This state of affairs has very real consequences for all asylum seekers, both those who get protection and those who are ultimately denied it; and for deciding what is an appropriate determination procedure to distinguish between the two.

A new Convention?

One response to this increased number of applications and grants of de facto status has been to consider reform of the Refugee Convention, leading to a variety of policy options. First, there are those who say that the Convention is too narrow; applicants needing protection do not get it, so a new Convention is required to give them that protection. Second it is said that the Convention is correctly and narrowly interpreted; those applicants who currently fall outside its ambit are rightly excluded and 'true' refugees are better protected by the maintenance of the distinction.[11] Third there are those, including Geoff Gilbert in this volume, who argue that the Convention is potentially wide enough for our purposes (or at least wider than is generally accepted) and that the problem is one of jurisprudential failure, following strict determinations by states.

These analyses often make reference to other international instruments, notably the Convention of the Organisation of African States and the Cartagena Declaration, but to justify a number of different arguments. To some these instruments, with their wider definition of persecution (including natural disasters, civil wars, famine etc) mark qualitative developments in the field and as such can be used to buttress the argument for a new, wider Refugee Convention; alternatively they can be used as examples of interpretations, rather than extensions of the Convention which therefore could be mirrored by Western European jurisprudence, if only the will were there.

On a more practical level it is said, particularly by governments, that there are asylum seekers in Western Europe who are merely in flight from civil war, or from economic collapse and are therefore not Convention refugees. On civil war, Kälin has argued that there are circumstances in which civil war victims can be included within the Refugee Convention (i.e., that their exclusion may be partly a question of interpretation).[12] Then again, others have argued that the Refugee Convention marks a useful boundary for states' obligations in this field. This approach may now be seen in practice in relation to former Yugoslavia as we see new categories of 'displaced persons' which are explicitly designed to fall on the wrong side of the refugee definition, with more limited protection and settlement rights.

Of course, for those people who are particularly conscious of the inadequacies of current determination procedures, a new Convention might be attractive in order to spell out in more detail the basic requirements of a determination system or to widen the refugee definition to include ELR cases. But even the 1977 UN Conference on Asylum failed to come to agreement on this point, and this at a time when opinion was generally more favourable to refugees. This and the current international climate on the asylum issue suggests that those seeking to assist asylum seekers should be reluctant to open up a debate upon the Convention at this time. One has only to look at the current European agenda to conclude that the outcome could well be to lower protection standards yet further, at both substantive and procedural levels. Even if the UK were to take the moral high ground on such a project, the current state of opinion elsewhere might well lead to a weakening of protection for asylum seekers.

The practical consequences of the increase: the rise (and fall?) of de facto status

The debate on a new Convention may seem rarefied, but it does address the fact that there is a large number of asylum seekers who pass through determination procedures, are not granted refugee status but nonetheless achieve some kind of tolerated status in Western

Europe. Some sort of determination of would-be refugees is necessary. But is there any point in Europe spending large sums of money (£10 billion in 1992 according to the *Financial Times*)[13] in determining whether somebody is a refugee of not if, in fact, in the most important sense of whether the applicant is allowed to remain, it does not matter whether the person is found to be a Convention or de facto refugee? Should we not be spending the budget elsewhere, perhaps in prevention work in countries of origin? And can we be confident that states will continue to allow the result to make little difference?

These questions are not just humanitarian and political but of practical relevance to determination procedures. In the UK there is a strong incentive for people who are granted ELR to re-enter the procedure immediately. This is for a number of reasons. There will always be hard cases requiring reconsideration; and flaws in the system and the uneven quality of advice mean that the initial decision may just be wrong. However, the climate of insecurity fostered by recent debate means that many applicants wish to obtain refugee status if at all possible because they feel more secure under the protection of the Refugee Convention than the state-driven political expediency of ELR. Moreover, many asylum seekers are men travelling alone who have left their families abroad. As Convention refugees they have an immediate right to family reunion. With ELR status they may wait for 4 or 7 years from decision before they can bring in their family and even then only in specific circumstances.

There is thus an incentive to re-apply to upgrade this status for a majority of applicants. Furthermore and most surprisingly, in any case of refusal of asylum and grant of ELR, an applicant has to re-enter either the determination or the appeal procedure (or both) before he or she can receive a reasoned decision. Thus it is possible for an asylum seeker interviewed in 1987 to find out only in 1992 that the interviewing Immigration Officer forgot to send vital documentary evidence provided at the interview to the determining authority, the Home Office, the only mechanism for that discovery being the lodging and prosecution of first a reapplication and then an appeal.

If one is trying to define a fair and efficient system, then one which invites most applicants to go through it twice and encourages lengthy appeals which only result in some achieving in (say) 2 years what most will achieve in 4 or 7 hardly seems sensible. Rather, it is a complete waste of resources.

It may be suggested that, in years to come, the numbers of applicants given de facto status will fall. This was for instance argued by the then Under Secretary of State in meetings about the first Asylum Bill in 1991 in respect of those cases where ELR is granted as a result of 'delay in consideration'. In my view he was over-estimating the number of cases in which delay is the determining factor. In fact, the growth of the ELR category in the UK has much to do with the Government's vain hope that the political situation in certain countries would ameliorate and allow the speedy return of some people with ELR (the classic example being Sri Lanka). I also think there is little doubt that in fact, although the Minister would not admit it, it was his hope that other applicants who would have, in the past, been candidates for ELR would not achieve that status under the new proposals.

In my view, however, it may well be difficult for states to reduce greatly the proportion of people granted de facto status and to implement a more vigourous expulsion policy. This is because, first, there is basic merit in a substantial proportion of the cases in which ELR is now granted. Reduce the possibility of ELR and you may see more grants of refugee status by the Courts. Second, however the candidates for removal are chosen, it will not be long before reports of human rights abuses inflicted upon returned asylum seekers filter back to determining countries. The UK Government faced exactly this problem when it developed the political will to try and return Tamils to Sri Lanka in 1987. The policy failed dismally and had (ironically through the case of *Vilvarajah*) a direct impact on the determination procedure debate which this paper now addresses. It will probably become easier to track returned asylum seekers in years to come. Where persecution does occur then a sophisticated analysis (in accordance with case-law) as to whether it was 'reasonably likely' that persecution would occur, or whether that persecution was in the end 'for a Convention reason', may satisfy some of the Courts, and some academics; but there is a real question as to whether it will satisfy public opinion.

This optimism should be tempered by the continued refinement by states of measures to prevent asylum seekers from reaching their borders in the first place and by the spread of public anti-refugee feeling. But if this general view is correct and these de facto refugees are in the end to be protected by states, then this has important consequences for the design of the determination system: is it then worth continuing the distinction between Convention and de facto refugees? Would not a process which simply decided whether someone should be protected, and which attached the same Convention protection and family reunion rights to either category, be more efficient, more cost effective and fairer than the current reliance upon the particular Refugee Convention definition and on individual state policy? The radical approach would be to apply a broader definition to identify those in need of protection, to provide reasoned decision in the case of refusal and to equalise the rights immediately available to all recipients of that protection in relation to family reunion etc. This would have a substantial effect in terms of the numbers of appeals and re-applications and would prevent any further drift towards the creation of a 'second class' of refugee in Europe.

At the very least there should be a change to incorporate a definition of ELR into the Immigration Rules. Until this occurs it is not possible even to litigate upon the grant or denial of ELR within the UK appeal structure, a vital check upon the states' use of the concept. Of course there are costs in defining such a fundamentally discretionary concept in the Rules, the arguments against incorporation at this time being similar to those against negotiating a new Convention. If, however, ELR were entrenched in law, then this might protect it from the attacks it is likely to face in any event in coming years.

Access to territory and to procedures

There has been increasing debate over *access* to procedures in recent years, with the development of concepts such as the 'International Zone' in mainland Europe which seek to exclude asylum applicants from local jurisdictions even after they have physically reached a safe country. Fortunately this issue has not been a live one in the UK for some time. The main area of debate here has been on carrier sanctions with which I shall deal below. There is another problem, however, which asylum seekers have to overcome before the difficulties which carrier sanctions raise.

Visas

The major and rather unquestioned plank of control of asylum seekers is the visa system. Historically some categories of travellers have been required to have visas together with a growing number of nationalities. The current moves towards a common European visa are well known. The problem for an asylum seeker attempting to travel to the

UK is that, as soon as any country begins to be seen as a refugee producing country, visas are imposed on its nationals. Thus, one of the worrying but predictable elements of the Maastricht Treaty is a scheme for the introduction of emergency visas in situations of mass influx.

If one looks at the countries upon which the UK has imposed visas over the last few years they are generally refugee producing (Sri Lanka, Ghana, Turkey, Bosnia to name the most obvious examples). However there is no provision within the UK Immigration Rules for the issue of visas to refugees as a category. The exceptional issue of visas to asylum applicants either in countries of origin or in third countries is often referred to by the British Government, but rarely seen. Interestingly, the Danes do have this provision in respect of applications from third countries although the requirement for a close connection with Denmark greatly reduces the advantages of this procedure, particularly as the asylum applicant is not in Denmark to participate in the determination process.[14] Generally the position in law of the asylum seeker seeking a visa in his/her own country is heavily circumscribed by the Convention definition which requires a refugee to be *outside* the country of origin.

The visa regime is thus a substantial barrier to asylum seekers. It encourages the use of false documents and deceit to circumvent it; yet the use of these documents is then used to attack the credibility of asylum seekers. It is a good example of one of the measures used to prevent asylum seekers from ever reaching the determination procedures of Western European countries. That said, visas are also a well established part of immigration control generally, which in international law is a legitimate concern of states. Once we accept that there are migratory pressures generally towards Europe, it might well be said that, if the UK sought to try to lift visa restrictions from asylum seekers or to have a 'refugee visa' in some sense, that change would have an effect on non-refugee migration patterns.

If a visa-national could go to an Embassy and escape the visa regime by setting out a desire to claim asylum in the UK, then there would be a strong incentive for would-be migrants who are not asylum seekers and who might otherwise have difficulties in satisfying the visa regime, to use that route, at least to reach the United Kingdom's borders. Moreover, few practitioners would relish the prospect of diplomatic posts abroad determining whether somebody really *was* coming to the UK to seek refugee status, given the suspect performance of those posts on other issues and the difficulty of challenging administrative decisions taken thousands of miles away. So the visa issue is fraught with difficulties.

It has been argued in respect of visas that there are obligations on states not to obstruct the right of individuals to flee from persecution. A variant of this argument is considered below in respect of carrier sanctions; I suspect that it will always succeed better on paper than in practice.

The unilateral abolition of visas alone might not act as a substantial pull factor in relation to asylum applicants so long as carrier sanctions remain. But there is little doubt that there would be a substantial pull factor if *both* carrier sanctions and visa controls were abolished in the UK, particularly if they remained in force in Europe. The UK is a popular flight destination and transit point from many parts of the world. A policy which greatly increases the liability of the UK to receive asylum applicants and is not accompanied by radical and effective burden-sharing proposals within the rest of Europe is doomed politically for the moment. Furthermore the chances of persuading our European partners by our unilateral policy to make this change multilaterally would seem rather small. Indeed the Draft convention on the crossing of external borders contains a common list of visa requirements.

Carrier sanctions

The second area of debate about access to procedures is around carrier sanctions. The tendency for states to impose sanctions upon carriers delivering undocumented passengers grew in the 1980s. Five European countries have already introduced a variety of such measures. The supplementary Schengen agreement will make them compulsory, as does the Draft Convention on the crossing of external borders. The current rash of carrier sanctions are however, by no means the first or the only sanctions upon carriers. In the UK the carrier has long been responsible for the detention costs and removal expenses of a passenger who is detained and refused leave to enter. Thus there was already an incentive upon a carrier to check documentation and/or admissibility of passengers prior to embarkation, before the introduction of the Immigration (Carriers Liability) Act 1987, the doubling of fines in 1991 and the extension of sanctions to transit visas in the new Act. This is not to say that the imposition of further carrier sanctions should not be opposed because it is merely an extension of an existing practice. Rather, it should be opposed as taking states further down an already objectionable road.

A discussion of the future of carrier sanctions can usefully commence with a consideration of the arguments currently deployed against them. The first is that they are in some sense in breach of international law and the spirit of the Refugee Convention. This argument relies on Article 14.1 of the Universal Declaration of Human Rights; 'to seek and enjoy in other countries asylum from persecution'; on the preamble to the Refugee Convention; and on the Vienna Convention on the Application of Treaties. Carrier sanctions, it is argued, are in breach of Article 31(2) of the Refugee Convention in that they are in some sense a *penalty* imposed upon an asylum seeker for illegal entry.

Close scrutiny is generally also given to the Chicago Convention on International Civil Aviation. The argument has mainly been defensive, attempting to limit the use of the Chicago Convention as a justification for sanctions. Feller argues, for instance, that the 'Chicago Convention requires compliance by passengers with entry formalities and calls on airlines to assist in this regard, not to enforce it'.[15] But at least one UNHCR document has stated that carrier sanctions are *not* necessarily against international law and elsewhere the arguments set out above have been dismissed, for instance by Hailbronner.[16] In my view it is unlikely that there is a legal forum in which carrier sanctions per se can ultimately be successfully challenged. There is important outstanding domestic litigation in a number of individual state jurisdictions. But if asked whether there is an obligation in law for states to facilitate access to territory (and therefore procedures), then in my view most domestic and international Courts will reply in the negative.

A further argument focuses on practicalities. Carrier sanctions encourage airline employees who are both untrained and probably unsympathetic (since driven by monetary considerations), to become the de facto determining authority; this is in breach of the spirit of the Convention, of specific Excom conclusions and of paragraphs of the *Handbook* which require determinations by a central authority. There are disturbing examples from the UK of airlines hindering or preventing the access of asylum seekers to the determining authority, even though the asylum seeker had reached UK territory. There is also evidence from the UK that the procedure for enforcing fines on certain state airlines may heighten the risk of revealing to that state the fact that the undocumented applicant has sought asylum and may cause retaliation against relatives who remain in the persecuting state.

The second argument focuses on the continuing increase in the number of asylum seekers in Western European countries despite the imposition of sanctions and poses the question whether carrier sanctions work. It must be said that the new wave of carrier sanctions vary in terms of detail and implementation from country to country with the UK leading the way in extent and enforcement. There is certainly no European homogeneity. A recent summary of litigation in relation to carrier sanctions points out that, in the countries studied (UK, Germany, Denmark, Canada and Belgium), the number of asylum applications made at airports has declined but only in the face of generally increasing numbers of applications elsewhere in the asylum system.[17]

These findings echo the warnings of those who refer to carrier sanctions as 'a forgers' charter' (since how else can most asylum seekers get beyond the airport) and the views of those who posit a 'zero sum' of migrants who, if thwarted in one way, reappear in another. Lord Mackie, in his report to the Council of Europe on the treatment of asylum seekers on arrival at European airports is of the view that carrier sanctions have increased the use of forged travel documents. However, in the final analysis the causality in the relationship between numbers and sanctions is not clear. The relationships between the changing pattern of applications and reduced internal border controls, unlawful removals and fraud in relation to welfare benefits have yet to be established. Suffice to say that there is a real question as to whether carrier sanctions are preventing or merely redistributing asylum applications.

UNHCR's position on sanctions[18] is that:

> while states have a legitimate interest in controlling measures, including visas, they are acting inconsistently with international obligations towards refugees when such measures hinder the access of refugees both to status determination and to asylum.

Feller argues that carrier sanction legislation threatens to undermine 'basic principles and refugee protection'. However, ultimately it is telling that she pays more attention to ameliorating the legislative approaches of states than to outlawing sanctions through arguments drawn from international law.

In a system where both Schengen and the Draft Convention on External Borders propose carrier sanctions it is difficult to foresee their unilateral abandonment. In my view, even if that were to happen, it would probably make little difference to access to procedures. Visa restrictions would remain, and these alone are a powerful protection for states. Moreover, it is difficult to imagine airlines which depart from 'refugee producing' countries ceasing their rigorous control of documentation on flights to London and Manchester to concentrate their resources on flights to Paris.

If carrier sanctions are to remain, there ought to be a system of rebates for airlines where undocumented applicants *are* granted leave to enter, or are deemed to have an arguable claim to asylum. Moreover, airlines should only be liable if they have been shown to be negligent. The French law required by France's Schengen obligations is a model in this respect. UNHCR has argued the need for a scheme requiring 'recklessness' on behalf of a carrier and which requires no judgement by airlines on the merit of a claim or the validity of documents.

Finally, it needs to be recalled that fair and efficient determination procedures for asylum seekers would be a substantial deterrent to those who seek to use asylum procedures only as a means of gaining admission to a territory, if speed is seen as integral to fairness and efficiency. This approach is attractive to those seeking to protect refugees since it at least has the merit of bothering to identify them. UNHCR also takes this view.[19]

In all the arguments which consider the role of carrier sanctions in a humane asylum determination system, the following quote from Hailbronner does ring true:

> Legislation which has the effect intended or otherwise of
> hindering the access of refugees both to determination procedures
> and to asylum is clearly inconsistent with the right of all persons
> to seek and enjoy asylum from persecution.

Visa and carrier restrictions may or may not be in breach of international law per se, but as Hailbronner has written of the Danish and German versions of the same:

> a framework of regulation had been constructed
> which...undermines the observance of the Convention by
> preventing the refugee from arriving at the border in the first
> place.[20]

I have found it difficult to come to a firm conclusion on this issue of access to territory and procedures. If there were no visas, and no carrier sanctions, then there would be substantially more migratory movements than at present. These would include people who would be recognised as Convention and de facto refugees, may of whom cannot as a result of these measures travel at the moment. But they would also include other categories of migrants in whose movements states have, under current international law, a legitimate interest in controlling. So the people whom we wish to protect from persecution would probably be protected—a significant advance from the present. But there would be no distinction between refugees and other migrants; in effect access to the border at least would be given to everybody who sought it. The political practicality of such a change is open to debate. At the very least it would be necessary to balance this easier access to the border with speedier determination procedures once it is reached.

It must be remembered that these measures clearly do not help determine who are and who are not refugees. They are indiscriminate in effect; everyone, refugees and migrants, are prevented from reaching the border. It is only the current political climate which makes indiscriminate access to the border so much more unacceptable than indiscriminate exclusion.

A less radical and more selective approach would be for states to countenance the lifting of fines and visa requirements on particular countries which are producing refugees at a particular time. Interestingly, this policy is exactly contrary to the policy currently adopted by European states. However, criticism can be made of this kind of 'list' approach. States are too slow to react to change; lists are politically controversial and do not help in the hardest cases. But this approach operated in a positive manner rather than a negative way, is worth considering.

UK determination procedures

There has been a wealth of research and policy work undertaken on the issue of asylum procedure, particularly during consideration of the recent Act. Some of this work is summarised below in tabular form. The most detailed proposals, those of Amnesty International in May 1992, are used as the yardstick by which other approaches are measured. Table 7.1 compares Amnesty International's recommendations with current UK practice, the Asylum and Immigration Appeals Act, the *UNHCR Handbook* and a recent UNHCR Statement, and with the pamphlet on procedures produced by the European Consultation on Refugees and Exiles in 1990.

Table 7.1 A Fair and Efficient Asylum Procedure; a comparison of proposals by agencies and by government

A. *Amnesty International* 'Towards a credible asylum process' May 1992	B. *European Consultation of Refugees and Exiles* 'A fair and efficient procedure for determining refugee status' October 1990	C. *UK procedure before 1993 Act*
1. Full interview for all applicants. Interview at Home Office not port.	Yes	Preliminary interview only for third country cases. Some interviews at port on arrival.
2. Knowledgeable determining officials.	Yes	Questionable re Immigration Officers interviewing at ports; less so re determining officers at Home Office.
3. Wider distribution of documentation.	Yes	Home Office documentation not available to Appellant.
4. Trained interpreters.	Yes	No formal training for interpreters.
5. Reasoned decision in all cases.	Yes	No reasoned decision where asylum refused and ELR granted.
6. Full oral appeal against negative determination with suspensive effect.	Decisions within a year normally.	No in-country appeal for Port Applicants. Judicial review only.
7. Independent adjudicator.	Yes	Yes
8. Adequate time to prepare for appeal.	Yes	Yes
9. Consultation re expedited appeals in case of 'safe third country' or no credible prima facie claim to asylum.	Yes	Opportunity to Home Office to prioritise appeals exist.
10. Further appeal on point of law.	Yes	If there is an appeal at all.

D. *Asylum and Immigration Appeals Act 1933*	E. *UNHCR 'Harmonisation in Europe' March 1992*	F. *UNCHR Handbook*
Preliminary interview only for third-country cases. Interviews for Port Applicants still done at ports.	Yes	Applicant to remain in-country pending a decision on initial request unless request is clearly abusive.
Unclear if practice will change.	Yes	Yes
As in C.	?	By implication.
As in C.	Yes	Competent interpreter.
As in C.	?	?
Oral hearings for all appeals.	?	A formal reconsideration of the decision either to a different authority, whether administrative or judicial. Appeal has suspensive effect.
Yes	?	See above.
Inadequate time limits for MUF cases. (2 days to appeal; 7 days to hearing.)	?	?
All expedited procedures—10 days; otherwise 45 days.	Accelerated procedures appropriate for MUF, 'fraudulent' and claims not related to refugee criteria. Safe country cases?	See 1.
Appeals for all.	?	?

Table 7.1 Continued

A. *Amnesty International* 'Towards a credible asylum process' May 1992	B. *European Consultation of Refugees and Exiles* 'A fair and efficient procedure for determining refugee status' October 1990	C. *UK procedure before 1993 Act*
11. Choice of representative; representatives' access to all interviews.	Opportunity to contact a lawyer/UNHCR representative/voluntary agency.	No Legal Aid for appeal otherwise choice between voluntary agency and private lawyer.
12. Detention only where identity or basis of claim is at issue, right to seek bail in all cases.	Yes	Relatively arbitrary use of detention; no right to bail for Port Applicants.

The conclusion to be drawn from this comparison of proposals is that there are some similarities between the model procedures and those now being implemented by the Government. Although the latter clearly leave much to be desired, the 1993 Act marks an improvement on the original 1991 proposals.

The context

The basic principles for a determination procedure should be that it is fair and efficient (for appellants and the determining authority) and that applicants who need assistance have it free of charge from a representative of their choice. Until the Government recently accepted the need for an in-country appeal for *all* applicants, the key change sought in the UK was for such an appeal for port asylum applicants.

D. *Asylum and Immigration Appeals Act 1933*	E. *UNHCR 'Harmonisation in Europe' March 1992*	F. *UNCHR Handbook*
LegaL Aid still available	UNHCR access at all stages; early counselling by UNHCR government, NGOs; assistance in providing routine statement prior to hearing.	
	Full interview leading to: 1) Convention status 2) Humanitarian status 3) Normal consideration 4) Entry into accelerated procedures.	
	Accelerated procedures leading to: 1) Refugee status 2) Re-entry to normal procedures 3) Denial Review of accelerated procedure.	
Increased detention part of package.	No detention unless absolutely necessary and in accordance with the law—not to be arbitrary, to be subject to review, not because of illegal entry only.	See 1.

Civil servants will admit to there being three main reasons for the change in position.

First, the Government took the view, in the first part of 1991, that there was a substantial likelihood that it would be defeated in the European Court of Human Rights in the case of *Vilvarajah* which attacked the existing UK determination procedure as being in breach of Article 13 (no adequate remedy). It was therefore necessary to have a preemptive policy change, if only as a damage limitation exercise, but with the details left sufficiently flexible to depend upon the result.

Second, a series of decisions in Judicial Review cases from 1987 onwards about the natural justice requirements of a determination system which did *not* have an in-country right of appeal on the merits, had complicated and lengthened the determination process by requiring additional safeguards. As a result, it seemed to Government that it could be more efficient to concede a (limited) right of appeal to all applicants in return for a faster procedure.

Third, it was obvious by 1991 that the existing determination procedure had all but broken down under the increased numbers of applications and that massive delays were occurring. The system had also failed to uncover a number of multiple applications apparently made for the purpose of benefit fraud.

The system which was proposed in the initial 1991 Asylum Bill was the minimum which the Government thought consistent with its obligations under Article 13, although ironically by the time the Bill was published the decision in *Vilvarajah* (to the surprise of most commentators and probably the Government) indicated that the existing UK appeal procedure *did* satisfy those obligations. In particular, the Bill proposed that all refused asylum applicants would have an in-country remedy, but only to the extent of being able to apply for *leave* to appeal, on the papers, to a special adjudicator. There was to be no oral appeal as of right.

The concerns of members of the UK protection community about these proposals are best understood if certain basic propositions are made clear. First, they want speedy decisions for their clients but not so speedy as to prevent adequate representation. Second, they did not have full confidence in the existing determination system either in terms of the good faith of the information gatherers and the decision makers, or in the quality of the information collected from asylum seekers. Third, they had great concern about the proposals to restrict access to legal advice under the Legal Aid System.

In October 1992, a new Asylum and Immigration Appeals Bill was published, now 'the Act'. On asylum issues the Act is broadly similar to its predecessor. However, it concedes a full appeal hearing to all refused applicants, albeit within tight time limits. These are extremely tight for a category of 'groundless' (that is MUF) cases defined as 'raising no ground under the Convention, or frivolous or vexatious'. No accompanying changes to the Legal Aid Scheme were announced (although threats are regularly voiced) so there is still no choice of representative for an appeal where the appellant cannot afford to pay for a representative. Almost all of the other objectionable aspects of the first Bill remain (the restrictive asylum rules, the introduction of finger printing, the restriction on access to housing, the collapsing of other appeal rights into the asylum procedure), along with a regrettable number of changes to non-asylum procedures.

The Act, although containing some concessions, marks no change of ethos. It is not the work of a government seeking to assist asylum seekers. In the hands of a determining authority looking to reduce the numbers of asylum seekers reaching the UK and achieving protection here, the changes will be a very considerable weapon.

The interview

It is trite but nonetheless important to re-emphasise that determination procedures need to be fair and efficient for both the asylum seeker and the determining authority. Putting this principle into practice, it is vital that full resources are put into the initial fact-finding interview. For this interview to be of maximum value the applicant must have a reasonable time to prepare for it and access to independent advice to assist in the efficient presentation of the salient facts. Equally, the interviewer must have sufficient knowledge of the country of origin. It is surely sensible for the actual decision-maker to conduct the interview (not current UK practice). Certainly immigration officers at ports should no longer be used for this fact-finding function. Properly trained interpreters must be used at interview. A representative of the applicant should be present. Written application forms can be completed within a reasonable time, providing that legal advice is made available before they are completed and that no negative decision is made without a full interview. Group determinations are acceptable if they are positive. Otherwise all cases must be individually considered (see below).

A determination procedure which is well resourced at this early stage should result in more correct decisions and fewer appeals. Advisers would not, as now, frequently have to elicit more and more detailed information from applicants at later and later stages in the procedure, in response to more and more detailed adverse decisions by the Home Office. It will result in quicker decisions which would benefit both applicant and the determining authority.

Advice

A recent comparative study of Legal Aid provision in EC countries by Hooghiemstra[21] concludes that all EC countries with substantial numbers of asylum seekers have some sort of publicly funded system of assistance for them, but that this system varies between those which treat asylum applicants like any other legally aided litigant and those which have a specialised pool of lawyers available to them. Changes in policy in Europe now reveal attempts by both the UK and France to reduce access to Legal Aid which are in keeping with the perceived 'rounding down' project of the Ad Hoc Group.

The requirement for proper advice is closely linked to the need for a full interview. Government should therefore not attempt to monopolise provision of advice, nor to cash limit it. Moreover, the faster a decision-making process the greater the need for advice; the more controversial the field, the greater the need for independent advice from more than one source.

ELR and de facto status

For the reasons set out above, ELR should be defined in the Immigration Rules. It should as a result be possible to raise the grant or withholding of this status on appeal. If however, the other proposals on ELR and family reunion were adopted, then arguably fewer upgrade appeals of this kind would take place since there would be a reasoned determination available at the time of the initial refusal, and the other existing incentives to appeal (the differing social and family reunion rights) would no longer apply.

Manifestly ill-founded (MUF) procedures

A central question is whether there should be some sort of accelerated procedure for MUF cases. Governments are pressing for them and most countries are introducing them. The concept of an accelerated appeal is clearly not an anathema to UNHCR which defines MUF cases as 'clearly fraudulent' or 'not related to the Refugee Convention' nor to 'any other criteria justifying the grant of asylum' and suggests that the review of cases rejected on this basis could be 'simplified' although it makes it clear that this should only be after a full interview by the body normally competent to make determinations.[22] UNHCR also emphasises that the main way of mitigating the effect of MUF applications on a determination process is to put more resources into the process to improve it, and to speed it up.

Clearly, the more confidence there is in the initial determination process, the less objectionable would be a 'simplified' appeal procedure for MUF cases. The Asylum Bill proposals in their initial form failed to win that confidence and in any event offered a fast procedure for all appellants with no guaranteed oral hearing. The Act modifies this approach and in effect introduces MUF procedures in the form of quicker truncated appeals. For the reasons set out below it is arguable that accelerated procedures with sufficient safeguards to protect asylum seekers can be 'efficient' enough to warrant their imposition. Given that the UK has a poor reputation for commitment to the principles behind the Refugee Convention, the new procedure is bound to be viewed with suspicion.

In the UK context, it was arguable that there was already the possibility of expediting particular categories of appeals within the existing procedure. There is no reason why the Home Office cannot dedicate its resources to preparing an appeal quickly where it thinks that the asylum applicant's case is particularly weak. It does this in other types of immigration appeals already (e.g. in the case of deportation). There is also a preliminary issue procedure which could be adapted[23] to dispose of cases which in law could never succeed and there is clearly no government reluctance to resource further courts; as the administrative changes that accompanied the Act make clear. It is therefore arguable that it was not necessary to design a special procedure for the UK to prioritise third-country cases or those which the Government considers to be MUF or otherwise unmeritorious, to end the delays which are reputed to attract the 'bogus' asylum seeker.

By deciding largely to rewrite the rules of procedure in respect of appeals under the Act the Government has abandoned a system broadly trusted by Appellants and practitioners and which has been widely tested in litigation over the years. The new rules raise many uncertainties and will no doubt be the subject of a great deal of litigation which will in effect wipe out the early months of the new regime.

In assessing the new appeal procedures, some general points may be helpful. Obviously the procedure must on its face be fair. However, as a procedure has to be interpreted through subsequent case law, it may not always be possible to predict at the outset how it will develop. In other areas of UK immigration law statutory concepts have taken on very different forms in the light of case law from that originally anticipated by commentators (and it is assumed by legislators). So there is a natural reticence amongst practitioners to approve new procedures, particularly where the anti-refugee ethos of the determining authority is so clear. The motivation and the commitment of the determining authority is very relevant to the efficacy of procedure to an appellant. Since the motivation thus far revealed by the Government is to reduce the number of asylum seekers, this makes the protection community more suspicious of the effect of change. It was argued above that the current appellate structure is wholly inadequate as it stands, for reasons set out above. But the procedure rules by which that structure works have been in place for many years and are broadly fair, in relation at least to in-country appeals.

Thresholds for appealing

The possibility of a threshold for access to the main appellate system is often raised in conjunction with the issue of MUF cases. In a recent research paper, Dr Renee Dedecker analysed such procedures.[24] It is noteworthy that her chosen model again posits a very detailed first interview. It also suggests early identification of MUF cases and cases in which humanitarian concerns will lead to protection. She adopts UNHCR's definition of 'MUF'[25] and calls for the harmonisation of interpretation throughout European countries. She is strongly of the view that the most efficient way to use the concept of MUF cases is *after* a full interview process and she proposes identifying MUF cases after interview and channelling them into a faster procedure with limited review, albeit with suspensive effect. Her comparative study did not suggest that the use of the concept of a pre-screening stage for MUF cases actually improved the efficiency of procedures. Thus she suggests satisfying the MUF determination as the threshold of the main appeal system.

There are general problems with thresholds. If a threshold is too high then either the system will shortly be discredited by examples of refoulement and/or the system will be clogged up by delays caused by judicial review applications to challenge threshold failures. The fairer the threshold procedure is, the more, in effect, it is going to duplicate a substantive appeal, to no great effect. Thus if the threshold is too low then there is no point in having it. This is very much the Canadian experience. As 92.8% of cases got through the first threshold it has, to all intents, been abandoned.

The Act gives all applicants an oral hearing, although the MUF procedure will be much quicker than the normal procedure. However it allows for a number of situations where the MUF procedure can be used without there being a full interview.

The objection in the end to MUF procedures and to thresholds for appeals is that, if they are too speedy and too high, they will not provide adequate safeguards. But once the safeguards that are required are built in, they cease to have their attraction. It may just be possible that in a determination procedure where real safeguards are given at the interview stages, a more limited (oral) appeal might be made available to some applicants. But neither the initial nor the appeal procedures in the current Act are adequate for this.

Safe countries of origin

A related area of debate is about the use of the concept of 'safe countries of origin' as a means of attempting to speed up the determination system. At its most basic, this system proposes certain countries which are deemed 'safe' and therefore whose nationals would either be refused access to asylum procedures altogether or channelled into MUF procedures. Hailbronner has given a detailed analysis of how this concept might be used[26] but is forced to conclude that the concept only has use if there is to be an abandonment of the fundamental principle of the individual determination of asylum applications. In the absence of such a controversial policy change to a cornerstone of the Refugee Convention, the notion really only has use as a procedural device or as a means of shifting the burden of proof.

Lists of countries that preclude individual consideration either on the basis of safe country of origin, or safe third country, are reactive. States may well find themselves either too slow or too fast in reacting to change in a particular country and therefore fail to consider the right applications. Political considerations may come into the exclusion or inclusion of a country on the safe list. Furthermore, the concept of a list ignores the fact that there will in every jurisdiction be hard cases which run counter to the general view about the safety of a particular territory. These are the cases which most need individual consideration.

Perhaps the most that can be said is that lists might be acceptable if they were of the inclusive rather than the exclusive kind, so that applicants from certain countries automatically *get* protection.

Safe third countries

The issue of safe third countries is another that is very much to the forefront of the debate in Europe. By this concept access to procedures is refused to applicants who have passed through safe countries en route to the country of application. 'Passed through' has been defined variously but can amount to a few minutes' presence on a territory and can include circumstances where no claim *could* have been made. In deciding the place of determination of cases within the EC, the Dublin Convention seeks to ensure that an asylum seeker will have their application considered by only one state and uses the principle of safe third countries to achieve that end. The Convention is still not ratified by all twelve countries although it is generally followed by the UK wherever its provisions allow it to divest itself of responsibilities for asylum seekers.

Current practice allows us to draw conclusions about what life under Dublin and proposed parallel conventions involving non-EC countries will be like. In deciding whether to consider an application from someone who has passed through a Convention country, no weight at all is given to Excom Conclusion 15(3) which states that, where possible, the asylum seeker's desire to go to a particular country should be taken into account. Rather, the very strict 'Eurocentric' definitions of family used means that families and communities are often split on the basis of one family member having spent two hours in a particular country although another may have spent years elsewhere. This encourages applicants to give inaccurate accounts of their route which in turn allows states to question their credibility.

Of course, the Dublin Convention only sets out the proposed relationship between EC States on this issue. Generally, however, European governments are also keen to pass on asylum seekers to other non-EC countries which might be described as safe. This is on the principle set out by Home Secretary Baker in June 1991 that 'the UK is not normally prepared to entertain claims from individuals who have failed to claim asylum in the first safe country that they have reached.'[27]

A number of substantive proposals can be made to try and improve the situation in relation to 'safe third country' legislation. The lawfulness of the removal must be for determination by an adjudicator on appeal, as under the Act, although doubts remain as to the scope of the appeal. In sharp contrast to the contents of the Asylum rules under the Act, it could be required that no asylum seeker be returned to an alleged safe third country without written assurance of guaranteed re-admission to that country and access to a fair and efficient determination procedure there. This latter point seeks to grapple with the problem of safe third-country cases where that country has limited determination procedures.

In addition, the problem of humanitarian concerns in a third country may arise (i.e., return to a safe but poverty stricken country) and perhaps could be litigated within the determination procedure. It should be required that the asylum seeker have access to internationally recognised civil, political and cultural rights and humane living conditions in the country of ultimate consideration. In addition, when considering whether the UK is the appropriate country, broader determining factors could be established, such as the presence of a spouse, dependent children of the family, siblings, parents, grandparents or other relatives who are considered close within the relevant culture. The presence of a cultural community in the UK and matters such as common language and education could also be considered. Certainly it could be stated that a short stay in another country should not preclude substantive consideration of an asylum application. In adopting such a position the UK would not be in breach of its obligations under Dublin since Article 9 allows a member state to examine an application for humanitarian reasons.

The iniquities of safe third-country procedures only emerge clearly with the visa regime and carrier sanctions referred to above. The latter make it very difficult for asylum seekers to travel directly to Western European countries. The safe third-country principle capitalises on this fact. There is also an important, but underused, argument that the safe country 'principle' has no foundation in international law and as such cannot be relied upon. This argument is founded upon the proposition that there is no requirement in international law to claim asylum in the first safe country which is reached. But it seems unlikely that the UK courts at least will reverse their position having already accepted the principle in a number of decisions.

Detention

There is likely to be an increased resort to detention both as a deterrent to asylum seekers and to aid speedy enforcement of refusals. More detention places are already being planned. Although the Act does not increase the powers to detain, by telescoping the existing appeals procedure once asylum has been refused, all refused asylum seekers are detainable. In the face of this increased power there should be a presumption of release and comprehensive bail provisions for all detained asylum seekers. These would include surety provisions which recognise, in the levels of surety required, the poverty of the refugee communities from which the guarantors will probably come. In fact, of course, detention should never be used as a general deterrent and much greater sensitivity is needed to the effect of incarceration on people who have fled persecution. Detention is probably already over used and is likely to be more so in the future.[28]

Children

During 1992, 185 children aged 17 or under, who were unaccompanied and without close relatives in the UK, applied for asylum when they arrived in the UK. In the course of the parliamentary debates on the recent Act a detailed series of amendments were put forward, unsuccessfully, to protect such children. Any asylum policy should take account of the suggestions to establish an agency to assist unaccompanied minors in their passage through asylum procedures.

Harmonisation of social conditions

There is clear evidence from the communication between EC States that it is felt that there must be harmonisation across Europe of social conditions achieved by refugees and persons with ELR. The policy is phrased in terms of 'burden sharing' but carries the thinly veiled threat that those countries which retain uncharacteristically generous provisions will become magnets for asylum applicants. The detailed requirements for civic rights for refugees are beyond the scope of this chapter but provisions which stigmatise these groups by excluding them from civic rights do not encourage good community relations. Rather they pander to xenophobic tendencies already too present in Europe. In a UK context this means that the housing and fingerprinting provisions of the Act are particularly objectionable, as are the limited terms of the protection given to 'displaced' Bosnians. It is all to easy to see how impoverishing refugees may encourage the 'liars, cheats and queue jumpers' analysis of refugees. To make asylum seekers and refugees even poorer than everyone else plays into the hands of anti-refugee sentiment.

It will be clear from the foregoing arguments that both in principle and for practical reasons there should be no distinctions between the civic rights of a Convention refugee and a de facto refugee.

Conclusion

In conclusion it is right that we return to thinking about policy at a European level. The climate of Europe is against both a liberal European and individual state policy on asylum seekers and refugees. A state which unilaterally adopts a liberal policy on access will find other states gratefully directing asylum seekers in its direction. A state which seeks to persuade Europe to adopt a more liberal policy on access multilaterally will have an uphill struggle, although this does not mean that this is a project which should not be commenced. Certainly, multi-lateral change is more likely to be achieved by a detailed engagement with other states in the European policy-making process than by a principled decision to withdraw from discussion. Nevertheless the portents are not good.

Elsewhere I have also sought to argue that if we are able to divorce ourselves somewhat from *Realpolitik*, then the continued obsession with dividing Convention from de facto refugees may not be a sensible use of resources. As states are about to launch an attack on the concept of de facto refugees I accept that this argument may not be timely but its force remains. I have however held to the view that there is much to be said for distinguishing these two categories of protection seekers from other migrants.

Finally, I have tried to show how, within the UK it may be possible to have a determination system which is both fairer and more efficient and that this might have been achieved more effectively by the adaptation of existing procedures than by the imposition of new ones.

8 FUTURE IMMIGRATION POLICY
Elspeth Guild

Family life

The importance of the family as a fundamental element of society has long been recognised by all political parties in the UK. Indeed, concern has been expressed across the political spectrum about the increasing divorce rate and the detrimental effect of family breakdown on the physical and emotional well being of children. Statistics which appear to indicate a co-relation between family breakdown and poverty have also been the subject of political comment.

The sanctity of the family is the subject of our international human rights obligations. Specifically the European Convention on Human Rights (ECHR) Article 8 states 'everyone has the right to respect for his private and family life'. Article 16 of the Universal Declaration of Human Rights states that 'everyone has the right to marry and found a family...the family is the natural and fundamental unit of society and is entitled to protection by society and the state.'

The policy of the UK Government in respect of immigration control has been to maintain a 'firm but fair' immigration system which limits as far as possible immigration to the UK for the purpose of settlement. Therefore, where someone settled in the UK seeks to exercise the right to family life with family members who have no independent right to enter or remain in the UK, a tension arises between these two policy objectives. On the one hand there is the obligation to respect family life and on the other the objective of limiting immigration for settlement. I shall examine the principles on which a balance between these two policy objectives can be achieved.

Principle of non-discrimation between classes of persons

The right to respect for private and family life as established in the ECHR applies to everyone in the territory of a signatory state such as the UK. It is further subject to Article 14 of the same Convention which, in respect of the rights and freedoms set out in the Convention, prohibits discrimination on any ground 'such as sex, race, colour, language, religion, political or other opinion, national or social origin, association with a national minority, property, birth or other status'. Accordingly, the principles of immigration policy in respect of family life should not discriminate between different classes and categories of people who have residence rights in the UK.

Further, if the right to family life is considered fundamental, on what grounds is state interference with that right justified simply because one spouse does *not* have residence rights? When two British citizens marry there is no state interference in respect of where they may or may not live. But when a British citizen marries a foreign national, the state, through immigration control, may interfere with their choice as to where to make the matrimonial home.

If discrimination is to be avoided, UK immigration policy must allow a right of entry for the purpose of exercising family life. For any limitations on that right to be acceptable they must be objectively justifiable and necessary to prevent abuse. Further, such limitations must be confined to the minimum necessary to satisfy the objective and must not constitute an unacceptable intrusion into private life.

Immigration policy in respect of family life is not an issue exclusively relating to ethnic minority communities. It affects all categories of residents in the UK and all classes of society. Nonetheless, first generation ethnic minority communities tend to have strong family ties with their country of origin and may therefore be disproportionately affected.

As recently as March 1992 the then Home Secretary reiterated the pride of the Government and previous Governments for 'two decades of progress in achieving harmonious race relations in this country'.[1] One of the principles of UK race relations policy is to encourage full and successful integration by immigrants into society. The Council of Europe's Committee of Ministers authorised a Committee of Experts to prepare a report on this issue, *Community and Ethnic Relations in Europe*, which was published in 1991. It found that, 'if immigrants are to be encouraged to integrate fully in the host society it is essential that they should benefit from security of residence and the right to family reunion'.[2]

To comply with international human rights obligations and to promote Government race relations policy, it is therefore necessary that immigration policy on family life applies equally to all persons with residence rights here. In achieving the balance of policy interests, it must also provide certainty to the interested parties and avoid unnecessary interference with private life. If there is a real and continuing risk that family life may be disrupted by administrative action, for instance by deportation of the foreign spouse in the event of reliance on public funds, then there will be discrimination between those who marry British (or EC national) spouses and those who do not.

Families are entitled to certainty in reaching decisions on their future. They are also entitled to respect for their privacy—a right not to have to answer humiliating and degrading questions about their married life or else risk separation. All too often immigration officials now feel entitled to examine love letters and ask impertinent questions about a couple's love life in order to satisfy themselves of the relationship. This clearly offends against the principle of non discrimination. Where *both* parties to a marriage have residence rights it is only in the most exceptional circumstances, primarily in the context of criminal investigations (for instance where there are allegations of abuse of children), that state interference of such a kind is considered permissible.

There is clearly a lack of balance if the act of seeking to be joined by a foreign spouse entitles the state to use techniques otherwise reserved for serious criminal investigations.

The definition of family

The concept of family is relatively elastic varying from all those persons related by blood or marriage who may be expected to participate in rituals relating to birth, death and marriage to the much more exclusionary definition of husband, wife and dependent minor children living together under the same roof.

In immigration policy, a balance must be struck between these two extremes which is consistent with a firm but fair immigration policy yet respects the emotional and economic ties between family members. Regard must also be had to the fact that the concept of family is not uniform throughout UK society. A simple example is the meaning of the term 'the Royal Family'. Traditionally, photographs of 'the Royal Family' include parents, grandparents, adult children and their spouses, their minor children and possibly other family members. This is certainly not the definition of family which is recognised as giving rise to expectations under UK immigration policy.

The issue is further complicated by the fact that the definition of family in respect of immigration control is not within the exclusive jurisdiction of the British Parliament. By virtue of the UK's membership of the EC, the British Government may not apply its narrow definition of family to persons exercising rights of residence in the UK under Community law. That is, almost all EC nationals working in the UK, and many British citizens who have lived elsewhere in the EC and returned to the UK may be joined by a wider circle of family members than those British citizens who have lived here all their lives.

This has the unfortunate consequence that the more restrictive definition of family members under UK legislation places most British citizens (and persons settled here) at a disadvantage in comparison with those persons exercising Community law rights where the definition of qualifying family members is wider. This peculiar situation offends against the principle of non-discrimination.

The problem of this disparity has become more acute since the decision of the European Court of Justice in July 1992[3] which permits British citizens who have exercised a free movement right and . travelled and resided in another Community Member State to claim the superior family rights under Community law when they return to the UK. Therefore even two British citizens may have differing rights in respect of which family members may join them in the UK.

Accordingly, in pursuit of a non-discriminatory UK immigration policy, the Community law definition of family must apply, that is spouses and descendants who are under the age of 21 years or are dependent, and dependent relatives in the ascending line of the resident and his or her spouse.

Under Community law there is a further requirement that Member States facilitate the admission of any member of the family not coming within the above definition if s/he is dependent on the resident or they lived under the same roof in the country the resident came from. Under Community law, the nationality of family members is irrelevant to the right to family life.

Finally, in considering the extent of family life, it would be wrong to overlook the question of same sex 'families'. In some European countries stable relationships between persons of the same sex are the subject of treatment equivalent with marriage. It may well be that the time has come for the UK similarly to acknowledge the seriousness of such relationships within the framework of family reunion law.

Private life and family life

The right to enjoy family life free of intrusion by the state is a principle both of Article 8 of the ECHR and Article 16 of the UN Declaration. Article 8 of the ECHR permits interference only where it is in accordance with the law and is necessary in a democratic society in the interests of national security, public safety or the economic well-being of the country, for the prevention of disorder or crime, for the protection of health or morals, or for the protection of the rights and freedoms of others.

Outwith immigration policy, the issue of state interference with family life has been the subject of very substantial policy debates particularly in the context of the rights of parents and safety of children. The issue also arises in respect of immigration policy. The UK Government has most forcibly argued it has a right to examine the genuineness of family life when considering the admission and residence of family members. On the other hand, the family is entitled to respect for its privacy. In terms of immigration policy this arises primarily in relation to the genuineness of marriages, and the genuineness of other family relationships.

Marriage

Immigration policy should benefit parties to genuine marriages where the intention is to live together permanently as husband and wife. Sham marriages where no such intention exists do not need protection. Two questions arise in respect of the genuineness of a marriage. First, is it sufficient as a test that the parties to the marriage intend to live together permanently as husband or wife as required by the Immigration Rules? If not, should there be a *further* requirement, as currently exists in UK immigration law, that at the time of marriage the parties to the marriage were not influenced as regards their choice of spouse by the possibility of coming to the UK?

The 'primary purpose test' requires the entry clearance officer to refuse entry to a spouse unless he is satisfied that the marriage was not entered into primarily to obtain entry to the UK. In practice it is difficult to administer. The Secretary of State said in Parliament on 2 March 1992:

> We all know that the primary purpose rule is difficult to interpret. I was at the Home Office when it was introduced and I do not think that I had any illusions then, but realised that it would cause difficulty. Anybody with a substantial number of immigrants—particularly Asian ones—in their constituency will know that it is not easy to interpret the primary purpose rule. Therefore on a practical level it may with justification be said that the test has not been an unqualified success.

In the light of the policy considerations set out above, is the test an unnecessary intrusion of privacy? In order to satisfy the test, parties to the marriage frequently must submit private correspondence, including love letters written both before and after the marriage, in order to show that the only purpose of the marriage was to enable two persons in love to found a family. Not infrequently other family members must make statements as to what they considered to have been in the minds of the parties at the date of the marriage.

The fact that the rule places the burden on the applicant to satisfy the official that the primary intention was *not* to obtain entry is particularly pernicious. Establishing what *is* in someone's mind at a specific time is difficult enough. To require someone to provide evidence of what was *not* in his/her mind is excessive and too subjective.

The test of the genuineness of the marriage can only be compatible with respect for private life when it does not require intrusion into that private life and gives rise to certainty on an objective basis. Further, as those persons entitled to family life under Community law cannot be subject to such an intrusive test the principle of non-discrimination set out above is violated.

Second, if it is agreed that no test beyond genuineness is acceptable, then to what extent may the state legitimately probe the genuineness of a marriage? Here the issue of the right to private life arises again. Parties to a marriage are entitled to respect and dignity. If they state their intention to be to live together as husband and wife they are entitled to be believed. Marriage is a serious commitment giving rise to emotional and financial obligations. All persons who take such a step deserve to benefit from a presumption in favour of the genuineness of the marriage. Further investigation should only be justified, if at all, on the basis of serious and compelling evidence to the contrary. The evidence and its source should be made available to the couple for their response.

Other family relationships

A substantial number of British citizens and men settled in the UK are refused family life in the UK with their wives and children because the authorities do not believe they are genuinely related. The circumstances arise almost exclusively in the context of family members in Bangladesh and Pakistan and cause a very substantial degree of distress and hardship to families. The allegation that minor children are not in fact related to the alleged parent is indeed a very serious one which pre-supposes either fraud or illegitimacy (used here in its colloquial meaning).

The introduction of DNA blood testing, which is generally accepted as having a very high level of accuracy as between parent and child, led to Home Office guidelines on the use of DNA tests in February 1989. Wherever the relationship is questioned (as occurs in a very substantial proportion of cases in Bangladesh), the parents and children undergo DNA testing. In 1992, for instance, 1043 DNA tests were carried out in Bangladesh, of which 7% revealed a child to be related to only one parent and 10% appeared to lack the claimed relationship.

The implications of such an intrusive measure can hardly be overestimated. The consequences for the families in those cases which revealed the lack of relationship may have been catastrophic. This is particularly the case when the child was related to the mother but not to the sponsoring father. An allegation striking at the very dignity and integrity of the family can only be justified if there is strong evidence of abuse. It is not the role of immigration policy to police the fidelity of wives. So long as children are accepted as the legal and moral responsibility of the parents such intrusion into private life is not justified.

Currently parents are only admitted to join their children settled in the UK where one parent is over 65, with an exception in respect of widowed mothers. Further, the parents must be wholly or mainly dependent on their children in the UK and have no other relatives in their own country to whom they may turn for support. The sponsor must also prove no recourse to public funds. This rule offends against the non-discrimination principle in that British and EC citizens who have exercised Community law free movement rights are entitled to be joined here by all dependent relatives in the ascending line irrespective of age. The only additional requirement is that the sponsor must have adequate housing available for these relatives.

A further problem arises with respect of the rights of minor children where a marriage between a person settled here and an alien spouse breaks down. The alien spouse may well not have acquired an independent right of residence. Where there are minor children, their right to family life with both parents may be breached if the alien spouse is expelled. The European Court of Human Rights has held that the expulsion of a divorced man could constitute a breach of the right to family life where it would result in the termination of his parental relationship with his child.

The rights of parents and children to enjoy family life must be protected. All other relatives are only admissible to the UK where they are living alone in the most exceptional and compassionate circumstances. Again they must be wholly or mainly dependent on the UK sponsor and without relatives in their own country to whom they could turn.

The rules applicable to EC nationals and to those British citizens who are exercising or have exercised free movement rights are different. These rules require the state to facilitate the admission of any member of the family if dependent on the sponsor or if the relative lived under the sponsor's roof in the country or origin. This provision is much more generous than the UK immigration rules and therefore gives rise to inequality. The very substantial benefit of the provision is that it is flexible enough to respect the concept of family as it may apply in different societies. Where a family lives together under one roof there is a clear indication of the concept of family which applies to the group.

Many people may not choose to live with their parents, in-laws or siblings but if their social responsibility as culturally defined requires that they do, those obligations deserve respect. Further, a family member who is dependent on a sponsor is necessary more vulnerable than one who is not. It is appropriate that vulnerable individuals should receive adequate protection whenever possible with the family on which they are economically or emotionally dependent.

Economic limitations on family life

The economic consequences of family life are a factor in determining immigration policy. At the moment, family life is to some extent the reward of economic independence in that current UK immigration law requires the family to show that it will have adequate support and accommodation without recourse to public funds before family life may be exercised in the UK. The purpose of this policy is undoubtedly to save the public purse, the view being that the introduction of family members from overseas should not increase the cost to the state.

It is unclear, however, whether this policy objective is achieved by the requirement that the family unit prove it can support itself *before* the overseas family members come to the UK. Government statistics on poverty and single parent families would seem to indicate that the presence of both spouses living together is likely to *reduce* the risk of reliance on state funds. The same may not be true for the admission of children and dependent parents. However there are humanitarian reasons why the exclusion of these two categories would in any event be undesirable. Further, it is inappropriate to penalise persons for involuntary unemployment if they have in the past been employed for many years paying national insurance contributions and tax.

The principle of non-discrimination also applies here. Those residents who can claim the benefit of Community law may not be required to support themselves without recourse to public funds. Most persons who are entitled to Community law family reunion rights must, of course, be engaging in an economic activity, even if the proceeds of that activity are insufficient to support them and therefore make them eligible for public funds. Those people with Community family reunion rights who are not engaging in economic activities must not be reliant on public funds. The requirement to provide adequate housing for family members applies to all those entitled to family life under Community law.

Independent residence rights and deportation

Currently, spouses and children who join a sponsor in the UK are subject to a probationary year, at the end of which they will be eligible for an independent right of residence and indefinite leave to remain, provided the family relationship is still intact and there is no reliance on public funds. This probationary year does not apply in respect of dependent parents or children joining both parents already in the UK.

In respect of spouses, the probationary year seems an adequate safeguard as to the genuineness of the marriage. Where a marriage has been entered into solely for reasons unrelated to family life it must necessarily take a very substantial amount of determination by both parties for them to remain together for a year. The probationary period may thus be seen as a test commensurate to the objective pursued and therefore justifiable.

The requirement that the family must not have been reliant on public funds during the first probationary year is not justifiable. Where the parties to the marriage are involuntarily unemployed for a period, it is disproportionate that the family should be forced to choose between the continued enjoyment of family life, which would require the family not to claim any public funds (and therefore possibly live in abject poverty), or to jeopardise their chance of family life by claiming welfare benefits. It should not be the role of public policy to force individuals to make such choices.

While the use of the probationary year is a useful safe-guard, it must be acknowledged that it places the spouse without an independent residence right in a dependent position. The spouse with residence rights will inevitably have a disproportionate amount of power over the other spouse. While this may be acceptable for a one year period it would not be proportionate for any longer term.

Immigration policy should not be permitted to become a tool whereby a UK resident spouse can dispose of his or her other spouse while keeping the British born children. As all family lawyers are aware, it is extremely difficult for someone who has been deported to prosecute family rights of custody or access to children once in a foreign jurisdiction.

Further, in considering the deportation of family members on family breakdown, regard must again be had to the ECHR as interpreted by the European Court of Human Rights. The Court has held that, where deportation of a family member will sever the parent/child relationship, even if the parent and child are not living together, it may be a violation of the right to family life.[4]

In conclusion, UK immigration policy in respect of family life should be based on three fundamental principles:

- International human rights obligations which the UK has undertaken;

- The principle of non-discrimination between classes of persons;
- The principle of respect for private and family life.

Within the limitations of these three principles a firm but fair policy should be pursued, protecting genuine family life.

Visitors and students

This section is based on the premise that overseas visitors and students are beneficial to the UK economically, socially and culturally and accordingly that this benefit should be reflected in UK immigration policy. The current policy of the Government is indeed to allow genuine visitors and students to enter the UK.[5] The question is how best to implement this policy in practice.

Visitors

In 1990, 46.4 million passengers arrived in the UK. Of this number, the majority were British citizens and European Community nationals, the first not being subject to immigration control and the second benefiting from the special legal order of the European Community. Eight million came from non-EC countries; 18,000 were refused leave to enter the UK.[6] British citizens and EC nationals present no particular problem in respect of immigration policy. It is the 5.5 million visitors and 202,000 students from countries outside the Community who are the primary focus of this chapter.

Visitors form an important part of the consumers of the UK tourist industry which earned the UK £5.6 billion in 1990.[7] In support of that industry, UK diplomatic posts abroad provide substantial amounts of information and encouragement to nationals of other countries to persuade them to come to the UK as visitors.

Further, the category 'visitor' in immigration law not only includes tourists but also business visitors coming to transact business in the UK. This is an important category which brings benefits to the UK economy in terms of increased import and export activity, investment, joint venture projects, etc.

The immigration category 'visitor' also includes persons coming to the UK for cultural purposes including those wishing to visit theatres in the UK or those attending short cultural studies courses. All of these activities enrich the UK both culturally and materially. Visitors inevitably spend money in the UK and through their contact with people resident here, participate in the fostering of cultural exchange, tolerance and understanding.

Visitors and visas

Visitors fall into two categories; those from countries whose nationals must obtain entry clearance (visas) from a UK post abroad before coming to the UK and those who do not require entry clearance to come as visitors. The majority of the countries whose nationals must obtain entry clearance are in the developing world while most of those visitors who do not require entry clearance are from the developed world.

On the introduction of mandatory entry clearance requirements for the nationals of India, Pakistan and Bangladesh, it was argued by the Government that the requirements were necessary in view of the increasing number of refusals of nationals from these countries at points of entry in the UK and their subsequent removal from the UK. It was further stated that the requirements actually helped nationals of these countries as it assisted them to find out in advance whether or not they were eligible for admission to the UK. The same argument was presented in 1989 when mandatory entry clearance requirements were adopted for nationals of Algeria, Turkey and Morocco.

A fee is payable for an application for entry clearance of between £10 for one entry where the applicant is under 25 and £85 for multiple entries valid for 5 years.[8] This is non-refundable if the application is refused. The imposition of mandatory entry clearance requirements on nationals of developing countries while refraining from doing so in respect of nationals of developed countries thus places a vastly disproportionate cost burden on the former when considered on the basis of average national income. Further, nationals of countries to which mandatory entry clearance requirements apply may not change their status once in the UK from visitor to student but must return abroad and seek entry clearance as a student before returning to the UK to take up a course of study. Nationals from those countries to which the requirements do not apply may switch from visitor to student status while in the UK.

Again, this places a disproportionate cost burden on nationals of developing countries who are least able to sustain those costs in addition to the costs of further education in the UK. It is not unusual for young visitors in the UK to investigate the possibility of further education here. Although the intention may not have been formed before leaving their country of origin, once in the UK, not unreasonably, the possibility seems much more real.

To discriminate against nationals of primarily developing countries in this way appears both wrong in principle and unnecessary. If mandatory requirements are accepted as necessary for effective immigration control it must be because they simplify the job of immigration officers at ports of entry. Where a passenger is in possession of entry clearance the immigration officer may still refuse admission but on the limited grounds that the officer is satisfied that:

- false representations were employed or material facts not disclosed for the purpose of obtaining the clearance;
- a change of circumstance since issue of the visa has removed the basis of the claim;
- there is restricted returnability, medical grounds, criminal record, or an outstanding deportation order.

Entry clearance is, therefore an administrative tool to speed up the work of immigration officers. The beneficiaries are the passengers but they have no choice whether or not to seek entry clearance before travelling. They must obtain it or the carrier will not normally allow the passenger to embark as it will be fined by the UK Government under the Immigration (Carriers' Liability) Act 1987. As entry clearance is of benefit primarily to the state, the cost should be born by the state, not the passenger.

Criteria for entry clearance or admission to the UK as a visitor

The criteria to obtain entry clearance or to obtain admission to the UK as a visitor are the same. The visitor must satisfy the entry clearance officer or the immigration officer that he or she:

- is genuinely seeking to come to the UK for a period less than six months;
- can maintain and accommodate him or herself and any dependants, or be maintained and accommodated by relatives or friends without working or recourse to public funds, and

can pay for the return journey from the UK;
- does not intend to seek employment and will not become a charge on public funds.

General considerations also apply in that admission may be refused on grounds of criminal record, health, an outstanding deportation order, failure to have complied with conditions on a previous visit or that his or her presence is not 'conducive to the public good'.

Until the enactment of the Asylum and Immigration Appeals Act, where entry clearance or admission to the UK was refused, the applicant had a right of appeal which could usually only be exercised while the applicant was overseas. The appeal took place in the UK and the applicant could instruct representatives to pursue the appeal here on his or her behalf. However, the Act removed all rights of appeal for visitors.

In view of the very large number of visitors who come to the UK each year, it is of great importance that consistency is maintained in decision making. If consistency is not maintained, then UK immigration policy is open to challenge on the basis that it permits improper discrimination on the basis of national origin or race. Such challenges can only be damaging to the tourism industry and to the UK's international reputation.

As can be seen, a great degree of discretion rests with the immigration or entry clearance officer, e.g. in determining the intentions of the proposed visitor. Intentions are notoriously difficult to assess objectively. As long as the burden of proof is on the intended visitor to satisfy an official as regards his or her intentions, the risk of unequal application cannot be controlled. Further, the removal of the right of appeal by the Act means that there is now no independent appellate authority with power to remedy the injustices which occur. Accordingly, two steps are required:

- The discretion of entry clearance and immigration officers to refuse entry clearance or admission to the UK to a visitor on the basis that the officer is not satisfied as to the intentions of the visitor must be limited.
- A right of appeal against a refusal to issue entry clearance or grant admission to the UK is vital in all instances. The appellate authority must have power to order that entry clearance or admission be granted on the next visit of the appellant.

Business visitors

There is no separate category in UK immigration law for business visits. Visitors who wish to come here to transact business must satisfy exactly the same requirements as persons seeking to come to the UK as tourists. This creates the absurd anomaly that business visitors must satisfy officials that they do not intend to engage in employment, paid, unpaid or self-employment, while in the UK. If the official considers that the proposed business activity amounts to employment, entry is refused.

By definition, business visitors are seeking to exercise business activities in the UK which in most circumstances could be classified as employment or self-employment. For instance, the employee of a multi-national company who is sent to the UK to investigate the performance of a UK subsidiary is necessarily doing so in the course of his or her employment. Nonetheless, he or she must seek admission to the UK as a visitor. A new category of business visitor is required in the UK immigration rules to accommodate persons transacting business here or undertaking short-term duties for an overseas company in the UK.

Visiting UK resident family members

Special problems arise in respect of visitors who have relatives in the UK. Unfortunately, all too often, the presence of close family members resident in the UK is perceived by officials as an incentive for the visitor to remain beyond the time permitted, and therefore leads to refusal. This gives rise to frustration and a sense of grievance on the part of both the prospective visitor and the family resident in the UK.

Unfortunately, it is often ethnic minority communities which encounter problems disproportionately to the rest of society. This in itself is contrary to the successful integration of those communities. The presence or absence of close family members in the UK should be irrelevant to the consideration of an application for entry clearance or admission to the UK as a visitor except insofar as it relates to accommodation and financial support.

Time limits

Currently there is a maximum period of six months that a visitor may remain in the UK. Extensions are only given on the most exceptional compassionate grounds or if the visitor is receiving private medical treatment. The reason for limiting visits to a specific period would appear to be to prevent visitors from becoming resident in the UK.

For visitors who have come for tourism and do not have access to the labour market, public funds or other social benefits, it is difficult to see what harm is caused by permitting them to extend their visit beyond six months. Provided that they are not reliant on public funds for maintenance and accommodation, their presence must be of benefit to the economy. It would seem sensible to permit people who wish to remain as visitors for the purpose of tourism to obtain successive extensions of their leave to remain, possibly for three months at a time so long as they fulfil the conditions necessary to be a visitor.

Students

The UK has a long tradition of educating students from across the world from primary to postgraduate levels. It is part of the cultural heritage of the UK and its colonial past that strong ties have developed through educational links. Overseas students also provide an important source of income for educational institutions in the UK. Increasingly at post-secondary level, educational institutions actively recruit overseas students because of the economic benefit of the high differential fees which they pay.

There were 84,600 overseas students in public sector institutions in 1992 and many more (490,000) in the private sector. The United Kingdom Overseas Student Association (UKOSA) estimates that a student spends in the region of £45,000 over a three year course, including college fees. In the case of Leeds University, those fees contribute £8.5 million, some 9.4% of its general revenue. David Wilson, the Principal of a college in the private sector, has estimated that the contribution of students in both sectors must amount to around £1,167 billion per annum. Officially, education is recognised as providing 4% of the UK's export earnings from services in 1990.[9] Wilson argues that it would be useful for an official estimate to be made of the foreign currency earnings generated by overseas students, including for instance their living expenses, 'if only to remind the powers-that-be of the vital role played by "British Education plc" to the economic life of the country'.

The Department of Trade and Industry, in recognition of the benefits to the UK economy, provides assistance to educational institutions which want to compete in the international market for students, for instance by subsidising the cost of their attending trade fairs abroad. It recently organised a conference on the Asia Pacific market for students, addressed by the Trade Minister Richard Needham, in which some 60 educational institutions participated.[10]

Overseas students are not only beneficial for the economy. Their presence at UK schools and universities also enriches the cultural diversity of these institutions. It is not uncommon for UK students to have their first contact with people from other cultures at school or university. This contact can only enhance understanding and tolerance.

For overseas students, not infrequently for reasons of language and culture, as well as the quality of education, the UK is often the first choice for the pursuit of training or studies in disciplines unavailable in the student's home country. The benefit which they take with them on their return to their country of origin may be extremely important. The increasing cost of education for overseas students in the UK has tended to make this the preserve of the wealthy or those who are able to obtain scholarships. However, some young people are able to study in the UK because a financial contribution to their studies is made by their whole extended family. In such circumstances, the students' successful completion of studies has an importance in social terms in their country of origin far beyond that of most British students.

In view of the importance of overseas students both to the UK economy and to the development of the countries from which they come, UK immigration policy should facilitate the admission of such students but does not always do so. Students from countries whose nationals must obtain entry clearance before coming to the UK, for instance may not change from being visitors to students while in the UK. They must return to their country of origin and apply for entry clearance as students and then return to the UK. This increases dramatically the costs for such students. It may be that visitors only consider whether or not it would be possible or desirable for them to study in the UK while here. To be required to return to their country of origin to obtain entry clearance, not only entails the cost of the air fare but the potential loss of an academic year if the formalities to obtain entry clearance cannot be completed in time.[11]

As in respect of visitors, overseas students must satisfy the immigration official of their intention to leave the UK on the completion of their studies. This leaves a large discretion to the officer to fail to be satisfied about an intention. In the interests of uniformity of application of the law, a diminution of that margin of discretion may be desirable.

The right of appeal against refusal of entry clearance or leave to enter which did exist has been removed by the Act where the student intends to take a course of study which is six months or less. This was an arbitrary attack on appeal rights, the effect of which can only be to discourage students from coming to the UK to study. Such an effect is counter productive in relation to the DTI's policy objective of increasing the number of students who come.

Two other problematic areas arise in respect of students. The first is the continued existence of overt sex discrimination in the immigration rules. While men students are entitled to have their wives with them in the UK while they study, women students are not permitted to have their husbands join them as dependants. In view of the commitment of the UK Government and the EC to the eradication of sex discrimination, this disparity should be eliminated by permitting women students the same rights as men.

Second, while students may work part-time during their studies and full-time during their holidays, they must obtain the permission of the Department of Employment before doing so. As this is normally granted, albeit after lengthy formalities, the requirement to obtain permission seems unnecessary. Further, it is not unusual, because of the nature of the endorsement in students' passports, that they are unaware how, or indeed that it is necessary, to obtain Department of Employment permission to take (or change) part-time employment. If they fail to do so, however, the penalty for failure is extremely severe: deportation.

In view of the fact that students are normally given permission to work part-time, the penalty for failure to obtain prior permission is disproportionate. Deportation necessarily means the end of their studies without completion of their course and the tragic loss of opportunity for these students. Accordingly, it would be preferable either for all students to be permitted to work part-time without requiring any further formality or for the penalty for working without permission to be a fine or some other measure proportionate to the offence.

Conclusions

Overseas visitors and students fulfil an important economic, social and cultural role in the UK. This role should be acknowledged and encouraged through UK immigration policy.

In order to do so, UK immigration rules in respect of both these two categories should be clear, simple and easily administered. The discretion of the entry clearance or immigration officer should be kept to a minimum as it relates to subjective criteria such as long term intention.

Appeal rights capable of providing an effective remedy must apply in all circumstances. In respect of students, failure to obtain prior permission from the Department of Employment before taking part-time work during term time or full-time work during the holidays should not render the student liable to deportation. Sex discrimination should be eliminated in respect of admission of dependants of students.

Rights of appeal

However well administered the present control may be, it is fundamentally wrong and inconsistent with the rule of law that power to take decisions affecting a man's whole future should be vested in officers of the executive, from whose finding there is no Appeal. *Wilson Committee under the Chairmanship of Sir Roy Wilson QC.*[12]

The Report of the Wilson Committee was published in 1967. On the basis of its recommendations the Immigration Appeals Act 1969 was passed setting up the appeals system currently in operation. It remains the most succinct statement of UK policy on rights of appeal in respect of immigration matters and the clearest justification. The position stated in that report is the foundation against which I shall measure current practice.

The current statutory provisions are contained in the Immigration Acts 1971 and 1988 and the Asylum and Immigration Appeals Act 1993 ('the Act'). A tribunal structure known as the Immigration Appellate Authorities was established, the purpose of which is to safeguard the lawfulness of administrative action, both procedural and substantive, in the administration of immigration control. A right of appeal arises primarily in five circumstances:

1. refusal of an application for entry clearance made at a British consular post abroad;
2. refusal of leave to enter the UK;
3. refusal of an extension or variation of leave to remain in the UK provided that, at the time of receipt of the application, the applicant still had leave (permission) to remain in the UK and the application was not subject to mandatory refusal under the Immigration Rules; alternatively on curtailment of leave;
4. decision to make a deportation order unless national security is invoked;
5. refusal of an application for asylum.

The Appellate Authority has three main duties when considering any appeal: to determine whether the immigration decision is in accordance with the law and Immigration Rules; to review the facts upon which a decision is based; and, where a discretion exists within the Immigration Rules, to determine whether that discretion has been correctly exercised. The two tiered nature of the authority ensures consistency and coherence of decisions.

Where an appeal right exists, in most cases it lies to an adjudicator at the first instance, then with leave to a three person Immigration Appeal Tribunal (IAT). In some cases the appeal lies to the IAT at first instance. Adjudicators and members of the IAT are appointed by the Lord Chancellor. One of the notable features of the appeal structure in respect of appeals arising under circumstances (1) and (2) above is the absence, in most cases, of the appellant. Although appellants are usually entitled to be present at their appeal, they cannot normally attend because they are not in the UK and cannot gain admission to the UK for this purpose. Most appellants refused leave to enter may only exercise their right of appeal after departure from the UK.

Following the refusal and lodging of notice of appeal, the Home Office or entry clearance officer prepares a written explanatory statement which counts as evidence. Oral evidence is rarely given by the respondent so that the IAT must rely on hearsay and documentary evidence rather than oral evidence and cross examination. Frequently the appeal turns on the credibility of the appellant, in which case the tribunal is particularly hampered by the inability to form its view on the basis of the appellants' oral evidence.

Only appellants in categories (3) and (4) will normally be able to attend their appeal hearings and give oral evidence. In respect of category (3), where a person applies for a variation or extension of leave to remain in the UK before the expiry of current leave, a right of appeal lies against a refusal while the appellant remains in the UK. The Act purports to remove the right of appeal where the refusal of the application is mandatory under the Immigration Rules. Where a person's leave to remain has expired before the application is received by the Home Office, no right of appeal exists. These distinctions do not appear to be consistent with the policy objective set out in the Wilson report that there be a right of appeal wherever an administrative act may affect the individual's whole future.

Deportation appeals

In respect of category (4), the Secretary of State may give notice of a decision to deport on one of three grounds:

- the passenger has not observed a condition attached to limited leave or remains beyond the time limited by the leave;
- the Secretary of State deems his deportation to be conducive to the public good or;
- if another person to whose family he belongs is or has been ordered to be deported.

The Secretary of State must first give notice of the decision to deport, whereupon the person may appeal. However, except where the deportation is 'conducive to the public good', if the person cannot satisfy the IAT that s/he was last given leave to enter the UK 7 years or more before the date of the decision, the tribunal cannot consider the merits of the case. The only exception is where the person claims to be a refugee. In 'conducive to the public good' cases, the person may appeal against the decision and the IAT may consider the merits. However, this right of appeal does not exist where the ground of the decision was in the interest of national security or of the relations between the UK and any other country or for other reasons of a political nature.

Certain rights of appeal also exist against refusal to revoke a deportation order and in respect of removal directions. In respect of the latter, it is limited to the ground that the person ought to be removed to a country or territory other than the one specified in the removal notice.

The distinctions which currently exist in respect of appeals against deportation lack coherence. Why should a person who has been in the UK for 7 years have a full right of appeal against a decision to deport, whereas someone who has been in the UK for 10 years but made a trip abroad in the middle of that period (and was granted fresh leave to enter on return) be unable to have the merits of the case considered?

The expulsion of persons long resident here in particular creates uncertainty in any ethnic community affected and hinders programmes towards integration. This view is supported by the Committee of Experts of the Council of Europe in its report *Community and Ethnic relations in Europe* (1991). Successful integration policies and the racial harmony which such policies engender depend on security of residence for non British citizens resident here.

Further, any policy on deportation must be consistent with the jurisprudence of the European Court of Human Rights as set out in the recent cases of *Beldjoudi, Moustaquim* and *Djeroud*.[13] The Court has consistently ruled that the expulsion of non-nationals who have spent substantial periods of time in a country is contrary to Article 8 of the European Convention on Human Rights, the protection of private and family life.

The most recent decision of this Court on deportation is *Beldjoudi v France*.[14] In a concurring opinion, Judge Martens states:

I believe that an increasing number of Member States of the Council of Europe accept the principle that such 'integrated aliens' should be no more liable to expulsion than nationals, an exception being justified, if at all, only in very exceptional circumstances.

Any decision to deport a person (whether lawfully in the country or not) must give rise to a right of appeal with suspensive effect. At that appeal, the tribunal must be able to assess the state's need to have effective enforcement of its immigration laws against the particular circumstances of the prospective deportee including length of residence, family ties, employment record, integration into the community and any other compassionate circumstances.

A judicial remedy is fundamental to both fairness and consistency of decision making. Deportation is a very serious penalty. Its consequences can include the division of families and the loss of education and employment prospects.

Asylum Appeals

In respect of category (5), the recent Act has introduced a special regime in respect of persons who claim that their removal from the UK would be contrary to the UK's obligations under the UN Convention on the Status of Refugees 1951 and the New York Protocol 1967.

The appeal which arises where such a claim is made is to a special adjudicator within the Immigration Appellate system. Such an appeal will lie against:

- Refusal of entry;
- A variation of (or refusal to vary) leave to remain;
- A decision to make (or a refusal to revoke) a deportation order;
- Removal directions as an illegal entrant.

The obligation of the UK under the Refugee Convention is not to return to the border a person who has a well founded fear of persecution in his or her country of origin on account of race, religion, nationality, membership of a social group or political opinion.

The introduction of this right of appeal for asylum seekers, which has suspensive effect in all cases, is a great improvement over the previous position. Unfortunately it is limited to the Refugee Convention and does not extend to the UK's obligations under the ECHR. In particular Article 3, the prohibition of torture, inhuman or degrading treatment, has been interpreted by the human rights court to preclude return to a country where the person is likely to suffer torture, inhuman or degrading treatment. Similarly it does not extend to the UK's obligations under the UN Convention against Torture and Other Cruel, Inhuman or Degrading Treatment or Punishment Article 3(1) which prohibits the return or extradition of a person to another state where there is substantial grounds for believing he or she would be in danger of being subjected to torture.

This problem is aggravated by the provision enabling a fast track procedure where an asylum claim is certified by the Secretary of State to be 'without foundation'. The definition that such a claim is without foundation contains two limbs: that it does not raise any issue as to the UK's obligations under the Refugee Convention; or that it is otherwise frivolous or vexatious.

Therefore, where an appellant is able to establish that s/he is likely to suffer torture, inhuman or degrading treatment in the proposed destination country but is not able to satisfy the definition of the Refugee Convention (that is to say that such treatment is on one of the five enumerated grounds of persecution), the appeal may be dealt with as one 'without foundation'. In accordance with the truncated procedure for such appeals, there is no further appeal to the second tier of the appellate authority, the Immigration Appeal Tribunal.

Circumstances in which no appeal right exists

There is no right of appeal if:

1. a Criminal Court has recommended deportation;
2. a deportation order has been signed;
3. a work permit application is refused by the Department of Employment;
4. an application for an extension (or variation) made after the applicant's current leave has expired or been refused;
5. before removal where the person is treated as an illegal entrant;
6. the Secretary of State certifies the decision is in the interests of national security, relations with other states or for other reasons of a political nature.
7. the application refused was to come to or enter the UK as a visitor or a student for a course of study of less than six months' duration, or the refusal is mandatory under the Immigration Rules.

I consider each of these circumstances in turn.

1. *Criminal Court recommendation:*
Where a suspect subject to immigration control is convicted of an offence, the court may recommend deportation as part of the sentence. Where it does so, a right of appeal lies only within the Criminal Court structure. It is open to the Secretary of State to proceed either directly to signing a deportation order or by way of his administrative deportation power.

This is inappropriate. The IAT should be responsible as it has the expertise and experience of considering the factors relevant to deportation appeals. Criminal Courts should not have a power to recommend deportation.

2. *A deportation order has been signed:*

Where notice of intention to deport is sent to the last known address of the proposed deportee, the right of appeal must be exercised within fourteen days. If no notice of appeal is received, the Secretary of State may sign a deportation order. If the whereabouts of a proposed deportee are unknown, it is open to the Secretary of State to serve notice 'on the file', that is to say without notification to the proposed deportee, who may then lose the right of appeal as s/he is unaware that the notice has been served. This can produce inequitable results, particularly where there is no fault on the part of the person subject to the order. The person will be unaware that a deportation order has been signed. If the person leaves the UK and subsequently seeks to re-enter, albeit ten years later as a visitor, s/he may be refused on the ground that s/he is a person named in a deportation order. If the immigration officer at the port of entry is unaware that a deportation order has been signed and admits the passenger, s/he will be an illegal entrant even though s/he was unaware that a deportation order had been signed and was, to the best of his/her knowledge, completely candid in responses to the immigration officer's questions.

The practice of servicing a notice of decision to deport 'on the file' should be discontinued and the time limit for appealing against such a decision should not start to run until the proposed deportee has actual notice of the decision.

3. *Refusal of a work permit:*

The work permit scheme is administered by the Employment Department Overseas Labour Section on an extra statutory basis. Where a work permit is refused, neither the business applying for the permit nor the proposed overseas worker has a right of appeal. This is not in the interests of the business community. Some sectors of the economy are suffering from skills shortages notwithstanding high unemployment in other skills sectors. Frequently, businesses are only able to find the necessary expertise outside the EC labour market. While the Department of Employment may make every effort to administer the work permit scheme fairly and efficiently, nonetheless businesses are not infrequently aggrieved by the decisions.

The work permit scheme should be brought within the Immigration Rules and the prospective employer have a right of appeal against refusal of a work permit (or training and work experience permit).

4. *Application for an extension or variation made 'out of time':*

Where a person's current leave expires before an application for an extension or variation is made, no right of appeal arises if the application is refused. This may occur in a variety of circumstances through no fault of the person—e.g. unexpected delays in renewal of his/her passport; loss of passport; error on the part of professional advisers.

It has been argued that the lack of a right of appeal in such circumstances is not critical as the person would then have an appeal right on merits should the Secretary of State serve notice of decision to deport. However, since the Immigration Act 1988, in many circumstances there has been no right of appeal on merits.

Accordingly, it is recommended that where an application for variation (or extension) of leave to remain in the UK is made unsuccessfully after the applicant's current leave has expired, the Secretary of State should have a discretion to allow an appeal. If he declines to do so, the applicant should still be entitled to exercise a right of appeal under the Act. However, the appellate authority should consider as a preliminary issue whether, on the merits of the case, the Secretary of State's discretion was correctly exercised. If the appellate authority is not so satisfied it should have power to substitute its discretion for that of the Secretary of State.

5. *Before removal where a person is treated as an illegal entrant:*

When the Immigration Act 1971 was first enacted, illegal entry was thought to include only cases of clandestine entry. However, since 1976 illegal entry has been held to include entry by deception.

An illegal entrant means a person who has entered or is seeking to enter the UK in breach of a deportation order or of immigration law. We are concerned here only with persons against whom the allegation is made that they entered by deception. The deception may be as to identity, entitlement, status or intention. However, to be an illegal entrant, the deception must have been the effective means of obtaining leave to enter.

The allegation of fraud is a serious one. The burden of proof rests on the immigration officer or Secretary of State alleging that deception. However, since the landmark decision of the House of Lords in *Khawaja*[15] setting out the burden of proof, no steps have been taken to establish an appropriate forum in which matters of fact can be determined. These are still being decided by the High Court in judicial review proceedings, requiring High Court judges to spend precious and expensive time determining matters of fact. Indeed, the courts themselves have commented on the unsatisfactory nature of the law, Mr Justice Hodgson stating,

> In very few cases is judicial review a satisfactory way to test whether it has been established that entry was illegal. It would, in my opinion, be a great improvement if illegal entry was added as a fourth reason for deportation to those already contained in S.5 of the Act. The factual question of whether the entry was illegal could then be tested on an appeal to an adjudicator.[16]

In my opinion such questions of fact would be more cheaply and effectively dealt with by the appellate authority within the context of an appeal right against an allegation of illegal entry.

6. *Conducive to the public good:*

The Immigration Act 1971 provides that a person who is not a British Citizen shall be liable to deportation if the Secretary of State deems his deportation to be 'conducive to the public good';[17] If this is for reasons of national security, there is no right of appeal.[18] This applies whether the decision is to refuse a variation of leave or to deport.

The decision is subject only to a review procedure under the Immigration Rules[19] which lacks fundamental characteristics of due process:

- The only 'appeal' procedure is by way of non-statutory review by a panel appointed by the Home Secretary, the recommendations of which have no binding effect and need not be notified to the appellant.
- There is no right to be informed of the allegations against the appellant.
- There is no right to legal representation.
- The burden of proof is on the appellant to show s/he is not a threat to national security.

Serious practical criticisms of the procedure were well ventilated in the press during the Gulf War when many Iraqi and other nationals were detained and threatened with deportation on national security grounds. The selection of persons for detention appeared to be based on information or rumour which was often unreliable. Even safeguards that the people named in the deportation orders were in fact those detained do not appear to have operated effectively. However of more fundamental importance are the civil liberties questions raised by lack of procedural safeguards and remedies. All the decisions to deport on grounds of national security issued against Iraqi nationals, Palestinians and others contained the same pro forma paragraph of reasons. These referred to Iraqi Government threats to take terrorist action in the event of hositilities and the deportee's 'links and activities in connection with the Iraqi regime'. No further reasons were provided nor any explanation which might guide the detainee as to the nature of the allegations or how to respond to them. The only course open to an appellant is to put before the Panel every conceivable instance that might or might not be relevant throughout his/her whole life. A phantom allegation is difficult to disprove.

On an unsuccessful challenge by way of judicial review of the sufficiency of the reasons and an application for habeas corpus on behalf of one such detainee, the Master of the Rolls rejected the argument that at least some disclosure was required by natural justice, holding that:

> the prospective detainee is not entitled to be given the fullest particulars of what is alleged against him. This would, in other circumstances, undoubtedly be objectionable as constituting a denial of natural justice. But natural justice has to take account of realities and something which would otherwise constitute a breach is not to be so considered if it is unavoidable.[20]

The Government argued that the denial of particulars is unavoidable in national security cases in order to protect the sources of the information. However, the refusal to give any indication of their substance renders it impossible for the detainee to prepare his/her defence. Natural justice cannot permit deprivation of liberty and deportation on any ground without requiring at least some substance of the allegations against the individual to be made known to him/her. Surely it is not beyond the abilities of civil servants to frame the particulars of allegations in such a way as to protect the sources of that information. The information was put to the appellants in examination: it could have been given in writing. There was no evidence that the cases had been considered individually before the decisions to deport or intern were made.

His Lordship accepted that the courts have a supervisory jurisdiction in such cases but stated:

> In the case of national security, the responsibility is exclusively that of the government of the day, but its powers are limited by statute and the courts will intervene if it is shown that the minister responsible has acted other than in good faith or has in any way overstepped the limitations upon his authority which are imposed by law.

Without any requirement to provide reasons it is difficult to see how a detainee could show a lack of good faith on the part of the Executive.

His Lordship also found that 'the advisory panel is susceptible of judicial review if, for example, it could be shown to have acted unfairly within its terms of reference'. As a recommendation of the Advisory Panel is confidential and in any event does not bind the Executive, this jurisdiction does little to reassure a detainee that the decision making process was fairly and properly conducted. Where the individual's liberty is concerned s/he is entitled to pursue all available remedies with the most effective means, including legal representation. Where additionally s/he may have difficulty with the language, surely there should be a right to legal representation: even the right to an interpreter was in the discretion of the panel.

The law in respect of persons detained and facing deportation on grounds of national security is thus unsatisfactory in that there is little semblance of due process.

The courts have held that it is a matter for Parliament to regulate the exercise of powers it has granted to the Executive in respect of national security. Therefore, Parliament should now remove the restriction on rights of appeal which currently apply where national security is pleaded. Until 1973 there was a full right of appeal in such cases: I can see no reason for not reverting to that situation. The immigration appellate authority is the appropriate tribunal to consider such appeals, having experience in considering all other deportation appeals. Any limitation on access by the appellant to full details of the allegations against him/her should be subject to judicial scrutiny on the basis that the burden is on the Executive to satisfy the court that each particular for which confidentiality is claimed would, on the balance of probabilities, prejudice national security. Legal representation should be allowed.

7. *Visitor and student refusals:*

The Asylum and Immigration Appeals Act has recently removed appeal rights for visitors who are refused visas or leave to enter the UK (with an exception for those visitors in possession of entry clearance but who are refused admission on arrival). Students also have no appeal rights if they are coming to the UK to study for less than six months.

As in respect of appeal rights on deportation these provisions create an anomalous situation where certain categories of visitors and students continue to have appeal rights while others, for no ascertainable or objective reason, are denied these rights. Such measures which fail a test of objectivity and consistency weaken the concept of the rule of law. A random appeal right which may attach, for instance, to the refusal of an application for a visa by a student enrolled on a course of six months and one week's duration but not his/her colleague enrolled on a course of five months' duration is certainly not unambiguously rational, the standard which should apply to all legislation.

Further, the vital role of appeal rights in regulating the consistency of decision making by public officials is undermined. If these provisions for visitors and students are an indication of future policy, the piecemeal dismantling of the immigration appeal system can be anticipated.

Bail

Under the 1971 Act, the Secretary of State and immigration officers are given wide powers of detention in respect of passengers, persons treated as illegal entrants and prospective deportees. Bail applications may then be made if the passenger has been detained for seven days without a decision on his/her leave to enter having been made;[21] or if they have an appeal pending.[22] However there is no presumption in favour of bail. Specifically the Bail Act 1976 does not apply unless the detainee has been charged with a criminal offence. This has given rise to inconsistency in the way in which bail may be granted or refused. In particular, a person charged with a criminal offence will benefit from the provisions of the Bail Act while a person not so charged cannot.

Further, the 1971 Act gives little guidance to the IAT on how to exercise its powers in respect of bail which further aggravates the problem of inconsistency. While some adjudicators grant bail with few conditions as a matter of course, others are reluctant to do so or inclined to require substantially higher sureties than their colleagues.

It is in the interests of justice that all bail applications be considered on the basis of uniform criteria. Such criteria have been set out in the Bail Act 1976 which should be amended so as expressly to apply to all bail decisions under the Immigration Act. All Immigration Act detainees should be entitled to apply for bail.

Administrative delay

In an area where fundamental issues of individuals' lives are at stake, delays in decision making are particularly perilous. When those delays apply unequally to situations of a similar nature, the allegation of discrimination is difficult to refute.

For instance, where a spouse applies at a British post abroad for entry clearance to come to the UK to join a spouse here, the application must be made in the country in which the overseas spouse is living. If that happens to be Bangladesh, the spouse will wait between three and nine months for a first interview. However, if the spouse was resident in Egypt, Cyprus or Nigeria, the wait from application to first interview is one day.[23]

Clearly there must exist discrimination in respect of the allocation of resources between these posts. How long after the first interview it may take before a decision is reached also varies dramatically. This may be the result of the issues raised at that interview. Nonetheless, in so far as delay is the result of administrative procedures, it should be eliminated where consistent with good management.

One solution is to set time limits with legal consequences. Where six months has elapsed from the date of application and no decision has been reached, at the applicant's election the application should be deemed to be refused and the applicant allowed to appeal immediately to the IAT. In this way at least the applicant may seek a remedy in the tribunal forum best equipped to consider the issues.

Conclusions

In view of the importance of a right of appeal both on the merits and the law in respect of matters relating to immigration and asylum there should be a right of appeal against every refusal to the Immigration Appellate Authority. It should have suspensive effect in all of the following circumstances:

- where the person is appealing against refusal to extend or vary leave to remain in the UK;
- where the person claims that removal will result in torture, inhuman or degrading treatment;
- in respect of any decision to deport;
- against any decision to treat the person as an illegal entrant;
- against refusal of leave to enter where the person was in possession of a current entry clearance or work permit.

The only circumstances in which such a right of appeal does not require suspensive effect is where it is against an application made at a British consular post abroad or is an application for leave to enter where the person is not in possession of entry clearance and no issue of asylum arises.

In all cases where a right of appeal arises, the Immigration Appellate Authority must have the power to consider the merits of the application as well as whether or not the decision was in accordance with the law. Wherever a discretion is exercised by the Secretary of State (or where he refrains from exercising a discretion) the Immigration Appellate Authority should have the power to substitute its discretion in place of that of the Secretary of State.

9 THE AGE OF INTERNAL CONTROLS?

Anne Owers

The age of external controls is over; we are now in the age of internal controls.
Senior official, Dutch Ministry of Justice, at a seminar in London, October 1990

Q. Is there any single person sitting at that table who now does not believe that the time has come for us to introduce a mandatory identity card and preferably one that is recognised and standardised throughout the European Community?

A. We are unified on that.

Q. Even if the external border checks were retained or only if they were abolished?

A. Regardless.

> *Representatives of the Association of Chief Police Officers, the Police Superintendents' Association and the Police Federation (APCO), giving evidence to the Home Affairs Select Committee, 12 February 1992*

The move towards internal controls

The Netherlands and the UK are the only European Community countries (apart from Eire) which do not use identity cards as part of a system of internal checks and controls. Both countries have traditionally resisted their introduction—the Netherlands because of the association with the Nazi occupation and the UK because of its common law tradition, which generally defines what is prohibited, rather than what is required.

The Dutch Government, however, now supports a 'voluntary' system of personal identification. There are two principal reasons for the shift: Dutch accession to the Schengen Agreement and the removal of frontier checks within the Schengen area; and a growing concern about possible migration from East and Central Europe into the Netherlands, which has the longest land border with Germany of any European country.

The British police evidence to the Home Affairs Committee in 1992 is evidence of a similar shift of opinion in the UK. Four years earlier, in response to a previous inquiry, the police service, and ACPO in particular, had been against identity cards, both because they would be ineffective and because they would be counter-productive and bad for community relations.

The official Home Office and immigration service position, in evidence to the 1992 committee, continued to be that border checks were more effective and less costly than internal controls. However, the Home Office has developed a fall-back position, with the prerequisites for a system of internal control which would be necessary if there were any substantial relaxation of frontier controls as a result either of the Maastricht Treaty or the intergovernmental negotiations taking place within the TREVI, Ad Hoc Immigration and Schengen groups. Its evidence to the Committee identified three kinds of 'compensating action' which would be necessary: increased resources for the enforcement side of immigration control (checking and deporting those here illegally); punitive sanctions on employers of unauthorised workers; and 'a requirement for people to establish their identity on demand'.[1]

The change in attitude, or emphasis, in the UK has the same causes as in the Netherlands: the increasing likelihood that the UK will be unable to sustain its present level of frontier checks (and will indeed for the first time have a land border once the Channel Tunnel is open); and the Europe-wide fear of mass arrivals from the East and South. The concept of a frontier-free space within Europe does not lead inevitably to the need for stronger internal controls, provided that there is confidence that the common external borders will be adequately policed. But there is no such confidence in the UK. First, like other northern European countries, the UK does not believe that countries in the south of Europe can or will enforce effective controls. Second, all continental European countries rely on a combination of external and internal checks because land borders are always permeable. Third, the so-called frontier-free space is a myth: the Single European Act gives freedom of movement within the common area *only* to nationals of EC countries; nationals of other countries, even if legally resident for many years, have no rights to live and work freely

265

in any other EC country save the one which granted them entry or residence rights. It is therefore not the case that, since 1 January 1993, all those within the EC area are entitled to cross its internal frontiers at will.

It is clear, therefore, that there is a growing, possibly irresistible, pressure for a system of internal checks and controls, including identity cards. Yet until now there has been little serious discussion in the UK of how such a system might operate, what problems it might be expected to solve and what effects it might have. The debate, particularly in relation to identity cards, is largely conducted in slogans, from prepared positions. For their proponents, identity cards are essential to prevent the flood of crime, terrorism, drugs and illegal immigration consequent on open borders; in addition, they are a simple and exciting application of new technology which will allow the law-abiding immediately to establish their status and travel freely. For their opponents, they are an infringement of civil liberties, an intimation of the Big Brother state and will provide an excuse for further harassment of the black communities.

This paper cannot provide a detailed comparative and analytical study. It attempts only to do two things: first, to look behind the slogans at the practicalities and consequences of setting up or strengthening internal control systems in the UK; secondly to test the claims that an internal control system, based on identity cards, is both a necessary compensatory measure for those policing the controls and a helpful protective measure for the public.

Systems of control

There are two major ways of enforcing internal immigration controls. The first is to require the carrying of personal identification which can distinguish those legally present from those illegally on the territory; to be effective, this requires random or systematic checks by enforcement agencies. The second is to spread the responsibility for enforcement among a variety of other agencies, both state and private, whose primary concern is not immigration: for example, employers, benefit and housing agencies and schools.

Scandinavian countries rely very heavily on the latter. In Denmark, each individual is given at birth (or on arrival) a unique, computer-held, personal identification number. This is fed into a series of linked data systems: a residence database (it is an offence not to report a change of address within six weeks), a tax and banking database (so that tax is deducted directly from bank accounts), medical, work and school records. Individuals need to provide their PINs when they register at a school or with a doctor, take up employment, open a bank account, rent or buy a house. There is felt to be no need for identity cards or overt checks, but hidden checks are part of people's daily lives.

This system appears to work because Denmark and other Scandinavian countries have traditionally been very homogeneous societies, with little distinction between the state and civil society. Other European countries with different traditions rely on a mixture of mandatory or voluntary personal identification and indirect immigration control enforcement through employer sanctions and entitlement to state benefits and services.

In practice, both mechanisms of control are already in existence in the UK, in an unregulated and piecemeal fashion. There is no requirement to carry personal identification; but it is very common, certainly within the Metropolitan Police area, for members of visible minority communities to be stopped, on the pretext of a check for a criminal or traffic offence, and asked for evidence of legal residence. Parliamentary questions elicited the information that in 1989 London police checked the immigration status of at least 6,800 people of whom only 2,400 were identified as immigration offenders.[2]

Similarly, since the 1980s, there has been a growing linkage between immigration status and access to state benefits and services. The clearest example is access to British citizenship itself, which since 1983 has been dependent on the immigration or nationality status of a child's parents. Others are the 'recourse to public funds' requirements in the immigration and benefit rules, and the effect of immigration status on entitlement to educational fees and awards and free hospital treatment. There is already, therefore, a network of devolved immigration controllers, from teachers trying to decide which children in a class can travel on a group British passport, to housing officials, benefits officers and education and health administrators. Some agencies, like hospitals, have clear and published instructions for staff doing immigration checks; others, like schools and local authorities, usually have none, and practice varies greatly.

The inter-relation between benefits and immigration is the clearest evidence of the growth of an unstructured, but increasingly visible, internal control system. Questioning about immigration status used to be ad hoc, varying from one benefit office to another. Now that records are kept on database and accessed centrally, it is very difficult for people to apply for a national insurance number for the first time, or to claim income support, in the absence of evidence of lengthy residence in the UK, without their immigration status being checked with the Home Office.

The treatment of asylum-seekers has greatly extended this form of control. The Asylum and Immigration Appeals Act means that all asylum-seekers have to be fingerprinted for benefit and housing purposes;[3] but even before the Act became law, the Home Office and Benefits Agency had agreed procedures, without any formal legislative change, whereby asylum-seekers were unable to obtain income support unless they obtained an identity document (with photograph) from the Home Office.

The creeping internalisation of immigration controls is therefore already evident in the UK. Two of the three Home Office proposals would extend this, by increasing the resources for direct enforcement of immigration controls and by bringing employers into the network of those responsible for indirect enforcement, by penalising them for employing unauthorised workers.

Enforcement is at present carried out by immigration officers, working with the police. There is no comprehensive system or programme for the detection of immigration offenders: there are no records of whether those admitted to the UK for a limited period in fact leave at the end of their stay. The immigration service therefore depends on three methods of enforcement: the stop and search activities described above, largely initiated by the police; denunciations by neighbours, family members and workmates; and 'major joint operations' (police/immigration service raids).

In the late 1980s, immigration officers at Isis House, the main enforcement office for London and the south-east, began to cultivate relations with the police on a more systematic basis. The Metropolitan police area was divided into sectors, with immigration officers detailed to each sector to encourage police to recognise and act on immigration offences. This resulted in the high level of police activity described above; it also, however, resulted in the passing on of so much information that immigration officers were unable to cope and had to run down the sector system. Individual denunciatory letters, also, are received in such numbers that the immigration service only acts if the information is recent and detailed. Action is undertaken without any further checks.

Joint police/immigration service raids are carried out on targeted premises. The immigration service recognises that such raids are not cost-effective as they tie up a great deal of police and immigration manpower; they are seen as necessary both *pour encourager les autres* and to draw political and media attention to a problem (as perceived by the immigration service). Raids have often been directed at language schools with a large number of African students or clothing or cleaning firms employing ethnic minority staff. There are no recorded instances of police/immigration raids on wine bars in Kensington employing large numbers of young Americans and Australians. According to the Home Office, better targeting of areas of suspected immigration abuse partly accounts for the increase in the number of people removed as illegal entrants in 1992; 3,600 compared to 3,200 the previous year.[4]

Employer sanctions are sometimes advocated as a means of protecting workers from exploitation, as well as enforcing immigration regulations. At present in the UK, employers are not obliged to check employees' right to be, or to work, in the UK. They can only be prosecuted if they knowingly aid or abet illegal entry or residence; such prosecutions are very rare and confined to those who systematically organise illegal immigration for work. However, many employers, particularly in low-paid, unsocial hours sectors like catering and cleaning, depend on illegal workers, who are the only people likely to accept the poor terms and conditions. This creates a low-wage employment sector, where workers have no rights, are not insured and often work in poor or unsafe conditions. If caught, they are criminalised and penalised, but their employers are not.

Immigration law is, however, an imperfect way of seeking to address other social problems (viz. the claim that the primary purpose rule protects young Asian women from unwanted marriages). Legal minimum wage levels, and additional sanctions and resources for health and safety enforcement are more likely to address employers' deficiencies than immigration sanctions. Other EC countries, which have employer sanctions, have more unauthorised workers than the UK; they are simply pushed further underground. In the UK, there would be additional problems. Most foreign residents in the UK are legally able to work, but very few have, or need, a work permit to do so (unlike in most other EC countries, which issue clear residence and work permits to non-nationals). Many employers already wrongly assume that foreigners need work permits to work and occasionally ask for them. If there was a legal responsibility to check, it is likely that many employers would, directly or indirectly, discriminate against non-British workers without work permits. Bona fide employment would then become more difficult for legally settled UK residents, while bad employers would continue to evade the regulations.

The first two Home Office proposals would be grafted on to a piecemeal system which already targets particular communities and ethnic groups, and which is insufficiently monitored and controlled. Increasing enforcement resources and informal checks, without creating a more systematic identification and control system, would increase the profile of immigration enforcement but would be unlikely to change the reality (viz. the UK-Mexico border, where people are visibly returned across the border, so that they can invisibly cross it again).

Identity cards

This therefore leads to the call for identity cards as a means of requiring and establishing legality. There are various systems of personal identification used in other European countries. Some are mandatory and some voluntary. However, evidence suggests that the difference is academic. It is not, for example, evident that a Turk in Germany (where the carrying of personal identification in mandatory) is any more likely to be stopped and checked than a Mahgrebian in France (where identity cards are voluntary). In practice, if a means of identification exists, then that is what both state and private agencies will ask to see if they wish to be certain of an individual's identity. Equally, it is clear that people who look or sound 'foreign' are much more likely to be asked to establish their identity, or to be the subject of random checks, particularly those related to immigration offences.

In theory, the advantage of a voluntary card is that non-possession is not a criminal offence and therefore does not provide a reason, or an excuse, for police checks. In practice, however, this is a technical rather than an actual distinction in countries where ID cards are allegedly voluntary. In France, for example, foreigners are required to have proof of residence or legality. Court decisions have held that it is illegal for the police to carry out random checks, but that they may ask for identification if there is a threat to public order or if they have reasonable suspicion that a person may be a foreigner. Such suspicion could arise from the person reading a foreign newspaper or being in the company of others speaking a foreign language.

Indeed, it can be argued that in practice a voluntary system bites hardest on ethnic minority communities who are likely to be the only legal residents to be targeted and disadvantaged by a failure to produce documentation. Given the UK's ability to develop extra-legal and in practice discriminatory systems both of external and internal control,[5] it is arguable that if identity cards are to be introduced, this should be done universally, with laws and regulations which provide clear and enforceable procedures, circumstances in which identification can be demanded, controls on detention powers, and statistics kept on the relative frequency of stops and the resulting detection of immigration offences.

The Home Affairs Select Committee has for some time been an enthusiastic advocate of voluntary ID cards, both for negative reasons (to combat crime and illegal immigration) and for positive reasons (as a means for UK citizens to establish their bona fides and move freely within the EC). In its 1992 inquiry, members of both political parties were dismissive of witnesses who failed to see the simplicity and the opportunities of hi-tech, instantly readable ID cards:

Why is it that when I go to a supermarket and buy a tin of peas the assistant goes 'like that' and it rings up how much it costs and it sends a message back to the shop to order another 10 cans of peas and all this can be done, and all your employers' sanctions or whatever, or proof that he is a bona fide man, proof that he pays his taxes, proof of everything....why cannot he have a bar code on his card like that which you just feed in, if he is challenged, to show his credentials? Why are you so objecting to modern technology? *Joe Ashton MP to Home Office witness, Minutes of Evidence taken before the Home Affairs Select Committee, 5 February 1992*[6]

The police service has also refined its definition of what an identity card, ideally mandatory, would provide. Speaking at the International Police Exhibition and Conference (IPEC) in October 1992, Ron Hadfield, Chief Constable of the West Midlands, said:

The essential features of an identity card, while not necessarily exhaustive, I would see as embracing the following eight features:
- it should be incapable of being forged and it should have a unique background and a computer-readable internal strip;
- it should incorporate the holder's fingerprint;

271

- the holder's place of birth and other suitable details, such as the holder's National Insurance number, should be included;
- the holder's photograph should be sealed into the card, which should be self-defacing if tampered with;
- the manufacture of the card should take into account current and developing technology;
- it should be the size of an ordinary credit card;
- it should be renewable at regular intervals;
- if the card were mandatory, there should be a requirement for the holder to produce the card on demand.[7]

Identity cards as an aid to establishing rights

One of the ironies about the identity card debate is that it sees the Home Office and immigration service lining up with immigration, race and civil liberties pressure groups in apparent defence of the status quo. Yet the latter groups have for years opposed the present system of border controls as arbitrary and unjust.

For example, the treatment of people seeking to enter the UK as visitors, and the powers of immigration officers to examine, detain and remove them have long been criticised. Well publicised refusals of Black Americans seeking entry to the UK in 1992 drew attention to this. The work of the Joint Council for the Welfare of Immigrants on the sudden and unexplained rise in refusals of Caribbean visitors in the late 1980s showed the growth of a self-fulfilling prophecy: once immigration officers perceive a group or nationality to be a 'problem', more of such people are refused, therefore providing 'evidence' for the suspicion.[8] Most visitors are refused entry simply because an immigration officer does not believe they intend to leave the UK at the end of the visit: the officer does not need to prove this, or find any evidence to support it.

Border control is tightened still further by the growth of mandatory visa requirements (so that people have to be checked before even setting off for the UK), fines on airlines to police such requirements and long and complex checks on family reunion cases (particularly the notorious primary purpose rule which is used to refuse two in every three young men from the Indian subcontinent). These intrusive and discriminatory checks are happening daily, but the threat to civil liberties and race relations is more easily ignored and less readily challenged because they happen at a distance.

Evidence cited above also shows how, in practice, members of ethnic minority communities are also subject to internal checks and controls in circumstances in which they may find it very difficult to prove their right to be in the UK.

It is therefore necessary to ask whether the introduction of a mandatory form of identification would provide positive benefits to those who are at present wrongly refused entry to the UK, to those seeking to travel within the EC or to those seeking to prove their right to be in the UK.

For the first group, it would be necessary to show that there would be 'reverse compensatory measures' if internal systems of control were adopted or strengthened—that border checks would become less harsh and unjust. All the evidence points in the opposite direction. Though intra-EC border crossings may become more relaxed, controls over travel into the common area from outside are being tightened. All the governmental fora discussing immigration and asylum are pressing for an increase in visa requirements, the exporting of immigration controls to points of departure and joint databases to ensure the exclusion of those defined as undesirable.

As far as travel is concerned, it is difficult to see what advantages a 'voluntary' ID card would have for British citizens over a passport. Most travellers would not wish to confine themselves to EC travel only and would therefore continue to need both. New British passports are computer-readable, already give free passage across Community borders and can be used for identity checks within other EC countries. It is possible that an identity card would have some advantages for non-British citizens legally resident in the UK who wished to visit other EC countries. It would provide clear evidence of their status in, and returnability to, the UK; though it would not, of course, confer on them any rights to be, or to work, in any other EC country.

It is also questionable whether in practice identity cards would be a quick and easy means for members of suspect groups to establish status within the UK. First, there is the assumption that a computer-readable card would be tamper-proof (which seems somewhat naive given the success of amateur computer hackers). Once there was any possibility of forgery, the card would have little face value for the people and groups most at risk (viz. the suspicion that West Africans have forged British passports and birth certificates). Second, and more importantly, is the Committee's assumption that an identity card would provide instant proof of identity and status. In practice, and particularly if the card held substantial amounts of computer-readable information, the card itself would not be proof: it would simply be the gateway to a series of checks, carried out by authorised officials accessing a series of databases. There would have to be powers to take and hold a suspect for questioning while these were carried out. In other words, the production of an ID card would be an occasion for further checks, rather than an end to checking. It would therefore not protect those who are now at risk of intrusive questioning or police detention.

Identity cards as a 'compensatory measure' in immigration control

The situation becomes even more complicated once the objectives of an ID card as an instrument of immigration control are considered. Mr Hadfield's finger-print and tamper-proof photograph card is clearly capable of establishing that an individual is the same as the person to whom the card was issued: in other words, if secure, it proves identity. But immigration status, for those subject to immigration control, is much more of a moveable target. Mr Ashton's tin of peas is always a tin of peas; all that the supermarket computer needs to know is its current price. British and EC citizens, who are actually or effectively exempt from immigration control, have an equally secure and unchanging status and it is therefore relatively easy to issue a machine-readable card which proves it. UK and EC citizens however are by definition not the people against whom external or internal immigration control is directed. They have a right to be and to work anywhere in the Community. It is the 15 million or so third-country nationals within the Community whose status is subject to checks. A form of identification which merely identified EC citizens would by implication cast doubt on the legality of every non-citizen and would not be an effective means of internal immigration control.

In order for them to be so, identity documents would have to be mandatory for non-citizens. What form would they take? Passports would be inadequate. Long-settled residents will not necessarily have a current passport, and even those who do are unlikely to have one which proves their settled status: settled people are readmitted to the UK without anything other than a date stamp. Temporary residents will have passports which show on what conditions they were originally admitted, but not necessarily whether they now have permission to be in the UK. For example, someone admitted as a student for a limited period and who is found to be in the UK after that period has elapsed could be a person who has overstayed leave and is therefore liable to deportation. However, s/he could also be someone with a current application for extension or variation of stay pending at the Home Office, who is legally here until a decision has been made on the application. Even if an application has been refused, and the passport marked accordingly, s/he would still be legally able to remain in the UK if an appeal had been lodged and was pending.

In order both to be effective as an instrument of immigration control and protective as a means for legal residents to establish their legality, a mandatory system of identification would need to ensure that the first group (permanent residents) had a document identifying them as such and that the second group (temporary residents) had a document which linked in to a constantly updated Home Office database.

The practical problems of both are enormous. It would be relatively easy to issue newly-settled residents with ID cards. But there are hundreds of thousands of existing settlers whose status would need to be meticulously checked if the system were universal. They would include children who originally came in on parents' passports, children born in the UK since 1983, and people from Commonwealth countries who entered the UK in the 1950s and 1960s before they were subject to immigration control.

Documentation establishing the current status of temporary residents would also raise problems. It would be wholly impractical to issue identity cards, of the type defined by Mr Hadfield, to the five million people who enter the UK every year as visitors. Yet it is from precisely this category of person that the greater proportion of those here illegally comes: people who originally entered the country for a short period and then stayed to live or work. Short-term visitors would presumably depend on their passports as evidence of identification (as in other European countries). Yet without compulsory border checks between EC countries, the passports of those entering the UK from within the EC would not be stamped with any indication of date of entry or period of stay.

Passports would, presumably, indicate a date on which and the purpose for which the person had initially been given permission to enter the territory of the EC as a whole, but there are still no agreed procedures for common policies in issuing a short-term 'Eurovisa' and it would therefore require a prolonged series of checks to establish the person's immigration history. Nor would it necessarily be the case that, even if such a person had remained without authority for a considerable period in other EC countries, he or she would not qualify for admission or stay for a six-month period as a visitor under UK immigration rules. In other words, mandatory identification would be useless as a means of immigration control over precisely the people, and in precisely the circumstances, for which compensatory measures are deemed to be necessary.

For other temporary residents, here for longer periods (for example students, work permit holders or spouses given an initial stay of one year as a preliminary to settlement), the ability to detect their legality would depend on the allocation of huge resources to the Immigration Department in order to computerise and keep up to date its paper records; poor filing retrieval systems and recording delays have been notorious in the Department for years. The need for such checks makes it certain that for most people who had originally entered for temporary purposes (which now includes nearly all family members) the production of an identity card for immigration purposes would merely be the preliminary to a detailed process of checking and not a means of establishing residence rights per se.

The practical difficulties of instituting a universal system of personal identification in the UK are huge. Unlike even the Netherlands, with its compulsory residence registers, the UK is unique in Europe in having no mandatory, or at least no enforced, personal registration system at all. The closest is the electoral register, which is known to be inaccurate and unchecked. In order to create an identity system of any value as an instrument of immigration control, it would be necessary to carry out an immigration census, checking the citizenship and immigration status of every resident. This scarcely seems either a political or a practical exercise. Yet without it, identity cards will in fact be of little value as a means of immigration enforcement or individual protection.

It is not only the practical difficulties however which cast doubt on the efficacy of identity cards as an effective means of immigration control. Countries which have universal systems of personal identification have larger populations of unauthorised immigrants than the UK. Other EC countries accept that systems of immigration control can no more prevent illegal immigration than systems of criminal justice can prevent crime; what is necessary in both cases is a selective, not a generalist, approach to enforcement.

This approach is indeed accepted in other areas of immigration control: for example, records are not kept on most travellers leaving the UK in order to check whether those granted leave for a limited period in fact left at the end of that period. The Home Office has always claimed that this is not a valuable use of resources, given that the vast majority of visitors do leave; it has therefore never been possible to assess how many, and what kind of, people overstay their leave to remain in the UK. This was emphasised in evidence to the Home Affairs Select Committee by a senior official in the Immigration and Nationality Department:

> There is not, in the United Kingdom, a comprehensive system to provide statistics of overstayers or any other category of unauthorised immigrant. At first sight this may sound surprising but if one thinks through what would be needed to provide the information in question one very soon has to face the fact that this could not be done except by a comprehensive entry recording and exit recording operation, conducted to a high standard of accuracy which would have to be pretty high for the information to be meaningful at all.[9]

Ed Grootaarts, head of the immigration police in the Hague, addressed the same IPEC conference as Ron Hadfield. He was somewhat bemused by the assumption of many of his questioners, from the British immigration and police services, that there is or can be a universal answer to the problem of uncontrolled or unauthorised migration:

> [In the Hague], we know that we have 49,000 aliens with a residence permit and between 15,000 and 30,000 aliens—and perhaps even more—without a permit....Above all, the legal rights of naturalised aliens and aliens with a residence permit have to be respected. Their population is vulnerable. The balance between the native and non-native populations is an unstable one.
>
> The conclusion has to be that there is no possibility of taking general measures. Police officers have to be sure of their cases. Aliens law enforcement is not a matter of arbitrarily keeping one's eye on everyone who looks like a stranger.
>
> That is why we think that general control policies are both ineffective and not the right police policy towards illegal immigrants. In the Netherlands we have set priorities....In the first place, we try to trace those illegal aliens who abuse their

position here (i.e., those committing criminal acts, or causing public disorder). We invest a lot of effort in their deportation. Then we are looking for those who take advantage of illegal aliens. In the criminal circuit we have prostitutes, drug couriers, pimps etc. In the big agricultural businesses in the Netherlands there is large-scale illegal employment of aliens without a work permit.

[However] in the Netherlands, control of the conditions for residence permits and for refused aliens is not very effective. It is a low priority.[10]

The UK's search for a perfect system of control may therefore be doubly deluded, both because it is ineffective as a means of enforcing control and because it may provide the excuse for a profound change in the relationship between the individual and the state.

This paper has argued that identity cards are of extremely limited value, particularly in the UK, as compensatory measures to reimpose border controls by other means. Failure to recognise this will allow the relaxation of internal EC frontiers to provide the excuse, not the reason, for the introduction of identity checks. This is clear from the opening quotation from police witnesses to the Home Affairs Select Committee inquiry: when pressed, they wanted identity cards *whether or not* border controls were relaxed.[11] The West Midlands Chief Constable was equally emphatic in his IPEC speech: 'the introduction of an identity card merits consideration independently of the issue of border controls'.[12]

The use and impact of an identity card in controlling drugs, terrorism and serious crime is outside the scope of this paper. But it is clear that the police case rests not on the need for a compensatory power, but for a new power for internal and international policing purposes. The emotive border control debate may persuade politicians to set up a system, ostensibly for one purpose, which will in fact have quite different uses.

Finally and importantly, the debate over identity cards in the UK raises wider issues about positive versus negative rights and responsibilities. The practical difficulties outlined above which would accompany the introduction of identity cards in the UK are not merely points of detail or problems to be solved; they are symptomatic of underlying constitutional and theoretical problems. At every stage, they challenge the UK system in which people do not require permission to be, or to work, or to live in a particular place: in which what is not prohibited by law is allowed. In continental European countries, by contrast, the relationship between the individual and the state is defined in constitutions which give the individual positive duties and positive rights.

In the UK context, a system of mandatory identity cards would place substantial new duties and penalties on citizens and residents. Yet these would not be balanced by any positive concept of the rights of the individual against the state, or any safety net of justiciable rights upon which individuals could call or below which laws and practices could not fall.

Conclusion

The development of internal systems of immigration control and enforcement is likely to continue. It is a process whose origins lie in the difficulty of controlling the movements of people at a time of easy and cheap international travel, as well as an increasing reluctance to share national benefits and facilities with non-nationals. It is likely that growing unemployment will give rise to demands for increased controls over employers, as increased pressure on the social security system has led to measures to exclude and invigilate foreigners' access to benefits.

However, there are powerful arguments against any further general extension of systems of internal control, particularly the introduction of identity cards. First, such measures inevitably target members of visible minority communities; not only does this reinforce feelings of exclusion and non-belonging among members of those communities, but it also creates and heightens prejudice and racism among the majority community. Second, all internal control measures are limited in their effectiveness and will inevitably be so without a level of checking and control which would be unacceptable outside a police state; it is therefore illusory to believe that a tamper-proof universal control can be created. Third, and consequently, the issue of increased internal controls should be separated from the perceived need to strengthen immigration controls in a frontier-free Europe; particularly in relation to the pressure for the introduction of identity cards, for which immigration is providing the excuse, not the reason. Fourth, the imposition on all UK citizens of an obligation to produce identification, backed up by penalties for non-production, would be to concede wide new powers to the executive, without the safeguard of positive constitutional rights against abuse of those powers.

The relaxation of internal frontier controls within Europe poses particular problems for the UK, which is accustomed to tightly policed sea and air borders and an immigration policy (or rhetoric) whose goal is the elimination of unauthorised entry or stay. However, the UK has in fact always had an unpoliced land border: that between the UK and the Republic of Ireland, which form a common travel area within which there are no immigration controls. This has not resulted in the transfer of the majority of the population of Ireland to the UK, even though Ireland has always been a country of emigration; nor has it led to immigration-related pressure for identity checks in order to prevent this.

Evidence from the Netherlands, and from the operation of the common travel area in the UK, suggest a flexible approach to immigration control in the new Europe. This should be based first on the grant of full free movement rights to third-country nationals legally resident in the community (since it is a nonsense to have a frontier-free zone in which 15 million legal residents cannot legally travel freely); second a requirement that temporary visitors crossing internal borders present themselves to an immigration officer within a given period (as happens with non-Irish travellers from Ireland to the UK at present); and third a more selective approach to enforcement, but one which is much more carefully monitored and regulated to avoid discrimination and arbitrary action. The principles on which such a system should be based are these:

- proportionality: the level of control and its effect on non-offenders (e.g., harassment, disincentive to use state systems) should be proportional to the mischief being addressed and the likelihood of success;
- non-discrimination: control should not bite disproportionately on any group (black people, women, the poor, users of state services or public housing);
- objective criteria: immigration control 'targets' (in relation to border controls as well as internal controls) are based on assumptions and anecdotes. If there is to be targeting, it should be based on statistical evidence (e.g., in a random sample of nationalities entering for visits, what kind of people left at the end of the visit).
- accountability and rights of challenge: this would include appeal rights, disciplinary offences for improper use of powers,

and ideally an Ombudsman-like authority with the power to redress individual complaints, call for reports on operational strategy and itself report on policy objectives and practices.

10 FUTURE CITIZENSHIP POLICY

Laurie Fransman

What is citizenship? What is nationality? Can or should there be a difference? What policies should apply and in what black-letter law should the application of those policies result?

To develop a discussion on these questions I go to the early part of this century and, to have working definitions, posit that nationality is a status identifying an individual as belonging to a community defined in terms of geography, geopolitics, religion and/or ethnicity (as in 'I am British and have such a passport'), whereas citizenship describes the relationship between an individual and the state whereby the individual enjoys civic rights and is bound by civic duties (as in 'I live in the UK and am a good citizen').

Development

The first comprehensive statute in British nationality law was the British Nationality and Status of Aliens Act 1914 which came into force on 1 January 1915. At this time the principal nationality category was British subject status and it was acquired by virtue of a sufficiently close connection with the Crown's dominions (the Empire, excluding those parts merely under Crown protection).

Regarding acquisition by birth, the 1914 statute enacted the common law rule of *ius soli*: all those born within the Crown's dominions and allegiance were British subjects. Those who were not born within the Crown's allegiance were simply the children of enemy aliens and diplomats and so numerically did little to detract from the clarity and certainty of the *ius soli* rule. The statute's reliance on allegiance was the continuation of a common law rule conceived back in the days of feudalism.

Regarding acquisition by descent, the common law (until 1914), provided for transmission through the legitimate male line to the first and second generations born outside the dominions. The 1914 Act proceeded on the basis that such generosity was not desirable and so a strict rule was enacted allowing only the first generation to acquire by descent. As a result of representations from expatriate communities abroad, amendments were later made to allow for transmission to the second generation and beyond (in particular circumstances) but automatic transmission to one generation only continued to be the broad principle.

Other policies embodied in the 1914 statute were a general prohibition against dual nationality and the requirement that the status of women and children should follow that of the husband/father. Nationality by grant was effected by naturalisation in a simple, administrative form but it was highly discretionary and conditional.

As to the consequences of British subject status, they included the civic rights that were available in the UK at that time and the right to come to, and reside in, the UK unfettered by any immigration restrictions. There was no freedom of movement of persons within the Empire as a whole as Dominion and colonial governments had the jurisdiction to legislate their own immigration policies. The rights of, and restrictions on, aliens were set out in the 1914 Act.

British Nationality Act 1948

The British Nationality Act (BNA) 1948 came into force on 1 January 1949. This statute was prompted by a new sentiment spreading through the Dominions (self-governing countries within the Crown's dominions) following the Second World War. These countries were no longer content to have British subject status as their only national identity and so wanted to enact their own citizenship laws. The agreement reached was that each such country (as well as the UK) would make statutory provision for citizenship of that country (including any territories dependent on it) and that British subject status would be retained as a status common to all citizens. British subject status was thus elevated to a sort of supra-national identity obtainable only by having or acquiring one of the local citizenships (of Canada, Australia, etc). Hence British subjects from New Zealand became citizens of New Zealand (and *ipso facto* remained British subjects), British subjects from the UK and British colonies became citizens of the UK and Colonies (CUKCs) (and *ipso facto* remained British subjects), and so on.

Allegiance, although no longer part of the definition of nationality, continued to be an important concept as all British subjects including the citizens of the independent Commonwealth countries, owed their allegiance to the Crown. India was the first country to reject the Crown as head of state and did so by drafting a republican constitution in 1950. This caused a constitutional crisis—was it not a contradiction in terms to have a republic within the Commonwealth?—ending with a Commonwealth Declaration confirming India's acceptance of the King as Head of the Commonwealth. The resolution of this crisis resulted in the British Commonwealth completing its evolution as an association of independent, equal, sovereign states.

So citizens of the UK and Colonies (*ipso facto* also British subjects) continued to owe allegiance to the Crown while citizens of the independent Commonwealth countries (*ipso facto* also British subjects) were gradually excluded from the duty of allegiance even though they retained British subject status. Although allegiance was still at the heart of British nationality as far as the UK's own citizenship laws were concerned, at the broader level it was no longer essential; British subject status (also known as Commonwealth citizenship) became a supra-national identity binding all citizens, without the need for allegiance.

As for the Commonwealth countries that continued to recognise the Crown as head of state, such clinging to the wreckage of empire bordered on farce. A person acquiring Australian citizenship had to swear allegiance to the Queen, leaving the individual in some doubt as to the significance and consequence of becoming Australian. Linked to the question of allegiance is the subject of dual nationality. In a very important policy change the UK abandoned the general prohibition against dual nationality in 1949. The main justification for a prohibition on dual nationality is the belief that one cannot simultaneously owe allegiance to more than one flag.

The UK boldly took a different view in the 1948 legislation, a path which may have been smoothed by the fact that, as of January 1949, all British subjects/Commonwealth citizens still owed a common allegiance to the Crown even though they were also to be citizens of Australia, Canada, or New Zealand etc. Nevertheless, even though a single allegiance was owed by an individual who was both a citizen of the UK and Colonies and, for example, Canada, the step was still a bold one as it permitted an individual at once to be both a British subject and an alien (i.e. a national of a foreign country). Further, there was no change in UK law when India ceased to be part of the Crown's dominions (though not part of the Commonwealth) in January 1950.

Regarding acquisition and loss rules from 1949 to 1982, acquisition by birth continued to be based on the *ius soli* principle[1] and acquisition by descent continued as a general rule to occur automatically in respect only of the first generation born outside the UK and Colonies. Regarding acquisition by grant, a simple but wholly discretionary naturalisation procedure was retained but, for the first time, a procedure was introduced to give rapid access to citizenship of the UK and Colonies in certain cases. This procedure was called registration.

Registration was introduced[2] to give citizens of the independent Commonwealth countries (as well as of Republic of Ireland and British subjects without citizenship) an entitlement to citizenship of the UK and Colonies dependent only upon 12 months' residence. As the policy towards British subjects in the diaspora changed, so did the original registration provision. The reference to 12 months became a reference to five years and then as of 1 January 1973 the entitlement became a mere discretion (save in respect of those settled in the UK on and ever since that date, or those with the right of abode in the UK). Thus 24 years after the original 'rapid access' provision came into force, that provision in substance had become identical to naturalisation.

The 1948 legislation abandoned the policy that the status of women and children should follow that of the husband/father. As a result, a woman did not automatically become a CUKC upon marriage to such a person. Instead, the Act gave any woman, irrespective of her nationality, an entitlement to register as a CUKC simply by virtue of being (or having been) married to such a man. The entitlement was not conditional upon any other requirement (such as residence) and it remained intact and unamended through to the end of 1982. There was no policy of sexual equality and so a man did not acquire citizenship of the UK and Colonies and was not in any way advantaged under British nationality law by virtue of his marriage to a CUKC.[3]

It will be perfectly plain that the 1948 legislation did not subscribe to the policy of equal access to citizenship irrespective of nationality or sex and it is just as plain that the Act made no apologies for favouring Commonwealth citizens (initially) over aliens, and women over men.

Although the automatic loss provisions of the earlier law were dropped when the prohibition against dual nationality was abandoned, in one particular respect automatic loss of citizenship of the UK and Colonies occurred on a massive scale during the currency of the 1948 Act. This was as a result of grants of independence.

Independence arrangements

Whereas independence had evolved in the Old Commonwealth (Australia, Canada, New Zealand, South Africa), there had been an instantaneous grant of independence in respect of India, Pakistan and Ceylon (Sri Lanka) during the two years before the commencement of the 1948 Act, and in Burma.[4] Once it had been agreed that India could constitute itself a republic but nevertheless remain a member of the Commonwealth, many other countries did the same when they took independence during the 1960s and 1970s. Some of the early grants of independence, taking place before British subjects were brought within the scope of UK immigration control by the Commonwealth Immigrants Act 1962, provided for the retention of British subject status/citizenship of the UK and Colonies with a generosity that seems quite astonishing by latter-day standards.[5]

The UK soon changed its tune, however, and independence arrangements by and large became standardised. The approach taken was that an independence constitution was agreed in consultation with the UK and that constitution made initial provision for citizenship of the new country. The UK's interest was to ensure (as much as it was able to) that citizenship of the new country would be broadly based so that those who had been CUKCs by virtue of their connection with that place would all automatically get citizenship on the basis of that same connection. The UK then legislated an independence statute providing, *inter alia*, that a CUKC becoming a citizen of the newly independent country on independence day would automatically cease to be a CUKC. Each such statute contained a standardised exceptions provision. This provided that a CUKC would not lose that citizenship if he or she retained a close connection with a place which remained within the UK and Colonies.

Difficulties occurred in certain instances: for example, the East African countries in effect refused to confer citizenship upon persons of Asian origin (whom the British had brought to East Africa in the first place) and so some wholesale retention of citizenship of the UK and Colonies did occur at times during the 1960s. The norm, however, was that the overall effect of the independence provisions was that all those who had been CUKCs (and/or British protected persons) by virtue of their connection with the territory attaining independence became citizens of that place following independence. They ceased to have British nationality save for British subject status which they only retained (or, in the case of BPPS, acquired) as a result of their new citizenship of an independent Commonwealth country.

Although much has been said of these independence arrangements, they do not in substance seem to be unreasonable. Where a people, formerly under the imperial yoke, wins independence and self-determination, it is difficult to argue that in addition to creating their own citizenship they should also retain the nationality of the former imperial power. It is difficult to see why they should even want to.

Right of abode

Moving on to the consequences of British subject status, the position regarding the right of abode after 1 January 1949 continued to be the same as it was before: any British subject/Commonwealth citizen enjoyed an unfettered right to enter and reside in the UK. The Commonwealth Immigrants Act 1962, however, subjected such persons to UK immigration controls for the first time and in doing so ran contrary to common law. The provisions were amended by the similarly titled Act of 1968 and were then replaced by the provisions of the Immigration Act 1971 which came into force on 1 January 1973.

The 1971 Act established the right of abode as a separate, free-standing immigration status and only the British subjects/Commonwealth citizens possessing it continued to have an unfettered entitlement to enter and reside in the UK. So British subject status and even citizenship of the UK and Colonies were no longer synonymous with these rights. The right of abode would be thought by any lay person to be a principal if not the principal consequence of having the nationality of a country; but the 1971 Act disembowelled nationality by cutting away the right of abode and constituting it as a separate immigration status obtainable on the basis of its own unique acquisition rules.

British subjects/Commonwealth citizens, insofar as they were

CUKCs, had the right of abode if they were born, adopted, registered or naturalised in the UK or had such a parent or grandparent.[6] Alternatively, they acquired the right of abode if at any time ordinarily resident in the UK throughout a five year period with no time restrictions (at least by the end of that period). All British subjects/Commonwealth citizens (whether or not CUKCs) acquired the right of abode if born to, or adopted by, a parent who was born in the UK; or if, being a woman, she was at any time married to a man who had the right of abode.

The citizenship given by nationality law was citizenship of the UK and Colonies and was given to those with a sufficiently close connection with any part of the UK and Colonies; the right of abode was given to those with a sufficiently close connection to the UK itself and that right posed as an immigration status but was effectively a UK nationality. The legislation did not have the sincerity to call a spade a spade—that was done 10 years later when the British Nationality Act 1981 simply relabelled CUKCs with the right of abode in the UK as 'British citizens'.

The right of abode phenomenon was a quite extraordinary one because it showed that the component parts of nationality can be separated and moved around like the inter-connecting units of a child's toy. So one permutation was that there could be an individual who as a CUKC could request protection while abroad and who as a British subject (rather than as a CUKC *per se*) could exercise civic rights in the UK, but who (despite being a British subject and a CUKC) did not have the right of abode in the UK without earning it in the form of an immigration status following five years' residence in this country.

The complaints of a racist agenda behind the right of abode provisions of the 1971 Act are legend and I need not dwell upon them here; I would rather look dispassionately at the exercise as a whole and acknowledge that the concept did seem to work in practice (in the sense that the objects of the legislation were all achieved). One might certainly make adjustments regarding the types of connections with the UK and there might even be adjustments as to whether the right of abode should arise automatically (as it did under the 1971 Act) or whether some sort of application should be made. But the device at the heart of it, that worked so well, was that one can confer upon an individual all or any of the component parts of a nationality cum citizenship and simply call it something else, thereby avoiding the political, sentimental and other difficulties that might otherwise arise.

A rose by any other name would smell as sweet...and would avoid many knotty difficulties relating only to roses.

So creating the right of abode in the UK as a status quite separate from nationality could perhaps play a role in the devising of future policy relating to nationality and citizenship matters.

Citizenship

Still on the topic of the consequences of British subject status from 1949 to 1982, there were some rights which related to all residents and not just to British subjects/Commonwealth citizens. Duties also became better defined. It is convenient to refer to the sum total of these rights and duties as constituting 'citizenship' and in doing so it is necessary to focus on the UK itself and not the UK and Colonies.

There are a number of points that can be made about citizenship in the sense in which that term is being used here (i.e., as distinct from nationality). First, citizenship is an individual and personal attribute and therefore cannot apply to purely legal entities such as companies. Further, whereas the community of nationals is clearly defined as comprised of individuals who have the legal status known as nationality, the community of citizens is fluid and forever changing as citizenship can come and go with physical presence in the country and can be possessed to varying degrees. The point becomes clearer the closer one looks at the content of citizenship.

Citizenship contains a philosophy about involvement, participation, the sharing of responsibilities and beneficial coexistence. Writing in 1950, T.H. Marshall in 'Citizenship and Social Class'[7] saw citizenship as having three elements: civil, political and social. He described them in this way:

> The civil element is composed of the rights necessary for individual freedom—liberty of the person, freedom of speech, thought, the right to own property and to conclude valid contracts, and the right to justice. The last is of a different order from the others because it is the right to defend and assert all one's rights on terms of equality with others and by due process of law. This shows us that the institutions most directly associated with civil rights are the courts of justice.
>
> By the political element I mean the right to participate in the exercise of political power, as a member of a body invested with

political authority or as an elector of the members of such a body. The corresponding institutions are Parliament and councils of local government.

By the social element I mean the whole range from the right to a modicum of economic welfare and security to the right to share to the full in the social heritage and to live the life of a civilised being according to the standards prevailing in the society. The institutions most closely connected with it are the education systems and the social services.

Regarding the civil element—civil rights enforceable through the courts—there is in the UK no clear set of such entitlements. We have no written constitution enshrining fundamental freedoms, nor a Bill of Rights. However, during the period 1949 to 1982 international instruments clarified our civil rights. In December 1948 we welcomed the UN's Universal Declaration of Human Rights and through the Council of Europe the UK was influential in drafting the European Convention on Human Rights which commenced in 1953 and gave individuals access to a European human rights court.

Civil rights, it will be appreciated, should be enjoyed by all within the jurisdiction irrespective of their nationality or even their immigration status; that is, by anyone physically present in the UK. Political rights, on the other hand, have long been confined to those with a particular nationality status. These political rights were enjoyed by all British subjects before 1949 and in substance there has been no change (to the extent that even nationals of the Republic of Ireland have expressly been given political rights in the UK though they ceased to be British subjects in 1949).

Regarding social rights, these should include the right to employment, to medical care and to other social and financial services all intended to guarantee a minimum standard of living and personal dignity. The European Social Charter (1965) contributed to the development of social and economic rights in Europe generally, but it will not be forgotten that this aspect of citizenship will always greatly be affected by the political model on the basis of which the society is functioning. The availability of social rights depends on various combinations of nationality and immigration status.

So much for a quick overview of some of the rights associated with citizenship; what about the duties?

Probably everyone would agree that in order to be a good citizen one must be law-abiding and pay one's taxes, stop at zebra crossings and serve on juries. Beyond this, the breadth of the duties of citizenship becomes moot. One must not commit treason to the extent that treason is prohibited by law but apart from this to what degree is there a duty to be loyal? To what extent is there or ought there to be a duty of allegiance?

Participation and involvement are aspects of citizenship and those who concern themselves with caring for the aged and handicapped are undoubtedly being good citizens, but to what extent is there a duty to provide voluntary services or to give old clothes to Oxfam or to donate blood? In modern Britain there is a duty to care for the environment because there are laws prohibiting pollution but to what extent are there environmental duties beyond those arising from black-letter law?

Another complicated aspect of the duties of citizenship concerns community norms. There is a duty to be law-abiding but to what extent is there a duty to obey norms that are not prescribed by law? Must all good citizens speak English? Must all good citizens keep to monogamous relationships? Defining the duties of citizenship can be exceedingly difficult in a multi-cultural society. Perhaps it would be neither possible nor desirable to attempt such a comprehensive description.

The 1981 Act and its legacy

Returning to British nationality and the chronology that began in 1914, we come to the BNA 1981 which came into force on 1 January 1983. At midnight on the previous day, CUKCs with the right of abode were renamed British citizens. Those without the right of abode became British Dependent Territories citizens (BDTCs) (if they had been CUKCs by virtue of a connection with a place which remained a colony) or British Overseas Citizens (BOCs) (if that place was no longer a colony).

The basic plan underpinning the 1981 Act is very different from that of the 1948 Act and well reflects the 24 years of changing politics and policy. The 1948 statute saw the UK and Colonies as a single territorial entity, gave citizens of the Commonwealth countries easy access to citizenship of the UK and Colonies and let everyone be joined together by British subject status, carrying with it the right of abode in the UK as well as political rights. The 1981 statute recognised as British citizens only those who in the interim had been defined as having the right of abode in the UK by virtue of their close connection with this country.

The reality upon which the present legislation is based is one in which the UK is no longer an imperial power. As of 1 July 1997 it will only be responsible for a few minor overseas territories with small populations incapable of self-determination. Provisions contained in the 1981 Act (as amended) already have the effect of extending British citizenship to persons from Gibraltar and the Falkland Islands. If it were not for Hong Kong, the legislation might well have taken this approach in respect of all the remaining dependent territories. However, as Hong Kong was (and until 1997 will be) still Crown soil, provision was made for a British Dependent Territories citizenship and, apart from British citizenship, it is the only British nationality status which can be perpetuated.

In general, British Overseas citizenship, British Protected Person status, British subject status under the Act and British National (Overseas) status (in existence since 1 July 1987 and relating only to Hong Kong) will all disappear in the fullness of time without any further legislation being necessary as the law relating to each such status has no mechanism allowing for perpetuation. So, in each category, as the present generation of such persons gets older and smaller, so the category is disappearing. This will leave British citizens (having such citizenship by virtue of their close connections with the UK and only the UK) and BDTCs. In less than five years, sovereignty over Hong Kong will terminate and at once the global number of BDTCs will be hugely reduced. Assuming that there is no change of policy in respect of Hong Kong over the next four years the questions for any future policy would be: what happens to the British dependent territories and British Dependent Territories citizenship after 1 July 1997 and how should our law cater for BOCs, BPPs, British subjects under the Act and BN(O)s pending the extinction of those categories?

Acquisition

Turning to the acquisition rules under the present law, the simplicity of *ius soli* has been abandoned in favour of *ius sanguinis* so that acquisition by birth now relies on the status of the child's parents (at the time of the child's birth). The argument for the change was this: why should a child whose parents have no real connection with the UK or no lasting or lawful connection, have citizenship of this country? Under the 1981 Act, those born stateless in the UK must wait at least 10 years before having the opportunity to acquire British citizenship on the basis of that statelessness.

Regarding acquisition by descent, sexual equality has been introduced (subject to a legitimacy requirement) so that any child born on or after 1 January 1983 will be a British citizen if at the time of that birth the child's father or mother is such a British citizen. As a general rule however, the parent must be such a citizen otherwise than by descent as the policy continues to be that transmission should only occur automatically to the first generation born outside the UK.

Regarding acquisition by grant, greater equality has been introduced in that naturalisation now applies to all adults irrespective of whether they are aliens or Commonwealth citizens, and spouses of British citizens are treated equally irrespective of their sex. However, there do continue to be many registration categories. The transitional registration provisions are now almost fully expired but there are permanent registration provisions relating to children born in the UK (but failing to acquire by birth), children born outside the UK (but failing to acquire by descent), minors generally (discretionary) and a registration entitlement on the basis of five years' residence in the UK when it comes to those who have some form of British nationality other than British citizenship.

Regarding the right of abode in the UK, except for a disappearing class of Commonwealth citizens in being prior to 1983, the right of abode is now reserved exclusively to British citizens and the Immigration Act 1971 has been amended to reflect that.

The 1981 Act further reduced the number of people eligible to obtain citizenship by right so that by 1992, 85% of the grants of citizenship were discretionary. Of the total of 42,200 people granted citizenship in 1992, 45% were granted citizenship on the basis of completing the 5 year residence requirement, 35% on the basis of marriage and 20% were minor children. Fifty-two percent of those granted citizenship were citizens of New Commonwealth countries, compared with nearly 80% in 1988. Six percent were from the Old Commonwealth, 9% from Europe and 32% from 'other foreign countries'.[8] Statistics are not given on the number of applications refused. Nor can the Home Office say how many of those eligible to apply for citizenship on the basis of five years' residence have done so.[9]

Statements of principle

The catalogue of principles or objectives on which to construct policies for nationality (and nationality-related citizenship matters) in a modern constitutional democracy would include the following:

1. *From discretion to objectivity*
Wide unqualified discretion is the breeding-ground for abuse and discrimination. A system based on objectivity serves the interests of the rule of law. Where discretion must exist it should be no broader than is essential and the office which is to exercise a discretion should be established or selected in a way which is most likely to guarantee impartiality.

2. *From complexity to clarity and simplicity*
Some of the provisions of the BNA 1981 are among the most complicated that the law has to offer (e.g. section 7(1)), making them unintelligible even to lawyers and Home Office staff. The quality of law and justice is eroded when provisions become inaccessible through complexity.

3. *From uncertainty to certainty*
This is a corollary of the previous point; an individual has the right to be certain as to his or her status and the ramifications of it.

4. *From allegiance to responsibility*
Allegiance contains loyalty and duty and (as has been seen) originally both were demanded in return for British subject status. I would argue that it remains legitimate to require loyalty in the limited sense of precluding unlawful acts of disloyalty (e.g. in time of war.) Emotional loyalty, however, or patriotism, is not available on demand and can only be earned, which means it can only be volunteered. For this view to prevail it is necessary to dispel the notion that allegiance, in that sense, has to be paid as a *quid pro quo* for nationality. Nationality status and citizenship rights exist quite independently of emotional loyalty. It is acceptable to see duties and responsibilities (e.g. jury service) arising from nationality status and indeed from membership of a community, but it is not acceptable to demand emotional allegiance, whether as the price of membership or otherwise. On this approach policies of dual and multiple nationality can be tolerated and individuals need no longer think that they must renounce their culture or religion in order to owe an allegiance to the Crown.

5. *From sentimentalism to respect*

This is closely associated to the previous point and involves an expansion of the thought that loyalty can be earned, and therefore volunteered, but never demanded. A difficult truth that history has shown is that allegiance can be blinding and excessive patriotism fatal for individuals and even whole communities. One need look no further than the front page of one's daily newspaper to see that the sentimentalism generated by national identity can be an enormously powerful force. Whether this force can be neutralised or perhaps even used constructively rather than destructively is surely the most difficult question of all to resolve. Perhaps the answer may lie in multi-culturalism—a community in which a plurality of identities and loyalties interact to keep in check the potentially destructive sentimentalism to which I am referring. If so, it becomes necessary to establish a well-balanced multi-cultural community, the hallmark of which would be self-respect and respect of others. Such a community could function at several levels, meaning that an individual may be a member of a local community within a national community within a European community.

6. *Multi-nationality*

Multi-nationality, an individual possessing the nationality (or, in traditional usage, citizenship) of more than one state, is to be accepted if not even encouraged. Air travel has shrunk the world and as a result many people divide their time between two or more countries. Where one will marry and where one's descendants will be born are no longer predictable. Multi-nationality is in the international interest and it becomes possible through point 4, above, and desirable further to point 5.

7. *The right to come and go*

The right to come and go at will is another principle to be honoured. In a sense it is a corollary to the need for multi-nationality, but it also implies that there are to be no restrictions on the departure of a national from the country of origin, no loss of nationality through absence from that country and no forfeiture of possessions.

8. *The non-denial of one's own nationals*

As already required by international law, a state cannot arbitrarily deprive its own people of nationality or deny them the right of entry.

9. *Avoidance of sexism, racism and favouritism*

The issue here is perhaps not quite as simple as it appears at first glance as even the most recent nationality statute, the BNA 1981, is riddled with instances of favouritism (e.g. persons from Gibraltar have instant access to British citizenship) and often favouritism is essential (e.g. advantages to stateless persons). So the point is a generalisation about fairness and cannot be taken too far; I do suggest, though, the extension to nationality law of the UK's abolition of the distinction between legitimacy and illegitimacy.

10. *Entitlement to passport facilities*

To leave passports in the realm of the royal prerogative is indefensible in this day and age; there should be a statutory or constitutional right to passport facilities, subject only to specified and necessary exceptions (e.g. to prevent a minor from being unlawfully removed from the jurisdiction).

11. *Avoidance of statelessness*

International law and British municipal law have so far taken the approach that stateless persons should be shown some mild favouritism. That is not enough; the approach should be the eradication of statelessness which can easily be guaranteed by a provision which automatically confers nationality on a person who, if all else fails, will otherwise be left stateless.

12. *Compatibility with European Union citizenship and possible devolution*

Policies for the UK should not lose sight of the fact that the UK is part of a greater entity, the European Community, and is made up of lesser entities (England, Scotland, Wales and Northern Ireland). The former is currently the dominant consideration given the provisions of the Treaty on European Union signed at Maastricht on 7 February 1992. Article 8 of Article G in part provides as follows:

Citizenship of the Union

Article 8
1. Citizenship of the Union is hereby established. Every person holding the nationality of a Member State shall be a citizen of the Union.
2. Citizens of the Union shall enjoy the rights conferred by this Treaty and shall be subject to the duties imposed thereby.

Article 8a

1. Every citizen of the Union shall have the right to move and . reside freely within the territory of the Member States...

Article 8b

1. Every citizen of the Union residing in a Member State of which he is not a national shall have the right to vote and to stand as a candidate at municipal elections in the Member State in which he resides...

Just the few words quoted above are enough to indicate how substantial and significant Union citizenship under the Treaty will be. The UK nationality and citizenship policies, including the policy underlying the definition of 'UK national' for Community purposes, must take account of the fact that our laws are part of a pan-European body of laws which will govern access (through local citizenship) to Union citizenship.

13. *Upholding international law and the rule of law*

International law and the rule of law, to the extent not already covered by the above points, must be upheld by nationality and citizenship policies. As to the rule of law, for example, secrecy should be avoided, there should be a general duty to give reasons and all decisions should be appealable or otherwise challengeable judicially. As to international law, it includes the Convention Relating to the Status of Stateless Persons 1954 and the Convention on the Reduction of Statelessness 1961, the Convention on the Nationality of Married Women 1957 and the Convention on Reduction of Cases of Multiple Nationality 1963. The 1963 Convention has been amended by protocol and at the date of writing it is understood that the Council of Europe is completing a further protocol which quite rightly will erode the principle of reduction to the point at which it is hardly a general rule any more. Nationality provisions in human rights instruments include Article 15 of the Universal Declaration of Human Rights (a right to nationality and no arbitrary deprivation) and Article 24(3) of the International Covenant on Civil and Political Rights (right to nationality).

Nationality, citizenship and the right of abode

Bearing in mind the meaning and development of these expressions and taking into account the above principles and objectives, how should these attributes be grouped together and what policies should apply? Should nationality, citizenship and the right of abode be kept completely separate from one another? Is the right of abode a characteristic of nationality or of citizenship (or neither)?

I think it has become clear that nationality and citizenship can coincide fully (a British citizen living in the UK) but do not have to: there can be a high degree of citizenship enjoyed by a person with no British nationality (e.g. an Irish citizen living in the UK) and there can even be nationality with only partial citizenship (a British citizen in prison or living abroad).

In policy there should be no attempt to force nationality and citizenship to coincide any more than they do naturally. Citizenship should be available as widely as possible and it should be dependent on nationality and even immigration status as little as possible.

The more difficult question is what should be done with the right of abode? At present it is part and parcel of nationality (i.e. the legal status known as British citizenship) and can only be acquired by the acquisition of nationality in that form. However, if the right of abode were to be severed from nationality (as it was from 1973 to 1982) then it might become a characteristic of citizenship thereby removing or reducing the need to acquire nationality. Although a citizen with the right of abode but no British nationality may sound a strange animal, they are among us even now. A person born in a Commonwealth country before 1983 whose mother was born in the UK would be such a creature; he or she would have the right of abode in the UK and living in this country would enjoy all the civil, political and social rights associated with citizenship.

To have an amalgam of citizenship and the right of abode, but no nationality, has a certain appeal—certainly sufficient to prompt a few moments' hesitation. Would not such a system help to deal with the problems of allegiance and sentimentalism (points 4 and 5 above)? Could it not take the place of nationality and become the real status of unity throughout the EC?

On the other hand, surely this is nothing short of a fantasy, overlooking, as it does, the fact that in reality all people (including the British) cling tenaciously to their national identity. Nationality, in addition to citizenship rights and the right of abode, gives the recipient a more tangible identity and sense of belonging than citizenship can convey.

I find it difficult to abandon the idea of resurrecting the right of abode as a separate immigration status and to use it, in conjunction with citizenship rights, as a common state of bliss throughout the Community (including third-country nationals). Probably, though, it must be abandoned. The result is that nationality remains intact and the right of abode in the UK would remain a characteristic of British nationality.

We are therefore left with a system virtually identical to the one already prevailing; British nationality automatically carrying with it the right of abode in the UK and a closely associated but quite separate body of citizenship rights and duties. It would be left to policies such as multi-culturalism and multi-citizenship to earth the negative sentimental charge that nationality can sometimes generate.

Access to nationality (including the right of abode)

If a British nationality (incorporating the right of abode in the UK) is to be retained, then the next issue to consider is what policies should govern access to such nationality.

Should the grant of nationality be a privilege—a wholly discretionary gift by the state? This would be the historical or traditional perspective. Should nationality be granted as an encouragement to integration or should it be seen as a right or discretionary reward earned by those who have successfully integrated?

The historical or traditional approach is unacceptable as it not only offends against the principle set out above (from discretion to objectivity) but its premise is the supremacy of the state and superiority of the indigenous population over all outsiders. This should not be the premise on which to base modern nationality policies as it leaves the way open to elitism, such as we see in Switzerland, and the attempt to enforce mono-culturalism, such as we see in Greece. In such countries an outsider may live and work for many years and still be denied access to nationality as a punishment for not having sufficiently assumed the culture of the state.

Therein lies the crux: nationality, on the basis of objective criteria, must be available to all those who have established a sufficiently close connection with the state. Nationality is not to be viewed as a privilege, an inducement or a reward and must not be linked to integration because to do so would at best be patronising and naive and at worst tantamount to dangerous elitism and cultural suppression. To have nationality widely available on the basis of objectively defined close connections (not including cultural conversion) would be good for democracy. It would also be a blueprint for future international law. It should not be open to any state to grant or withhold nationality as it pleases but, rather, each state should be seen as having the responsibility to grant nationality to the persons most closely associated with that state. In so doing it must be accepted that close connections are now generated more by a frequent ebb and flow of migrants than by a single momentous exodus to a promised land. So a state with which an individual is most closely connected *at a given time* is a state which, in pursuance of such a global responsibility, should grant that individual its nationality.

Access to citizenship

De facto residence here at any given moment should continue to be synonymous with citizenship as far as duties and civil rights are concerned. A citizen in this sense is already bound by duties, such as that of obedience to the law, and simply by being in the jurisdiction already enjoys all the civil rights.

A particular objective in the field of civil rights might be the adoption of a Bill of Rights.

Turning to political rights, these are enjoyed by all Commonwealth citizens (British nationals, excluding British protected persons, and all citizens of the Commonwealth countries) and all citizens of the Republic of Ireland. As for policy it should be observed that the more extensive the political rights in the society, the better for democracy. Political rights therefore should not be removed from any Commonwealth citizens nor from citizens of the Republic, but in the 1990s it becomes increasingly difficult to justify distinctions between Commonwealth citizens and citizens of the Republic on the one hand and aliens (particularly Community aliens) on the other.

It is also to be appreciated that there are Community political rights, exercisable in the UK, as well as domestic political rights. Voting and candidacy rights of Union citizens have already been referred to, above, and it should just be a matter of time before third-country nationals throughout the Member States enjoy Community political rights too. The establishment of political rights for Community aliens and even non-Community aliens is further reason why political rights for Commonwealth citizens and the Irish, but not for others, cannot be sustained.

Regarding social rights, residential and nationality considerations dictate when they arise and this is not the place for a detailed analysis of the rights and their prerequisites. Suffice it to say that if social rights are enhanced, if the quality of social citizenship is improved, then surely the beneficiaries would function as better citizens—they would be more likely (if they are solvent, employed and educated) to exercise political rights, participate in the community and thereby improve the quality of democracy.

Regarding citizenship rights, the Report of the Commission on Citizenship recommended 'a review and codification of the law relating to the legal rights, duties and entitlements of the citizen in the United Kingdom'[10] and perhaps codification of the various rights and duties associated with citizenship would be a good thing; the arguments for and against are similar to those for and against the adoption of a Bill of Rights.

Categories of British nationality

The only British nationals who, under current law, have the right of abode in the UK are British citizens. Those from existing colonies are BDTCs and by virtue of the colony's immigration laws will normally have the right of abode in that colony. BOCs, British subjects, BPPs and BN(O)s have no right of abode anywhere and each such status is designed to become extinct with the mere passage of time. Commonwealth citizens and citizens of the Republic of Ireland continue to occupy privileged positions in our nationality law.

The principles of clarity, simplicity and certainty demand that there should be a single British nationality, the holders of which have the right of abode in the UK. In effect, therefore, British nationality (or, using the term 'British citizenship' in its present legal sense) should be extended to all BDTCs, BOCs, British subjects, BPPs and BN(O)s. British nationality should be available by virtue of a sufficiently close connection with the UK or any British dependent territory and it would accordingly be logical for all British nationals to be deemed to have that status by descent (and thus be unable to pass it on to the next generation) except for those born in the UK or a colony.

In practical terms it is only in respect of BDTCs from Hong Kong that the above suggestion is bold because it is only such persons who constitute a numerically large group—a little under 3.5 million. When sovereignty ends on 1 July 1997 the group of BN(O)s and BOCs from Hong Kong will be virtually as large (although it will at once begin to shrink) and so those concerned about numbers will undoubtedly remain opposed to universal British citizenship for a long time to come.

It hardly needs saying that a single UK nationality would fit in neatly with European Union citizenship; all UK nationals would be British citizens and all British citizens would *ipso facto* be Union citizens. Regarding Commonwealth citizens and citizens of the Republic of Ireland it is difficult to see why such persons should continue to have a separate identity in British nationality law. Indeed, in the case of the Irish this separate identity seems to fly in the face of Southern Ireland's rejection of constitutional links with the UK in 1937 and 1948.

Acquisition and loss rules

The typical rules regulating the acquisition of nationality concern birth, descent and grant (naturalisation/registration).

Objectivity, simplicity, certainty and the avoidance of statelessness would dictate that acquisition by birth should occur on the basis of *ius soli* (nationality by place of birth). The argument against *ius soli* is that, in a number of instances, it exceeds generosity and defies common sense to grant British nationality simply because one's birth occurs in the UK. On policy grounds the children of diplomats and enemy aliens should not benefit from birth in the UK and why should nationality be given to the children of those who are here unlawfully? Even the children of those who are here lawfully should not take nationality if the parents are only temporarily present in the UK.

This is the argument of states possessive about bestowing the privilege of their nationality. States of the view that each has an equal role to play in discharging a global responsibility by giving nationality to the persons most closely connected with it at any given time would surely take a different view. The logic of the 'objective close connection' test would dictate that, like domicile, no person should ever be without nationality and the best starting point would therefore be the universal granting of nationality by the place of birth at the moment of birth. If compromises are necessary, then recourse to the Australian system would be preferable to an abandonment of the *ius soli* principle; in Australia *ius soli* applies, but the child loses citizenship if he or she leaves the country within five years of birth and does not return.

Finally, if *ius soli* results in an increase in dual or multiple citizenship then that in my definite view is a further advantage of the doctrine and not a disadvantage.

Turning to the acquisition of British nationality by descent, as a matter of principle descent provisions should operate to prevent statelessness and equality of the sexes demands that a child should acquire nationality by descent from either parent. The non-discrimination principle would even eradicate the distinction between legitimacy and illegitimacy (where such a distinction still remains).

Subject to these points, the major consideration is where a line should be drawn between an ancestral connection with the UK and Colonies which is sufficiently close for present purposes and one which is insufficiently close. In the UK since 1915 the general rule has provided for transmission only to the first generation and this is probably right. The difficult question concerns the exceptions to the general rule—how should they be defined?

One exception should concern the prevention of statelessness. Another should concern descendants born abroad in the course of a parent's service for, or on behalf of, the government of the UK or a colony. Remembering the relationship between British nationality and Union citizenship, arguably a descendant born in one of the other Member States should take British nationality at least if Union citizenship is not acquired at birth in any other way.

Further exceptions should arise from the appreciation that people now come and go in complex patterns and so it is not necessarily the case that the second generation born outside the relevant territory will have a weaker connection than the first, or that the third generation will be more remote than the second. UK ancestry is a connecting factor of variable strength and, taken together with other such factors, might therefore warrant the conferment of British nationality on the basis of an overall close connection. The difficulty in practice with this approach is that identifying the sufficient combinations of connecting factors would be an unenviable task and the difficulty in principle is that allowing for transmission to successive generations in this way might leave the law open to allegations of favouritism (i.e. hidden racist agendas).

303

Nationality by grant

Turning to acquisition of nationality by grant, it has been stated that nationality should be widely available on the basis of sensible and objective access rules with little or no discretion.

Acquisition of nationality by grant is normally based on a period of residence (or a similar period of service abroad on behalf of the state). The periods in question vary from three years (Australia, Canada) to five years (Italy, USA) and even to eight to ten years (Greece, Hungary). Proposals for a new Hungarian nationality law, however, specify only a three year residential period where certain other connecting factors are present. I believe that countries such as Australia and Canada correctly identify a three year period of residence as constituting a sufficiently close connection to warrant acquisition by grant but I also believe that Hungary is perhaps setting the tone for a modern alternative to the traditional residential requirement. Close ties such as the birth or presence of relatives in the UK, business connections and the like might wholly or partly be acceptable in lieu of a period of residence.

If residence remains relevant (and to a certain degree it should), then it becomes necessary to consider the relationship between nationality laws and immigration laws. Should nationality be available solely to those with indefinite leave to remain or should it be available, too, to those with merely limited leave? Most importantly, immigration laws must not be employed so as to frustrate or undermine nationality policies. The point is well illustrated with reference to Gibraltar: it may sound fair to allow Moroccans to be naturalised as BDTCs after five years' residence in Gibraltar, but any hint of fairness disappears when it comes to light that there can be no naturalisation without indefinite leave and under the colony's immigration laws it is often impossible ever to attain that immigration status.

To this extent the formulation of nationality policies cannot be undertaken in isolation. Not only must there be provision for a natural and equitable progression from the most superior immigration status to nationality, but the very nature of that superior immigration status must be carefully determined. If that status gives complete security of tenure, such as the right of abode in the UK under present law, then that may be very agreeable for the most part but serve to discourage applications for nationality. If the most superior immigration status gives little security, such as limited leave (or even indefinite leave as presently formulated) then arguably more people would seek nationality sooner. This relates to the suggestion that the right of abode should be a characteristic of nationality and not of citizenship.

As to the other requirements, 'good character' should be of less significance because the duty to grant nationality to an individual closely connected with the state is not a duty that should be lightly avoided. If the good character requirement must apply, then perhaps it should take account of criminal convictions only—this would certainly put the requirement firmly onto an objective basis. As for the language requirement, proficiency in any Community language should definitely suffice. With a positive multi-culturalism policy perhaps languages commonly used in the UK (other than English, Welsh or Scottish Gaelic) should be acceptable.

Registration

In British nationality law there is, in addition to the mainstream method of acquisition by grant (i.e. naturalisation), a fast-track procedure known as registration. Registration may be discretionary or by entitlement and is available to certain favoured groups. Notwithstanding the principle of avoidance of favouritism it is likely that it will always be necessary or desirable to advantage certain persons in this way; in which case it is essential to monitor closely the policies underlying such favouritism. Present UK law, for example, gives a registration entitlement to certain persons who are two generations removed from the UK (and therefore one generation too remote to benefit under the descent provisions). This seems to be acceptable favouritism.

On the other hand, recent British nationality law has favoured Commonwealth citizens and citizens of the Republic of Ireland. Such favouritism was based on history, tradition and habit and surely can no longer be justified. However, rising above the selfish interests of the UK itself and looking at the interests of peoples and states on a regional or global basis, favouritism along novel lines may indeed be desirable or even necessary. It may be desirable, for example, for UK nationality law to favour Union citizens and perhaps even third-country nationals settled in the Community. It may be necessary, from a global perspective, for our nationality as well as immigration laws to favour persons from the third world, but not simply along historical Commonwealth lines.[11]

Loss of nationality

Moving from the acquisition rules to the rules governing loss of nationality, this undoubtedly is a simpler and less contentious subject.

Renunciation must always be an entitlement, subject only to the avoidance of statelessness, and should never be qualified in any other way. In some systems, though not in the UK, renunciation cannot be effected if the individual still owes income tax or otherwise has undischarged liabilities to the state. The right to renounce ought to be viewed as a fundamental freedom as there should be no constraints on one's resignation from membership of a club.

Regarding deprivation of nationality, loss in such a form, which must include treating a grant as *void ab initio*, should always be rare and reviewable on appeal or by the courts. Finally, the UK does not provide for any sort of automatic loss through absence abroad and I think that is absolutely right. The individual will always be entitled to renounce any nationality, but otherwise, completely unlike the domicile concept, nationalities should be cumulative throughout one's life. Although it might be essential to have one's personal law governed by only a single legal system at any given time, returning to the theme that multiple citizenship should be encouraged, an accumulation of nationalities would be pleasing for the individual, would tend to divide his or her loyalties internationally and so enhance non-partisanship, and the community benefits as the ebb and flow of peoples promotes multi-culturalism and enriches society. British citizenship once acquired is, unless expressly renounced, already a life-long attribute; so should it remain and so should it be with all nationalities.

11 THE IMPLICATIONS OF IMMIGRATION POLICY FOR RACE RELATIONS

Sarah Spencer

Successive British governments have argued since the mid 1960s that, in the words of a Conservative Home Secretary, 'Good race relations are heavily dependent on strict immigration control.'[1] Labour similarly, when in government in 1965, used race relations as the justification for extending immigration controls on Commonwealth immigrants, arguing that 'without limitation, integration is impossible'.[2] In its White Paper of that year, the two arms of government policy which are retained today were set out: maintenance of strict controls on immigration on the one hand; on the other, implementation of measures to tackle discrimination and promote equal opportunities for ethnic minority people.

The justification for the 'no integration without limitation' argument has been the strength of public opinion against black and Asian immigration. In fact, research on public opinion in the early years of immigration control was inconclusive on the breadth and degree of public hostility to immigrants and the extent to which politicians themselves whipped up the ill-feeling. Certainly there were areas in which public hostility was very vocal, particularly after the 'race riots' in Notting Hill and Nottingham in 1958.[3] However, at least one respected authority on race relations argued in the 1960s that the emphasis on the need for control 'helped to create the anxieties it was intended to calm, with the curious result that public concern was eventually prayed in aid of policies that had helped to create it'.[4] Saggar similarly concludes that curbs on immigration 'did not so much follow popular sentiment as actually precede and create it'.[5]

By the late 1950s, immigration became an electoral issue and Labour's earlier opposition to controls on Commonwealth immigrants wavered. When the Labour shadow Foreign Secretary lost his seat in 1964 to a candidate who used the slogan 'If you want a nigger neighbour, vote Labour', it was clear that responding to public concern about immigrants or, from an alternative perspective, exploiting voters' prejudices, could win votes.[6] The new Labour government, with a fragile majority of 5, joined the Conservatives in supporting immigration controls in order to reassure the concerned/prejudiced voter.

The controls which were introduced in 1962, extended in 1968 and 1971 and effectively consolidated by the 1981 British Nationality Act were designed to restrict the number of New Commonwealth (that is, largely black and Asian) people who, for historic reasons, had previously enjoyed the right of entry to the UK. The indirect race discrimination in immigration controls, and the continuing hardship inflicted by rules which prevent or delay family reunification, has been censured by the European Commission on Human Rights and is well documented elsewhere.[7] At the same time, legislation was introduced in 1965 and strengthened in 1968 and 1976 to outlaw racial discrimination in employment and the provision of services, although immigration control was, and is, exempt.[8] The recent Asylum and Immigration Appeals Act, while providing certain new, limited, safeguards, continued the trend towards more restrictive immigration controls.

No government has acknowledged that immigration control is largely intended to exclude black and Asian immigrants.[9] Justifying the recent Act, for instance, the then Home Secretary used the argument that open entry to the UK 'would lead to terrible pressures on our employment, on our housing, on our social services, on our health service and on our education service'. But he supported this argument with no statistics or research evidence.[10] Indeed, the research programme of the Home Office Research and Planning Unit, where such research might be expected to be initiated, reveals that no research on the impact of immigration on the labour market or public services has been carried out.[11] Nor is such evidence available from nongovernmental sources. Thus the government is not in a position to know whether immigrants, on balance, make a positive contribution to the British economy or constitute a drain on public services and resources. It does not, and did not, have the information to know whether any of the public fears about immigration, for instance that immigrants would take scarce jobs and houses, were justified, or whether these were myths which should be firmly refuted.

The argument which has in practice fuelled political pressure for immigration controls since the late 1950s was most clearly articulated by Mrs Thatcher when, as leader of the Opposition in 1978, she spoke on television about 'The British people's fear' of 'being swamped' by people with 'alien cultures'.[12] Her message to the public was unambiguous—your fears about alien cultures are justified—but it was also selective. (There was no suggestion that she was referring to the spread of American fast-food chains.)

Many critics have pointed out the inconsistency in a government policy which discriminates on race grounds at the point of entry while seeking to outlaw discrimination against those already here.[13] They have argued, with reason, that the effect of the first arm of the policy, immigration control, has been to counter rather than support the second.[14] By accepting public concern about immigration as a legitimate grievance, and seeking to remedy that grievance by restricting the entry of black and Asian people, governments have reinforced the view that such people are undesirable and undermined their own efforts to eradicate discrimination.

While accepting that immigration policy and the attitudes of some politicians have exacerbated public hostility to ethnic minority immigrants, however, one could not argue that no hostility existed prior to introduction of controls nor that it would dissolve if the controls were removed. Racism is pervasive[15] and academics who argue for greater efforts to eradicate discrimination, such as Zig Layton Henry, also argue that 'there seems no political alternative for the [Labour] party other than to continue its support for stringent immigration controls, even though these are inevitably open to attack as in some respects racist....There is no easy way to escape this dilemma except perhaps to try to displace the responsibility for immigration policy from the United Kingdom Government to the European Commission'.[16]

It is my intention to argue that there is an alternative strategy to current immigration policy which neither displaces responsibility for immigration controls onto an already unpopular European Commission nor involves abandoning immigration control. My contention is that it is the inherent race discrimination (and other key aspects) of our immigration controls, and the way in which immigration policy is presented, which are harmful rather than immigration controls per se. I shall argue that, in order to achieve its objective of improving race relations and ending discrimination against members of ethnic minorities, the government must make key changes in the content and presentation of immigration and asylum policy.

Discrimination, harassment and race relations

It is not necessary here to demonstrate the need to tackle discrimination and racial violence, nor indeed to consider whether government policy should go beyond tolerating cultural differences to encourage cultural diversity[17] (though such an argument, if accepted, would raise interesting questions for immigration policy). Reports from the Commission for Racial Equality alone make it clear how much has to be achieved before members of ethnic minority communities enjoy full equality of opportunity, free from racial harassment and violence.

The kind of racist attacks which are frequent occurrences in Germany and other parts of Europe[18] for instance, are also happening here, including three recent murders in South London. Racial harassment, the CRE reports, occurs on a significant scale.[19] A government research report in 1991 estimated that as many as 7000 racial incidents may have occurred between January 1988 and June 1989 in one area of London alone.[20] The attitude of some offenders leaves no doubt that their offence was racially motivated. The man convicted of murdering a 15-year-old Asian boy in October 1992 gave a nazi salute when told that he had seriously injured the boy and his uncle and is reported to have said 'Good, I hope they die. My name is Conroy. Good English name that. What am I going to get for doing a couple of Pakis? I am Anglo-Saxon.'[21] Racism is a threat to public order as well as imposing a blight on the lives of many black and Asian people.

Research confirms that discrimination in employment, services and the criminal justice system has been endemic.[22] As a result of discrimination in the labour market, skills and experience are lost to the British economy. For reasons which include discrimination:

> large proportions of people belonging to ethnic minorities remain economically vulnerable, concentrated in lower job levels and subject to higher rates of unemployment than the white population, even among the more successful minority groups, and even within qualification levels.[23]

Periodically, the frustration in some sections of the black and Asian communities spills over into disorder.[24]

Implications for immigration and asylum policy

Government race relations policy has evidently not achieved its objectives and immigration policy must, as I have argued, bear some responsibility for this. If immigration policy is to contribute to, rather than damage, race relations, government must first establish what the real social and economic impact of immigration is (as argued in Findlay) and the implications of our obligations under international law (see Storey, Dummett and others). Armed with the facts, government should:

- initiate an informed public debate about the form which immigration and asylum policy should take;
- redraw its policy and controls on immigrants and asylum seekers;
- present its immigration and asylum policy in a way which both convinces the public of their rationale and fosters the self respect and sense of security of members of ethnic minority communities.

Informed public debate

The UK is far from being the only country in which immigrants find themselves blamed for the country's socio-economic problems. In Australia, for instance, a high level committee was set up in 1987 to advise on the country's immigration policies in part because 'community consensus in favour of immigration is at risk'.[25] The Fitzgerald Committee found that immigrants were being blamed unjustly for unwelcome social change:

> When there are forces moving our society which people seem not to be able to identify, or to understand, or to halt, immigration as a cause seems easier to pinpoint, the change it brings becomes negatively perceived, and it is felt that by manipulating immigration in this way or that way we can avoid having economic or social problems.[26]

Such attitudes, it argued, must be recognised by the government and met with decisive leadership, education, and presentation of the facts about non-European immigration.

This Committee found, however, that public misunderstanding

was not the whole problem. Surveys revealed that the immigration programme 'is not identified in the public mind with the national interest and must be given a convincing rationale'. That is, if the public were to be convinced that immigrants were not to blame for socio-economic problems, the government must be able to demonstrate both that there were sound reasons for allowing the immigrants to enter, and that the immigrants were not subsequently contributing to these problems. Moreover, if support for the humanitarian and family unity categories of immigration were to be retained, selection criteria for other immigrants needed to be sharpened so that those with the technical and entrepreneurial skills needed were, and could be seen, to be chosen. 'The sounder the economic rationale', they argued 'the better the compassionate and humanitarian objectives can be served'. If the public are not convinced that there is an economic justification for immigration, serving the national interest, then the humanitarian parts of the immigration programme are at risk.[27]

In the UK, similarly, people need to be convinced that the immigration which is allowed or encouraged is justified according to criteria which have been publicly discussed and have broad agreement. The government should propose, on the basis of research on the economic and social impact of migration, what kinds and levels of immigration would, in its view, be appropriate to meet its economic, social and political objectives; then it should make its data and analysis available.

Public discussion is needed, for instance, on the balance which should be drawn between allowing companies to select employees from overseas, and the need to provide jobs for existing residents. Although the rules for inter-company transfers were recently relaxed, significant barriers are still put in the way of companies who wish to recruit, and keep, even skilled staff from overseas. The Confederation of British Industry (CBI), whom we consulted on this issue, and who in turn consulted some of their members who employ overseas workers replied that:

> Employers also raised the issue of the need for a global workforce if business is to operate successfully in a global business environment. For example, a multi-national company with a UK headquarters may wish to recruit in the US, bring the trainee to the UK to gain UK HQ experience before deploying him in the US or elsewhere in the Company's global network. *Restrictions via the Work Permit Scheme on such recruitment and*

training strategies may result in multi-nationals moving their HQ
operations to countries where work permit restrictions are
considered less onerous.[28] [our emphasis]

In this example, the operation of immigration control could be working against the general national interest (though not necessarily against the interests of sections of the workforce), but there is no forum in which business interests or trade unions may raise their concerns and have them discussed. At a recent Anglo-German seminar on the economic impact of migration, German economists could not understand how UK labour immigration policy could have been devised without regular consultation with these representatives of business and employees' interests, as happens in Germany.[29]

Is it the case, for instance, that the decline in the population of working age throughout Europe means that we shall become reliant on overseas labour once again; or could this shortfall be met by more women entering the labour market and by retraining the unemployed? Solicitors have told us of the difficulties which entrepreneurs wishing to start up small businesses in the UK now face because to obtain entry they must have £200,000 to invest; and of would-be tourists from the Indian subcontinent with money to spend unable to obtain visas to take their holidays here. Would it be in the public interest for the rules restricting these categories of people to be relaxed? Equally, there has been no consideration of the damage which has been done to the UK's international standing by the reservations which it has entered when ratifying international human rights instruments, such as the UN Convention on the Rights of the Child, because its immigration law is known to contravene them. A full enquiry is needed into these issues, backed by research and public consultation.

One issue which needs to come out into the open is the potential conflict between the interests of sections of the public and the perceived interests of the country as a whole. The priority given to protecting the existing workforce over the needs of companies for overseas labour is one example of this, as are potential conflicts of interest created by residents wanting to be joined by dependent relatives for whom they are unable to provide financial support and who would therefore be a burden on the tax-payer. A balance needs to be found and priorities agreed and this can be done more satisfactorily through informed public debate than behind closed doors. Consultation contributes both to the quality of the decisions taken and to their public acceptability.

Advocating a public debate on immigration policy is not likely to be popular. While a minority of politicians have responded to, and whipped up, anti-immigrant sentiment, the leaders of the two major parties have (with notable exceptions) sought to maintain a fragile consensus that the immigration issue be kept out of public debate and electoral politics. Believing that avoiding debate was more likely to keep the lid on anti-immigrant feelings, they have not created a forum for the public including members of ethnic minorities to be consulted on immigration policy. Saggar argues that it was this suppression of debate which led to the growth of support for the far-right National Front, 'an extra-party mode of articulating political interests which had been largely smothered by the major parties' [30] until Mrs Thatcher broke the consensus in 1978.

If the government is to seek to change public attitudes on immigration, and members of ethnic minority communities are to be given an opportunity to influence those policies, the public should be consulted and a forum provided for continuing discussion. Parliament cannot as yet provide an adequate forum as there are so few MPs from ethnic minority communities. The Fitzgerald Committee in Australia came to this conclusion and, as a result of its report, the Bureau of Immigration Research was set up in 1989 to conduct and promote research into immigration issues and foster public understanding and informed discussion on immigration. Its research covers such topics as the micro-economic effects of immigration and the impact of illegal entrants on government services and benefits. Its first national conference attracted 700 people.[31] The fact that the UK has fewer immigrants than Australia[32] should not be used as an excuse to dismiss such initiatives as irrelevant here. Immigration has had, and is likely to go on having, major social, political and economic implications for the UK and it is this, rather than the relative numbers involved, which merits the kind of research, consultation and policy development which the issue has always lacked.

Controls on immigrants and asylum seekers

Informed by research and public debate, the government will be in a position to redraw immigration controls and policy on asylum seekers. Controls must, as has been argued elsewhere in this volume (e.g., Storey, Guild, Findlay) be based on clear, defensible criteria which reflect the capacity of the UK to absorb immigrants on the one hand and its international obligations on the other. To be defensible, the criteria used must be based on factual evidence, e.g., on skill shortages, the impact of migrants on the housing and labour market and so forth. Not only can controls thus be free of charges of discrimination; any restriction placed on the exercise of basic human rights (e.g. family life) can be justified as required by international law (see Storey, Guild).

Second, the immigration service must be brought within the scope of the Race Relations Act. As the CRE notes,

> in relation to immigration control...there is apparently a wide freedom to discriminate so far as the remedies under the 1976 Act are concerned. The Commission believes that this is wrong. This lack of remedy occurs precisely where the individual is most vulnerable. In the private sector, if there is discrimination at one source, the individual generally has both the opportunity of going elsewhere to another provider of services and also has a remedy under the Act. There appears to be neither opportunity when the individual is facing an immigration officer, prison officer or police officer prepared to discriminate improperly in exercising control functions.[33]

The wide discretion which immigration officials are allowed under the Immigration Rules, which in practice allows so much discrimination, should in future be based on objective criteria, not on guesses about people's motives or intentions.

Summary

I am thus not arguing that immigration controls should be abolished. If it is correct that a government should put the interests of existing residents, including the interests of its ethnic minorities, before those of people from other countries, then there are criteria which can be used to determine who should be allowed/encouraged to come and who should be excluded. If there are objective reasons why the UK cannot accept all those who would like to enter, and there are, these reasons should be given with supporting evidence. Only thus will the impression be countered that it is people from particular countries who are undesirable and the possibility be created of a new dawn in British race relations.

Presentation of policy

Once immigration policy is set, the public needs to be informed of its rationale. Labour immigration through the work permit scheme, for instance, is currently limited almost entirely to those with essential skills or experience, admitted for posts which cannot be filled internally. Yet the public are largely unaware of the benefits which these immigrants bring, if aware at all that immigration of this kind exists. This constitutes a lost opportunity for the government to argue the potential benefits of immigration, in the general public interest.

There are other examples which could be cited. Foreign students bring short-term income to our universities and long term goodwill when they return to influential positions in their own countries. Yet this is not how they are viewed. More public attention is given to the few who work without permission and are deported than to the benefits which the majority bring. Refugees, similarly, are portrayed either as vulnerable dependants in need of our help (and resources) or as scroungers who defraud social security. We could instead be informed of the skills and experience which they bring, from which in the long term we shall benefit. In the presentation of policy, moreover, government must be scrupulous in referring to the objective criteria on which individuals are allowed to enter or excluded, taking care to avoid fuelling any prejudices about particular immigrant groups.

The relationship between anti-immigrant or racist ideology and historical, structural conditions is of course complex and racism cannot be tackled effectively without removing the structural causes which feed it: including the conflicts over resources in the deprived areas in which immigrants first settle; shortage of housing and jobs, hospital places and schools. The *source* of the problem is not public attitudes but the conflicts which give rise to those attitudes.

One cannot, however, conclude from this that a change of attitude by government accompanied by positive initiatives to change public attitudes to new and past immigrants would not be worthwhile. In a recession, there may be limits to the action which government can take to improve conditions in deprived areas although there is no shortage of suggestions of general policies which would particularly benefit members of ethnic minority communities.[34] But government can act to stop immigrants and members of ethnic minorities being blamed for those conditions. The ideology is not free floating; but it can be influenced. After Mrs Thatcher's 'swamping' speech the percentage of the public who thought that immigration was an 'urgent issue facing the country' went up from 9% to 21%.[35]

In contrast to his predecessor's intervention, the Prime Minister John Major did recently speak in positive terms about the role of ethnic minorities in the UK:

> I know from personal experience what a vital and rich contribution people from the ethnic minorities can make

and went on to argue, not for a uniform society in which everyone is like everyone else but for an integrated society which he described as:

> like a successful team, all the different players have recognised roles to play, they have contributions to make and they are accepted by each other as equal parts of the whole...we must harness to the full the potential of all our citizens. Capabilities and not colour is what must matter and will matter in the future.[36]

Significantly, however, he was speaking only to a meeting of one sympathetic organisation. This is not a message which, in the UK, has received strong public backing by government.

In contrast, the governments of some other countries have made conscious attempts to change public perception of immigrants and foreigners. While the German Government is undoubtedly open to criticism for its handling of right-wing hostility to immigrants and refugees,[37] and is thus a poor model in other respects, it is interesting to note the publicity campaign which it launched in November 1992 to change public attitudes to these groups. Afraid of the consequences of the rise of racism, the President spoke out against it at a demonstration and the Interior Minister announced a public information campaign 'to inform the public of the dangers of extremism and xenophobia'. This includes the provision of material for schools and advertising through posters, youth magazines and TV slots in which well known popular figures appear to state their opposition to racism. Companies have been encouraged to sponsor initiatives such as the national football team wearing T shirts with the logo 'My friend is a foreigner' (sponsored by Opel) and Stuttgart taxi drivers likewise (sponsored by Mercedes). Local government has followed suit with, for instance, placards on the underground in Berlin. Companies such as Daimler-Benz and Bosch have written to their employees urging tolerance towards foreigners and the media have taken up the theme so that it is a frequent topic of chat-shows. The initiative was backed by 'tough' new measures against right-wing violence.[38]

Sweden, in contrast, has had a long term policy of informing the public about immigration and immigrants;[39] while in the Netherlands an ongoing public debate was initiated by the government in 1991 on the shape a multicultural society should take and on its values and norms, the government itself arguing that society should be flexible and prepared to absorb new cultural elements. The Dutch Government subsidises anti-discrimination consultations held by the churches, trade unions and organisations for minority groups, provides grants for one-off information campaigns and encourages people in inner-city neighbourhoods to exchange information and engage in joint activities, for instance by inviting people living in the same apartment block to participate in discussions.[40] In France, again not always a model in other respects, the government of the mid-1980s was supportive of the SOS Racisme rallies and the slogan '*ne touche pas a mon pote*'.

It is of course true that it is not possible to measure the impact of such initiatives as other variables are involved. In Germany, for instance, opinion polls in December 1992, after the government's initiative had begun, recorded a drop in anti-foreigner sentiment among West and East Germans, the proportion supporting the slogan 'Foreigners Out' having dropped from 69% to 43%. It is argued, however, that this could be attributed to the effect of the murder of three Turks in Mölln in November.[41]

Electoral impact

In contrast to other European countries, parties of the extreme right in the UK have not enjoyed any significant electoral support in recent years. They achieved a maximum of 3.1% of the votes in the general election of October 1974 and went into decline in the late 1970s, which was variously attributed to the success of the popular campaign against them and to Mrs Thatcher's willingness to champion the cause of the prejudiced voter. As Saggar puts it, the National Front found 'its political message and most popular policies stolen by the respectable right'. If the mainstream political parties were to adopt the approach which I propose, what would be the likely impact on public support for the extreme right?

The first answer must be that there is no guarantee that support will remain low even if governments maintain the present policy. Where immigrant numbers are perceived as the problem, and the pressure of numbers of refugees and migrants is likely to grow, there will always be the potential for public hostility to be inflamed. While there is any immigration, it is unlikely to disappear.

If, however, the basis of immigration control is based on criteria which are supported by serious research, pursuant to national economic and social policies, the government will at least be able to provide positive reasons for its policy. Numbers only increase if it is broadly in the national interest for them to do so. Moreover, if the change of policy is accompanied by initiatives to change public attitudes, the situation is less likely to deteriorate. Nor should we over-estimate the extent of public hostility to foreigners. Although a recent Eurobarometer survey found that 54% of the UK public thought that there were too many non-EC people living in Britain, 40% did not take that view.[42] Moreover, the British Social Attitudes Survey found that the number of people who thought that there would be more prejudice in 5 years time fell from 42% in 1983 to 21% in 1991.[43]

Conclusion

I have argued that a government policy which discriminates against ethnic minorities at the point of entry while seeking to remove discrimination against them internally, is inconsistent. The negative message of the first policy has damaged the positive impact of the second. The dangers posed by racism to public order and to the well-being of members of ethnic minorities necessitate urgent government action to reverse this position. A new approach is needed.

In immigration policy, government has the right to put the interests of its existing residents, including members of ethnic minorities, before those of individuals who want to settle here. The government should, first, initiate research to establish the socio-economic implications of immigration—the costs and benefits for different sections of society—and should assess the full implications of our obligations under international law, as argued in more detail elsewhere in this volume.

Second, it should initiate an informed public debate on the form which future immigration and asylum policy should take. Consultation improves the quality of decisions and their public acceptability.

The consensus to keep immigration out of public debate has not succeeded in stemming anti-immigrant feeling but has ensured that neither those against nor those in favour of immigration have been properly consulted. An enquiry now, and a continuing forum, are needed in which the kinds and levels of immigration can be discussed, research considered, conflicts of interest aired. A public debate fuelled only by sensational reports about the next group of immigrants or asylum seekers would not achieve our objectives. A government initiated debate, informed by new research data and guided by the sense of priorities I have proposed, could both inform policy making and contribute to changing public attitudes to immigrants.

Third, government should redraw immigration controls so that decisions on entry and residence are based on research based, defensible criteria such as employment skills and family connections, regardless of the country of origin of the individual. The immigration service should be brought within the scope of the Race Relations Act and the wide discretion allowed to immigration officers in the Immigration Rules should be based on objective criteria.

Finally, government should seek to change attitudes through its public presentation of policy, drawing attention to the rationale for immigration and asylum policy, and to the economic and social contribution which immigrants and refugees make. This will only be successful, and resentments be allayed, if any sections of the public whose standard of living is genuinely affected feel that their concerns have been addressed by the revised policy which is adopted and they are convinced that immigrants and asylum seekers who are allowed to enter either make a positive economic contribution or have the right to the public resources they use.

Although the impact of such initiatives is difficult to measure, and it is of course true that attitudes are not independent of their historical origins and structural causes, it is nevertheless worthwhile to counter the negative views encouraged in the past by discriminatory immigration policy and publicly aired prejudices.

The electoral risks for a government seeking to initiate public debate and to change attitudes towards immigrants are considerable. Even leaving aside the humanitarian reasons for reform, however, and the potential benefits to the economy, the dangers inherent in maintaining the current approach justify the political risk. The pressures to migrate to Europe over coming decades are likely, as we have seen, to be enormous. Where a negative, ill-informed public debate focuses solely on numbers, the potential hostility fuelled by any increase in immigration could present a serious threat to public order. The government should move to shift the debate away from such narrow, negative concerns before it is too late.

CONCLUSION AND RECOMMENDATIONS

Sarah Spencer

With the exception of asylum seekers, the UK has remained relatively immune from the growing migration pressures which are being experienced elsewhere in Europe. Although it is not possible to make accurate predictions of migration flows, population growth and other push factors are expected to lead to mass migration on an unprecedented scale. While the UK will not be the first country to feel this pressure, it cannot expect to be immune.

The UK thus needs immigration and refugee policies capable of anticipating and responding to potentially large, and changing, migrant and refugee flows. The dramatic increase in the number of asylum seekers which has already taken place (not withstanding the significant fall in numbers in 1992) is not the only difference from the early 1960s when current immigration policy was adopted. Migration from former Commonwealth countries for family reunion, once highly significant, is declining, while skilled migration for professional and managerial posts has become an area of expansion, not least because of the growth of international companies, many based in the UK. The free-movement provisions of the European Community have increased the numbers of EC nationals coming to live and work in the UK.

The contributors to this report have been highly critical of the form which current UK immigration and refugee policies take, from many different perspectives. They have criticised the philosophy on which immigration policy is based; the failure to meet international obligations; the failure to address the causes of refugee flows; the failure to relate immigration policy to any serious study of the economic impact of migrants and the consequent inadequacy of policy tools; the discrimination, lack of fairness and due process in some immigration and asylum procedures and the disproportionate measures used to enforce immigration control; the negative consequences of current immigration controls for race relations and, overall, the failure to recognise the implications of immigration, refugee and citizenship policy for wider government economic and social objectives.

There is no one country which can provide an attractive model for reforming UK policies. But in this last respect the so-called countries of immigration have a positive approach in that they set clear objectives for their immigration and asylum policies. The Canadian Immigration Act (1978) for instance, begins with the list of objectives which the Act is intended to fulfil. These include the need to 'enrich the cultural and social fabric of Canada; facilitate reunion between Canadians/permanent residents and their relatives abroad; foster the development of a strong and viable economy, and fulfill international legal obligations'. The UK could usefully set itself the task of identifying what the objectives of UK immigration and refugee policy ought to be.

Drawing on the papers in this report, I suggest here what the central tenets of future immigration and refugee policy should be. I use the term refugee policy to include the policies covering the refugees' countries of origin; asylum policy refers to policies towards individuals who have already become asylum seekers. The first tenet of future policy reflects that terminology: that government should address not only the symptoms of migrant and refugee flows, but the causes.

Causes before symptoms

The immigrants and asylum seekers who reach the UK are but the tip of the iceberg of migrants and displaced persons world-wide. Refugees are involuntary migrants and many other emigrants would not choose to leave their country of origin if they could achieve satisfactory living conditions there. It makes no sense for Europe to attempt to shut the door unless it takes effective steps to ameliorate the conditions which cause migration and refugee flows.

In this volume we have looked only at the causes of refugee (as opposed to migrant) flows and advocated many measures to create conditions under which such flows would be less likely to occur. The size and complexity of the problem leave no alternative but for the international community to take responsibility for averting refugee flows and for the international bodies and individual states to adopt a holistic, co-ordinated approach, ensuring that each arm of their policy contributes towards that end.

Attention must first be focused to a greater extent on the country from which refugees are being, or are likely to become, displaced. New international arrangements are needed to establish obligations on states to co-operate in removing the causes of refugee flows, to adhere to procedures for managing flows and help secure voluntary repatriation, in return for assistance from the international community. Negotiation is more likely than confrontation to secure co-operation but sanctions and other means of enforcement, including use of the international human rights machinery, must be explored. Arms trade restrictions, aid, debt and trade policies should be co-ordinated and focused on the objective of averting refugee flows, in the interests of the potential refugees but also of the countries to which they would flee.

In this context, the British Foreign Office should establish a unit with responsibility for co-ordinating refugee policy internally within that department and with the Department of Trade, Ministry of Defence, Overseas Development Agency and Home Office. Its role would involve both long term planning and crisis management. In relation to asylum seekers in the UK, co-ordination is also needed between the Home Office, the Departments of Environment, Social Security, Health and Employment, and local government, if the reception and long term needs of both refugees and migrants are to be met, a point to which I return below.

The UK should encourage the development of the EC and UN early warning systems and, to increase the pressure for action to be taken, ensure that the information is made public. It should give greater support to the international agencies dealing with refugee flows and press for greater competence for the International Fact Finding Commission. Means of protecting minority rights should continue to be pursued. States should be encouraged to ratify the international agreements protecting refugees, and knowledge about the Conventions and their enforcement mechanisms should be disseminated. Conventions are of course only as good as their enforcement mechanisms and states (including the UK) need encouragement to endorse them, particularly rights of individual petition. Chapter 1 ends with a checklist of steps which the UK and the EC should take to implement this integrated approach.

International migration experts provide a similar list of urgent measures to curb mass migration from the developing South. The International Organisation for Migration's package includes targeting international trade, investment and development aid to migration producing countries to increase job and wealth creation and foster development. Improving living conditions may, in the short term, increase migration pressures by giving people the resources and the knowledge necessary to leave. In the long term it is the only solution. Potential migrants, in turn, must have clear, credible information about the opportunities in receiving countries, to dispel misleading myths. (A recent survey found that 48% of Albanians, for instance, thought that they were eligible to apply for asylum if the economic conditions in their country were intolerable.)[1]

A holistic approach must do more than address the causes of migrant and refugee flows. European states must, for instance, consider the impact which their asylum policies are having on those states to whom the asylum seekers are being displaced, in developing countries and in Eastern Europe. Asylum seekers should not be returned, for instance, to countries without the resources and procedures to consider their claims for refugee status. The impact of large numbers of asylum seekers on the fragile economies and democracies of Eastern and Central Europe must be a consideration.

Working with our European partners

Addressing migration and refugee flows is only one aspect of policy on which it is unrealistic to identify a United Kingdom policy in isolation from the approach adopted by other countries. As a European country, and a member of the European Community, it must be a principal objective to work with our European neighbours on these issues of mutual concern. Indeed, the UK has accepted this in relation to the EC in signing the Single European Act and ratifying the Maastricht Treaty (Chapter 5). The future of the EC states is bound together and they need to find a common approach and common solutions to the problems they face. Free movement within the EC necessitates a joint immigration policy for its external borders, raising the question how long there will be a distinct UK immigration and asylum policy. There are, however, good grounds for seeking to define it now. Although the UK's role within the EC is to contribute to making policy for 12 countries, not simply to pursue its own interests, the UK does need to identify what those interests are. It also needs to be confident of its own practice and to be clear in which direction it wants to influence EC policy. Nevertheless, there is no longer any question of developing policy in isolation nor of 'going it alone' once new directions are identified.

The UK needs to develop a new style of thinking about the Community. It should see the development of policy as comparable to that of a government providing for the varying needs of its regions. Such co-operation and burden sharing is necessary if internal free-movement is to work successfully, without major migratory movements from one member state to another, including movement of illegal immigrants.

This is not to say that harmonisation of immigration and asylum policy should be the over-riding priority. The UK needs to ensure that harmonisation is not simply a process of levelling down but one in which international human rights standards are identified and protected before further agreement is reached. It must stand out against illiberal or unworkable proposals. Priority should be given to achieving free movement rights for all long term residents in EC states, necessary for the single market to work as intended. A company which employs some non-EC nationals should not be at a disadvantage compared to one which does not, leaving aside the humanitarian reasons for such free-movement rights.

Internally, the government should reform UK policy so that it moves towards convergence with those policies of the EC and EC states which are progressive, for instance recognising the EC's wider definition of family for the purposes of family reunion. EC nationals who are exercising their right to work (or study) here, and many UK nationals who have similarly lived in other EC countries, may be joined by a wider circle of family members here than UK nationals who have lived here all their life (e.g., by children up to 21 years and elderly dependent relatives). This is simply unfair and the rules should be changed to end that discrimination. The UK should also reform the administration of its own immigration controls, for instance strengthening rights of appeal, so that it can be confident of its own practice when advocating good practice in EC negotiations. Ann Dummett sets out detailed proposals at the end of Chapter 5.

The insistence by the UK and other states on using inter-governmental machinery to develop common policies, rather than negotiations under the auspices of the EC, reflects their unwillingness to accept this shared responsibility and the EC's authority in this area of policy. The Maastricht Treaty paves the way for greater EC competency and the UK should press for this. Not only would this facilitate long-term forward planning for the whole community, rather than negotiations between individual states. It provides for more open decision making, makes it more likely that policy will reflects the principles of the European Convention on Human Rights (which the EC is committed to uphold) and provides a means of redress to the European Court of Justice. Where the policy agreed has such major implications for human rights it is simply unacceptable for the decisions to be taken in secret, unaccountable fora. On the contrary, basic principles of open democratic decision making must be adhered to.

Respecting international human rights standards

In the UK, as in the EC, international human rights standards should form one of the cornerstones of policy reform. Migrants and asylum seekers are without question a vulnerable group whose rights require protection. They have no powerful interest groups to defend them and face media, and sometimes public, hostility. It is an emotive area of policy subject to influence by racism, xenophobia and nationalism and the rights of migrants and refugees should be protected by grounding the law and its administration firmly in international human rights principles. These provide only minimum standards and should be seen not as an obstacle to be surmounted but as a prerequisite to good practice.

It must also be said that our respect for these principles influences our standing in the world and the confidence with which the government can call on other states to improve their human rights record. Like much of the approach advocated here, to give effect to these human rights standards does not imply an abandonment of British self-interest but a re-evaluation of where that self-interest lies.

One major implication of acknowledging the authority of international standards is that any restriction on these rights must be proportional to the harm being addressed and defensible by objectively justified criteria. If rights are curtailed there must be an effective remedy. Thus, if family life is to be restricted by denying entry to family members or deporting them, evidence must be provided that the exclusion is necessary on grounds specified in the relevant Conventions, such as to protect the 'economic well-being' of the country (Article 8, ECHR). The research has not yet been conducted, nor data collected, which would make this possible (nor should it be assumed that to allow family life is uneconomic, as we argue below). Similarly, where a marriage breaks down, can the government justify excluding the alien father and separating him from his children?

The primary purpose rule, excluding spouses from a genuine, permanent relationship who nevertheless cannot demonstrate that their primary purpose in marrying a British person was not to obtain entry to the UK, is disproportionate to the harm it seeks to avoid. It would be more reasonable to investigate the marriage only if there is evidence that it is not genuine, and avoid the infringement of privacy which current investigations involve. A probationary year to establish that a marriage is genuine is appropriate, but not a longer period. DNA tests to establish whether children are genuinely related to the parent they are seeking to re-join should also be carried out only if there is evidence of abuse. If a child is accepted by an adult as their moral and legal responsibility, this intrusive test (which may, for instance, reveal, unnecessarily, that the wife has been unfaithful), is not justified.

The government should change those aspects of the law which conflict with the judgments of the bodies charged with supervising international human rights standards, and use those standards as a yardstick against which to measure other provisions. It should reconsider its record of non-ratifications, reservations and derogations and specifically justify those which remain, using research and data which demonstrate the ongoing necessity for those exemptions. The UK's international obligations should be reflected in our own statutes and rules. Storey proposes a means of selecting those which should be incorporated in statute.

Government alone cannot be charged with responsibility for protecting the rights of these vulnerable groups. A monitoring body should be established to review immigration and asylum law and its administration in order to ensure that they give full effect to international law. Experts on international human rights law should be among its members.

Responsibility for protecting human rights of migrants and refugees should not be restricted to a body which is not well placed to compare their treatment with the treatment of other groups. The Human Rights Commission, advocated by many, should therefore also include these groups within its brief, seeking to avoid a situation in which treatment which would be considered quite unacceptable for existing residents is tolerated for migrants (e.g., confinement in detention camps).

Identifying the socio-economic impact of migrants

Human rights principles are advocated as minimum standards, not as the only consideration in immigration and asylum policy. Refugees who fall within the UN Convention definition of refugee are of course *entitled* to protection, and we would argue that many of those excluded by that definition are nevertheless refugees and should be given sanctuary. For those who are not entitled to enter on humanitarian grounds, however, the government must take into account broader considerations in deciding whether to welcome or reject the applications of those who want to come.

Successive governments have, in their assessment of UK interests to date, allowed narrowly conceived social, political and economic considerations to determine immigration and asylum policy without carrying out the investigation of the socio-economic impact of migration on which to make reasoned judgements. A serious economic investigation of the consequences for the economy of different immigration scenarios is long overdue. Government should know, in as much as research can supply the answers, not only what the broad impact of different categories of migrants is, for instance, on the labour market, but their impact on the living standards of existing residents. It cannot make reasoned policy unless it knows who will gain and who, if any, will lose.

How, for instance, should the skill shortages of tomorrow be addressed? Should the UK actively promote immigration to fill such shortages, as certain other Western countries do, and should the UK be seeking investors and entrepreneurs? Would it be in the long term interests of the economy for companies to be able to select the employee which they feel will do most to enhance their business, or should the domestic work-force be given priority when job vacancies occur? Does the import of skilled labour reduce the need for skill training in the UK, and thus the opportunities for indigenous workers? At present, the data is not available on which an informed discussion of these issues could be based, nor is there a forum in which interested parties can put their point of view.

Allan Findlay concludes that the UK government's negative attitude to immigration has sold the country short. It has failed to reap the economic benefits from selective skilled migration, forgone the investment and jobs which entrepreneurs could provide and prevented companies from benefitting fully from inter-company transfers. For these companies the question is not whether a local person *could* do the job but whether the long term benefits would be greater of allowing one of their own employees to spend a period working at their UK branch. The work permit system serves primarily as a form of entry control, restricting temporary migration from outside the EC, not as a system which seeks on an informed and rational economic basis to achieve labour market adjustments through immigration to meet the broader needs of the British economy. If the needs of the economy are to be met, he argues, government must conduct systematic research on skill shortages so that it can welcome, or indeed encourage, those who are needed to come.

There is no suggestion that the UK is likely, even in the longer term, to need substantial numbers of migrants to fill labour shortages. A large company unable to get the labour it needs at the price it is prepared to pay is more likely to relocate abroad than to look to immigration for its employees. Economic considerations are likely to be grounds for constraining immigration policy rather than for any broad relaxation. Nevertheless, where particular categories of migrants are needed, it would be in the UK's interests to adopt a system which signals to potential migrants the UK's desire to mould its labour market in a positive way and that they might be welcome to make a contribution. That is, it should switch its philosophy from one of excluding migrants to protect the status quo, to a system of positive selection of those immigrants with most to contribute.

The UK could not adopt this approach without consideration of the needs of the migrants' countries of origin. In 1989, £66.6 billion per annum was earned in remittances from migrants, but the loss of skilled workers also damages the development potential of their countries of origin. The impact of emigration on developing countries is not one of the aspects of immigration policy which we have studied (albeit its importance is integral to an understanding of the causes of migration) but it is one which the government should take into account, and consult those states on, if intending to encourage migrants with particular skills and qualifications.

Labour migration taking place under the work-permit system is seen by the government as a temporary skill transfer. Those with valuable skills are not encouraged (and may not want) to stay (only 14% of work permit holders obtaining right of settlement). In contrast, immigrants entering for family formation and reunification are seen as permanent residents but, stereotypically, as uneconomic.

The system fails to recognise the positive economic potential in many of those who enter under humanitarian categories or to assist them to reach that potential.

The assistance which immigrants and refugees need in order to settle successfully and make their full contribution to society is also not one of the aspects of policy which we have studied in detail but we have become convinced that this is an issue to which government should attach some priority. It is in the interests of the UK, as well as those of the newcomers, that they are as productive and as little reliant on public resources as possible. Not only does this mean that they should, for instance, be assisted to acquire English language skills and employment training if needed. Government should also consider whether existing immigration controls are interfering with this objective. Where children are entitled to come to the UK, for instance, delays in entry clearance which reduce the number of years spent in British schools will affect their later employment and earnings potential. Similarly, common sense would suggest that two parent families are more likely to earn enough to be self-supporting than single parent families where one spouse is excluded from the UK.[2]

Labour market impact is not the only consideration which government must take into account. The implications for housing, the balance between taxes paid by migrants and the costs they incur in education, welfare and health services, should be the subject of serious research and analysis. The assumption is often made that immigrants are a drain on public resources but this is by no means supported by research abroad.[3] Broader cultural contributions should also not be discounted.

If the government is to take these broad economic criteria fully into account it must, first of all, be better informed. Inadequate research and a poor statistical base is a source of misinformation and weak policy making. The government currently has no adequate research base to justify its economic objections to higher levels of immigration; nor does the data exist to support its policy tools such as the work permit system. When we suggested to Home Office officials that such knowledge would be valuable in future policy development they were sceptical. As ministers had already decided what immigration policy should be, it was not clear what purpose new research would serve, they said. They doubted that Ministers would reconsider their approach. Yet it cannot be right to continue to enforce a policy in ignorance of its impact and without considering alternative options.

An adequate research and statistical base is a pre-requisite for any further policy developments, regardless of their objectives (not least if restrictions are to be justifiable by international human rights standards). The use in the UK of statistics on ethnic minorities, many of whom are second and third-generation immigrants, rather than on current stocks and flows, is but one example of the inadequacy of current information. The kind of data which is needed on current and recent immigrants is collected in some countries and has enabled the kind of research we recommend to be conducted; e.g., on language proficiency, participation rates, occupational status, take up of welfare benefits and so forth. The collection of this information should not entail any unacceptable intrusion into privacy. Increasing the sample size of some existing surveys such as the International Passenger Survey would provide some necessary data. Independent studies, seen to be separate from immigration control, are needed to provide more detail, e.g., on the effect which language ability has on employment and earnings potential.[4]

Public consultation

In an attempt to avoid the expression of anti-immigrant views, politicians have largely sought to keep immigration and asylum policy out of public debate, a policy which has prevented those for and against immigration from being consulted. Moreover, in the absence of information on the economic impact of immigration, government has not been in a position to provide the public with the facts and draw a distinction between legitimate concerns and unfounded prejudice.

Consultation improves the quality of decisions and their public acceptability and an enquiry now, and a continuing forum, are needed in which the kinds and levels of immigration can be discussed, research considered and conflicts of interest aired. A public debate fuelled only by sensational press reports would not be helpful. A government-initiated debate, informed by research and guided by the priorities outlined in this chapter, would assist government in determining the objectives which it should seek to achieve through its immigration, citizenship and asylum policies.

Redrawing immigration and asylum controls

Armed with information on the socio-economic impact of migrants, informed by the views of the public and interested parties, and clear as to its obligations under international law, the government will be in a position to rewrite immigration, citizenship and asylum policy. In so doing, it should ensure that the measures it proposes are based on defensible criteria reflecting the known economic impact of migrants and the UK's international human rights obligations. They should be non-discriminatory, fair and clear. The means of enforcement should observe due process and be proportionate to the harm they are intended to redress.

Criteria for entry clearance

Entry controls must be based on criteria which reflect the socio-economic impact of migrants and the UK's obligations under international law. To be defensible, the criteria used must be based on factual evidence, e.g., on skill shortages, the impact of migrants on the housing and labour market, and so forth. Not only can controls thus be free of charges of discrimination; any restriction placed on the exercise of basic human rights can be justified, as required by international human law.

Fairness, clarity and due process

There is a strong argument that fair procedures are also efficient procedures. A procedure which accurately determines the refugee status of an applicant, for instance, and does so quickly, will deter those who seek to use the procedure to obtain entry for other reasons. The recommendation that those conducting the interviews should be well informed about the applicants' country of origin, and thus in a position to assess the veracity of their persecution claim, is one of many detailed recommendations which Chris Randall makes in Chapter 7 to improve both the fairness and efficiency of the asylum procedure.

The government must consider whether it is sensible to spend time and resources determining whether an individual may have full refugee status or Exceptional Leave to Remain (ELR), when those with ELR are allowed to remain anyway, albeit under restrictive conditions. The numbers allowed to remain despite refusal of refugee status only demonstrate the inadequacy of the international definition and we would advocate adoption of a broader humanitarian test, attaching the same Refugee Convention and family reunion rights to both categories. If this is rejected, ELR should at least be a category in the Immigration Rules so that decision to grant this status is subject to appeal.

Visa requirements and carrier sanctions clearly prevent some asylum seekers from reaching Europe as well as migrants. Calling for the removal of carrier sanctions may not be realistic, but there should at least be a system of rebates to airlines where the application for refugee status is successful or one in which the airline is liable only if negligent (as in France). Visa requirements should be lifted temporarily when a country experiences a sudden mass exodus of refugees, a policy which would need to be implemented throughout the Community.

The notion that it is possible to identify safe countries from which no application for asylum could be legitimate must be rejected. It breaches the principle of individual determination of each case and ignores the reality that there may always be exceptional cases. All of the countries which Germany deems 'safe', for instance, are criticised in Amnesty International's most recent report on human rights abuses.

The widely accepted policy that asylum seekers should be required to apply for asylum in the first safe country they reach, even if they are there in transit for only a few hours, should also be reconsidered. It contradicts UN advice that the individual should, if possible, go to the country of their choice and the common sense underlying this must be acknowledged. Where the refugee knows the language of a country or has family there, s/he is far more likely to prosper and avoid being a burden on the public purse than in a country where s/he does not have these advantages. This could not be the only consideration if there is to be any equity between EC states in sharing the 'burden' (itself an unhelpful, negative term). Nor would it be feasible to give asylum seekers a continuing right to seek asylum after they had lived for some time in a safe country. But allowing individuals to settle where they believe they can prosper most quickly is surely more likely to be in the long term interests of states than the present policy.

Appeal rights are essential to fairness and consistency in decision making (but will be exercised less frequently if those with a just case are treated fairly first time round). If we do no more than accept the conclusion of the last official enquiry into immigration appeal rights, that

> it is fundamentally wrong and inconsistent with the rule of law that power to take decisions affecting a man's whole future should be vested in officers of the executive from whose finding there is no appeal,[5]

there are many instances where UK procedures fall short. In many cases there is *no* appeal (e.g., against refusal of a work permit); in others the difference between those without an appeal (e.g., students seeking to attend courses of less than six months) and those for whom there is an appeal (where the course is over six months) lack justification and coherence. Asylum seekers who claim not that they will, if returned, be subject to persecution as defined in the UN Convention, but that they will be subject to torture, would have their claim for asylum treated as 'without foundation' and have no right of appeal to the Appeal Tribunal. The procedure for those subject to deportation for reasons of 'national security' fails every test of due process. In Chapter 8, Elspeth Guild sets out the reforms which are needed in each case, arguing for a right of appeal against all immigration and asylum decisions, in most cases requiring a suspension of the decision until the appeal is resolved.

Long delays in decision making (e.g. on entry clearance), impose stress and hardship and long periods of family separation. The extreme differences in waiting times in different countries opens the government to allegations of discrimination. It should increase its resources in those areas to remove the discrepancies. A time limit should be imposed for decisions in all such applications, after which it would be deemed to be accepted. (Alternatively, it could be deemed to be refused, opening the way for an appeal. This course, however, puts the burden onto the applicant and applies less pressure on government to speed up its handling of applications.)

Consistency

The position of overseas students demonstrates the need for greater consistency in government policy making. The Department of Trade assists education institutions to compete in the international market for students, recognising that they are a significant export earner, some 4% of earnings from services in 1990. The Foreign Office is known to consider overseas students a valuable means of ensuring UK contacts and good will abroad, and of providing assistance to developing countries. Yet Home Office and Department of Employment regulations impose unnecessary obstacles for students seeking entry and the right to work part-time. Concern to limit the numbers who enter appears, for the Home Office, to dominate its thinking to the exclusion of other priorities. In this case, visa regulations and appeal rights should be reformed, women should be allowed to be accompanied by their husbands, and employment regulations (or at least the penalties for abuse) relaxed, to reflect the benefit which these students bring to the UK.

The treatment of visitors illustrates the same point. While it is government policy to encourage tourism, visa requirements and the removal of appeal rights for visitors who are refused entry may deter or exclude potential big spenders. While UK policy is to welcome genuine visitors, in practice the uneven visa requirements favour those from the developed world, and immigration officials have, and use, their considerable discretion to refuse entry if they are not satisfied that the visitor intends to return home. The scope for discrimination, inevitable with such wide discretion, and the absence of appeal rights, are of course also unacceptable on due process and humanitarian grounds. While discretion is necessary to avoid the inflexible application of rules, discretion to refuse entry should be based on objective criteria, not supposition about an individual's motives or intentions. Moreover, if visitors want to stay beyond six months, without any reliance on employment or public funds, what is the justification for refusing to extend their visit?

These examples of procedures which appear to act against the policies of other government departments, illustrate the need for co-ordination between departments which deal with immigrants, asylum seekers and visitors to ensure that they are all working in the same direction.

Proportionate measures

Measures taken to enforce immigration control should be proportionate to the harm they are intended to address. The most obvious imbalance in this respect is the treatment of illegal immigrants, an imbalance which is reflected in their portrayal by government and the press.

Whatever system is introduced to regulate the entry of immigrants and asylum seekers, many will be rejected. Unskilled workers, in particular, are unlikely to be accepted unless on humanitarian grounds. But it is recognised that the incentive to enter, or to stay beyond a permitted time, is so strong that many will attempt to do so undetected and some will succeed.[6] The question is how the UK should respond.

The first point must be to recognise whom we are dealing with. 'Illegal immigrants' are associated in the public mind with drug dealers and other serious criminals. Illegal entry is indeed defined as a 'serious offence' under the Police and Criminal Evidence Act. Yet the vast majority are people of no criminal intent (other than their breach of immigration law) who are simply seeking to improve their living conditions or rejoin family members from whom they have been separated. Many take low paid work which resident workers will not do; they come, in part, because demand exists for their labour. These 'irregular migrants' are neither criminals, in the common sense of the word, nor are they necessarily taking jobs from existing workers. We accept the need for control of illegal immigrants but the measures adopted to prevent and detect them should be proportionate to the perceived harm which they do.

The treatment of Joy Gardner, the Jamaican woman who died in August 1993 following her arrest by police for over-staying her visitor's permit illustrates the disproportionate measures which are used in some cases. Overstaying, in contrast to illegal entry, is not classed as a serious offence although it is treated as though it were. The exact circumstances of her death remain disputed, but the Metropolitan Commissioner confirmed that she had been arrested by officers from a special deportation unit (deployed to help immigration officers in cases where resistance or violence was anticipated), and that these police officers were authorised to use a restraining belt with attached hand-cuffs which is not permitted to be used by any other officers.[7] It defies belief that alleged illegal immigrants, including this middle aged woman whose five year old child was present, could be considered potentially more dangerous than known violent criminals; yet the mythology is such that they are seen to require more severe measures, and (as outsiders) to be entitled to less protection from normal due process requirements. The fact that the Bail Act does not apply to those held under immigration law, so that there is no presumption of bail, is but a further example of this disproportionate treatment.

Anne Owers shows convincingly that some of the control measures proposed for the future would be neither feasible nor successful. ID cards to establish immigration status, for instance, could only be introduced after a comprehensive, expensive and intrusive survey of the immigration status of the existing population and would require regular updating to record applications to extend a visit, pending appeals and so forth. Moreover, such a system would not cover those who enter from the EC without entry controls nor those temporary visitors whose over-staying causes the most concern. Enforcement would be likely to target visible minorities, reinforcing their feelings of exclusion and heightening the prejudices of the majority.

The support for such measures in Parliament and now among senior police officers suggests that the abolition of border controls may be used to justify their introduction. In signing the Single European Act, Britain accepted that EC territory was to form an area without internal frontiers. Movement within it is intended to be like movement within a single state although, in practice, Britain is not alone in resisting the dismantling of its border controls.

There is no question that dismantling of border controls is what was intended by Article 8a of the Act, nor that it is necessary if there is to be genuine free-movement of goods, services and labour. Even to retain border formalities (while allowing EC nationals to exercise their free-movement rights) would take time and time, it is argued, costs money and therefore amounts to unfair competition. Moreover, the absence of border formalities is one of the most attractive aspects of EC membership for the general public. However, if the absence of *formalities* itself is to be the grounds for extensive new internal controls, in order to detect irregular migrants, we have to ask whether despite the costs it would be preferable to retain them. (It could, however, be argued that the pressure for new internal controls is such that they will be introduced regardless).[8] The absence of such formalities would, of course, also make it much more difficult to obtain the kind of data on migrants which we believe is necessary to develop a more informed, rational, immigration policy. However, such a decision would appear to require renegotiation of Article 8a with our EC partners.

Race relations, democracy and citizenship

Immigration and asylum policy, as we have seen, have implications for other areas of government policy which must be taken into account. (Perhaps most significant is the impact of these policies on race relations).

Successive governments have argued that 'firm' immigration control is essential for good race relations but the *form* which that control has taken, and the way in which policy has been presented, has had the opposite effect. To discriminate against non-white people at the point of entry, while seeking to end discrimination against them internally, is inconsistent. The negative message of the first policy damages the positive impact of the second. The perception that black and Asian people (in particular) are undesirable members of British society is endorsed, while members of existing minority communities have been made to feel unwelcome and insecure.

Much of what has already been recommended will redress that damage. Government will be informed about the true impact of migration and able to separate fact from fiction. Public debate will allow those with strong views to voice their concerns and have them answered or addressed in the revised policy. The redrawing of immigration and asylum controls on the basis of defensible criteria will both remove the scope for discrimination and the suggestion that it is people from particular countries who are undesirable.

Such a change in policy will enable the government to take the lead in changing public opinion towards immigrants and asylum seekers through its presentation of policy, drawing attention, for instance, to the economic and social contribution which immigrants and refugees make. Care in drawing a distinction between the minority of irregular migrants who are involved in crime, and the majority who are not, is a further example. Although the impact of such initiatives is difficult to measure, it would contribute to creating a more positive climate with immediate implications both for new arrivals and existing minority communities.

On this and other areas of government policy the voice of all members of the population should be heard but many members of minority communities are disenfranchised. Although citizens of Commonwealth countries and Eire, unusually in Europe, can participate in elections with UK nationals, other non citizens cannot, yet they pay taxes and their lives are influenced by the decisions which national and local government reach. This undermines democracy and the extent to which former immigrants can identify with the society in which they now live. Government should therefore encourage long term residents to become citizens, should they wish to do so.

There is a distinction between the legal status of British nationality and the concept of citizenship. The strength of society and its democratic system rests on the extent to which its residents enjoy *citizenship* rights—civil, political and social—and not on the number who hold the legal status of British national. The government should consider the further extension of civic rights beyond Commonwealth and Irish citizens to those who do not, or cannot become British nationals. It should end its opposition to the extension of voting rights in the Community to third-country nationals in this position.

The days when holding British nationality rested on a notion of *allegiance* are over. Permitting dual nationality demonstrated that *duty* to a state is now a more appropriate term. But receipt of nationality status is still viewed as a privilege rather than a right for those who have achieved a close relationship with the state. Three years residence in the UK should, in our view, normally be sufficient to obtain nationality status, or birth in the UK. Criteria for rejecting applications should be objective (e.g., having no serious criminal convictions rather than being 'of good character') and decisions should be subject to appeal.

Rather than states jealously protecting nationality status, bestowing it only at their discretion, should we not be moving towards an obligation in international law on states to grant nationality to those with a close connection with the state? Should they in fact be encouraged to allow dual and multi-nationality in recognition of the extent to which individuals may live parts of their lives in a number of different states and have rights in, and obligations to, them? Within Europe, we should be seeking to harmonise the conditions under which residents can obtain nationality status, this being the only means by which they can become citizens of the European Union. It will not be fair if a Turk in Germany has to wait, say, 10 years to obtain German citizenship and thus European citizenship if a Turk arriving in the UK could obtain both after only five years, the current residence requirement.

There may, however, be a real conflict between seeking to harmonise conditions and seeking to improve them. Other European states do not favour *ius soli* (obtaining nationality by birth in a country), for instance, and in relation to residence requirements the UK may have to resist pressure to harmonise by increasing, rather than decreasing, the period required.

Summary of conclusions and recommendations

1. The UK needs flexible immigration and refugee policies capable of anticipating and responding to potentially large and changing migrant and refugee flows.
2. The global migration context in which the UK government should be developing its immigration and refugee policy has changed significantly since the 1960s when the current approach to immigration policy was adopted (Chapters 2, 5, 6).
3. Current immigration and refugee policies are open to substantial criticism from many different perspectives (page 321).
4. There is no country which can provide an attractive model for reforming UK policies but the UK should, like some 'countries of immigration', identify the positive objectives which its immigration, citizenship and refugee policies are intended to fulfil (page 322).

Causes before symptoms

5. It makes no sense for Europe to attempt to shut the door unless it takes effective steps to ameliorate the conditions which cause migration and refugee flows. The international community should assume responsibility for attempting to avert refugee flows and international bodies, as well as individual states, ensure that each policy arm contributes to that objective—defence, aid, trade, arms sales and debt (Chapter 1).
6. The Foreign Office should have a unit responsible for co-ordinating action on refugees both within that department and with the DTI, MOD, ODA and Home Office, both for long term planning and crisis management.
7. International arrangements should be sought which clarify the responsibility of the source state for removing the causes of refugee flows, establishing obligations on states to co-operate in removing those causes and, where necessary and appropriate, in managing flows and securing voluntary repatriation of asylum seekers in return for assistance from the international community.
8. The UK should encourage the development of international early warning systems; give greater support to international refugee organisations; press for greater competence for the International Fact Finding Commission; and encourage states to ratify human rights Conventions and their enforcement mechanisms (rectifying

its own flawed record in this respect).

9. A similar, holistic approach should be adopted in relation to migration flows (page 323).

European Community

10. As a European country and a member of the EC, working with our European partners on these issues of mutual concern should be a principal objective. Within the EC, the UK is contributing to policy for 12 states, not simply pursuing the UK's sectional interests (Chapter 5).

11. Free movement within the EC necessitates harmonisation of entry rules at external frontiers. Harmonisation should not be a process of levelling down but one in which human rights standards are protected before further agreement is reached.

12. The UK should press for free movement rights for third-country nationals who are permanently resident within the EC.

13. Internally, the government should reform UK immigration and asylum policy so that they move towards convergence with those policies of the EC and other EC states which are progressive, e.g., on family reunion.

14. Where policies have such major implications for human rights it is unacceptable for decisions to be taken in secret, unaccountable inter-governmental bodies. The UK should press for greater EC competency in immigration and asylum policy to facilitate long term planning for the whole Community, to make it more likely that decisions will reflect the principles of the ECHR, and to provide a means of redress to the European Court of Justice.

International human rights standards

15. International human rights standards should form a cornerstone of immigration and asylum policy reform. These minimum standards should be seen not as an obstacle to be surmounted but as a pre-requisite to good practice (Chapter 4).

16. In order to comply with international human rights standards, all measures which infringe rights must be proportional to the harm they are intended to redress and be justified by objective criteria (Chapters 4, 8).

17. The primary purpose rule, and the intrusive means used to administer it, are not proportional to the mischief it is intended to avoid. The validity of a marriage should be questioned only if

there is evidence of abuse; marriages in which one partner is an immigrant may be subject to a one year probationary period (Chapter 8).

18. The government should amend those aspects of immigration law which conflict with the judgments of the bodies charged with supervising international human rights standards. Immigration policy cannot be termed 'fair' while it continues to ignore the failings identified by such bodies.

19. The government should reconsider its record of non-ratifications, reservations and derogations from international human rights provisions and demonstrate the on-going necessity of those which it decides must remain. Some international rules should be incorporated into our own statutes.

20. A monitoring body should be established to review immigration and asylum law and its administration to ensure that it gives full effect to international human rights standards.

21. If a Human Rights Commission is established it should include immigration and asylum law and practice within its remit to ensure that treatment which would be considered unacceptable for existing residents is not tolerated for migrants and refugees.

Economic impact of migrants

22. For those migrants and asylum seekers who are not entitled to enter on humanitarian grounds, the government must taken into account wider considerations in deciding whether to welcome or reject their applications.

23. Successive governments have allowed narrowly conceived social, political and economic considerations to dominate immigration and asylum policy without carrying out the investigation of the economic impact of migration which would have enabled it to make reasoned judgements (Chapter 6).

24. A serious economic investigation of the grounds for immigration policy and the consequences for the economy of different immigration scenarios is long overdue.

25. Substantial numbers of migrants are unlikely to be needed to fill labour shortages in the UK. Economic considerations are likely to be grounds for constraining immigration policy rather than for any broad relaxation. Recognising that particular categories of migrants are needed, however, government should switch its philosophy from one of excluding migrants to protect the status

quo to a system of positive selection of those migrants with most to contribute.

26. The work permit system currently serves primarily as a form of entry control, not a system which seeks on an informed, rational economic basis to achieve significant labour market adjustments through immigration to meet the broader needs of the British economy.

27. Before deciding to encourage skilled migration, government should consult the governments of the migrants' countries of origin (page 32).

28. Government should recognise the economic potential of many of those who enter under humanitarian categories. It should ensure that families' ability to be self supporting is not hampered by the exclusion of an adult breadwinner, and ensure that immigrants and refugees receive language and employment training to enable them to reach their economic potential (Chapter 6; page 159).

29. Government must also take into account the impact of migrants on housing, the balance between taxes paid and costs incurred in education, welfare and health services, and so forth. These must therefore be the subject of serious research and analysis and any negative, as well as the positive, impact on the public purse or the living standards of particular sections of the public taken into account in developing policy.

30. If government is to take these broad economic criteria into account, it must be better informed and refine its policy tools. Inadequate research and a poor statistical base is a source of misinformation and weak policy making.

Public consultation

31. The absence of a forum for public debate on immigration and asylum policy has prevented those 'for' and 'against' immigration from being consulted. The absence of information on the economic impact of immigration has meant that government has not been in a position to provide the public with the facts and draw a distinction between legitimate concerns and unfounded prejudice.

32. Consultation improves the quality of decisions and their public acceptability. Before revising immigration policy government should establish an enquiry, and a continuing forum, in which the kinds and levels of immigration can be discussed, research considered and conflicts of interest aired.

Redrawing immigration and asylum controls

33. Entry controls must be based on clear, defensible criteria which reflect the economic impact of migrants and the UK's obligations under international law. The criteria must be based on factual evidence (e.g., skill and housing shortages) in order to be free of charges of discrimination and to justify any restriction placed on the exercise of basic human rights (Chapters 4, 8, 11).

34. Fair asylum procedures would also be efficient procedures, deterring those without a legitimate claim and reducing the number of appeals. Details of a fair procedure are outlined (Chapter 7).

35. The number of people given Exceptional Leave to Remain (or an equivalent status in other Community countries) demonstrates the inadequacy of the narrow UN definition of refugee. The government should adopt a broader humanitarian test, attaching the same Refugee Convention rights to both categories. ELR should at least be a category in the Immigration Rules so that a decision to grant this status is open to appeal.

36. Visa requirements and carrier sanctions prevent some refugees reaching Europe as well as migrants. Carrier sanctions should be operated more leniently, being imposed only if the airline is negligent, or fines reimbursed if the application for asylum is successful. Visa requirements should, in co-operation with other receiving countries, be lifted temporarily when a country experiences a sudden mass exodus of refugees.

37. It is not possible to operate fairly a 'safe country' policy from which no asylum application will be considered.

38. Refugees are most likely to prosper if allowed to go to the country of their choice where they may be able to speak the language, have family or contacts. Requiring them to apply for asylum in the first safe country they reach in transit is thus neither in their interests nor that of the receiving country. Flexibility is needed to enable asylum seekers to apply in the country of their choice. Provision would, as now, be needed to ensure equitable 'burden sharing' between receiving states.

39. Appeal rights are essential to fairness and consistency in decision making. There are many instances where UK appeal procedures are lacking or inadequate. There should be a right of appeal against all immigration and asylum decisions, in most cases with suspensive effect (Chapter 8).

40. Long delays in decision making impose hardship and family separation. Government should increase administrative resources to avoid such delays and impose a six month time limit on applications (e.g. for entry clearance) after which it would be deemed to have been accepted (Chapter 8).

41. Consistency is needed between the policies of different government departments. Those Home Office and Department of Employment regulations which impose unnecessary obstacles on overseas students, despite the fact that they are recognised to bring many benefits to the UK including export earnings, should be removed (Chapter 8). Regulations which hinder genuine visitors should similarly be withdrawn.

42. The treatment of illegal immigrants is disproportionate to the harm which the legislation is intended to redress, an imbalance which is reflected in their portrayal by government and the press.

43. The incentive for migrants to enter developed countries is so strong that some will enter illegally despite border controls. Only a small minority will be of further criminal intent; the majority will be people seeking to improve their standard of living, often taking jobs indigenous workers will not do, or to be reunited with their families They can more appropriately be called 'irregular' migrants. Measures to prevent and detect such migrants are necessary but must be measured and proportionate to the harm which they are intended to redress.

44. The official procedures made use of in the treatment of Joy Gardner, the Jamaican woman who died in August 1993 following her arrest for over-staying her visitor's permit, illustrates the disproportionate measures which are used (page 336).

45. Some of the control measures proposed for the future would be neither feasible nor successful. ID cards to establish immigration status could only be introduced after a comprehensive, expensive and intrusive survey of the status of the whole population, regularly updated to take account of changes in status. Temporary visitors, whose over-staying causes most concern, would not have ID cards, while enforcement is likely to damage race relations (Chapter 9).

46. The support for such measures in Parliament and the police is such that the abolition of border controls may be used to justify their introduction. If the absence of border *formalities* is to be the grounds for extensive new internal controls, it may be preferable to retain them (while maintaining rights of freedom of move-

ment). This may necessitate re-negotiation of Article 8a of the Single European Act.

47. Permitting EC residents who are not EC nationals to take up employment in other EC states would cut down the number of irregular migrants (Chapters 5, 9).

Race relations, democracy and citizenship

48. The implications of immigration and asylum policy for other areas of government policy must be taken into account, in particular for race relations.

49. Government argues that 'firm' immigration control is good for race relations but the form immigration control has taken has had the opposite effect. Discrimination against non-white people at the point of entry has undermined attempts to discourage discrimination internally. The perception that such people are undesirable has been endorsed and members of existing minority communities made to feel unwelcome and insecure (Chapter 11).

50. Much of what has already been recommended will redress that damage (page 338).

51. Immigration control should be covered by the Race Relations Act and the discretion exercised by immigration officials should be based on objective criteria, not supposition about individuals' motives and intentions.

52. Government should take a lead in changing public attitudes towards immigrants and refugees. It should demonstrate the rationale for its revised policies and the contribution made by those immigrants and refugees who are allowed to enter. In its presentation of policy it should be aware of the need to change attitudes, e.g., by avoiding portraying irregular migrants as 'criminals', and stressing the importance of the UK honouring, and being seen to honour, its international commitments.

Citizenship

53. The fact that many long term residents in the UK cannot participate in elections undermines our democracy and the extent to which former immigrants can identify with the society in which they now live. Government should encourage them to become citizens, if they choose to do so, and end its opposition to granting voting rights throughout the Community to third-country nationals in this position. It should also consider the

extension of civic rights (beyond Commonwealth and Irish citizens) to those long term residents who do not, or cannot, become British nationals.

54. Citizenship should be granted on the basis of objective criteria such as three years' residence, or birth, in the UK, with clear criteria for those rejected, such as conviction for serious criminal offences. Reasons for rejection should be given and the decision subject to appeal. To encourage applications, the cost (particularly for a family) should be reduced.

55. We should be looking towards a development in international law imposing on states a duty to grant nationality status to those with a close connection with the state, allowing dual and multi-citizenship in recognition of the extent to which individuals may live parts of their life in a number of different countries and have rights in, and obligations to, them.

56. Within the Community we should seek harmonisation of the conditions under which citizenship can be obtained so that all EC residents can obtain European Union citizenship on an equitable basis. However, there may be a conflict between seeking to harmonise conditions and seeking to improve them.

APPENDIXES

Appendix 4.1

Table of Relevant International Instruments and UK Ratifications, Reservations, Declarations, etc.

[NB: Present draft covers position as at 1 January 1993]

This catalogue excludes: EEC/EC and 'paracommunitarian' instruments; instruments dealing with special categories, e.g. diplomats, as well as those under the CSCE process; and UN Security Council Resolutions. It does not list all International Labour Office (ILO) instruments nor all instruments on nationality *stricto sensu.*

[*Texts of reservations, declarations, etc., do not include 'territorial' clauses covering UK dependencies or other territories for which the UK has accepted a treaty responsibility.*]

[NB: Unless expressly stated to the contrary, the UK has ratified all the instruments cited.]

General conventions

Universal/global

Universal Declaration of Human Rights, 1948 [42 AJIL (1949) Supp. 127]

International Covenant on Economic, Social and Cultural Rights, 16 December 1966 (United Nations, Treaty Series [UNTS], vol.993, p.3); entry into force: 3 January 1976.

International Covenant on Civil and Political Rights, 16 December 1966 (UNTS, vol.999, p.171); entry into force: 23 March 1976.

UK Government reservation:

> The Government of the United Kingdom reserve the right to continue to apply such immigration legislation governing entry into, stay in and departure from, the United Kingdom as they

may deem necessary from time to time and, accordingly, their acceptance of article 12(4) and of the other provisions of the Covenant is subject to the provisions of any such legislation as regards persons not at the time having the right under the law of the United Kingdom to enter and remain in the United Kingdom. The United Kingdom also reserves a similar right in regard to each of its dependent territories.

The Government of the United Kingdom reserve the right not to apply article 13 in Hong Kong in so far as it confers a right of review of a decision to deport an alien and a right to be represented for this purpose before the competent authority.

The Government of the United Kingdom reserve the right to enact such nationality legislation as they may deem necessary from time to time to reserve the acquisition and possession of citizenship under such legislation to those having sufficient connection with the United Kingdom or any of its dependent territories and accordingly their acceptance of article 24(3) and of the other provisions of the Covenant is subject to the provisions of any such legislation.

Optional Protocol to the International Covenant on Civil and Political Rights, 16 December 1966 (UNTS, vol.99, p.171); entry into force; 23 March 1976—*UK not ratified.*

Second optional Protocol to the International Covenant on Civil and Political Rights aiming at the abolition of the death penalty, 15 December 1989 (United Nations, G.A. Res. 128); not in force—*UK not ratified.*

Declaration regarding article 41 of the International Covenant on Civil and Political Rights (competence of the human rights Committee to receive communications by a State Party against another State Party); entry into force: 28 March 1979.

Torture

Convention against torture and other cruel, inhuman or degrading treatment or punishment, 10 December 1984 (United Nations, G.A. Res. 39/46, Doc. A/39/51); entry into force: 26 June 1987.

Declaration regarding article 21 of the Convention against torture and other cruel, inhuman or degrading treatment or punishment (competence of the Committee against torture to receive communications by a State Party against another State Party); entry into force: 26 June 1987.

Declaration regarding article 22 of the Convention against torture and other cruel, inhuman or degrading treatment or punishment (competence of the Committee against torture to receive communication from individuals); entry into force: 26 June 1987. *UK has not made declaration.*

Slavery, traffic in persons, forced labour
Convention for the suppression of the traffic in persons and of the exploitation of the prostitution of others, 21 March 1959 (UNTS, vol.96, p.271); entry into force: 25 July 1951—*UK not ratified.*
NB: Two other UN instruments (on slavery) and two ILO instruments (on forced labour) are omitted from this list for reasons of insufficient relevance.

Refugees, stateless persons
Statute of the Office of the United Nations High Commissioner for Refugees, G.A. Res. 428.
Convention relating to the status of refugees, 28 July 1951 (UNTS, vol.189, p.137); entry into force: 22 April 1954.

UK Government reservation:
(i) The Government of the United Kingdom of Great Britain and Northern Ireland understand articles 8 and 9 as not preventing them from taking in time of war or other grave and exceptional circumstances measures in the interests of national security in the case of a refugee on the ground of his nationality. The provision of article 8 shall not prevent the Government of the United Kingdom of Great Britain and Northern Ireland from exercising any rights over property or interests which they may acquire or have acquired as an Allied or Associated Power under a Treaty of Peace or other agreement or arrangement for the restoration of peace which has been or may be completed as a result of the Second World War. Furthermore, the provision of article 8 shall not affect the treatment to be accorded to any property or interests which, at the date of entry into force of this Convention for the United Kingdom of Great Britain and Northern Ireland, are under the control of the Government of the United Kingdom of Great Britain and Northern Ireland by reason of a state of war which exists or existed between them and any other state.
(ii) The Government of the United Kingdom of Great Britain and Northern Ireland accept article 17, paragraph 2, with the

substitution of 'four years' for 'three years' in subparagraph (a) and with the omission of subparagraph (c).

(iii) The Government of the United Kingdom of Great Britain and Northern Ireland cannot undertake to give effect to the obligations contained in article 25, paragraphs 1 and 2, and can only undertake to apply the provision of paragraph 3 so far as the law allows.

UK Government Commentary:

In connection with article 24, paragraph 1, subparagraph (b) relating to certain matters within the scope of the National Health Service, the National Health Service (Amendment) Act, 1949, contains powers for charges to be made to persons not ordinarily resident in Great Britain (which category would include refugees) who receive treatment under the Service. While these powers have not yet been exercised it is possible that this might have to be done at some future date. In Northern Ireland the Health Services are restricted to persons ordinarily resident in the country except where regulations are made to extend the Service to others. It is for these reasons that the Government of the United Kingdom while they are prepared in the future, as in the past, to give the most sympathetic consideration to the situation of refugees, find it necessary to make a reservation to article 24, paragraph 1, subparagraph (b), of the Convention.

The scheme of Industrial Injuries Insurance in Great Britain does not meet the requirements of article 24, paragraph 2, of the Convention. Where an insured person has died as the result of an industrial accident or a disease due to the nature of his employment, benefit cannot generally be paid to his dependants who are abroad unless they are in any part of the British Commonwealth, in the Irish Republic or in a country with which the United Kingdom has made a reciprocal agreement concerning the payment of industrial injury benefits. There is an exception to this rule in favour of the dependants of certain seamen who die as a result of industrial accidents happening to them while they are in the service of British ships. In this matter refugees are treated in the same way as citizens of the United Kingdom and Colonies and by reason of article 24, paragraphs 3 and 4, of the Convention, the dependants of refugees will be able to take advantage of reciprocal agreements which provide for the payment of United Kingdom industrial injury benefits in other countries. By reason of article 24, paragraphs 3 and 4, refugees will enjoy under the scheme of National Insurance and Industrial Injuries Insurance certain rights which are withheld from British subjects who are not citizens of the United Kingdom and Colonies.

No arrangements exist in the United Kingdom for the administrative assistance for which provision is made in article 25 nor have any such arrangements been found necessary in the case of refugees. Any need for the documents or certifications mentioned in paragraph 2 of that article would be met by affidavits.

Protocol relating to the status of refugees, 31 January 1967 (UNTS, vol.606, p.267); entry into force: 4 October 1967.
[NB: This list omits Convention on Diplomatic Asylum, 1954, Declaration on Territorial Asylum, 1967 and two other UN agreements on refugee seamen.]
Convention relating to the status of stateless persons, 28 September 1954 (UNTS, vol.360, p.131); entry into force: 6 June 1960.

UK Government Commentary:

In connection with article 24, paragraph 1, subparagraph (b), which relates to certain matters within the scope of the National Health Service, the National Health Service (Amendment) Act 1949 contains powers for charges to be made to persons not ordinarily resident in Great Britain (which category would include some stateless persons) who receive treatment under the Service. These powers have not yet been exercised but it may be necessary to exercise them at some future date. In Northern Ireland the Health Services are restricted to persons ordinarily resident in the country except where regulations are made to extend the Services to others. For these reasons, the Government of the United Kingdom, while prepared in the future, as in the past, to give the most sympathetic consideration to the situation of stateless persons, find it necessary to make reservation to article 24, paragraph 1, subparagraph (b).

No arrangements exist in the United Kingdom for the administrative assistance for which provision is made in article 25 nor have any such arrangements been found necessary in the case of stateless persons. Any need for the documents or certifications mentioned in paragraph 2 of that article would be met by affidavit.

Convention on the reduction of statelessness, 30 August 1961 (UNTS, vol.989, p.175); entry into force: 13 December 1975.

UK Government reservation:

Notwithstanding the provision of article 8, paragraph 1, the United Kingdom retains the right to deprive a naturalised person of his nationality on the following grounds, being grounds existing in United Kingdom law at the present time: that, inconsistently with his duty of loyalty to Her Britannic Majesty, the person

(i) has, in disregard of an express prohibition of Her Britannic Majesty, rendered or continued to render services to, or received or continued to receive emoluments from, another state; or

(ii) has conducted himself in a manner seriously prejudicial to the vital interests of Her Britannic Majesty.

Family, marriage, children

Convention on consent to marriage, minimum age for marriage and registration of marriages, 10 December 1962 (UNTS, vol.521, p.231); entry into force: 9 December 1964.

Convention on the rights of the child, 20 November 1989 (United Nations, G.A. Res. 44/25); entry into force: 2 September 1990.

UK Government reservation:

The United Kingdom reserves the right to apply such legislation, in so far as it relates to the entry into, stay in and departure from the United Kingdom of those who do not have the right under the law of the United Kingdom to enter and remain in the United Kingdom, and to the acquisition and possession of citizenship, as it may deem necessary from time to time.

Women

Convention on the elimination of all forms of discrimination against women, 18 December 1979 (G.A. Res. 34/180, UN Doc. A/34/46); entry into force: 3 September 1981.UK Government reservation:

The United Kingdom reserves the right to continue to apply such immigration legislation governing entry into, stay in, and departure from, the United Kingdom as it may deem necessary from time to time and, accordingly, its acceptance of article 15(4) and of the other provisions of the Convention is subject to the provisions of any such legislation as regards persons not at the time having the right under the law of the United Kingdom to enter and remain in the United Kingdom.

The British Nationality Act 1981, which was brought into force with effect from January 1983, is based on principles which do not allow of any discrimination against women within the meaning of article 1 as regards acquisition, change or retention of their nationality or as regards the nationality of their children. The United Kingdom's acceptance of article 9 shall not, however, be taken to invalidate the continuation of certain temporary or transitional provisions which will continue in force beyond that date.

Convention on the political rights of women, 20 December 1952 (UNTS, vol.193, p.135); entry into force: 7 July 1954.

Convention on the nationality of married women, 20 February 1957 (UNTS, vol.309, p.65); entry into force: 11 August 1958—*UK not ratified.*

Freedom of information, private life

Convention on the international right of correction, 31 March 1953 (UNTS, vol.439, p.191); entry into force: 24 August 1962.

Convention for the protection of individuals with regard to automatic processing of personal data, 28 January 1981 (Council of Europe, European Treaty Series [ETS], no.108); entry into force: 1 October 1985.

Migrants

International Convention on the protection of the rights of all migrant workers and members of their families, 18 December 1990 (United Nations, G.A. Res. 45/158); not in force—*UK not ratified.*

ILO Convention (No.97) concerning migrant workers, 1 July 1949 (United Nations, Treaty Series, vol.120, p.71); entry into force: 22 January 1952.

NB: Note companion Migration for Employment Recommendation (Revised) 1949: No.86.

Fairly recent ILO Recommendation (No.169: Employment Policy [Supplementary Provisions] Recommendation 1984) recommends measures to help developing countries improve in order to 'reduce the need to emigrate to find employment'.

This list omits certain other ILO instruments relevant to immigration: see further: R. Plender (ed.), *Basic Documents on International Migration Law*, 1988, pp.271–373, which covers relevant ILO Conventions and Recommendations.

Social security
ILO Convention (No.102) concerning minimum standards of social security, 28 June 1952 (UNTS, vol.210, p.131); entry into force: 27 April 1955.

ILO Convention (No.143) concerning migrations in abusive conditions and the promotion of equality of opportunity and treatment of migrant workers, 23 June 1975 (ILO, Official Bulletin, vol.LVIII, 1975, Ser.A., no.1, pp.36–43); entry into force: 9 December 1978—*UK not ratified*.

N.B. Note companion Migrant Workers Recommendation 1975, No.151—*UK not ratified*.

Genocide, war crimes, crimes against humanity
London Agreement on Prosecution and Punishment of Major War Criminals and its Annex; The Nuremburg Charter.

Convention on the prevention and punishment of the crime of genocide, 9 December 1949 (UNTS, vol.78, p.277); entry into force: 12 January 1951.

Convention on the non-applicability of statutory limitations to war crimes and crimes against humanity, 26 November 1968 (UNTS, vol.754, p.73); entry into force 11 November 1970—*UK not ratified*.

Combatants, prisoners and civilian persons in time of armed conflict
Geneva Convention for the amelioration of the condition of the wounded and sick in armed forces in the field, 12 August 1949 (UNTS, vol.75, p.31); entry into force: 21 October 1950.

Geneva Convention for the amelioration of the condition of the wounded, sick and shipwrecked members of the armed forces at sea, 12 August 1949 (UNTS, vol.75, p.85); entry into force: 21 October 1950.

Geneva Convention relative to the treatment of prisoners of war, 12 August 1949 (UNTS, vol.75, p.135); entry into force: 21 October 1950.

Geneva Convention relating to the Protection of Civilian Persons in Time of War (UNTS, vol.75, p.287).

[Omitted here are two additional protocols of 1977 relating to the protection of victims of international and non-international armed conflicts *(neither of which the UK has ratified)*.]

Extradition and terrorism
Not covered here.

Others/miscellaneous
International Convention on the elimination of all forms of racial discrimination, 21 December 1967 (UNTS vol.660, p.195; entry into force: 4 January 1969. (The UK has not made a declaration under Article 14 which has been in force since 3 December 1982.)

UK Government reservation:

> the United Kingdom does not regard the Commonwealth Immigrants Acts, 1962 and 1968, or their application, as involving any racial discrimination within the meaning of article 1, paragraph 1, or any other provision of the Convention, and fully reserves its right to continue to apply those Acts.

Other conventions concerning discrimination omitted here for insufficient relevance.

Convention on International Tracing Service, 1955 [219 UNTS 79].

Regional
Only Council of Europe treaties included here. This list also omits Assembly recommendations and Committee of Ministers resolutions.

Convention for the Protection of Human Rights and Fundamental Freedoms (European Convention on Human Rights), 4 November 1950 (Council of Europe, ETS, No.5); entry into force: 3 September 1953.

Declaration regarding article 25 of the European Convention on Human Rights (right of individual petition); entry into force: 5 July 1955.

Declaration regarding article 46 of the European Convention on Human Rights (jurisdiction of the European Court of Human

Rights); entry into force: 3 September 1958.

Protocol to the European Convention on Human Rights: March 1952 (Council of Europe, ETS, No.9); entry into force: 18 May 1954.

Protocol No.2 to the European Convention on Human Rights conferring upon the European Court of Human Rights competence to give advisory opinions, 6 May 1963 (Council of Europe, ETS, no.44); entry into force: 21 September 1970.

Protocol No.3 to the European Convention on Human Rights amending articles 29, 30 and 34 of the Convention, 6 May 1963 (Council of Europe, ETS, no.45); entry into force: 21 September 1970.

Protocol No.4 to the European Convention on Human Rights securing certain rights and freedoms other than those already included in the Convention and in the first Protocol thereto, 16 September 1963 (Council of Europe, ETS, No.46); entry into force: 2 May 1968— *UK not ratified.*

Protocol No.5 to the European Convention on Human Rights amending articles 22 and 40 of the Convention, 20 January 1966 (Council of Europe, ETS, No.55): entry into force: 20 December 1971.

Protocol No.6 of the European Convention on Human Rights, concerning the abolition of the death penalty, 28 April 1983 (Council of Europe, ETS, No.114); entry into force: 1 March 1985.

Protocol No.7 to the European Convention on Human Rights, 22 November 1984 (Council of Europe, ETS, no.117); entry into force: 1 November 1988—*UK not ratified.*

Protocol No.8 to the European Convention on Human Rights, 19 March 1985 (Council of Europe, ETS, No.118); entry into force: 1 January 1990.

Protocol No.9 to the European Convention on Human Rights, 6 November, 1990 (Council of Europe, ETS, No.140); not in force— *UK not ratified.*

Protocol No.10 to the European Convention on Human Rights, 25 March 1992 (Council of Europe, ETS, No.146); not yet in force.

European Agreement relating to persons participating in proceedings of the European Commission and Court of Human Rights, 6 May 1969 (Council of Europe, ETS, no.67); entry into force: 17 April 1971.

Convention for the protection of individuals with regard to automatic processing of personal data, 28 January 1981 (Council of Europe, ETS, No.108); entry into force: 1 October 1985.

European Social Charter, 18 October 1961 (Council of Europe, ETS, no.35); entry into force: 26 February 1965.

Additional Protocol to the European Social Charter, 5 May 1988—*UK not ratified*. (Council of Europe, ETS, No.128); not in force.

Protocol amending the European Social Charter, 21 October 1991 (Council of Europe, ETS, No.128); not yet in force.

Torture

European Convention for the prevention of torture and inhuman or degrading treatment or punishment, 26 June 1987 (Council of Europe, ETS, No.126); entry into force: 1 February 1989.

Refugees

European Agreement on the abolition of visas for refugees, 20 April 1959 (Council of Europe, ETS, No.31); entry into force: 4 September 1960.

UK Government reservation:

> The Agreement is ratified, subject to the reservation...that in accordance with the provisions of paragraph 1 of Article 14 of the Agreement, the United Kingdom of Great Britain and Northern Ireland declares that insofar as it is concerned, transfer of responsibility under the provisions of paragraph 1 of Article 2 of the Agreement shall not occur for the reason that it has authorised the refugee to stay in its territory for a period exceeding the validity of the travel document solely for the purposes of studies or training.

European Agreement on transfer or responsibility for refugees, 16 October 1980 (Council of Europe, ETS, No.107); entry into force: 1 December 1980.

Children and young persons

European Agreement on Travel by Young Persons on Collective Passports between the Member countries of the Council of Europe (ETS, No.37).

UK Government declaration:

> At the time of ratification the Government of the United Kingdom hereby declare, with reference to Article 11 of the Agreement, that one additional copy of the collective passport

will be required if the party is not composed solely of nationals of the Contracting Party which issues the document.

The Government of the United Kingdom further declare, with reference to Article 12 of the Agreement, that the authorities of the United Kingdom...will require each person aged sixteen years or over who travels in a party using a collective passport covered by the Agreement to be in possession of an official identity document bearing a photograph (e.g., an identity card, driving licence, certificate of nationality for travel purposes or a passport which has expired not more than three years previously) or, alternatively, a certified photograph of each such member to be affixed to the Collective passport opposite his or her name. These photographs may be certified by the organising body or by the leader of the party and after they have been affixed to the collective passport, must be stamped by a British Visa Officer in such a way that the photograph cannot be removed and replaced by another. It would also be of considerable assistance to the immigration authorities of the United Kingdom and of the above-named territories if young persons under the age of sixteen years travelling in parties using a collective passport could carry with them some sort of official identity document, but this is not essential.

The Government of the United Kingdom finally declare, with reference to Article 13 of the Agreement, that, for the purpose of admission to and stay in the United Kingdom...and subject to reciprocity, the provisions of the Agreements are hereby extended to young refugees and young stateless persons lawfully resident in the territory of another Contracting Party, subject to the following conditions:

1. The inclusion of young refugees or young stateless persons on a collective passport commits the issuing Government to the re-admission without time-limit of such persons to its own territory even when a young refugee or young stateless person does not return with the party.

2. The names of young refugees and young stateless persons must be listed separately from those of nationals and their status clearly shown.

3. The collective passport must bear a clear indication at the top that the party is not composed solely of nationals but includes young refugees or young stateless persons.

4. A copy of the collective passport must be provided for the

immigration authorities.
5. Each young refugee or young stateless person aged sixteen or over must carry an identity card bearing a photograph.

European Convention on the Adoption of Children 1967 (ETS, No.58).

European Convention on the legal status of children born out of wedlock, 15 October 1975 (Council of Europe, ETS, No.85); entry into force: 11 August 1978.

Migrants

European Convention on the legal status of migrant workers, 24 November 1977 (Council of Europe, ETS, No.93); entry into force: 1 May 1983—*UK not ratified.*

European Agreement on Regulations Governing the Movement of Persons between Member States of the Council of Europe, December 1957.

European Convention on Establishment 1955 [529 UNTS 141]; entry in force: 23 February 1965.

Social Security

European Convention on Social & Medical Assistance (1953 ETS No.14).

European Code of social security, 16 April 1964: (Council of Europe, ETS, No.48); entry into force: 17 March 1968.

Protocol to the European Code of social security, 16 April 1964 (Council of Europe, ETS, No.48); entry into force: 17 March 1968—*UK not ratified.*

European Code of social security (revised), 6 November 1990: (Council of Europe, ETS, No.139); not in force—*UK not ratified.*

UK Government declaration:

The Government of the United Kingdom do not regard Article 73 of this Code as binding them to become a Party to any Convention, Agreement, or other instrument governing questions relating to Social Security for foreigners and migrants concluded pursuant to it.

Supplementary Agreement for the application of the European Convention on social security, 14 December 1972 (Council of Europe, ETS, No.78); entry into force: 1 March 1977.

Genocide, war crimes, crimes against humanity
European Convention on the non-applicability of statutory limitation to crimes against humanity and war crimes, 25 January 1974 (Council of Europe, ETS, No.82); not in force—*UK not ratified.*

Extradition
[not covered here].

Others/Miscellaneous
Convention on the Participation of Foreigners in Public Life at Local level, Strasbourg, 5 November 1992 (ETS, No.144)—*UK not ratified.*

European Charter for regional or minority languages, 5 November 1992 (Council of Europe, ETS, No.148); not in force—*UK not ratified.*

Appendix 6.1

Definitions of immigration—a note

The Office of Population Censuses and Surveys (OPCS) in its annual report on *International Migration* defines an immigrant as 'a person who has resided abroad for a year or more and on entering has declared the intention to stay in the United Kingdom for a year or more'. By this definition, as Table 6.1 shows, 40% of all immigrants in 1990 were in fact British citizens. Treatment in the rest of this paper of the term 'immigrant' excludes British citizens, even although they are both an integral part of the international migration system in which Britain is just one destination, and despite the difficulty of understanding the economic behaviour of foreign nationals migrating to this country without evaluating first the interdependent relationships which exist between the organisation of foreign and British migration systems.

The popular use of the term 'immigrant' differs in numerous respects from the statistical definition of Table 6.1. Most importantly, many conceive of immigrants in terms of Britain's non-white 'ethnic minority' populations such as Indians, Pakistanis, Chinese and Afro-Caribbeans who in total account for 2.58 million persons.[67] Robinson[68] has shown how many other large ethnic groups exist within Britain outside the much discussed 'ethnic minorities'. These include over 100,000 Poles, 336,000 Jews, 850,000 Irish, and 98,000 Italians. While all these ethnic groups are significant in terms of the structure of Britain's population and economy, many of them are not, and have never been during the course of their lives 'immigrants' in the OPCS sense of the term. This is because many ethnic groups are made up largely of second, third or fourth generation populations.

The differences of definition illustrated above (and many more could be cited) are responsible for some of the differences which exist between economic and demographic forecasters, concerning the implications for Britain of immigration. Table 6.2 for example shows that Britain has only a modest foreign population. In 1989 only 1.8% of the population resident in Britain were non-EC nationals, compared with 5.7% in Germany and 4.4% in France. By contrast with these statistics, some government population projections based on ethnic definitions (as opposed to nationality ones) have suggested that 7% of the British population by 2001 will be made up of black or Asian minorities.[69]

NOTES

Introduction
Sarah Spencer

1 Home Office, *Immigration and Nationality Department*, Annual Report, 1991–2; Home Office, *Statistical Bulletin (SB) Control of Immigration Statistics*, 14/93. Department for Education, *Statistical Bulletin*, 3/93, January 1993. International Passenger Survey, MN *International Migration*, OPCS, 1991. Figures have been rounded to the nearest hundred.

2 Home Office, *Immigration and Nationality Department Report*, London, 1991–2.

3 Home Office official, Asylum Policy Unit, in conversation with the author, 17 August 1993.

4 Home Office evidence to the Select Committee on Race Relations and Immigration, February 1971.

5 J. Salt, International Migration and the United Kingdom, unpublished report of the United Kingdom SOPEMI correspondent to the OECD, 1992.

6 See J. Purcell, Director-General of the International Organization for Migration, keynote address to the CSCE ODIHR Seminar on Migration including Refugees and Displaced Persons, Warsaw, 20–23 April 1993; and J. Widgren, 'International Migration and Regional Stability', *International Affairs*, vol.66, no.4, 1990, pp.749–66.

7 OECD, *Trends in International Migration, Continuous Reporting System on Migration (SOPEMI)*, 1992, p.13.

8 Purcell, op.cit., and Widgren, *International Affairs*, op.cit., Widgren is coordinator and head of the Secretariat in Geneva of the Inter-governmental Consultations on Asylum, Refugee and Migration Policies in Europe, North America and Australia, currently involving 16 states. He is a former Swedish Under-Secretary of State for Immigration.

9 Widgren, 'The Need to Improve Co-ordination of European Asylum and Migration Policies', paper given to the Conference of the Trier Academy

of European Law: Comparative Law of Asylum and Immigration in Europe, March 1992; and his paper Existing fora for Inter-governmental Co-operation on Asylum, Refugee and Migration Problems in the European Region', 1993, unpublished.

10 For example, see Purcell, op.cit., and Widgren, 'The Need to Improve Co-ordination of European Asylum and Migration Policies', op.cit.

1 Tackling the Causes of Refugee Flows
Geoff Gilbert

1 See IEDSS, *After the Soviet Collapse: New Realities, Old Illusions*, cited in the *Guardian*, 14 January 1992, p.8: 'The refugees are an unwelcome reminder that the definition of Europe may be determined one day not by officials in Brussels, but by the people of the continent, literally with their own feet.' In the first six months of 1992 over one million Bosnians left their homes due to the armed conflict: *Guardian*, 15 July 1992, p.1, and 21 July 1992, p.22. For the strategic implications of refugee movements, see Institute for Strategic Studies, *Refugee Movements and International Security*, Adelphi Paper, no.268, summer 1992.

2 The CSCE Helsinki Document, 10 July 1992, accords the same rights to refugees and displaced persons in Europe: Decisions, pt VI, paras 39–46; hereinafter, Helsinki Document.

3 Preventive action should not be aimed at keeping refugees out of Europe, but should be undertaken for humanitarian considerations, even if the former may be an incidental result. In the wake of the Gulf conflict, the British government spoke of setting up safe zones throughout the world where refugees might flee, but the unstated aim was to deny those refugees the chance of applying for asylum in Europe.

4 Conclusions adopted by the Executive Committee on the International Protection of Refugees, 40th session, 1989, no.56, para.(b)(ii) (UNHCR, 1990); hereinafter, Conclusions. See also 36th session, 1985, no.40, para.(c): 'The aspect of causes is critical to the issue of solution and international efforts should also be directed to the removal of causes of refugee movements.'

5 May 1991, proposal 1990/91:195, p.1. See also Inter-Governmental Consultations on Asylum, Refugee and Migration Policies in Europe, North America and Australia document, Strategy Platform, September 1991; hereinafter, Strategy Platform. This group of 16 states, including the United Kingdom, holds regular informal consultations.

6 189 UNTS 50. And see the 1967 Protocol, 606 UNTS 267.

7 Article 1(2) 1951 Convention, as amended by 1967 Protocol.

8 G. Goodwin-Gill, *The Refugee Regime: A Perspective on the 1951*

Convention and 1967 Protocol relating to the Status of Refugees, SIM Special, December 1991, p.33–4.

9 See J. Hathaway, *The Law of Refugee Status*, 1991, pp.101–5. I am grateful to Professor Dan Steinbock, School of Law, University of Ohio at Toledo, and Alex Neve, Toronto, for their thoughts and illuminating discussions on this topic in 1991 at the Human Rights Centre, Essex. Needless to add, any errors and views expressed here are mine alone.

10 That is 'race, religion, nationality, membership of a particular social group or political opinion'. See also Article 3 UN Convention Against Torture and Other Cruel, Inhuman or Degrading Treatment or Punishment, 1984, 23 INT.LEG.MAT.1027 (1984) and 24 INT. LEG.MAT.535 (1985), which protects anyone from *refoulement* if they would face torture on their return.

11 The Soviet bloc withdrew from the drafting process leaving the West to define a refugee in terms of those fleeing human rights violations in Eastern Europe and the USSR. See J. Hathaway, *Reinterpreting the Convention Refugee Definition in the Post-Cold War Era*, SIM Special, The New Refugee Hosting Countries, December 1991, p.38; hereinafter, SIM Special.

12 The Universal Declaration of Human Rights, article 14 of which declares that everyone has the right to seek asylum from persecution, contains civil and political as well as economic, social and cultural rights. I am indebted to Alex Neve for sharing his thoughts with me on this point.

13 Of course, claims to be refugees on the basis of social group membership are often combined with other article 1 grounds. See also *UNHCR Handbook on Procedures and Criteria for Determining Refugee Status*, 1979. Para.79 explicitly states that it will only be in exceptional cases that social group membership on its own will qualify an applicant for refugee status.

14 57 International Law Report 324 at 326, 1966.

15 See generally, Compton, 'Asylum for Persecuted Social Groups: A Closed Door Left Slightly Ajar', 62 *Washington Law Review* 913 at pp.926–9, 1987.

16 297 F.2d 744, 746, 1961.

17 I am grateful to Professor Dan Steinbock, op.cit., for his help in relation to US materials.

18 407 F.2d 102 at 107, 1969.

19 Fein, 'Lives at Risk', *Monitoring Human Rights Violations*, ed. Schmid and Jongman, 1992, p.41, and the PIOOM Report, vol.4, no.1, 1992, p.21, found, *inter alia*, that 49 states with bad human rights records produce 96% of the world's refugees and that in the seven countries with the worst human rights record 19% of the population, on average, was uprooted.

20 D. Bronkhorst, 'The "Realism" of a European Asylum Policy: A Quantitative Approach', *Netherlands Quarterly of Human Rights*, 1991, p.142.

21 See Hathaway, *The Law of Refugee Status*, op.cit., pp.108–12. Again, I am grateful to Alex Neve for his assistance in formulating these ideas. The corollary is that an act permitted by the duly declared derogation will not be persecutory in nature—not all human rights violations amount to persecution. On the limits of derogation, see Higgins, *Derogation under Human Rights Treaties*, 48 British Year Book of International Law 281, 1976–7.

22 *Possible Swiss Strategy for a Refugee and Asylum Policy in the 1990s*, 1989, p.13 (hereafter Swiss Policy Document).

23 Cf. article 1(2) of the OAU Convention on Refugee Problems in Africa, 1969, 691 UNTS 14, which includes in the term refugee those fleeing external aggression, occupation, foreign domination or events seriously disturbing public order. See also, OAS, Cartagena Declaration on Refugees, 1984.

24 *UNCHR Handbook*, 1979, op.cit., paras 164–6.

25 See Swiss Policy document, op.cit., p.8, also Italian firm's denial that it dumped toxic waste in Somalia: *Guardian*, 11 September 1992, p.10.

26 *Guardian* and Oxfam's Earth Supplement, 1992. See also, *Guardian* 23 April 1992, p.24.

27 See generally, Swiss Policy Document, op.cit., pp.22–3.

28 The emphasis in this paper is on state responsibility for refugee flows, rather than on the individual perpetrators of the violations, such as torturers. However, individual responsibility does exist under articles 4 and 5 of the UN Convention Against Torture and Other Cruel, Inhuman or Degrading Treatment or Punishment 1984, 23 INT.LEG.MAT.1027 and 24 INT.LEG.MAT.535. Prosecuting torturers for their crimes is one means by which human rights guarantees can be enforced. See also, 'Introduction', *Amnesty International Annual Report*, 1992.

29 See below, p.33.

30 For example, the European Convention on Human Rights, ETS, 5, 1950; hereinafter, ECHR. The American Convention on Human Rights, 9, INT.LEG.MAT.,673, 1969; hereinafter ACHR.

31 For example, the Human Rights Committee under the International Covenant on Civil and Political Rights, UNGA Res.2200A(XXI), UNGAOR, 21st Sess., supp. no.16, p.52, 1966. See also D. McGoldrick, *The Human Rights Committee*, 1991.

32 Advising an asylum seeker to take a case before one of these committees or tribunals may not be warranted, however, since it alerts the persecuting state as to his whereabouts and may endanger family members left at home.

33 See the work of the CSCE in this field, especially its 1990 Copenhagen Document: *Document of the Copenhagen Meeting of the Conference of the Human Dimension of the CSCE*, Pt IV; see also, 11 *HRLJ*, 1990, p.232.

34 The following text is taken from G. Gilbert, *The Legal Protection of Minorities in Europe*, [1992] 23, *Netherlands Year Book of International Law*, 1992, p.67.

35 Principle VII of the Helsinki Final Act 1975. 14 INT.LEG.MAT.1292, 1975. See also *Madrid Concluding Document* 22 INT.LEG.MAT.1395, 1983.

36 Para. 19. 28 INT.LEG.MAT.527, 1989.

37 *Document of the Copenhagen Meeting of the Conference of the Human Dimension of the CSCE*, Pt IV; see 11 *HRLJ* 232, 1990. See H. Hannum, 'Contemporary Developments in the International Protection of the Rights of Minorities', 66, *Notre Dame Law Review*, 1991, 1431, pp.1440 et seq.

38 Hannum, op.cit., p.1440.

39 Copenhagen Document, op.cit., para.32.1; see also para.32.5 on the dissemination of information in the mother-tongue of the group.

40 'The effectiveness of the system of protection of minorities in Europe will not be determined exclusively by legal means, but also by other factors: the international climate, the economic possibilities of interested states, the success of democratization in Central and Eastern Europe and progress in the construction of a common European home.' Symonides, Collective Rights of Minorities in Europe', *The Changing Political Structure of Europe*, ed. Lefeber, Fitzmaurice and Vierdag, 1991, p.123, n.39.

41 See M. Galenkamp, 'Collective Rights: Much Ado About Nothing?: A Review Essay', 1991, *NQHR* 291.

42 See the German–Danish Declaration of 28–29 March 1955.

43 Report of the CSCE Conference of Experts on National Minorities, Geneva, 1991 (CSCE/REMN.20). See also Roth, 'Comments on the CSCE Meeting of Experts on National Minorities and its Concluding Document', 12 *HRLJ* 330, 1991, p.331.

44 See also para.IV, which again 'notes' that local and autonomous administrations have proved useful.

45 Helsinki Document, op.cit.

46 Helsinki Document, op.cit., Decisions, pt II, paras 2 and 3.

47 Some might argue that one of the main causes of refugee flows in the past has been the formation of the 'nation-state'. However, this viewpoint ignores the fact that secessionist tendencies have only arisen where minority groups in larger states have suffered discrimination, forcing them to consider moves towards self-determination. The minority rights guarantees considered above will not prevent secession in every

case, but they will reduce the number of cases where mono-ethnic states are established.

48 See Symonides, op.cit., p.123. 'Some believe that only all-European citizenship and a rejection of state logic may definitively solve the minorities problem.' Further, it should not be part of British policy to encourage mono-ethnic states in E.Europe. See also, Helsinki Document, op.cit., Declaration, para.12.

49 J. Garvey, 'Toward a Reformulation of International Refugee Law', *Harvard Journal of International Law* 26, 1985, 483.

50 And possibly the ACHR as well. See n.30 above.

51 29 INT.LEG.MAT.1378, 1990, pp.1381–2.

52 App.No.6950/75, 1975.

53 Emphasis added.

54 See Swiss Policy Document, op.cit., p.23.

55 See the German government's decision to stop selling arms to Turkey because of its treatment of the Kurdish community. See the *Guardian*, 3 April 1992, p.4.

56 See the *Independent* 17 September 1991 and 9 November 1991; the *Guardian*, 29 August 1992, p.7. It seems that Russia and Cyprus have played a large part in allowing Serbia to breach the arms embargo, that Austria and Germany financed Croatian arms purchases and that Bosnians received arms from Iran and Turkey: see the *Guardian*, 12 September 1992, pp.1 and 21.

57 For the strategic implications of refugee movements, see Adelphi Paper, no.268, op.cit.

58 See *The Times*, 3 October 1991, and 27 November 1991; and the *Guardian*, 16 July 1992, p.4. See also the Scott Inquiry.

59 See A. Roberts and R. Guelff, *Documents on the Laws of War*, 2nd edn., 1989.

60 See Geneva Convention IV.

61 As at 30 June 1992, 112 states were party to the Protocol. Moreover, this figure includes all the states in the Eastern bloc and most states in Africa and South-East Asia: see Roberts and Guelff, op.cit. See also, F. Kalshoven, *Constraints on the Waging of War*, 1987, p.61. My thanks are due to my colleague Françoise Hampson for the up-to-date figures.

62 See Articles 50 and 51 for a negative definition of a civilian.

63 See F. Hampson, 'Proportionality and Necessity in the Gulf Conflict', [1992] ASIL PROCEEDINGS (in preparation).

64 There is special protection from incendiary weapons in Protocol III of the 1981 UN Weapons Convention.

65 As at 30 June 1992, 103 states had ratified Protocol II: see Roberts and Guelff, op.cit., pp.459–62. Again, I am indebted to my colleague, Françoise Hampson, for the up-to-date figures.

66 See Kalshoven, op.cit., pp.143–4.

67 For example, El Salvador or Peru.

68 See note 4 above.

69 See 33rd Session, no.27, 1982; 34th Session, no.32, 1983; 37th Session, 1986, No.45; and 38th Session, no.48, 1987.

70 'Debts add to pressure on countries to destroy the environment': see R. Cowe, 'Banks Dip their Toes into the Green Pond', *Guardian* 25 April 1992, p.31.

71 Research by Christian Aid. See the *Guardian*, 4 February 1992, p.5.

72 See Strategy Platform, para.8, op.cit., n.5.

73 See Hansard (HL) vol.532, no.1592, cols. 1274–6, 26 November 1991. See also Swiss Policy Document, op.cit., p.24; and the *Guardian*, 9 June 1992, p.22. It must always be borne in mind that in the short term aid and development may allow the better educated members of that society to emigrate to the first world, impoverishing their state of origin. See M.S. Teitelbaum, 'The Effects of Economic Development on Outmigration Pressures in Sending Countries', unpublished paper presented at the OECD International Conference on Migration, Rome, 13–15 March 1991.

74 See the *Guardian*, 15 May 1992, p.25. 'During the last horrific year of African hunger, 1985, when Live Aid focused British people's generosity on the world's most desperate people, the hungriest African countries gave twice as much money to the developed world as we gave to them— all in interest payments. And [1991's] Red Nose Day, which raised 12 million, served to pay just one day of interest payments from the 44 poorest countries.'

75 See Garvey, 'The New Asylum Seekers: Addressing their Origin', *The New Asylum Seekers*, ed. D. Martin, 1987, p.185.

76 Executive Committee on the International Protection of Refugees, 36th Session, 1985, op.cit.

77 See the *Independent*, 18 December 1991, p.8. The UN Department of Humanitarian Affairs was established in April 1992 to meet this role.

78 Although it is arguable that states only act out of self-interest or embarrassment, it was the Gulf allies who encouraged the Kurds to rebel, but who then failed to provide military and logistical aid, leading directly to the displacement of so many people. Their current situation, where they are assisted in an area of the state in which the state is denied control, as Iraq is, cannot last indefinitely. Furthermore, safe havens must protect the displaced persons. Arguments that more people can be assisted and that repatriation is easier if the refugees stay close to their old homes only make sense if those people fleeing can be effectively protected close to what may now be a war zone: see the *Guardian*, 30 July 1992, p.22.

79 See the Moscow Final Act, CSCE/CHDM.49/rev.1, and the *Guardian*, 5 October 1991, p.8.

80 Helsinki Document, op.cit., Decisions, pt II.

81 Helsinki Document, op.cit., pt III, para.52.

82 The European Community (EC) and the United Nations (UN) considered measures ranging from diplomatic and trade sanctions to armed intervention against Serbia to protect the civilian population of Bosnia: *Guardian*, 25 May 1992 p.1, and 31 July 1993, p.1.

83 Under chapter 7 of the Charter of the United Nations it is arguable that the UN should have its own forces rather than having to rely on action by its members. Dr Boutros Ghalli, UN Secretary-General, has recommended to the Security Council that it is now time for a permanent force to be established. Among the industrialised states France and the United States seem to support the idea, although British support is said to be lukewarm; the question is not simple and the British Foreign Secretary has raised queries about the necessary level of commitment. See paras.34–45 (esp. 42 and 43), *Agenda for Peace*, UN Doc.A/47/277, S/24111, 17 June 1992; and *The Times*, 20 June 1992, p.1; the *Guardian*, 27 June 1992, p.22, 22 September 1992, p.20, and 23 September 1992, p.8, and 28 January 1993, pp.1, 8, 20.

84 See the reasoning in Gallagher, 'The Two Faces of Humanitarian Action in Countries of Origin', *Refugee Policy Group Review*, 1922, July, p.1.

85 There is a movement to reduce the powers of the five Permanent Members and to change the composition of the group: *Guardian*, 4 September 1992, p.7. See also the Campaign for a Democratic United Nations (CAMDUN), which seeks to remodel the UN to give power to peoples rather than solely to states.

86 The Boutros-Ghali document, op.cit., recommends a peace-making role for the UN. In some cases, this may be the only way to intervene because economic or diplomatic sanctions would have little effect.

87 See Swedish Policy Document, op.cit., p.4. See also the third Lomé Agreement (OJ 1986 L 86/3; and Reg. 1825/87, OJ 1987 L 173/6), which, in part, attaches human-rights criteria to EC aid: the fourth Lomé Convention (29 INT.LEG.MAT.783, 1990) again included provisions relating to human rights. See also Resolution of the Council and of the European Community Member States Meeting in the Council on *Human Rights, Democracy and Development*, paras 6,7 and 10.

88 See the *Guardian* 11 May 1992, p.6. See also, *Human Rights, Democracy and Development*, op.cit., para.9.

89 Swiss Policy Document, op.cit., p.18.

90 See E. Mortimer, 'Foreign Aid as a Vote Winner', *Financial Times*, 18 March 1992.

91 See Gordenker, 'International Organization for Dealing with Refugees', SIM Special, December 1991, p.13 at p.14.

92 The ICRC and the UNHCR are involved in co-ordinating relief in Bosnia-Herzegovina, for example, see the *Guardian*, 13 April 1992, p.22.

93 See Gordenker, op.cit., pp.14–16.

94 See Lee, 'The Right to Compensation: Refugees and Countries of Asylum', 80, *American Journal of International Law*, 532 p.550, 1986, for 1984 figures of donor state contributions.

95 See Hocke, 'Refugee Problems', *Refugees and International Relations*, ed. Loescher and Monahan. I am indebted to Danny Heilbronn for his thoughts on this matter.

96 See Lee, op.cit., p.549.

97 Gordenker, op.cit., p.16.

98 See the call for greater burden-sharing in Helsinki Document, op.cit. Declaration, para.14. And see Strategy Platform, op.cit., para.8.

99 See note 6 above.

100 Gordenker, op.cit., p.18; see also pp.19–20.

101 See UNHCR Executive Committee Conclusion 1990, para.2(a)(i), Doc.A/AC.96/760.

102 That is Department of Humanitarian Affairs established in April 1992. See Goodwin-Gill, op.cit., p.34 n.16. See also, *Agenda for Peace*, op.cit., paras 26 and 27; *The Times*, 20 June 1992, p.1. See also Strategy Platform, op.cit., para.8.

103 See Gordenker, op.cit., p.21; footnotes added by author.

104 The number of children would be extremely useful information, since it would help in the planning of medical assistance.

105 The reason for this sort of information seems only to alert the industrialised states as to whether the refugees will try to seek asylum with them.

106 Helsinki Document, op.cit., Decisions, pt II, paras. 11–16 (minorities), and pt III generally.

107 This form of work has been carried out in Sri Lanka, Yugoslavia, Albania and Northern Iraq.

108 Cf. the UNHCR Executive Committee's 1990 Conclusion, op.cit., para.2(a)(vi), states that countries of origin should 'assume a significant responsibility', including addressing root causes' and 'voluntary repatriation'. See UNHCR Executive Committee's 1991 Conclusion, Doc.A/AC.96/783, para.21(h) and (j). See also Garvey, op.cit., p.181, and esp. p.182.

109 See Garvey, ibid., pp.185 et seq., and Lee, op.cit.

110 *UNHCR Handbook*, op.cit., para.65.

111 Once again I am grateful to Alex Neve for his thoughts on this matter.

112 See *Causes of Refugee Flows*, op.cit.

113 *Velasquez-Rodriguez* v *Honduras*, Inter-American Court of Human Rights, 29 July 1988, series C, no.4, p.154.

114 Of course, there are still problems where the state is in such disarray that it does not effectively exist, as Somalia for example.

115 UNGA, Res.194 (III), 3 UNGAOR Pt1, Res. at 21, UN Doc.A/810, 1948.

116 See Lee, op.cit., pp.534–5.

117 See Lee, ibid., pp.545–6. Cf. G.A.Res.36/148, 16 December 1981, para.3, which speaks of 'adequate compensation' rather than just damages for property loss.

118 However, as Lee, ibid., p.546, points out: 'Affirmation or reaffirmation of the right of refugees to compensation under international law is one thing; implementation of such a right is quite another.' He goes on to suggest pressure to enforce compliance be put on the source state by withholding aid, but his approach is fraught with difficulties, as discussed above. See also ILA Declaration of Principles of International Law on Compensation to Refugees Report of the 65th ILA Conference, Cairo, 1992.

119 General Assembly Declaration, G.A.Res.2625 (XXV), 24 October 1970, on Principles of International Law Concerning Friendly Relations and Co-operation Among States in Accordance with the Charter of the UN, article.1, principle VI.

120 *US* v. *Canada*, 1938 and 1941, 3 RIAA 1905.

121 See Lee op.cit., and Garvey, op.cit.

122 Jennings, 'Some International Law Aspects of the Refugee Question', 20, *British Yearbook of International Law*, 98, 1939, p.111, cited in Garvey, op.cit., p.188.

123 See Lee, op.cit., pp.559–60.

124 See Lee, op.cit., pp.560, *et seq*.

125 See the *Guardian*, 11 March 1992, p.7.

126 Bangladesh, in line with the new-found vigour of the Security Council, sought assistance in that organ: see note 125 above.

127 And it must not be turned into a tool for industrialised states to impose yet more burdens on developing states, although the breach of international law will usually only arise after a mass trans-border influx, which would mean that only a neighbouring state would ordinarily be given a right of action.

128 See Garvey, op.cit., pp.189, 190.

2 Current and Future Migration Flows

Reuben Ford

1 Much of the material for this paper came from J. Salt, 'International Migration and the United Kingdom', unpublished report of the United Kingdom SOPEMI correspondent to the OECD, 1992, kindly made available to the author by Dr John Salt, Department of Geography,

University College, London.

2 D.A. Coleman, 'UK Statistics on Immigration: Development and Limitations' *International Migration Review*, no.21, 1987, pp.1138–69.

3 Some authors, for example M.S. Teitelbaum, 'The Effects of Economic Development on Outmigration Pressures in Sending Countries', unpublished paper presented at the OECD International Conference on Migration, Rome, 13–15 March 1991, argue that aid acts to encourage rather than discourage emigration, at least in the short-medium term.

4 D.A. Coleman, 'Does Europe need Immigrants? Population and Work Force Projections', *International Migration Review*, no.26, 1992, pp.413–61.

5 It is assumed that only a small proportion of adult migrants from these countries will be retired. Only 4800 immigrants of retirement age were picked up by the IPS in 1990, and a substantial proportion of these will have been British.

6 D.A. Coleman, 'The United Kingdom and International Migration: A Changing Balance', paper presented to conference on Mass Migration in Europe, Implications for East and West, Vienna, 5–7 March 1992.

7 J. Salt, 'International Migration and the United Kingdom', unpublished report of the United Kingdom SOPEMI correspondent to the OECD, 1991 and 1992.

8 J. Salt and R. Kitching, 'Labour Migration and the Work Permit System in the UK', *International Migration*, September 1990, pp.267–94.

9 Coleman, 'The United Kingdom and International Migration', op.cit.

10 'Migration: The Demographic Aspects' Paris, OECD, 1991, p.13.

11 Ibid.

12 Coleman, 'Does Europe Need Immigrants?', op.cit.

13 This estimate assumes some 20% of those who currently do not participate in the labour market continue not to do so.

14 'Migration: The Demographic Aspects', op.cit.

15 D.A. Coleman and J. Salt, 'The British Population: Patterns Trends and Processes', Oxford University Press, 1992.

16 C. Chatfield, 'The Analysis of Time Series', 3rd ed., Chapman and Hall, London, 1984.

17 P.J. Harrison and S. F. Pearce, 'The Use of Trend Curves as an Aid to Market Forecasting', *Industrial Marketing Management*, no.2, 1972, pp.149–70.

18 Where the forecast is taken as the product of the last known year's estimate and the change occurring a set number of years previously, e.g., where i_x is the estimate for year x:

$$i_{1991} = i_{1983} \times \frac{i_{1990}}{i_{1982}}$$

19 Where the forecast is taken as the sum of the last known year's estimate

and the change T occurring a set number of years previously, e.g., where i_x is the estimate for year x:

$$i_{1991} = i_{1990} + (i_{1983} - i_{1982})$$

20 Forecast 3 is based on a sum of past observations. The most recent observation is weighted 0.727, the second most recent 0.21 and the third most recent 0.063.

21 J. Widgren, 'International Migration and Regional Stability', *International Affairs*, vol.66, 1990, pp.749–66.

22 Coleman and Salt, op.cit.

23 Coleman, 'The United Kingdom and International Migration', op.cit.

24 G.J. Borjas, *Friends or Strangers. The Impact of Immigrants on the US Economy*, New York, Basic Books, 1990.

25 The National Front (NF) and British National Parties (BNP) between them fielded 24 candidates in the 1992 general election. In those seats, NF polled less than 0.7%, BNP less than 1.1%, all candidates losing their deposits. The low level of influence such parties have had on the British political scene in recent years can be seen by the small number of seats contested (14 by NF in 1992, none in 1987) and their negligible share of the vote (fewer than 11,000 votes combined).

Bibliography

Eurostat (1992 and earlier) *Demographic Statistics*, Luxembourg, EC.

Eurostat (1993) *Labour Force Surveys*, Luxembourg, EC.

Haskey, J. (1990) 'The ethnic minority populations of Great Britain: estimates by ethnic group and country of birth', *Population Trends*, 60, pp.35–38.

Home Office (1993a), *Asylum Statistics: United Kingdom 1992*, Statistical Bulletin 19/93, HMSO.

Home Office (1993b) *Persons Granted British Citizenship: United Kingdom, 1992*, Statistical Bulletin 16/93, HMSO.

Home Office (1993c) *Control of Immigration Statistics: Third and Fourth Quarters and Year 1992*, Statistical Bulletin 14/93, HMSO.

Hovy, B. (1992) *Asylum Migration in Europe: Patterns, Determinants and the Role of East-West Movements*, paper presented to conference on Mass Migration in Europe, Implications for East and West, Vienna, 5–7 March 1992.

OPCS (1989) *Population Projections: Mid-1987 Based*, Monitor PP2 89/1, OPCS, London.

OPCS (1991) Birth Statistics 1989, series FMI No.18, HMSO.

OPCS 'Overseas travel and tourism', *Business Statistics Office Business Monitor MA6*, 1981–92 annual, HMSO

3 Three Theories of Immigration

Bhikhu Parekh

1 I am grateful to Sarah Spencer for her advice and comments.

2 M. Oakeshott, *On Human Conduct*, Oxford, Clarendon, 1974, pp.108 ff.

3 B. Ackerman, *Social Justice in The Liberal State*, New Haven, 1980, p.95.

4 H. Sidgwick, *Elements of Politics*, London, 1981, p.295.

5 Ackerman, op.cit., p.95.

6 M. Walzer, *Spheres of Justice*, Basic Books, New York, 1983, p.62.

7 Ibid.

8 Ibid., p.41.

9 For a detailed discussion of the New Right, see B. Parekh, 'The New Right and the Politics of Nationhood', *The New Right: Image and Reality*, ed. G. Cohen, *et al*., London, Runnymede Trust, 1986.

10 The extraordinary idea of turning long-settled British immigrants into guest workers was proposed by J. Casey, 'One Nation: The Politics of Race', *Salisbury Review*, autumn 1982.

11 *Spheres of Justice*, op.cit., p.46.

12 Ibid, pp.41 ff.

13 See 'Genetics Provide Clues to History', *Financial Times*, 27 August 1992.

14 The mistaken objectives of this policy are discussed in B. Parekh, 'Britain and the Social Logic of Pluralism', *Citizenship*, ed. G. Andrews, Lawrence and Wishart, London, 1992.

15 The British immigration policy was at first grounded in the liberal and later in the ethnic view of the state. Unlike France and the Netherlands, the communitarian view had very little influence in Britain. Although the post-war British government preferred white immigration, the latter soon dried up, and the labour-hungry industries turned to the New Commonwealth. Thanks to the influence of the liberal view, every Commonwealth immigrant had a right to enter Britain and enjoyed full rights of citizenship on arrival. In 1962, Britain imposed the first set of restrictions on immigration. But they were economic in nature and remained within the liberal framework. The ethnic view of the state was first evident in the 1968 Immigration Act, which denied entry to the British passport-holding Kenyan Asians. The 1971 Immigration Act introduced the concept of patriality and reinforced the ethnic view. For the first time in British history, the British Nationality Act of 1981 defined British citizenship in ethnic terms, subject, of course, to the limits set by the messy legacy of colonialism.

16 In this chapter I have only concentrated on who should be admitted to the country. The legal and moral implications of admission and the kinds of

implicit commitment that the state makes raise important questions, but they fall outside my concern.

4 International Law and Human Rights Obligations

Hugo Storey

Unless otherwise stated all judgments of the European Court of Human Rights (ECHR) cited are published in *E.Ct.H.R. Ser.A* as well as in *EHRR* (*European Human Rights Reports*) and the *HRLJ* (*Human Rights Law Journal*).

1 Report of European Commission of Human Rights, *X (Abdulaziz), Cabales and Balkandali* v. *UK Cases*, March 1983, para. 108. 1984 6 *EHRR*, 23.

2 9214/80, 9473/81, 9474/81, *Abdulaziz, Cabales and Balkandali* v *UK* (cited throughout as *Abdulaziz*), 1985 7 *EHRR* 471.

3 W.R. Bohning and J. Werquin, *Some Economic, Social and Human Rights Considerations concerning the Future of Third Country Nationals in the Single European Market*, WEP Research Working Paper, International Labour Office, 1990.

4 See *People on the Move: New Migration Flows in Europe*, Strasbourg, Council of Europe Press, 1992.

5 See R. Plender, *International Migration Law* (2nd rev. edn), Dordrecht, 1989; G. Goodwin-Gill, *International Law and the Movement of Persons between States*, 1978; G. Goodwin-Gill, *The Refugee in International Law*, 1983; G. Goodwin-Gill, 'Immigration, Nationality and the Standards of International Law', *Towards A Just Immigration Policy*, (ed.) A. Dummett 1986. For texts of relevant instruments in full or in extract form up to 1988, see R. Plender, ed., *Basic Documents on International Migration Law*, Nijhoff, 1988. Appendix 4.1 contains an up-to-date list of most relevant instruments.

6 See *East African Asians Cases*, 1981, 3 *EHRR* 76; *Abdulaziz*, 1985, op.cit.; *Min* v. *UK* 10204/82 7/10/86; *Uppal* v. *UK*, 8244/78 (no.1) 1979 3 *EHRR*, 391; *Fadele* v. *UK* 13078/87; *Yousef* v. *UK*, 14830/89, 8/10/1990; *Lamgunidaz* v. *UK* 16152/90; for the Commission's rebuke of discretionary aspects of UK law and practice, see its Report on *Abdulaziz*, 1983, op.cit., para.130–7; *Alam* v. *UK*, 2991/66, YB (Yearbook) 10, 478; *Amekrane* 5961/72 CD 44, 101; *Caprino* v. *UK* (1980) 4 *EHRR*, 97; *Zamir* v. *UK* 9174/80, DR (Decisions and Reports) 40, 42. All the foregoing cases resulted in admissibility decision against the UK. So did the *Vilvirajah* case in admissibility decisions of 7 July 1989. The report of 8 May 1990 considered there had been a

violation of article 13. But the Court eventually concluded that the UK was not in breach: Ser. A 215; 12 [1991] HRLJ, 432. In the Soering case, on extradition, the Court made an adverse judgment against the UK under article 3 (concerning inhuman and degrading treatment of a young adult facing the 'death row' phenomenon in Virginia, USA): See Soering v. UK, Ser. A, vol.161, judgment of 7 July 1989 (1989) 11 *EHRR* 439. A further important case against the UK is *Kandiah* v *UK* 9856/82, DR52/70, in the course of which the UK government made its 'Kandiah concession' relating to the position of overstayers facing deportation.

7 Even at judicial review level it is only recently that there has been express recognition of the indirect 'victim' in an immigration context: see *Sumeina Masood* [1992] Imm. A.R. (CA), p.70.

8 I. Macdonald and N. Blake, *Immigration Law and Practice* (3rd edn), Butterworths, 1991, pp.140–78.

9 See J. Madureira, 'Aliens' Admission To and Departure From National Territory: Case-law of the Organs of the ECHR and the European Social Charter', Strasbourg H (89), 1989 (H.89 4E).

10 On 'Greater Europe', see European Parliament Resolution of 12 December 1990 on the Constitutional Basic of Europe [1991] *HRLJ* 54, Preamble and para. E.

11 The term 'paracommunitarian' is used to describe the increasing practice of EC states of making agreements and conventions at an intergovernmental level, rather than within the normal machinery of EC law-making.

12 On human rights in community law, see H. Schermers, 'The European Communities bound by Fundamental Rights', CMLR 255, 1990; A. Clapham, 'A Human Rights Policy for the European Community', 10 YEL 309, 1990.

   The Maastrict Treaty (Treaty on European Union) has as one of its Common Provisions (F2) a commitment to respect fundamental rights as guaranteed by the ECHR. On criticism of Schengen and other paracommunitarian instruments, see Meihers *et al.*, *Schengen, Refugees, Privacy, Security and the Police*, Kluwer, 1991; D. O'Keefe, 'The Free Movement of Persons and the Single Market', CMLR 3–19, 1992; Free Movement of Persons in Europe: Problems and Experience (Proceedings at the TMC Asser Institute, Colloquium of 12–13 September 1991, Nijhoff, 1992); also report by E. Rule, *Immigration and Nationality Law and Practice*, vol.7, no.1, pp.24–6.

13 See L. Fransman, 'Future Citizenship Policy', ch.10.

14 See A. Dummett, 'United Kingdom Objectives for Future European Community Policy', ch.5; also T. Hammar, *Democracy and the Nation State*, 1990.

15 See G. Gilbert's 'Tackling the Causes of Refugee Flows', ch.1. On UK

foreign policy, see 'Human Rights in Foreign Policy', Document no.215, 1990; speech by Mrs Lynda Chalker to the ODI, Chatham House, 25 June 1991, and FCO, 'Human Rights in Foreign Policy': Foreign Policy Document, no.215.

16 On human rights and EC foreign policy, see, for example, text of Declaration made at meeting of Foreign Ministers of EC Member States in Brussels on 16 December 1991 reprinted in [1992] *ICLQ*, 477.

The EC's disregard of its own 'Badinter Report' strategy in dealing with the recognition of new states in the former Yugoslavia raises doubts about the operation of its new recognition criteria (on the latter see C. Warbrick, [1992] *ICLQ*, 477).

17 *Abdulaziz*, para. 67; *Berrehab*, Ser. A, vol.138 (1989) 11 *EHRR*, 322; *Moustaquim* Ser. A. vol.193 12 *EHRR* (1991) para.85; 13 *EHRR* 1992, para.43 (p.802); *Beljoudi*, Ser.A.234, para.74.

18 It is important however, not to ignore customary international law developments in this field entirely: see Goodwin-Gill, *International Law and the Movement of Persons between States*, op.cit., and Plender, *International Migration Law*, op.cit.

19 On the right of individual petition as an essential propeller, see P. von Dijk and G. van Hoof, *Theory and Practice of the ECHR*, 2nd edn, Kluwer, 1990, p.37.

20 For example see Madureira, op.cit., pp.4, 5, 112; Macdonald and Blake, op.cit., pp.320–41; H. Storey, 'The Right to Family Life and Immigration Case Law at Strasbourg', 39 *ICLQ* 1990, pp.328–44; 'The European Court of Human Rights and UK Immigration and Asylum Law: An Analysis of Implementation', ILPA, July 1993.

21 For periodic survey of ratifications of most of the relevant instruments, see J.-B. Marie's series in *HRLJ*, the latest available being in 13 *HRLJ*, 1992, 55. For a list of relevant global and European instruments, see appendix 4.1.

22 See J. Polaciewicz and V. Jacob-Foltzer, 'The ECHR in Domestic Law: The Impact of the Strasbourg Case Law in States where Direct Effect is Given to the Convention', 12 *HRLJ*, pp.65–85, 125–42. The same claim *vis-à-vis* Community Law would seem more controversial.

23 See Macdonald and Blake, op.cit. In a 12 May 1987 decision the German Constitutional Court found that the eight years' residence requirement for a spouse to be reunited in the FRG complied with article 8 of the ECHR: Eu GRZ 1987, 449. Shorter time-spans would seem to be envisaged by the European Court of Human Rights in *Berrehab*, Ser.A., vol.138, 1989, e.g. para.29.

24 See Polaciewski, op.cit. See earlier study of both incorporating and non-incorporating states by A. Drzemczewski, *ECHR in Domestic Law*, Oxford University Press, 1983.

25 On *Alam*, see note 6 above.

26 See C. Humana, *World Rights Guide*, 3rd edn, Oxford University Press, 1992, pp.346–9: the UK receives a 93% 'human rights rating'.

27 See appendix to this chapter for UK reservations, etc.; under UN system generally, see Multilateral Treaties Deposited with the Secretary-General: Status as at 31 December 1989, 811 UN Document St/Leg/ERR.E/1990.

The UK's current reservations and declarations relating to immigration and nationality are in the Appendix to this chapter. For background analysis of reservations etc., in relation to human-rights treaties, see I. Maier, ed., *Protection of Human Rights in Europe*, Muller, 1982, pp.87–121.

28 See appendix to this chapter.

29 See e.g. 1985: CCPR/C/SR, 597, para. 24; Consideration of Third Periodic Report 2nd of the UK (CCPR/G/SR 1045 4 April 1991, paras 39,56; April paras 35; 1050 paras 9,12,53.

30 For text, see UNGA, Res.45/158.

31 H. Kellerson, 'International Labour Convention and Recommendations on Migrant Workers' in A. Dummett (ed.), *Towards a Just Immigration Policy*, op.cit., p.32.

32 FCO correspondence with author dated 10 November 1992.

33 Despite turbulence caused to its own constitutional case law and to interpretation of its Community Law obligations by the case of *Attorney General* v. *X (Irish High Court and Supreme Court)* (1992) Common Market Law Reports, 277 (concerning 14–year-old rape victim seeking an abortion in the UK).

34 In FCO correspondence with the author, 10 November 1992.

35 Protocol no.7: Explanatory Memorandum, Strasbourg 1984 7 *EHRR*, 1985, 7.

36 Articles 2 and 3. For further background see Macdonald and Blake, op.cit., pp.322–3.

37 This Bill lapsed, but its successor has now passed into law as the Asylum and Immigration Appeals Act 1993.

38 1977 European Convention on the Legal Status of Migrant Workers, ETC 93, see, for text, Plender, *Basic Documents on International Migration Law*, op.cit., p.192.

39 The UK government's current attitude towards and reasons for not signing the Schengen Convention (or earlier Schengen Agreement) were stated before the Home Affairs Select Committee at paras 58–9 of appendix I to session 1991–2, 215–i,ii and iii: 'Migration Control at the External Borders of the European Community; Minutes of Evidence, 5,12, 26 February 1992.

40 See Free Movement of Persons in Europe: Problems and Experiences, op.cit.

41 Geneva Conventions Act 1957. For a cogent analysis of the situation of

Iraqis in the UK during the Gulf conflict, see F. Hampson 'The Geneva Conventions and the Detention of Civilians and Alleged Prisoners of War', *Public Law* [1991] 507–522.

42 Aviation and Security Act 1990; Aviation Security Act 1982; Diplomatic Privileges Act 1964; Visiting Forces Act 1952; International Headquarters and Defence Organisations Act 1968; International Organisations (Immunities and Privileges) Act 1950; Merchant Shipping Act 1970.

43 The Act involved was the Immigration Act 1988, s.5(2) Immigration (Restricted Right of Appeal Against Deportation) (Exemption) (No.2) Order 1988 (SI 1988/1203). See now Asylum and Immigration Appeals Act 1992, s.2 and Sch.5, s.2.

44 *Kandiah* v. *UK* 9856/82, DR 52,70.

45 See Cmnd 4298, para.58. For current rules, see HC 725, 5 July 1993. The UK government's justification for not incorporating the 1951 Convention into English law by way of statute has constantly been based on its view, in relation to treaties generally, that no formal change in the law is necessary or desirable if existing provisions of the law appear to cover new treaty obligations: Hansard, 25 May 1979, col.1376 (Mr Raison). On UK policy on treaties generally, see F.A. Mann, *Foreign Affairs in English Courts* (Oxford University Press, 1986) and R. Higgins, in F. Jacobs and S. Roberts, *Effects of Treaties in Domestic Law*, 1987. For a critique of UK policy as applied to human rights treaties, see Goodwin-Gill, in Dummett, ed., op.cit., pp.8–10; See also J. Williams, 'Treaties and Municipal Law' in J.P. Gardner, ed., *United Kingdom Law in the 1990s*, 1990, pp.255–69.

46 See, for example, I. Macdonald and Blake, op.cit., pp.31–3.

47 For further background, see indexes to Hansard for 1992–3. References to the 1951 Convention in the Asylum and Immigration Appeals Act 1993 are at s.2 and Sch.5, s.2, as well as in July 1993 Immigration Rules (HC 725).

48 See *Chundawara* (1988) Imm. A.R. 161 (CA); *Thakrar* v. *SSHD* (1974) 2 all ER, 261; *Chung Chi Cheung* v. *R* (1983) 4 All ER 786.

49 *Derbyshire County Council* v. *Times Newspapers* (*The Times*, Law Report, 20 February 1992). (CA) But cf. HL judgment on same case [1993] 1 All ER 1011.

50 T.H. Bingham, 'There is a World Elsewhere: The Changing Perspectives of English Law', *ICLQ*, 1992, pp.513–29; see also Lord Browne-Wilkinson, 'The Infiltration of a Bill of Rights', *Public Law*, 1992, pp.397–410.

51 The UK government's 'snailspace' programme for eliminating sex discrimination has to be viewed not only in the context of its commitments to reform made in the light of the *Abdulaziz* case but also its written assurances given in the course of Commission post-admis-

sibility deliberations on the *Min* v. *UK* case (see note 6) and, more broadly, its obligations under the UN Convention on the Elimination of Discrimination Against Women. On the UK position up to 1988, see E. Guild, 'Sex Discrimination in UK Immigration Law', Immigration and Nationality Law and Practice, vol.2, no.4, January 1988, pp.82–5.

52 Conclusions XII-1, Provisional Edition, Strasbourg, 1991, p.199.

53 XII-1, Provisional Edition, Strasbourg, 1992, pp.187–96. For further background on the 1961 European Charter, including recent moves to strengthen its implementation machinery, see D.J. Harris, 'A Fresh Impetus for the European Social Charter', *ICLQ*, 1992, pp.659–76.

54 I have already noted some examples of continuing sex-discrimination. See above: p.16 and n.51.

55 *Cruz-Varas*, para. 5 69,70.

56 See Storey, op.cit., n.20.

57 See von Dijk and van Hoof, op.cit., pp.532–48.

58 9973/82 v UK 5 *EHRR* 296. The Commission's own qualification of this ground on the basis that: 'in all immigration applications the Secretary of State has an overriding discretion to accord entry clearance in cases of hardship' appears to be at odds with its own specific critique of just this feature in its report on *Abdulaziz*, see note 6.

59 The court in *Vilvirajah* did not demur from the Commission's detailed criticism of pre-judicial review stages of remedy available to the applicants: on Report of Commission, see note 6.

60 *Bulus* v. *Sweden* Report of 8 December 1984, DR 39, 75; *Sanchez-Reisse*, Ser. A. 107 1986 *EHRR* 71.

61 *Berrehab*, para.29; also *Yousef* v. *UK* case (see n.6). Significantly new instructions issued to Home Office officials in January 1993, on enforcement of immigration control by deportation, reflect increased acceptance of ECHR case-law.

62 Handbook on Procedures and Criteria for Determining Refugee Status. For example *R* v. *SSHD ex p. Hidic Gunes* 1991 Imm AR 298.

63 *R* v. *C.I.O., Heathrow Airport, ex p. Salamat Bibi* 1976 3 All ER 843.

64 See references at n.20 above.

65 For a concise summary of the main options, see A. Bradley, 'The Sovereignty of Parliament', *The Changing Constitution*, ed. J. Jowell and D. Oliver, 92nd edn, 1989, pp.45–50. See also IPPR publications: A. Lester, *et al.*, *A British Bill of Rights*, December 1990, and *The Constitution of the United Kingdom*, 1991.

66 See E. Jaconelli, 'Incorporation of the ECHR: Arguments and Misconceptions' *Political Quarterly*, vol.59, 1988, p.343.

67 On statistics showing nationality of applicants taking cases to Strasbourg, see European Commission of Human Rights, *Survey of Activities and Statistics, Council of Europe*, 1992, pp.14–15.

68 A point made forcibly in numerous articles by A. Lester, e.g.

'Fundamental Rights: The United Kingdom Isolated?', *Public Law*, 1984, pp.47ff; see also F.G. Jacobs, 'The Convention and the English Judge', *Protecting Human Rights: The European Dimension: Studies in honour of G.J. Wiarda*, ed. F. Matscher and Herbert Petzold, 1988, pp.273–80.

69 This is further suggested by the UK government's assertive approach to its rights as a state in the sphere of immigration throughout its experiences as a respondent government at Strasbourg: see, for example, Series B pleadings in *Abdulaziz* and in *Vilvirajah*.

70 See A. Drzemczewski, Human Rights Files no.7, Directorate of Human Rights, Strasbourg, 1984, p.29.

71 For example, Justice Comments on the UK second Periodic Report to the Human Rights Committee under the ICCPR, March 1985.

72 The declaration is not to conflict with obligations under other international instruments, and it must state 'the special reasons justifying the derogation with regard to receiving capacity': art.12 (3). 1977 European convention on the Legal Status of Migrant Workers, *ETS*, 93; see Plender, *Basic Documents on International Migration Law*, op.cit., 192 at 196–7.

73 On interpretation of restrictions, see von Dijk and van Hoof, op.cit., pp.573 ff.

74 See R. Pekkanen and H. Danelius, 'Human Rights in the Republic of Estonia', 13 *HRLJ*, 1992, 236 at 242.

75 As was required of the UK government by the Strasbourg organs in the proceedings on the *Abdulaziz* cases: see Storey, op.cit., pp.338–9.

76 For a recent example broadly embodying this approach to family reunion, see Second Report of the (Australian) Joint Standing Committee on Migration Regulations, on 'Change of Status on Grounds of Spouse/De Facto Relationships', May 1991, which explicitly based itself on the various provisions of the ICCPR that protect family life.

77 A point also made by Interrights in appendix 3 to the Home Affairs Committee's Inquiry into Migration Control at External Borders of the European Community, (op.cit.) For further background on the effect of treaties generally in UK law, see Mann, op.cit. and R. Higgins, op.cit.

78 See A. Dummett and A. Nicol, 'The Law and Human Rights', *Subjects, Citizens, Aliens and Others: Nationality and Immigration Law*, 1990, pp.260–81.

79 On the workings of extra-statutory policy on adoption and its operation, see *Khan (Asif) v. IAT* [1985], 1 All ER and Macdonald and Blake, op.cit., pp.276–81.

80 On the ability of ICCPR protection to deal more extensively with discrimination issues, see Mauritian Women case: R.9/35, HRC 36/134, para. 9.2(b)(2)(i)(2). On the HRC, see D. McGoldrick, *The Human Rights Committee: Its Role in the Development of the Interna-*

tional Covenant on Civil and Political Rights, 1991, and M. Nowak, *Commentary of the UN Covenant on Civil and Political Rights*, 1993.

81 See n.45 above.

82 For text of relevant ILO instruments, see R. Plender, *Basic Documents in International Migration Law*, op.cit., pts VII and VIII.

83 On European Convention on Establishment, see A.H.J. Swart, 'The Legal Status of Aliens: Clauses of Council of Europe Instruments Relating to the Rights of Aliens', *NYIL*, vol.11, 1980, pp.3–64.

84 Surinder Singh, Case 370/90, judgement delivered on 7 July 1992.

85 On EC-EFTA Agreement, see [1992] 1 (MLR 921 and Draft EEA Treaty Implementation Reg [1992] O.J. (339/11), 22 December 1992.

86 For example with Hungary and Poland. For direct applicability of comparable freedom of movement provisions in existing Association and cooperation agreements, see EC Association Agreement with Turkey—ECJ Art. 177 ruling in s.2 *Sevince* v. *Staatssecretaris Van Justitive*, Case C192/89 [1992] 2 CMLR 57; *KUS* Case, judgement 16 December 1992. On the readiness of the ECJ to regard provisions (dealing with social security) in the EC cooperation agreement with Morocco, see Case No. 18/90 *Kziber*, judgement of 31 January 1991.

87 On UDHR, see A.H. Robertson, *Human Rights in the World*, Manchester, 1982.

88 On CSCE instruments, see D.M. Goldrick, 'Human Rights Developments in the Helsinki Process', *Emerging Rights in the New Europe*, ed. R. Beddard and D.M. Hill, Southampton Papers in International Policy, no.2, University of Southampton, 1992; R. Brett, 'The Development of the Human Dimension Mechanism of the CSCE', University of Essex, Human Rights Centre, 1992.

89 The 1990 Charter of Paris for a New Europe reaffirmed that: 'Free movement and contacts among our citizens...are crucial for the maintenance and development of free societies and flourishing movement.' The October 1991 Moscow Meeting on the Human Dimension reiterates this objective.

90 1975 Helsinki Final Act (HFA) Basket III: all such applications are to be dealt with 'in a positive and humanitarian spirit'; 1989 Vienna Concluding Document (VCD) [*HRLJ*, vol.10, 1989, pp.270–97], Principle no.41 requires that the Basket II provision for migrant workers had to be discussed with reference to its 'human dimension'; Basket III, 5, 7 (applications relating to family meetings to be decided normally within one month); 6, 13 (applications relating to family reunifications or marriage normally to be decided within three months), 10 (special precautions are to be taken for the reunification of minor children with their parents).

91 (VCD) (Principle no.20 requires state assurance that refugees may return in safety to their homes); Helsinki Document 1992, VI, 39–46—dealing

with *easing of visa processing formalities and the abolition of entry visas*. See also—on displaced persons—Helsinki Document 1992: 'The Challenge of Change', [1992] *HRLJ*.

92 Helsinki Document 1992, VI, p.557.

93 To give just one illustration of possible pitfalls: consider simple insertion of a rule requiring the Secretary of State to ensure that in deciding whether to exercise his discretion to depart from the immigration rules he should pay regard to the UK government's obligations under the ECHR. Without further amendment of s.19 of the Immigration Act 1971 (or its equivalent in any fresh statute), such a change would mean that immigration appeal adjudicators and tribunal members were precluded from reviewing any refusal by the Secretary of State to so depart (s.19(2)). The latter section would also need amendment.

94 The Foreign Affairs Committee has examined, *inter alia* the future of Hong Kong (Second Report, HC281-1 91988-89) and migration aspects of the changes of Central and Eastern Europe: at para.110–14 in Central and Eastern Europe: Problems of the Post-Communist Era: First Report, Session 1991–92, HC21-1, 1992.

95 The proposed derogation relevant to the sphere of immigration is from article 19(4)(c).

96 On Australian reform programme, see the Fitzgerald Report: *Immigration: A Commitment to Australia: A Report of the Committee to Advise on Australia's Immigration Policies*, 2 vols (AGPS, 1988). Also see paper by K. Cronin, 'The Australian Immigration System: Controls and the Migration Programme', London, IPPR, 1992 (unpublished).

97 See, for example, Home Affairs Select Committee, Session 1991–92, 215-i, ii and iii: Migration Control at the External Borders of the European Community: Minutes of Evidence', 5, 12 and 26 February 1992, and appendices. See also Report of the House of Lords Select Committee on the European Communites, '1992: Border Control of People', Session 1988–9, 22nd Report (H.L. Paper 90). (The House of Lords displayed its most explicit and thorough analysis of UK obligations under the ECHR in the field of immigration in its 'Proposed New Immigration Rules and the ECHR', First Report, Home Affairs Committee 1979-80, 11 February 1980). For critique of human-rights aspects of the Schengen and Dublin Conventions, see Maijers *et al.*, and other references at n.12 above.

98 US Immigration Act 1990.

99 On the Australian reforms, see notes 76 and 96 above.

100 On Social Security Advisory Committee.

101 Legomsky, op.cit., C. Harlow and Rawlings, *Law and Administration*, 1984, pp.503–8.

102 See n.96 above. The first 5 of the 11 reports are especially pertinent. See also Department of Immigration, Local Government and Ethnic Affairs

Background Information Paper for Participants in Community Consultations by the Minister on the Size and Structure of the 1991–2 Migration Programme, January 1991.
103 'Humanitarian' is used here in a non-technical sense to cover both human-rights law and humanitarian law *stricto sensu*.

5 Objectives for the Future European Community Policy

Ann Dummett

1 The Single European Act was an amendment to the Treaty of Rome. Article 8A of the amended Treaty says that the Community 'shall adopt measures with the aim of progressively establishing the internal market over a period expiring on 31 December 1992...an area without internal frontiers in which the free movement of goods, persons, services and capital is ensured in accordance with the provisions of this Treaty'.
2 Commission Communication to the Council and the European Parliament on Immigration, Brussels, 23 October 1991, SEC (91) 1855 final.
3 Ad Hoc Group Immigration, Brussels, 3 December 1991, SN 4038/91 (WGI 930).
4 However, the meeting of immigration ministers in Copenhagen in June 1993 adopted a document on family reunion, whose tone was much more restrictive.
5 W.R. Böhning and J. Werquin, *The Future Status of Third-Country Nationals in the European Community*, Churches' Committee for Migrants in Europe Briefing paper no.2, Brussels, 1990 (abridged version of an ILO Working Paper).

6 An Economic Audit of Contemporary Immigration

Allan Findlay

1 B. Maan, 'The New Scots', Edinburgh, Donald, 1992.
2 Peach, 'Immigrants and the 1981 Urban Riots in Britain', *Contemporary Studies of Migration*, ed. P. White and B. Vander Knaap, Geobooks, pp.143–54.
3 Maan, op.cit.
4 L. Foster, A. Marshall and L. Williams, 'Discrimination against Immigrant Workers in Australia', *World Employment Programme Discussion Paper*, no.34, Geneva, ILO, 1991.

5 R. de Beijl, 'Discrimination of Migrant Workers in Western Europe', *World Employment Programme Discussion Paper*, no.49, Geneva, ILO, 1990.

6 J. Salt and J. Kitching, 'Foreign Workers and the UK Labour Market', *Employment Gazette*, no.98, 1990, pp.538–46.

7 K. Jones and A. Smith, 'The Economic Impact of Commonwealth Immigration', Cambridge University Press, 1970.

8 T. Hammar, 'Comparing European and North American International Migration', *International Migration Review*, no.23, 1989, pp.631–7. A. Zolberg, 'The Next Waves: Migration Theory for a Changing World', *International Migration Review*, no.23, 1989, pp.403–30.

9 Population Reference Bureau, *Intercom*, May 1978.

10 B. Heisler and M. Heisler, 'From Foreign Workers to Settlers', Sage, Beverley Hills, CA, 1986. L. Bacci, 'South-North Migration: A Comparative Approach to North American and European experiences', Conference paper presented to the OECD International Conference on Migration, Rome, 13–15 March, 1991.

11 G. Urbani and E. Granaglia, *Immigrazione e diritti di cittadinanaza*, Rome, Editalia, 1991.

12 P. White, 'International migration in the 1970s', *West European Population Change*, ed. A. Findlay and P. White, Croom Helm, Beckenham, 1986.

13 R. Bohning, *The migration of workers in the United Kingdom and the European Community*, London, Oxford University Press, London, 1972.

14 R. Lawless, A. Findlay and A. Findlay, *Return migration to the Maghreb*, London, Arc, 1982.

15 White, op.cit.

16 J. Salt, 'Europe's Foreign Labour Migrants in Transition' *Geography*, no.70, 1985, pp.162–8.

17 'Population Issues and Australia's Future', National Population Council (Australia), Canberra, 1991.

18 *Economic outlook 1960–90*, Paris, OECD, 1992.

19 A. Findlay, 'From Settlers to Skilled Transients', *Geoforum*, no.19, 1988, pp.401–10.

20 D. Massey, *Spatial Divisions of Labour*, London, Macmillan, 1984.

21 A. Champion and A. Townsend, *Contemporary Britain*, London, Arnold, 1990.

22 D. Owen, 'Migration and employment', *Migration Processes and Patterns*, no.2, ed. J. Stillwell *et al.*, London, Belhaven, 1992, pp.205–24.

23 F. Frobel *et al.*, *The New International Division of Labour*, Cambridge University Press, 1980.

24 Owen, op.cit., p.223.

25 A. Green, 'Changing Labour Processes and Internal Migration', *Migration Processes and Patterns*, no.1, A. Champran *et al.*, London,

Belhaven, 1992, pp.105-18.

26 Green, op.cit., p.6.

27 J. Lonnroth, 'Labour Market Policies for the 1990s', unpublished paper presented at the OECD International Conference on Migration, Rome, 13-15 March 1991.

28 Ibid, p.13.

29 Ibid. p.15.

30 J. Seymour, 'Labour Migration and the UK Work Permit Scheme', unpublished paper presented at the IPPR/Frierich Ebert Foundation seminar on The Economic and Social Impact of Migration, London, 6-7 March 1993, p.7.

31 Ibid.

32 J. Salt, 'International Migration and the United Kingdom', report of the United Kingdom SOPEMI correspondent to the OECD, 1992 (unpublished), p.10.

33 Findlay, op.cit., J. Salt and A. Findlay, 'International Migration of Highly Skilled Manpower', *The Impact of International Migration on Developing Countries*, ed. R. Appleyard, OECD, Paris, 1989, pp.159-82.

34 M. Kritz and F. Cases, 'Science and Technology Transfers and Migration Flows', *International Migration Systems*, ed. M. Kritz *et al.* Oxford, Clarendon Press, 1992, pp.221-43.

35 J. Onslow-Cole, 'Work Permits, A Review of Changes to the Scheme', *Immigration and Nationality Law and Practice*, no.5, 1991, pp.50-2.

36 Written answer, 5 February 1993.

37 *Home Office Statistical Bulletin*, issue 14/93, London, Government Statistical Service.

38 J. Buchan, I. Seccombe and J. Ball, 'The International Mobility of Nurses', *Institute of Manpower Studies Report*, no.230, Brighton, IMS, 1992.

39 P. Trott, 'Practical Problems for Businessmen', *Immigration and Nationality Law and Practice*, no.4, 1990, pp.73-4.

40 Ibid., p.111.

41 T. Straubhaar and K. Zimmermann, 'Towards a European Migration Policy', *Munchener Wirtschaftswissenshaftliche Beitrage*, 92/2, Ludwig Maximilians University, Munich, 1991. K. Zimmermann, 'European Migration Policy', *International Economic Insights*, no.3, p.9, 1992. F. Rivera-Batiz, *et al.*, 'US Immigration Policy Reform in the 1980s', New York, Praeger, 1991.

42 G. Borjas, *Friends or Strangers?*, Basic Books, New York, 1990. J. Simon, *The Economic Consequences of Immigration*, Oxford, Blackwell, 1989.

43 Straubhaar and Zimmermann, op.cit.

44 A. Gieseck, V. Heilemann and H.D. von Loeffelholz, 'Economic and Social Implications of Migration into the F.R. of Germany', paper presented to the IPPR/Friedrich Ebert Foundation Seminar on the

Economic and Social Impact of Migration, London, 6–7 March 1993. R. Ulrich, 'The Impact of Foreigners on the public purse in Germany', paper presented to the IPPR/Friedrich Ebert Foundation seminar on the Economic and Social Impact of Migration, London, 6–7 March 1993. K. Zimmermann, 'Labour Market Impacts of Immigration', paper presented to the IPPR/Friedrich Ebert Foundation seminar on The Economic and Social Impact of Migration, London, 6–7 March 1993.

45 S. Baron, 'Blut und Boden', *Wirtshaftswoche*, no.44, 25 October 1991.

46 A. Phizacklea and R. Miles, *Labour and Racism*, London, Routledge and Kegan Paul, 1980. R. Miles, *Capitalism and Unfree Labour*, London, Tavistock, 1990.

47 M. Cross, *Vocational Training of Young Migrants in the United Kingdom*, Luxembourg, Official Publications of the EC, 1986. A. Newnham, *Employment, Unemployment and Black People*, London, Runnymede Trust, 1986. J. Brennan and P. McGeevor, *Ethnic Minorities and the Graduate Labour Market*, CRE, London, 1990.

48 de Beijl, op.cit.

49 V. Robinson, 'The Internal Migration of Britain's Ethnic Population', *Migration Processes and Patterns*, ed. A. Champion *et al.*, New York, Belhaven, no.1, 1992, pp.188–200.

50 Salt and Kitching, op.cit.

51 Ibid., p.545.

52 A. Fielding, 'Inter-regional Migration and Social Change', *Transactions*, IBG, no.14, 1989, pp.24–36.

53 Salt and Kitching, op.cit.

54 A. Green, op.cit.

55 M. Pearson, S. Smith and S. White, 'Demographic Influences on Public Spending', *Fiscal Studies*, no.1, 1989, pp.48–65.

56 J. Bailey, 'International migration', *Population Trends*, no. 67, 1992, pp.29–34.

57 Jones and Smith, op.cit.

58 F. Hawkins, *Critical Years in Immigration: Canada and Australia Compared*, Montreal and Kingston, McGill-Queens University Press, 1989.

59 Economic Council of Canada, *Economic and Social impact of Immigration*, Information Canada, Ottowa, 1991, p.51.

60 National Population Council (Australia), op.cit.

61 Buchan, Seccombe and Ball, op.cit.

62 Salt, op.cit.

63 CBI, 'Review of the Work Permit System', *Employment Affairs Report*, no.29, 1989, pp.12–15.

64 Department of Employment unpublished data reproduced in Salt, op.cit.

65 National Population Council (Australia), op.cit.

66 Economic Council of Canada, op.cit.

67 J. Haskey, 'The Ethnic Minority Population of Great Britain', *Population Trends*, no.60, 1990, pp.35–8.
68 Robinson, op.cit.
69 Immigrant Statistics Unit, 'Population of New Commonwealth and Pakistant Ethnic Origin', *Population Trends*, no.16, 1979, pp.22–8.

7 An Asylum Policy
Chris Randall

1 For a good recent summary of these see L. Druke, *Asylum Policies in a European Community without Internal Borders*, no.9, Churches Committee for Migrants in Europe (CCME), October 1992; and A. Cruz, *Schengen, Ad hoc Immigration Group and Other European Intergovernmental bodies*, no.12, CCME, 1993.
2 Dated 3 December 1991.
3 *Handbook on Procedures*, UNHCR, 1979, para. 189–205.
4 *Vilvarajah* Series A 215;12 [1991] HRLJ, 432.
5 M. Mousalli quoted by Earl Ferrers *Hansard* 12 February 1993 p.457.
6 Stolenburg, 'The Ratification Process of Schengen', quoted in Ian Guest, 'The United Nations, the UNHCR and Refugee protection: A Nonspecialist Analysis', *International Journal of Refugee Law*, 3:3, 1991.
7 Ibid.
8 Home Office Statistical Bulletin, 19/93.
9 The UN definition of refugee is limited to those with a 'well-founded fear of being persecuted for reasons of race, religion, nationality, membership of a particular social group or political opinion, is outside the country of his nationality and is unable or, owing to such fear, unwilling to avail himself of the protection of that country'.
10 Letter from Under Secretary of State to Bishop Shepherd, August 1992.
11 K. Hailbronner, 'The Concept of "Safe Country" and expedient asylum procedures', Report to CAHAR (91)2, September 1991.
12 W. Kälin, 'Refugees and Civil Wars. Only a matter of Interpretations?', *International Journal of Refugee Law*, 3:3, 1991.
13 Dated 4 March 1992.
14 Nona Mallet, 'Deterring Asylum Seeker: German and Danish Law on Political Asylum Part II', *Immigration and Nationality Law and Practice*, 6.I, January 1992.
15 E. Feller, unpublished paper at a seminar on the effects of carrier sanctions on the asylum seeker in Europe, Copenhagen, 28 November 1991.
16 Hailbronner, op.cit.
17 A. la CourBodtcher and J. Hughes, 'The Effects of Legislation Imposing Fines on Airlines for Transporting Undocumented Passports', *The Effects*

of Carrier Sanctions on the Asylum System, Danish Refugee Council and the Danish Centre of Human Rights, 1991.

18 A document entitled, 'Harmonisation in Europe', UNHCR, March 1992.

19 See also Excom conclusion No.30/1983.

20 See Hailbronner, op.cit.

21 Hooghiemstra, *A Comparative Study of Publicly Funded Legal Services to Asylum Seekers in the Twelve Member States of the EC*, ILPA, 1992.

22 Excom Conclusion 30.

23 The Immigration Appeals Authority has the ability and has also shown the inclination to list particular types of appeals together, although, of course it regulates its own procedures.

24 R. Dedecker, 'The Right of Asylum in Europe: Some Proposals on Accelerated Procedures for the Twelve Member States', working document prepared with support of the UNHCR, January 1992.

25 See n.19 above.

26 Hailbronner, op.cit.

27 1990 Immigration Appeal Reports, 573.

28 See M. Ashford, *Detained Without Trial*, JCWI, 1993.

8 Future Immigration Policy
Elspeth Guild

1 Hansard, 2 March 1992, col.24

2 Community and Ethnic Relations in Europe, 1991, para.266.

3 R v. *Immigration Appeal Tribunal ex parte Surinder Singh*: *The Times*, 7 July 1992, also Imm A R [1992]4 565.

4 *Berrehab* [1989] 11 *EHRR*.

5 Immigration and Nationality Report 1991–2.

6 According to the Immigration and Nationality Department Report 1991–2.

7 DTI Overseas Trade Services Report, *Invisibles*, May 1992.

8 The Consular Fees (Amendment) Order 1990.

9 Conversation with Maeve Sherlock, Director of UKOSA, 29 March 1993; conversation with Anne Honeyman, Leeds University administration, 5 April 1993; D. Wilson, Overseas Students in the UK Private Sector', *International Journal of Education*, vol.3, no.2, July 1992; Department of Trade, *Invisibles*, May 1992.

10 'The Education and Training Markets of the 1990s', DTI Asia-Pacific Group conference, London, May 1993.

11 If the individual intends to become a student but has not yet secured a place on a course they may enter as a 'prospective student' and switch to student status within six months.

12 Report of the Wilson Committee of Enquiry, Cmnd. 3387, HMSO,

1967.

13 *Beljoudi* v. *France* [1992] 14 *EHRR* 801; *Moustaquim* v. *France* [1991] 13 *EHRR* 802; *Djeroud* v. *France* [1992] 14 *EHRR* 68.

14 Hansard, 26 March 1992, p.27.

15 *Khawaja* v. *Secretary of State for the Home Department* [1984] AC.74.

16 *R* v. *Secretary of State for the Home Department ex. p. Kwame Addo*, (1985) (transcript p.10).

17 Section 3(5) (b) of the Immigration Act 1971 (as amended).

18 Section 14(3) and Section 15 of the Immigration Act 1971 (as amended).

19 Currently HC 251.

20 *R* v. *Home Secretary ex p. Cheblak* CA 6 February 1991, *NLJ* 200.

21 Immigration Act 1971 (Sched 2, para.22(1)).

22 Immigration Act 1971 (Sched 2, para.29(1)).

23 Hansard, 13 July 1992, Cols 437 and 438.

9 The Age of Internal Controls?

Anne Owers

1 HC215–i,ii and iii, p.67, para.45.

2 *Official Report*, 24 July 1989, cols 494–8.

3 Asylum and Immigration Appeals Act, section 3.

4 Home Office Control of Immigration Statistics, 14/93.

5 See, for example, the uneven impact of the primary purpose marriage rule, rarely if ever invoked against American spouses, but used to refuse two out of every three fiancées and husbands from the Indian subcontinent; or the targeting of nationals of different Third World countries for visit refusals (*Target Caribbean*, JCWI, 1990).

6 HC215, p.12, para.71.

7 Speech given by Ron Hadfield at the International Police Exhibition and Conference (IPEC), 15 October 1992.

8 *Out of sight*, JCWI 1987, *Target Caribbean*, JCWI 1990.

9 Anthony Langdon (Grade 2) HC215, p.5, para.23.

10 Speech given by Ed Grootaarts at IPEC Conference, 15 October 1992.

11 HC215, p.29, paras 176–8.

12 See Hadfield, op.cit.

10 Future Citizenship Policy

Laurie Fransman

1 Anyone born within the UK and Colonies was a CUKC by birth subject to what in effect were the same exceptions as at common law—British

Nationality Act 1948 section 4.

2 Under the British Nationality Act 1948, section 6(1).

3 Regarding children, discretionary registration provision were introduced by section 7 of the Act.

4 Burma, unlike India, was not permitted to be a Republic within the Commonwealth.

5 Hence many Burmese remained British subjects and, for example, all CUKCs from Penang and Malacca remained such citizens when those colonies became part of independent Malaya.

6 Maternal as well as paternal.

7 Cambridge University Press, 1950.

8 'Persons Granted British Citizenship, UK 1992', Home Office Statistics, 16/93.

9 Written answer, 29 March 1993.

10 HMSO, 1990, recommendation no.10.

11 A final point on acquisition rules is that, although acquisition by grant must in all probability at least mainly occur as the result of the making of an application, perhaps some provision should be made in respect of lost opportunities (that is, where an individual at a given moment had the eligibility to apply but through ignorance or for some other reason failed to do so). This system can operate very unfairly and a device ought to be conjured up whereby an individual may be invited to apply at the right time or, in this situation, somehow be advantaged at a later time.

11 The Implications of Immigration Policy for Race Relations

Sarah Spencer

1 Kenneth Clarke, then Home Secretary: Second Reading debate on the Asylum and Immigration Appeals Bill, 2 November 1992, Hansard, vol.213, no.64, col.21. See also the remarks by Winston Churchill MP widely reported in the press on 19 July 1993.

2 Roy Hattersley MP quoted in E.J.B. Rose, *et al.*, *Colour and Citizenship. A Report on British Race Relations*, Oxford University Press, 1969, p.229.

3 For example the *Daily Express* survey after these riots showing high levels of support for immigration control, quoted in Z. Layton-Henry, *The Politics of Immigration: Immigration, 'Race' and 'Race' Relations in Post-war Britain*, Making Contemporary Britain, ed. A. Seldon with P. Hennessy, Oxford, UK and Cambridge, USA, 1992, p.73.

4 E.J.B. Rose, *et al.*, *Colour and Citizenship*, op.cit., p.228.

5 S. Saggar, *Race and Politics in Britain*, Contemporary Political Studies,

ed. J. Benyon, Hemel Hempstead, Harvester Wheatsheaf, 1992, p.175.

6 See Layton-Henry, op.cit., p.77.

7 For example, see Hugo Storey's chapter, International Law and Human Rights Obligations, in this volume and the first comprehensive legal textbook on immigration law: L. Grant and I. Martin, *Immigration Law and Practice*, London, Cobden Trust, 1982. Its concluding chapter begins with the words: 'The immigration law and practice set out in the preceding chapters is racially discriminatory in its motivation and in its effect,' p.347. See also A. Dummett and A. Nicol *Subjects, Citizens, Aliens and Others: Nationality and Immigration Law*, Law in Context, ed. R. Stevens, W. Twining and C. McCrudden, London, Weidenfeld and Nicolson, 1990, who show how the operation of the law in practice was and is discriminatory; for example under the Commonwealth Immigrants Act 1962, those Commonwealth citizens whose British passport was issued by the UK government (mainly white) rather than by a colonial government (mainly black and Asian) were exempt from the entry restrictions: see p.183. More overtly, the Commonwealth Immigrants Act 1968 provided that a British subject would be free from immigration control only if he, or at least one of his parents or grandparents, were born, adopted, registered or naturalised in the UK. East African Asians could not meet this requirement, see p.203.

The European Commission of Human Rights found the Commonwealth Immigrants Act 1968 and the Immigration Act 1971 to be in breach of article 3 of the European Convention (discrimination amounting to degrading treatment). See East African Asian cases: 4626/70 and others, 4783/71, 4827/71 (Oct-Dec 1970) DR vol.13, pp.5 and 17 (re. admissibility decisions); and 1981 3 EHRR 76 (re. the merits).

8 *Second Review of the Race Relations Act 1976*, CRE, 1992, p.31.

9 A. Dummett and A. Nicol report some of the early discussions on the dilemma: how to keep out 'coloured people' while appearing not to discriminate, for example, Sir Alex Douglas-Home, later to be Conservative Prime Minister: 'On the one hand it would presumably be politically impossible to legislate for a colour bar and any legislation would have to be non-discriminatory in form. On the other hand we do not wish to keep out immigrants of good type from the old Dominions.' (1955, Cabinet Papers) quoted in *Subjects, Citizens, Aliens and Others. Nationality and Immigration Law*, London, Weidenfeld and Nicolson, 1990.

10 Clarke, op.cit., col.22.

11 Home Office Research and Planning Unit, *Research Programme* for the years 1987 to 1992 (in separate volumes). The programme concentrates on the mechanics of the immigration control system.

12 *World in Action*, Granada TV, January 1978, quoted in Saggar, op.cit., p.121.

13 See for example, R. Miles and A. Phizacklea *White Man's Country*.

Racism in British Politics, London, Pluto, 1984.

14 The CRE, the body that has statutory responsibility in the UK for promoting good race relations, undertook a formal investigation into immigration control procedures and concluded in its 1985 report that: 'The interests of race relations in the UK had been damaged, because by the logic of the "pressure of immigration" argument those most adversely affected by the operation of the immigration controls have included members of groups which form substantial ethnic minority communities as part of our multi-racial society.'

15 For example, see *Eurobarometer*, no.35, Commission of the European Communities, Brussels, 1991.

16 Layton-Henry, op.cit., p.177.

17 Bhikhu Parekh, for instance, argues that government must recognise that cultural differences are a valuable asset, preservable only within ethnic communities that do not threaten our social cohesion but enhance it. It should, he argues, make the public aware of the value of cultural differences that widen the range of lifestyles open to all and bring new traditions and ideas into a creative interplay with existing ones whether musical, culinary, literary or artistic: 'Communities educate and even "civilise" each other in subtle and elusive ways, provided, of course, that none is too overbearing and self-righteous to welcome a dialogue.' Immigrants, moreover, bring new skills, new forms of social organisation, new talents that can be harnessed in business, management, industry, government and sport. To prevent these valuable communities being atomised, Parekh argues, 'We need to explore a more imaginative and pluralist vision of Britain and develop a new social and cultural policy capable of nurturing ethnic identities within a shared cultural framework.' Far from undermining ethnic minority ties, government should be encouraging them and strengthening them. 'Britain and the Social Logic of Pluralism' published in the CRE's Discussion Paper 3, *Britain: A Plural Society, Report of a Seminar*, London, 1990.

18 See, for example, IRR, *European Race Audit*, nos 1 and 2, 1992–3; and almost any edition of *Migration News Sheet* and the *European* for reports on these widespread incidents.

19 *Second Review of the Race Relations Act 1976*, op.cit., p.27.

20 W. Saulsbury and B. Bowling: *The Multi-agency Approach in Practice: the North Plaistow Racial Harassment Project*, paper 64, Home Office Research and Planning Unit, 1991.

21 Quoted in IRR, *European Race Audit*, no.1, from articles in the *Independent*, 30 October 1992, and the *Guardian*, 3 November 1992.

22 For example see C. Brown, *Black and White Britain. The Third PSI Survey*, London, Heinemann, 1984.

23 T. Jones, *Britain's Ethnic Minorities*, London, Policy Studies Institute, 1993.

24 For example see *Report of the Moss Side Enquiry Panel to Greater Manchester Council* on the Moss Side disturbances in July 1981, which concluded that, in the case of black youths, one contributory factor was their 'bitterness against white society due to experience of insults and discrimination in many fields' (para 44.2).

25 *Immigration: A Commitment to Australia: The Report of the Committee to Advise on Australia's Immigration Policies* (Fitzgerald Report), Canberra, Australian Government Publishers' Service, 1988. The five person committee sat under the chairmanship of Stephen Fitzgerald, an academic, businessman and former Ambassador to China.

26 Ibid, p.3.

27 Ibid, p.16.

28 Letter from Sue Shortland, Manager of the CBI Employee Relocation Council, to Sarah Spencer, IPPR, dated 15 February 1993.

29 'The Economic and Social Impact of Migration in the UK and Germany', seminar organised by IPPR and the Friedrich Ebert Stiftung, London, 6–7 March 1993.

30 Saggar, op.cit., p.179.

31 Department of Immigration, Local Government and Ethnic Affairs, *Review '91*, Annual Report 1990–91, Canberra, Australian Government Publishing Service, pp.159–71.

32 J. Salt, 'International Migration and the United Kingdom, report of the United Kingdom SOPEMI correspondent to the OECD, 1992, shows that Australia accepted 124,000 permanent settlers in the year 1990–1 compared to the United Kingdom's 52,000 in 1990.

33 *Second Review of the Race Relations Act 1976*, op.cit., p.32.

34 See, for example, Lustgarten's list in his chapter, 'Racial Inequality, Public Policy and the Law: Where Are We Going?' *Discrimination: The Limits of the Law*, ed. B. Hepple and E. M. Szyszczak, London and New York, Mansell, 1992.

35 NOP poll in 1978, quoted in Saggar, op.cit., p.125.

36 John Major speaking to the Windsor Fellowship in London, 25 September 1991.

37 New York based Helsinki Watch went further in its criticism and blamed the government for the attacks, citing frequent official references to the influx of refugees and passive attitude of the authorities in the face of right-wing violence. The government rejected the report. *Migration News Sheet*, Brussels, November 1992.

38 Press release from the Embassy of the Federal Republic of Germany: 'Ministers Toughen Measures against Right-wing Violence', 3 December 1992; also 'Never One to Back Down from a Fight', the *European*, 12–15 November 1992 and subsequent conversation with the author of the article, the head of the *European's* German desk, Tony Paterson. Also reported in *Migration News Sheet*, Brussels, November 1992 and January

1993. A criticism of the form the publicity has taken has been that, while encouraging friendship to foreigners it has emphasised that they are separate from rather than an integral part of German society.

39 T. Hammar, 'Sweden', *European Immigration Policy: A Comparative Study*, ed. T. Hammar, Cambridge University Press, 1985.

40 'The Netherlands Government's Policy on Minorities Examined in the Light of the Report of the CSCE Meeting of Experts on National Minorities, Geneva 1991', paper tabled at the CSCE ODIHR seminar, 'Case Studies on National Minorities issues, positive results', Warsaw, 24–8 May 1993.

41 Survey conducted by the Enmid Institute, reported in *Migration News Sheet*, Brussels, January 1993.

42 *Eurobarometer*, no.35, Commission of the European Communities, Brussels, June 1991.

43 *British Social Attitudes: The 9th Report*, ed. R. Jowell, L. Brooke, G. Prior and B. Taylor, Dartmouth, Aldershot, Hants, and Brookfield Vermont, Social and Community Planning Research, 1992, op.cit.

Conclusion and Recommendations

Sarah Spencer

1 J. Purcell, Director General of the IOM, Geneva, in a talk entitled 'Towards a Comprehensive Approach to the Migration Challenges of the 1990s', Chatham House, 4 May 1993. See IOM questionnaire on Albania, 1993.

2 Draft papers prepared for IPPR on these issues by R. Sondhi, 'Training and Employment Needs of Immigrants and Refugees', 1992, and A. Dubs, 'Refugee Settlement in the UK', 1993.

3 For example see papers on the economic impact of migrants in Germany prepared for the IPPR/Friedrich Ebert Stiftung seminar 'The Social and Economic Impact of Migration', 5–7 March 1993, London, Trentham Books (in preparation).

4 For example see summary of such research in a number of countries in *Bulletin*, no.55/56, London, Centre for Economic Policy Research, February/April, 1993.

5 Wilson Committee, 1976, ch.9.

6 For example UN Population Fund, *The State of the World Population*, 1993.

7 E. Pilkington and S. Weale: 'Police halt deportation unit amid anger at death', *Guardian*, 4 August 1993, p.1.

8 The Chairman of the European Parliament Intergroup on frontier

Controls, Christopher Jackson MEP, demonstrated the enthusiasm for internal controls in the *Independent on Sunday*, 15 August 1993. He noted the Danish system in which everyone lawfully in the country has a personal identification number without which they cannot get a job, receive benefit, get medical attention etc. and without which it is difficult to stay long in Denmark. Britain, he argued, 'should examine ways of making illegal stay here virtually impossible. This done, we could sensibly relax our immigration controls at borders with other EC countries.'